John Donne's Performances

John Donne's Performances

Sermons, poems, letters and *Devotions*

Margret Fetzer

Manchester University Press
Manchester and New York

distributed in the United States exclusively
by Palgrave Macmillan

Copyright © Margret Fetzer 2010

The right of Margret Fetzer to be identified as the author of this work has been asserted by her in accordance with the Copyright, Designs and Patents Act 1988.

Published by Manchester University Press
Oxford Road, Manchester M13 9NR, UK
and Room 400, 175 Fifth Avenue, New York, NY 10010, USA
www.manchesteruniversitypress.co.uk

Distributed in the United States exclusively by
Palgrave Macmillan, 175 Fifth Avenue,
New York, NY 10010, USA

Distributed in Canada exclusively by
UBC Press, University of British Columbia, 2029 West Mall,
Vancouver, BC, Canada V6T 1Z2

British Library Cataloguing-in-Publication Data is available

Library of Congress Cataloging-in-Publication Data is available

ISBN 978 0 7190 9561 0 paperback

First published by Manchester University Press in hardback 2010

This paperback edition first published 2014

The publisher has no responsibility for the persistence or accuracy of URLs for any external or third-party internet websites referred to in this book, and does not guarantee that any content on such websites is, or will remain, accurate or appropriate.

Printed by Lightning Source

For Severin

Contents

Acknowledgements	ix
Introduction – Beginning Donne	1
1 Pulpit performances – Sermons	25
2 Promethean and protean performances – Worldly poems	77
3 Passionate performances – Poems erotic and divine	138
4 Patronage performances – Letters	185
5 (Inter)Personal performances – *Devotions*	225
Conclusion – Being Don(n)e	271
Bibliography	276
Index	307

Acknowledgements

This book originated as a doctoral thesis at the Ludwig-Maximilians-University of Munich, Germany. During the years of writing my PhD, I have profited enormously from my supervisor's insightful commentary and advice, and I would like to use this opportunity to thank Professor Tobias Döring for so thoroughly encouraging and supporting my work on Donne. I am also grateful to Professor Andreas Höfele and Professor Ina Schabert, both of whom were likewise involved in reviewing my thesis.

Parts of this study were presented at the universities of Munich, Tübingen, Berlin and Bonn, and I would like to thank the convenors of these conferences for giving me the chance to present my work in front of a larger academic audience. On these occasions and after, I have learnt much from such distinguished Donne critics as Professor Ramie Targoff, Professor Raymond J. Frontain, Professor Tom Healy, Professor Brian Cummings and Professor Wolfgang G. Müller.

Thanks go also to my colleagues and students at Munich, who contributed to the pleasant and inspiring working atmosphere at the department. In particular, I would like to mention Dr Daniella Jancsó, who read an early draft of the project, and Kathleen Rabl, who proof read the final version of my PhD. Moreover, I would like to thank Manchester University Press for their friendliness and patience in answering all my questions concerning the publishing of this book.

Even though they may not at all times have known what exactly I was studying or working on, my parents, Dr Peter and Elisabeth Fetzer, have never hesitated to invest in my education. I would hereby like to acknowledge both their generosity and their patience in empathising with the developments of their daughter's academic career. Moreover, I would like to thank my own daughter Magdalena for waiting to enter this world only two weeks *after* the manuscript of this book was sent to Manchester University Press.

This book would not have been completed without my husband Severin's altogether non-academic support. Whenever I was overly preoccupied with my research, he managed to cheer me up and distract me – for example by admonishing me to 'for God's sake, hold my tongue, and let us love'. It is to him that I dedicate *John Donne's Performances*.

Introduction – Beginning Donne

Good wee must love, and must hate ill,
For ill is ill, and good good still,
But there are things indifferent,
Which wee may neither hate, nor love,
But one, and then another prove,
As wee shall finde our fancy bent.

('Communitie', ll. 1–6)

Since 1921, the year of T. S. Eliot's review of Grierson's *Metaphysical Lyrics and Poems of the Seventeenth Century*, John Donne's poetry has been of central interest for a large 'Communitie' of critics. That Donne's writing is 'good' and should thus be loved, has rarely been disputed – when it was, as by Fish, others have been eager to counter charges of Donne's egocentricity by exposing the critic's own self-centredness instead (Fish, 1999; Brett, 1999; Strier, 1995). The majority of the critical 'Communitie' would however agree that not everything Donne wrote is deserving of the critic's 'love'. The poem under consideration, a rakish celebration of polygamy, is rarely included either in poetry anthologies or writing on Donne. In order to preserve the poet's name, it has repeatedly been argued that Donne could not have been in earnest when composing poems like that quoted above (Guss, 1966; Zunder, 1982). The Donne canon has been sieved, but critics, of course, seized upon their own individual criteria as most adequate and determined selections as they found their 'fanc[ies] bent'. What is true of literature studies generally is particularly striking in the case of Donne: the subjective preference of the critic surfaces in even the most perceptively argued accounts of his writing. What goes for Donne's work has even more relevance for his biography: more than is customary, his oeuvre has been scrutinised for traces of the writer's precise religious allegiances – and this holds not only for straightforwardly religious works, like the sermons or *Devotions*, but also for his divine and erotic poems (Martz, 1954; Lewalski, 1979; DiPasquale, 1999).

The present study is no exception. I, too, have shown a preference for some of Donne's poems over others, and, although my approach strives for greater comprehensiveness by focusing not only on Donne's *Songs and Sonets* but also on his divine poetry, as well as his sermons, letters and *Devotions*, one cannot presume this to be 'All Donne'. My approach in the subsequent pages is to read Donne's texts as performances. I shall pay less attention to the underlying 'meaning' of each text than to the ways in which Donne's writing performs, creates and communicates. The primary 'fancy' of this book is 'bent' less on estimating the conceptual content of some of Donne's writings than on concentrating on how what is said is articulated, transmitted, effected and received. Rather than speculate on his personal convictions, my thesis is that even Donne's apparently most contradictory utterances, whether in poetry or prose, whether concerned with erotic love or religious worship, are related to one another: each of them constitutes just one of *John Donne's Performances*.

Why performances?

In his 1955 lecture series *How to Do Things with Words*, the language philosopher J. L. Austin revealed that some utterances, instead of stating something, actually perform an act simply by being uttered (Austin, 1975). Moreover, they are not subject to truth-conditions, as they cannot be defined as either true or false. These so-called *performatives* include utterances made in marriage services or in christenings; thus an implicit link to (church) rituals is established. In the course of his lecture series, however, Austin gradually deconstructs many of the distinctions he drew initially: first the one between explicit and implicit performatives, and then the one between performatives and constatives, the latter term referring to utterances he originally judged to be concerned only with description and thus not performative in themselves.

If Austin's self-correction implies that every utterance is performative, this also refers to those utterances he previously excluded as 'misfires' or 'abuses', since they failed to meet the felicity conditions introduced by him before he extended his focus to all utterances. If language is generally performative, then Austin's felicity condition that 'a person participating in and so invoking the procedure must in fact have those thoughts or feelings, and the participants must intend so to conduct themselves' (Austin, 1975: 15) is also undermined: performativity is no longer limited to the originally described procedures. This would include literary utterances, too, as they do not necessarily presuppose an equivalence between what is said and what is taken to be true, nor need any immediate consequences arise as regards the conduct of any producer of literary utterances. Although Austin himself insisted on excluding literature from his scope of analysis, Derrida's discussion of speech act theory has shown that its supposedly non-serious character as well as its reliance on iterability is by no means unique but applies to language in general (Derrida, 1986; Culler, 1994). In fact, those utterances which Austin initially used to introduce his notion of *How to Do Things with Words*, namely the words used in christenings or marriage services, strongly depend on citationality to be efficacious at all.

What could be the use of Austin's theory for the study of literature? First of all, there may be cases where literary utterances, sometimes more, sometimes less explicitly, make reference to the power of language, and, as they do so, they may develop a notion of language that is very similar to that of Austin – Manfred Pfister even defines such poetic auto-reflexivity as 'the most subtle and incisive dimension of the performative' (Pfister, 2005: 222). Many speakers in Donne's *Songs and Sonets*, not considering their utterances as bound by any external truths, consciously exploit their linguistic potency as they strive to be performative and engage in creations not only, through metaphysical conceit, of worlds but also of truth and self.[1] They are herein illustrative of how 'saying makes it so', as are many of Donne's letter writing personae who, by suggesting parallels between themselves and their superior addressees, implicitly work towards a subtle undermining of social hierarchies. The Bible, notably one of the major influences on Donne's writing, likewise exemplifies the performativity of verbal utterance, when, in Genesis, God speaks the world into existence.

Secondly, performance theory allows for a concept of self that differs significantly from (post-)Enlightenment notions of identity (cf. Reiss, 2003: 1) which postulate a clear separation of external and internal (Sawday, 1997: 38), of body and soul, and which have also exerted a strong influence over the ways in which literary critics of the twentieth and twenty-first century have conceived of Donne. Performance is more than just a show of something that may or may not be there, as it does not function merely as an image of human behaviour but constitutes life itself (Fischer-Lichte, 2004: 360). If, as Judith Butler maintains, gender identities are created through repetitive performative acts (Butler, 1990), self and identity as such may likewise be created via performance (Krämer, 2001: 260). Such performances may of course also include verbal acts like those of Donne's sermons, poetry, letters or *Devotions*, in which speakers come into being and evolve through what they are saying – according to Stephen Greenblatt, '[s]elf-fashioning is always, though not exclusively, in language' (Greenblatt, 1980: 9).

When accepting that self and identity are importantly affected by and effected via words, such performance should not be confused with the faking of a self in order to deceive, a criticism which has frequently been voiced against Donne.[2] Instead, there may be ways in which initially merely external performances bring about and enable the 'sincere' performance of the required act. This is true also, or perhaps even especially, of religious identity. In 1595, Samuel Ward, a contemporary of Donne's, writes in his diary: 'Remember God's mercy toward thee, in giving thee grace at the end of thy prayer to pray heartily unto thee, whereas in the beginning thou wast blockish' (Cressy/Ferrell, 1996: 121). Not only may the performance of prayer thus coincide with the 'thing itself', the performance may actually effect this 'essence' in the first place (cf. Targoff, 1997), a performance of prayer that began only 'as if' sincere may enable the supplicant to 'pray heartily' at the end. The idea of performativity therefore encourages us to pay attention to how it may come about not only that 'saying' but also 'playing makes it so'. Religious worship 'is not only expressive as the devotees of sincerity insist, it is also [. . .] instrumental in creating emotions that ought to be felt' (Horton Davies, 1996: I, 528).

Playing invokes the context of the theatre – and this suggests the third reason why an analysis of literary texts in the context of performance theory may be worthwhile. Theories of performativity were first seized upon by theatre studies. Theatre cannot do without an audience – and Austin's categorisation of speech acts into illocutionary acts and perlocutionary effects illustrates the relevance of a social context for the performance of an utterance. While the illocutionary force of an utterance may be determined in advance, the perlocutionary effect almost exclusively depends on the audience's reaction (Austin, 1975: 102). As Sandy Petrey insists, '[t]he collectivity can be as small as two people, but performative speech can never be the unilateral act of a single individual' (Petrey, 1990: 5). This point is valid also for the 'audience' of literature because '[t]he [literary] text too does things through and with those to whom it speaks' (Petrey, 1990: 55). Many of *John Donne's Performances* are theatrical in that internal communicative systems, the relations between speaker and addressee, are in complex ways entangled with and reflected by those between writer and reader/listener, that is a text's external communicative situation.

How can we justify an analysis of early modern texts such as Donne's in the light of late twentieth-century theories of performativity? Even though performance theorists such as Erika Fischer-Lichte are interested mainly in the increasing theatricalisation of the modern world, the early modern period, too, was conscious of the ways in which both 'saying' and 'playing', what Sawday calls 'embodiment' (Sawday, 1997: 48), may make it so. The idea that saying something brings about that which is said in actual fact is at the centre of Roman Catholic concepts of transubstantiation. Upon the utterance of 'Hoc est corpus meum', bread and wine are believed to be made into the body and blood of Christ. Muir describes rituals such as the Eucharist as processes where *'matter'*, here the host, has to be combined with the adequate *'form'*, that is the correct words, and meet with the appropriate *'intention'* so that *'grace'* can be conferred (Muir, 1997: 155–6). These four elements echo Austin's felicity conditions, what is required for the successful performance of a speech act: Austin's insistence that there 'must exist an accepted conventional procedure having a certain conventional effect, that procedure to include the uttering of certain words by certain persons in certain circumstances' as well as his emphasis on this procedure having to be 'executed by all participants both correctly and [. . .] completely' rehearses Muir's notion of *'form'*. Austin's theory also lists '*intention*' as an essential element of a felicitous speech act (Austin, 1975: 14–15), the perlocutionary effect of which, in the case of the Eucharist, would be the conferring of '*grace*' on those participating – at least if they are ready and willing to receive it. Although Austin nowhere addresses the speech acts involved in the Eucharist, he does discuss two of the rituals Muir mentions as 'rites of passage', namely marriage and baptism (or rather, the christening of a ship), and the links between Muir's account of ritual and Austin's speech act theory are therefore hard to deny – despite the fact that Muir's study never even acknowledges or engages with this correspondence.

Muir characterises the Reformation as the period when 'the generalized concept of *ritual* as a distinct kind of activity came into being', most notoriously so in the course of the 'theoretical debate about presence and representation' surrounding the Eucharist (Muir, 1997: 7–8). While Luther's theory of transubstantiation still claimed that body and bread were simultaneously present in the consecrated host, Zwingli took a more radical approach, translating the dogma of 'This is my body' into 'This signifies my body', hence ridding the Eucharist of its last traces of divine presence and entering the realm of mere representation. Calvin suggested a compromise between the Lutheran and the Genevan extreme by accepting Zwingli's concept of the bread merely signifying or pointing to the body of Christ but insisting that Christ was at least spiritually present in the host (cf. Muir, 1997: 171–5). However, there is evidence that, even as late as 1634, the question of the Eucharist had not been satisfactorily settled. In a clearly rhetorical question, Robert Skinner, in a sermon preached before King Charles I at Whitehall in that year, wonders: 'Is it not deep infidelity and heresy, to think Christ to be absent from his body and blood?', and concludes: '[m]ost certainly present he is, though not by his glorious, yet in a singular way, by his gracious presence' (Cressy/Ferrell, 1997: 173).

Although the long process of English Reformation commenced as early as 1534, Donne's contemporaries were still preoccupied with questions of presence and representation. If the English Church's oft-bespoken *via media* places it between the extremes of either Protestantism or Roman Catholicism, the concept of the performative, situated at the interface of representation and ritual, may reveal itself as a useful approach to such religiously informed texts as Donne's, all of which were written when the English Reformation, far from being completed, was still very much under way. Performative power is, however, not limited to a clearly demarcated context of ritualistic ceremonies such as the Eucharist. In fact, the revolution in ritual, which took place during and after the Reformation, to some extent corresponds to J. L. Austin's gradual realisation that, to be performative, language does not necessarily have to be framed within rigorous structures and conventions. Whereas ritual and the strictly regulated language connected with it had been at the heart of the Roman Catholic service, the Reformation disputed the coincidence of saying and doing, of pronouncing Christ's presence in the Eucharist and thereby effecting it in actual fact. Instead, the holy word of Scripture in general, and the sermon as the words concerned with the interpretation of Holy Writ, gained relevance. As the physical presence of Christ in bread and wine became an increasingly contested issue, both Biblical and homiletic utterances became more and more significant for the enactment of Christian sacrament. These words were not only considered to be saying something, or to be serving a merely representational function – their capacity for actually having an effect, their performative value, gradually supplemented and partly even replaced acts of ritual (cf. Cummings, 2002), as my discussion of Donne's 'Pulpit performances' sets out to demonstrate.

From here, it is only a small step to the recognition of the performative power of all language. Such an awareness is not only at the core of Donne's writings but is also testified to by early modern poetics such as Puttenham's *Arte of English Poesie* and Sidney's *Apology for Poetry*. Whereas Puttenham claims that '[a] Poet is as much to say as a maker' (Puttenham, 1959: 3) and partakes of divine verbal power in speaking the world into existence, Sidney goes even further, suggesting that, whereas the realm of nature is 'brazen, the poets only deliver a golden [world]' (Sidney, 1547: 7). Poetic texts are no less endowed with performative power than ritualistic utterances – their interrelatedness is suggested in Donne's 'The Canonization', which negotiates cultural practice and ritual: it reflects the (Catholic) practice of canonisation, but only in the act of establishing a new mode of that ritual, a canonisation that is 'self-created'.

There are other ways in which 'The Canonization' diverges from ritual; its speaker does not revitalise an event that takes place outside of himself and which he was not originally included in, nor does he aim at making present anyone apart from himself (or perhaps his beloved). Quite the contrary is true for the celebration of the Eucharist: it is the re-enactment of the Last Supper, an event at which none of the participants was originally present, and, most significantly, it is intended to effect Christ's presence in bread and wine. By simultaneously drawing on and modifying traditional Catholic ritual, 'The Canonization' is illustrative of Puttenham's characterisation of poets, whose work, at the same time as it engages in imitation and mimesis, also allows them to be original, being as they are '(by maner of speech) as creating Gods' (Puttenham, 1959: 4). The ambiguity of this statement is telling: poets are 'so to speak' 'as creating Gods' – they are so '(by maner of speech)', through (performative) language.

The speaker of 'The Canonization' both cites and appropriates traditional ritual, and the poem may herein be said to combine Roman Catholic and reformed tendencies. The emphasis placed on the lovers' singularity may be rooted in the context of the Reformation which encouraged individuality to enable a more personal relationship to God, as a gradual shift from the 'experience of passively watching the celebration of the liturgy' towards the (admittedly) 'disciplined activity of interpreting the meaning of a text' (Muir, 1997: 150), or, in the present case, a hermeneutics of ritual, was taking place. Words gained in relevance, and not only for ministers of the English Church but for all members of the congregation since Protestantism believed in the 'priesthood of all believers' (Muir, 1997: 180). 'New pieties were forming, and something of the old sense of the sacred was transferring itself from the sacramentals to the scriptures' (Duffy, 1992: 586). The rising influence of the Biblical word also seems to have exerted its influence on Donne's *Devotions*, which encourage their readers individually to engage with their God, as does the speaker in his own utterances. Approaching Donne's literary work as a progeny of the Reformation, we find that the personae of his poetry and prose distinguish themselves by an active individuality, frequently employed in the service of theological dispute as in one of his 'Holy Sonnets': 'Thou hast made me, And shall thy worke decay?' (l. 1).

If the idea that 'saying makes it so' gained currency for Donne's contemporaries, a similar claim holds for the efficaciousness of playing: even though one's inner state might not correspond with the external actions one is undertaking, the mere participation in them could nevertheless affect also the inner man or woman – thus the complicated functions that ritual, according to Muir, was and still is supposed to serve. Muir distinguishes between 'models' and 'mirrors': 'Many rituals work like models. They present a standard or a simplified miniature for society to follow', whereas '[m]irrors [...] present the world as it is understood to be' (Muir, 1997: 5). He is quick to point out that hardly any ritual is either one or the other. Although he groups marriage under 'mirrors' since this rite of passage can be said to 'have a declarative character', as in '*she* is my wife in a wedding' (Muir, 1997: 5), it is clear that marriage, by its insistence on monogamy also works as a model. Similarly, while baptism may be read as a ritual which mirrors humanity's being cleansed of sin through the sacrifice of Christ, it also presents this state as the model way of leading one's life as a Christian. Even though the ritual of marriage or baptism does not ensure the participants' faithfulness and freedom from sin, there is a silent expectation that the external ritual celebration of such impeccable models will have actual consequences for the attitude of those included in it. By an external re-enactment of the model, one may be encouraged to strive to mirror this ideal – and such a hope is implicit in Donne's sermons wherever they encourage their listeners to identify with Biblical examples.

A 'profound conviction in the transformative power of public performance' (Targoff, 1997: 50) governed the measures taken by the early English Church in order to ensure ecclesiastic conformity, and such strategies seem to be informed by what Greenblatt has called 'an increased self-consciousness about the fashioning of human identity as a manipulable, artful process' (Greenblatt, 1980: 1). Attention at services was obligatory, for, although one could not possibly have looked into people's hearts, divines such as Lancelot Andrewes placed considerable 'faith in the physical display of devotion' (Targoff, 1997: 57). Krämer characterises the rigid separation of signifier and signified as Protestant, a separation which finally established the victory of representation over epiphany in the course of the Enlightenment (Krämer, 2002: 323–5). Her argument, together with Targoff's observations, supports Duffy's view of the English Reformation as a very gradual process (Duffy, 1992; Ferrell, 2004), as the early representatives of the church for a long time clung to strategies of creating devotional presence which did not rely on as rigid a separation between external and internal spheres. With regard to the study of early modern texts as replete with contemporary religious debate as Donne's, the performative concept therefore suggests a promising alternative to representational approaches.

Contemporary concerns as the debate on presence and representation, and discourses on identity and self are interrelated (cf. Paster, 1993: 4). Early modern men and women imagined their bodies as predominantly humoral, 'characterized by corporeal fluidity, openness, and porous boundaries' (Paster, 1993: 8; Schoenfeldt, 1999). Not only was each person's humoral balance influenced by their sex, individual passions or diet – the permeability of the humoral body 'suggests a material embeddedness of self and surround' (Selleck, 2001: 150). If behavioural changes can be brought about 'outside-in', the playing of a part may actually make one so, one may come to coincide with one's role, by way of 'acting-as-becoming' (Selleck, 2001: 155). The utterances produced in this context need not constitute a potential articulation or dissembling of an essence of self. Rather than subjecting a previously existent self to manifold performances, selves may come into being through performance.

Reading Donne's *Devotions*, Kuchar notes that Galenism had to face the challenges of mechanistic models of the body, promoted by Paracelsus and his followers (Kuchar, 2001: 19; Paster, 1993: 2). The flexibility afforded by humoral models has its drawbacks, since it fails to guarantee a secure resting place: when it comes to religion, for example, the self has to engage repeatedly in converting itself to God, as it can never be assured for long of finding itself in harmony with the divine (Questier, 1996: 3). Such anxiety is central to Donne's 'Holy Sonnets', but it is also lurking in his sermons and *Devotions*. Most of the time, Donne's speakers put considerable trust in the powers of performance – but hesitation, doubt, sometimes even panic as to its efficaciousness, surface on a regular basis, and at such moments a notion of inwardness as opposed to external manifestation (Maus, 1995) betrays itself. Pfister alludes to the potential falseness or immateriality of performance by drawing attention to the different meanings of 'to perform', which may refer either to the actual carrying out of an act or to the mere pretence of doing so (Pfister, 2005: 220; Barish, 1981: 155). Not the opposition between something internal and external to performance but the very concept of performance itself comprises these two mutually contradictory dimensions.

Donne's texts are at their most vivid whenever they question whether saying or playing actually make it so, when they function not only as 'the expression of the codes by which behavior is shaped' but 'as a reflection upon those codes' (Greenblatt, 1980: 4). What Greenblatt asks of Shakespeare, '[h]ow did so much life get into the textual traces' (Greenblatt, 1990: 2), is of interest also with regard to Donne. *The Circulation of Social Energy* is most of the time marked by fragmentation and conflict. If this is true of concrete instances of cultural practice, such as the Renaissance stage, it is also translatable to early modern culture in general. The 'relation between mode and individual performance' (Greenblatt, 1990: 4), influential as it doubtless was for early moderns, will not always be harmonious, mode and individual performance will hardly ever smoothly coincide, and it is this very unevenness which Greenblatt calls 'social energy', following Puttenham's reappropriation of the Greek term *'Energia,* of *ergon'* as a concept of 'strong and vertuous operation' (Puttenham, 1959: 148). The same is true for the linguistic energy of Donne, whose writing, in adopting and negotiating a process of 'acting-as-becoming', reflects the contemporary 'revolution in ritual theory' (Muir, 1997: 155) brought about by the Reformation. At the end of *Renaissance Self-fashioning*, Greenblatt declares himself amazed at 'the extent to which my identity and the words I utter coincide' (Greenblatt, 1980: 256), whereas, at the beginning of *Marvelous Possessions*, he is much less enthusiastic. Greenblatt's awareness of their 'uneasy marriage in a world without ecstatic union or divorce' (Greenblatt, 1991: 7) probably constitutes one of the major reasons why his work has proved so influential in early modern studies, and contributed substantially to the approach to Donne's works in the present book.

The question as to whether role-play and acting actually make the man or woman invokes the context of the theatre, whose early modern heyday may partly be accounted for by its ways of doubling the impact of the humoral model as it negotiates 'the indeterminate, variant relationship between two ambiguous and mutable social texts – between the actor's body, natural and social, and the specific attributes, natural and social, of his fictionalised being' (Paster, 1993: 20). As Fischer-Lichte suggests, the popularity of the seventeenth-century notion of the world as theatre, the 'theatrum mundi', indicates that distinctions between being and seeming were not yet all that definitely maintained (Fischer-Lichte, 2002: 292–3; Greenblatt, 1990: 15). Post-Enlightenment attitudes to the theatre, by contrast, are far less ambiguous: almost all metaphors 'borrowed from the theater – *theatrical, operatic, melodramatic, stagey*, etc. tend to be hostile or belittling' (Barish, 1981: 1).

Targoff establishes a direct link between church services and the theatre as both significantly depend on public performances. But whereas the authorities hoped that, by exposing people to liturgical rites, the denominationally appropriate devotion might be created in their hearts, they were at the same time afraid that, by the same mechanism, the theatre's 'hypocritical performance would become a transformative experience' for actors and audience alike (Targoff, 1997: 52). That the communicative processes of both church and stage should be more closely related than the religious authorities would have preferred them to be may at least partly have been their own fault; while the spectacle of the Roman Catholic Eucharist, with the elevation of the host and the ringing of bells at the moment of transubstantiation, had provided parishioners with considerable visual and aural enticement, reformed services were much less sensually oriented. '[F]or the most of the first Elizabethan adult generation, Reformation was a stripping away of familiar and beloved observances' (Duffy, 1992: 591) – and this seems to have been the reason the theatre gained greater influence (cf. Montrose, 1980; Barber, 1988; Schwartz, 2008: 13).

In spite of the predominantly Puritan railings against the theatre, church and stage were not that far apart. While Jeffrey Knapp is interested particularly in the ways in which theatrical performances recreated and appropriated religious modes (Knapp, 2002; Diehl, 1997), I would like to suggest that theatricality and religion, interrelated as they were, permeated almost all areas of early modern experience. They certainly do so in Donne's writing. If it is true that early modern preachers would have assumed that 'people who went to plays also went to sermons and would go to sermons more often if there were fewer or no plays to go to' (Lake/Questier, 2002: 429), this should encourage us to read sermons such as Donne's with an eye to the ways in which they were conceived as theatrical performances. Donne's poetry, much of which was written for and accessible only to a coterie of friends, frequently reproduces theatrical situations in that it relies on the interactions between external and internal communicative systems. Although the letter was considered a mirror of the writer's soul, early modern epistolography at the same time touches upon questions of role-play, hence encouraging a reading of Donne's letters as performances. Finally, in that they have recourse to meditative patterns, both Donne's 'Holy Sonnets', but even more so his *Devotions*, credit a notion of the self in need of repeated religious performances – for only thus can there be hope of ever fully communicating, indeed of communing with both Father and Son. A theory of performance and performativity offers both valuable and historically valid insights into the communicative conditions of early modern literature – particularly as they concern the writings of John Donne.

Why John Donne?

If I have argued for the merits of a performative analysis especially regarding texts from the early modern period, this does not account for the choice of John Donne as a case in point – particularly since, although he wrote prolifically in both poetry and prose, he was no playwright. To date, performative readings of early modern literature have focused chiefly on dramatic texts – Döring's *Performances of Mourning* concentrates primarily on the drama of Shakespeare and his contemporaries, and in her discussion of 'sincerity and theatricality in early modern England' Targoff uses *Hamlet* as her reference text.[3] Scholars in theatre studies were first to introduce performative theory to literary texts, so it is no coincidence that drama should still predominate in studies of literary performativity. The often inflationary use of the term has caused Carlson to insist that only theatrical performance and performance art ought to be considered performative: '[performance] is a specific event with its liminoid nature foregrounded, almost invariably clearly separated from the rest of life, presented by performers and attended by audiences both of whom regard the experience as made up of material to be interpreted, to be engaged in' (Carlson, 1996: 198–9). What Carlson fails to acknowledge is that his definition also serves well to describe the performative processes of poetry, at least of poetry such as Donne's, which may be defined as a linguistic event that 'presents, not character in a dramatic situation but the theatrical ego on a private stage, whose player and audience are equally the self' (Stevie Davies, 1994: 35). Despite the numerous controversies of Donne criticism, one thing which almost all readers of Donne agree on is the dramatic dynamics of his writing (Stevie Davies, 1994: 1; Herz, 2006: 104).

Lines like 'For Godsake hold your tongue, and let me love' ('The Canonization', l. 1) or 'Busie old foole, unruly Sunne' ('The Sunne Rising', l. 1) are the most famous examples of the proverbial energy and vigour by which Donne's language has long been considered to distinguish itself. It is on lines like these that his fame rests and that make his writing so unmistakably Donne – but so far, no study of Donne's writings has attempted to analyse this vitality systematically. Remarks on Donne's dramatics hardly ever amount to more than a commentary made in passing, for example on how he likes to begin his poems *in medias res*. Much as this may be true of the greater part of Donne's poetry, referring to this quality as 'dramatic' involves rather a vague usage of the term, taking it to mean something like 'sudden', 'immediate' or, more negatively, 'exaggerated', 'histrionic'. In a more narrow sense, however, drama distinguishes itself through an interplay of external and internal communicative systems, which can be seen to be at work also in many Donne texts. The personae of Donne's writings should not be confused with the person of John Donne, nor the (implied) addressee with the (empirical) audience, which are known to differ most notably with regard to his erotic poems. In many of his poems, one may identify both an internal and an external communication system as well as complex overlaps of the two, and in his letters or sermons one likewise encounters theatrical structures. Similarly, Donne's *Devotions* do not only theoretically discuss the need to empathise with one's neighbour but as a whole encourage their readers to identify with the sick speaker by whom they are articulated. In order to analyse systematically how this specific quality of Donne's writing is effected, I have chosen to read his oeuvre from a performative point of view. In virtually all of Donne's texts, we are faced with a speaker who foregrounds himself for example by the way in which lines such as 'I / Except you'enthrall mee, never shall be free, / Nor ever chast, except you ravish mee' (ll. 12–14) isolate the 'I' and the 'mee' at the end of a line and poem. Such self-dramatisation takes place in front of and for the sake of an audience – and these listeners or readers decisively contribute to the re-enactment of each of *John Donne's Performances*.

Manfred Pfister's 'Skalierung von Performativität' (scale of performativity) (Pfister, 2001: 302) makes it possible to evaluate the performative quality of Donne's writings: this list of concrete linguistic indicators such as frequency of personal pronouns, progressiveness, dialogisation, audience-orientation and self-reflexiveness helps to focus on performance as a theoretical concept that is more than a fashionable label. Apart from providing a useful tool for the practice of performative criticism, it also clarifies why Donne's texts promise a particularly rich field of research: personal pronouns abound in poems such as 'The Canonization', not without the same pronoun shifting from one referent to another as the poem continues. Donne's marriage letters are no less ambiguous in their use of personal pronouns and adjectives.

Apart from the performative properties of his texts, there is another reason why an interpretation of *John Donne's Performances* may be more promising than that of other early modern writers. In his youth, Donne had apparently been 'a great frequenter of plays' (Baker, 1641: 156) – but there is also another way in which his biography encourages a performative reading of his works. Donne was a convert from Catholicism who, by the end of his life, had risen to the rank of Dean of St Paul's, a position in which he was revered as one of the most influential preachers of the English reformed Church. His familial background had not been that of an average Roman Catholic. His mother, living with her son at the deanery of St Paul's, remained a staunch Catholic to her death. Moreover, Donne was the great-great-nephew of Sir Thomas More who, as he refused to take the Oath of Supremacy, died a martyr in 1535. Extraordinary as Donne's biography may be, it epitomises processes which, a few generations earlier, had been central to the lives of all English people (Stevie Davies, 1994: 9): thus much of what is particularly true of Donne applies in similar ways to a large part of early modern English society and culture.

Conversion can mean at least three things: not only does it refer to the process by which bread and wine may or may not turn into Christ's body and blood, it also characterises the relationship each individual ought to cultivate towards God, namely again and again to turn to God and Christ, striving to become more and more like them. Thirdly, conversion refers to England's and each English individual's move from Catholicism to English Protestantism. A central category of all Christian faith, conversion is thus inseparably bound up with matters of religious denomination. Religious denomination, in turn, is closely related to the ways in which one imagines the conversional processes of the Eucharist. Not only are these three notions of conversion difficult to separate from one another, they also share an emphasis on process rather than product, on becoming rather than being, and all of them are thus, in the widest sense, performative (cf. Cummings, 2002: 365).

Marotti has noted how conversions both to the reformed faith as well as to Catholicism often had 'a theatrical visibility' (Marotti, 2005: 97). Former Roman Catholics such as Donne would have been particularly sensitive to the ways in which performance and role-play mattered (Jagodzinski, 1999: 27; Maus, 1995: 23). Before 1534, all the English had been Roman Catholics, who were then increasingly forced to convert to reformed doctrines, at least until the persecution of Protestants under Mary. By 1558, when Elizabeth ascended the throne and re-established the reformed Church in a more moderate form, many an English man or woman may have experienced their lives and selves as a matter of performance. Donne's writings, therefore, are a case in point.

While ritual significantly relies on previous institutionalisation and on the re-enactment of a past event, Donne's texts present us with the here and now of a speaker whose self is performed and evolves as we are reading – a process which, at the same time, differentiates his work from artefacts of mere symbolic representation. Performance and performativity offer a third mode between real presence and representation, and one suspects that such a stance may have been particularly attractive to a man like Donne, who, although born and raised a Catholic, at some point converted to the English Church, probably for reasons of professional preferment. Donne's religious position would have been far from clear-cut – and this may be why, as Colin Burrow suggests, '[a] sense of performance, rather than of confession, runs through almost every word he wrote' (Burrow, 2006: 9) and may have been characteristic of his life also.[4] At the same time, in spite of its reformed basis, the early English Church itself retained many Catholic liturgical elements and occupied a middle position between Catholicism and more radically reformed Protestantism.

So religiously turbulent a life as Donne's is nevertheless unusual even by early modern standards. The select (!) bibliography of the *Cambridge Companion to John Donne* lists no fewer than twelve entries under biographies, not including Carey's *John Donne: Life, Mind and Art*, which, although the work of a literary critic, draws extensively on the man's life to illuminate his art, nor John Stubbs's 2006 biography on *Donne: The Reformed Soul*. As these latter two examples easily illustrate, Donne biographies differ from each other primarily with regard to the 'actual', 'real' or 'innermost' religious convictions they ascribe to their subject. Whereas Carey considers Donne a religious 'apostate' who never fully recovered from his official and, as Carey claims, merely superficial conversion to the English faith, Stubbs's title suffices to indicate the denominational thrust of 'his' John Donne: a man of reformed conviction, who was, by and large, tolerant also of other denominations (cf. Dean, 2007). The rampant controversy about Donne being a camouflaged Roman Catholic or staunch Protestant extends not only to biographical accounts but also to the literary analysis of his writings. Most notorious is Martz's 1954 reading of the 'Holy Sonnets' in the same vein as Ignatian spiritual exercises, which was countered by Lewalski's *Protestant Poetics* in 1979. Although, in a later publication, Martz attempts to reconcile Lewalski's criticism with his own claims (Martz, 1994), recent criticism of Donne's sermons, 'Holy Sonnets' and *Devotions* indicates a trend towards viewing Donne as more conformist and reformed than has hitherto been assumed (cf. Papazian, 2003).

In this study, I intend to avoid assigning either Donne's writings or their author to any one religious faith. Not only is it problematic to conclude definitely from literary, albeit religiously informed, utterances anything about the confessional leanings of their writer – I also share Ben Saunders's observation that many critics may not only be analysing the desires of Donne but actually be all too immediately involved with *Desiring Donne* themselves

(Saunders, 2006). To some extent, Donne scholars engage in yet another kind of conversion, namely that of making themselves like Donne – or, 'conversely', in creating Donne in their own image, so that the religious preferences assigned to Donne are mirroring those of his critics. By not approaching Donne as either Roman Catholic or reformed, I attempt to follow Saunders's demand for 'a greater self-consciousness on the part of the critic about the role of desire in his or her own interpretive practice' (Saunders, 2006: 32). In that they place some emphasis on *imitatio Christi* as a recurrent phenomenon in Donne's religious writing, the following pages may seem to imply a latent Catholicism in Donne and thus appear to be counteracting the recent denominational trends of Donne criticism. The faiths of early modern Catholics, Anglicans and Puritans were, however, all strongly Christo- and cruco-centric (Horton Davies, 1996: I, 79) – no fewer than seven of the sixteen translations of Thomas à Kempis's *Imitatio Christi* were of Protestant origin, and there may have been several more translations in manuscript (Crane, 1975: 79). Early modern notions of personhood and self may be more closely related to identifications with the suffering Christ than has hitherto been explored (Sawday, 1997: 35), as such imitations of Christ effected 'a simultaneous affirmation and effacement of personal identity' (Greenblatt, 1980: 77).

Pronouncing a verdict on John Donne's religious allegiance is problematic also because the denominational factions in early modern England were by no means as distinct from one another as might be expected, considering the heated, sometimes bitter arguments Donne and his contemporaries were both involved in and exposed to. What is more, for Donne and his contemporaries, the term 'fashion' takes on the meaning of 'the forming of a self' (Greenblatt, 1980: 2). The humoral fluidity and instability of the self entailed that it had to be re-created over and over again – and clearly, this also meant that no performance was quite like another. As each of them had to be credited and accepted by its audience, there are, particularly in the 'Holy Sonnets', various instances where the powers of performance, rather than the advantages or drawbacks of any one particular religious confession, are doubted and questioned. By suggesting that the self is most significantly fashioned through the ways in which both saying and playing make it so, a performative approach to Donne's writings eliminates the possibility of interpreting his utterances as articulations of the writer's 'innermost' religious and denominational attitudes.

Why sermons, poems, letters and *Devotions*?

In attempting unambiguously to establish Donne's religious affiliation, critics have frequently been tempted deliberately to ignore some of his writings in order to bolster their argument. By contrast, my reading of *John Donne's Performances* is subject only to limitations of space, as it not only treats Donne's worldly and divine poetry but attempts a discussion of his oeuvre at large. Clearly, the choices I have made are also determined by my thematic interest, but, by analysing sermons, poems, letters and *Devotions* as *John Donne's Performances*, I hope to be as open in approaching his writings as the speaker of Donne's 'Holy Sonnet' 'Show me deare Christ' imagines Christ's true church to be. Since the final couplet of this poem, which takes literally the idea of Christ being married to his church, figures the church as a prostitute which would accommodate men of all denominations, she is associated with the type of woman that '[g]oes richly painted' (l. 3) and that is identified with the visual abundances of Roman Catholicism (Erne, 2001: 22). The kind of Catholicism which is at stake in the poem's final lines, is, however, as Erne suggests, universal rather than Roman. Just as such a church would be 'open to most men' (l. 14), so may a reading of Donne's works as performances be more suitable for accommodating the many different personae featured in his various utterances than would be an approach aimed at interpreting them as the articulations of a man fixated on only one type of woman or religious confession. The speaker of 'The Indifferent', notably a little discussed poem, boasts that he 'can love both faire and browne, / Her whom abundance melts, and her whom want betraies' (ll. 1–2), whereas the love celebrated in 'The good-morrow', or the love of God advised by the sermons, seems to be of a more exclusive and monogamous kind: when reading Donne, one hears not one but 'many voices' (Greenblatt, 1990: 20).

The majority of Donne monographs considers his oeuvre too cumbersome to address it in its entirety – Targoff's 2008 monograph is a notable exception. Both the different texts' strategies and readers' expectations are importantly shaped by generic properties. 'Literature is defined by the conventions organizing the community that recognizes it as literature' (Petrey, 1990: 55; Krämer, 2002: 343). Although I can only mention in passing *Biathanatos, Paradoxes and Problems, Ignatius His Conclave, Pseudo-Martyr* or *Essays in Divinity*, I hope to show how Donne's sermons, his worldly and divine poems, as well as his letters and *Devotions* distinguish themselves from and contextualise each other, while all of them confront their listeners or readers with the performances of their various speaking or writing personae, as these feature 'in several habits, and at several ages, and in several postures' (Walton, 1675: 53).[5] In the hope of avoiding biographical speculation, I shall throughout eschew referring to Donne as the articulator of these various utterances. Instead, I shall focus on the generic differences between the articulators of the words in Donne's poetry and prose. Donne's 'Holy Sonnets' are to be read against the background of his *Songs and Sonets* and sermons, and his letters will be considered in close relation to the *Devotions*. Although it appears an obvious procedure to analyse an author's writings in the context of his own works, it has so far not been common in studies on Donne where it is rare to discuss both Donne's erotic and divine poetry in one and the same book, let alone chapter. Nevertheless, close links exist between Donne's worldly and divine poetry, as well as between the patronage concerns of his letters and the (inter)personal performances of his *Devotions*. The sequence of the subsequent chapters is deliberately not chronological. Donne's writing did not become more or less performative as he grew older; rather, his performances are genre-specific.

Donne's 'Pulpit performances' are paradigmatic for my argument. I shall address a selection of sermons where ritual is negotiated and gradually superseded by homiletics. Theories of ritual (Catherine Bell, 1992; Humphrey/Laidlaw, 1994) and rhetoric (Vickers, 1988; Shuger, 1989) are to supplement my reading. More extensively than any other genre, the sermons elaborate on God's relationship to humankind, presenting it as reliant on mutual cooperation. The preacher is to realise and make vivid the need for each individual's contribution, and listeners are encouraged to respond as actively to the sermon as they ought to God's demands for spiritual and moral conversion. The theatre became the sermon's most serious competitor (P. W. White, 1993; Lake/Questier, 2002). Instead of distancing itself from theatrical practice, the rhetoric of Donne's sermons is significantly theatrical. The sermons constitute stagings of the Biblical word, and listeners are expected to convert themselves to the various examples offered there. The preaching persona's position as intermediary parallels that of St Paul, but also of Christ – albeit not always harmoniously so.

Donne's worldly poems seize upon the creative, indeed Promethean potential of language, as poetic worlds, truths and selves are spoken into being. Many *Songs and Sonets* debate their own linguistic efficacy and performativity. Apart from being Promethean, these worldly poems are also protean as their speakers engage in re-enactments of a considerable variety of roles and plots. Most of these poems were conceived for a predominantly male coterie or worked as commendatory poetry for a particular patron or patroness. Like the sermons, these texts are therefore considered in their social dimension. In the light of Austin's and Searle's speech act theory, I shall analyse the ways in which these poems' illocutionary forces may have exerted perlocutionary effects on contemporary audiences or readers, and how, for example in 'The Canonization' and 'The Curse', an anxiety as to how the performative might of words might come down also on the speaker's head is rehearsed there.

Donne's *Songs and Sonets*, as well as many of his 'Holy Sonnets', at the same time also constitute 'Passionate performances'. Both Roland Barthes's and Niklas Luhmann's conceptualisations of love and passion are distinctly performative. Although love is determined by a certain code, its distinguishing mark is excess, an outgrowing of all convention. The paradox of such systematic violation of a code is one of the passionate common features of Donne's erotic and divine poems, concerned as they are with amorous passion and the passion of Christ respectively. In the latter case, various passion problems arise: the speaker's potential self-interest proves a stumbling block to divine meditation, nor do the speakers of the 'Holy Sonnets' appear as confident with regard to the working mechanisms of passionate performances as those of the erotic poems. Moreover, God is not easily fitted into gendered models of amorous passion, and far-reaching communication difficulties ensue from the communicative situation of the divine poems which contrasts markedly with that of most *Songs and Sonets*. In functioning as theatres of their own, the 'Holy Sonnets' differ both from Donne's erotic and his homiletic performances.

The last two chapters provide a comparative reading of Donne's *Letters to Severall Persons of Honour* and *Devotions Upon Emergent Occasions* as 'Patronage' and '(Inter)Personal performances'. Donne's letters constitute material tokens of loyalty not only between friends but also in transactions between client and patron or patroness. They are presented as commodities, to compensate for the material benefits their writer may have been granted by his social superior. Early modern epistolography, such as Erasmus's *De Conscribendis Epistolis* (1536) and Angel Day's *The English Secretary* (1599), assumes that close connections hold between writer and letter, although Day in particular also places great emphasis on the conventions to be observed if the writer is to play the part adequately. Donne's writing personae often take literally the notion of the letter as a mirror of the soul. They repeatedly strive towards becoming the word, and, in a second step, attempt to become as one with their various addressees. Owing to these efforts at 'communion', Donne's epistolary writing is illustrative of a religion of letters, a kind of devotion which, however well it may have worked at other times, was not crowned with success concerning Donne's epistolary pleading with his (former) employer Sir Thomas Egerton and Sir George More after his clandestine marriage to the latter's daughter.

Particularly in the *Iland* passage, Donne's *Devotions* display an overwhelming interest in becoming the other. Despite the work's unambiguously theological thrust, each individual devotion's movement from meditation and expostulation towards prayer, from communication towards communion recalls the processes of Donne's letters. The *Devotions* contain some of Donne's most detailed commentary on the complexities and difficulties surrounding the Eucharist, considered in its typological relation to the Fall. Communion allegedly amounts to an identification with Christ, and a similar kind of identification ought to take place between the reader and speaker of Donne's *Devotions*. As Donne wrote letters in both prose and verse, we may also consider his *Devotions* as generically related to the 'Holy Sonnets'. A discussion of Donne's use of verse as opposed to prose concludes this chapter.

Notes

1 Webber notes how self and language are closely connected to each other in the early modern period (Webber, 1968: 10).
2 Thomas Docherty professes to be interested less in ethics than in cultural poetics, but moral judgement creeps in when he labels the self of Donne's poems 'fundamentally *hypocritical*' (Docherty, 1986: 118, italics original). John Carey likewise criticises the falseness behind Donne's writing (Carey, 1990; Oliver, 1997; Healy, 2005: 77).
3 Moreover, although Donne features prominently in Shami's essay collection on *Renaissance Tropologies* of 'journey, theater, moment, and ambassadorship' (Shami, 2008a: 1), none of his writings is considered within a theatrical and hence performative context.
4 Donne's posing for his effigy in his shroud constitutes the most famous 'performative' instance of the writer's biography. One nevertheless ought to refrain from questioning 'the sincerity of an attitude which seems to us ... almost theatrical' (Gosse, 1899: II, 286). Theatricality does not necessarily entail insincerity.
5 Despite this recognition, Izaak Walton was interested primarily in Donne as a dignified preacher, who allegedly made great haste to convert to the reformed faith – much greater haste than is suggested by Gosse.

1

Pulpit performances – Sermons

We pray you in Christ's stead, be ye reconciled to God. (2 Cor. 5.20)

This short verse epitomises the major purpose of Donne's sermons. Humankind's reconciliation with God is their central concern. There were two major channels through which such a conversion might be achieved: the sermon and the Eucharist. Despite their interrelatedness, homiletic and ritual elements of the early modern English service did not readily coexist – which is why an analysis of how Donne's sermons combine homiletics with ritual starts off my discussion of his pulpit performances.

Moreover, the above quotation places Christ in a humble position, picturing him, together with the speaker of this verse, in the act of praying. Donne's sermon on this text observes Christ acting here 'as though God needed us, to intreat us to be reconciled to him', 'he proceeds with man, as though man might be of some use to him, and with whom it were fit for him to hold good correspondence' (X, 5, 120). The relationship between God and humankind is imagined as one of mutuality, even interdependence, where giver and recipient, God and each man or woman, can hardly be distinguished – just as in the Bible, where often 'the phrase is such in doing a curtesie, as though the receiver had done it, in accepting it' (X, 5, 119). Such a view of the relationship between God and the self proves typical of Donne's sermons.

If God and the self are mutually dependent on one another, in that salvation cannot take place unless one first accepts God's offer of reconciliation by consenting to be converted to him, and if the preacher's task is to encourage such consent in his hearers, this relationship corresponds to that between preacher and listener. The *divisio* of Donne's sermon on this text announces how its focus will be on the preacher as God's intermediary: 'our parts will be three: *Our* Office towards *you*; *yours* towards *us*; and the Negotiation it self, *Reconciliation* to God [...] for, in the two first (besides the matter) there are two kinds of *persons*, *we* and *you*, The *Priest* and the *People* (we *pray you*.) And in the last there are two kinds of persons too, *you* and *God*; *Be ye reconciled to God*' (X, 5, 120).[1]

The sermon constitutes a theatrical re-enactment of the Biblical word, especially concerning the ways in which it encourages listeners to imagine themselves in the examples offered by the preacher. The last part of this chapter focuses on the theatrical structures inherent to Donne's sermons – as, for example, when the preacher encourages his listeners to re-enact the Biblical script and take St Paul's part in his dialogue with the blinding light of Christ by responding to Christ's question '*Cur me?*' with the words of the Apostle: 'Answer this question, with *Sauls* answer to this question, by another question, *Domine quid me vis facere? Lord what wilt thou have me do?*' (VI, 10, 222). As dramatic (re-)enactments, Donne's sermons strongly depend on the rhetorical concepts of *enargia* and *energia*, in order to make present that which is otherwise non-presentable, the divine. What is particular to Donne's preaching is the way in which it adapts the communicative system of the theatre to the genre of the sermon in order to re-enact Christ's sacrifice and resurrection.

Whenever Donne preached, he would have been aware of that other institution which competed with him for listeners – the theatre (Lake/Questier, 2002: 430; Michael O'Connell, 1985: 306). There were two ways of meeting this challenge: the most straightforward was to use the pulpit for a thorough denunciation of the stage as the epitome of heresy and ungodliness, in order to dissuade listeners from going anywhere near a theatre at any time, let alone on a church day. The other possible response was to seize upon the potential of dramatic communication in order to equal or even outdo the theatre on its own terms. Although the unknown author of the 1625 'short treatise against stage plays' does not share this view, he concedes that some playgoers 'will say, that sometimes the sacred Scripture is or may be acted by players on the stage, and thereby a man may learne more then at a sermon' (Davison, 1972: 11; Lake/Questier, 2002: 447). In his youth, Donne himself had been 'a great frequenter of plays', and not only 'a great visitor of ladies' (Baker, 1641: 156).² Although no evidence exists as to whether Donne and Shakespeare ever met, Bald suspects that Marlowe may have 'made a deeper impression on Donne than any other English contemporary' (Bald, 1970: 47). Just as Donne did not leave behind his erotic passions when approaching God in his divine poetry, so did he retain his predilection for the theatrical mode in his preaching. Although Puritans denounced the theatre for the way it manipulated the senses of its audiences, its great potential in doing so did not go unnoticed (cf. P. W. White, 1993: 173). Preaching and stagecraft are closely linked, for '[a]t the center of Protestant worship stands an essentially dramatic performance: the sermon' (Döring, 2005: 20). The relatedness of Donne's sermons to the theatre was a consequence of the liturgical shifts that were still taking place in the aftermath of the Reformation: 'the Reformation insistence on the centrality of the spoken word reintroduced an element of theater into the liturgy – albeit theater of a different order from the theatricality of which the medieval liturgy stood accused' (Crockett, 1995: 6).

The preacher's persona functions 'in Christ's stead', meaning that he is importantly associated with Jesus, who was both God and man. Christ's passion features significantly here and is not limited to the preacher alone, as listeners are encouraged to re-enact his suffering. But despite the preacher's reliance on Biblical example, there are some instances where the inherent risks of acting by precedent come to the surface and will not be contained, as will be illustrated by a detailed analysis of two individual sermons which is to conclude this chapter.

Although I shall be quoting from a broad variety of Donne's sermons, this chapter draws on three sermons in particular: first, I have chosen the above-mentioned sermon on the conversion of St Paul (Acts 9.4), since this event was of evident interest to the convert John Donne. It is one of four sermons he preached, in various years, on the Conversion of St Paul at St Paul's. In furthermore choosing an earlier sermon on the Psalms (Psalm 38.4 (Lincoln's Inn, 1618)) and one on the Epistles, namely the one on 2 Corinthians 5.20 (St Paul's, of unknown date), I have followed Donne's own preference. He claims to favour those two Biblical books over all others 'because they are Scriptures, written in such forms as I have been most accustomed to; Saint *Pauls* being Letters, and *Davids* being Poems' (II, 1, 49). What he does not mention is that the poetic style of the Psalms often resembles his own: the dramatic immediacy with which these texts confront their implied addressee (i.e. God) and the dynamics with which they often move from an accusation of God to an avowal of his eternal trustworthiness is typical also of many 'Holy Sonnets', and it is probably no coincidence that Donne should have chosen Psalm 38 as the textual basis for a series of no fewer than six sermons at Lincoln's Inn in 1618. Psalm 38 is a grand display of a sinner's penance: 'For mine iniquities are gone over mine Head: as a heavy burden they are too heavy for me. / My wounds stink and are corrupt because of my foolishness' (Ps. 38, 4–5) – and this performance of iniquity, the speaker hopes, will be witnessed by God, so that he will eventually relent towards him: 'For in thee, O LORD, do I hope: thou wilt hear, O Lord my God' (Ps. 38, 15). Although the whole Psalm represents quite a thorough declaration of transgression, the speaker promises not to waver in this performance of penance, '[f]or I will declare mine iniquity; I will be sorry for my sin' (Ps. 38, 18). The Epistles, on the other hand, probably aroused Donne's interest not least because he liked to align himself with St Paul as a prominent preacher, and frequently he considers the Epistles as sermons in themselves.

Ritual performativity

In their introduction to Protestant preaching, Albrecht and Weber characterise Reformation theology fundamentally as a theology of homiletics, so much so that the sermon gradually came to surpass the relevance of the Eucharist, as its words increasingly acquired the status of sacrament (Albrecht/Weber, 2002a: 2; Targoff, 2008: 158). In England, even fairly close to the beginning of the Reformation, the sermon also gained in significance: 'The Book of Common Prayer has from its first version in 1549 prescribed a dual ministry of word and sacrament' (Carrithers, 1972: 10) – under different monarchs, one or other of these ministries was emphasised more (McCullough, 1998: 6). As a priest of the English Church under King James I, Donne appears to have 'favoured communication over Communion' (Ferrell, 1992: 63), and, clearly, the differences between the celebration of the Eucharist as an instance of ritual and the sermon as an act of performative language cannot be denied. In a sideswipe at Roman Catholic priests, the speaker of one sermon confesses that 'whereas these men make man, and God too of bread, naturally wholly indisposed to any such change, for this power we confess it is not in our Commission', but, 'for that power, which is to work upon you, to whom we are sent, we are defective in nothing' (X, 5, 129). Since this sermon is explicitly concerned with the function of preaching, the 'power' referred to here is that of the pulpit.

In the following, I shall explore the differences between sermon and sacrament while at the same time drawing attention to the ways in which reformed homiletics echo the practices of ritual, how the English sermon's *'newly embodied* word superseded the traditional sacraments, refiguring in the physical presence of the speaker the Word that had been incarnate in bread and wine' (Crockett, 1995: 6; Whalen, 2002: 85; Webber, 1963: 133). '[R]itual is a distinctive way in which an action, probably any action, may be performed' (Humphrey/Laidlaw, 1994: 3; Catherine Bell, 1992: 7). This implies that preaching may also be subject to processes of ritualisation, especially if we assume that an action's being 'intrinsically directed' marks the 'difference between ritualized and unritualized action' (Humphrey/Laidlaw, 1994: 4). Sermons are directed in that they are minutely planned and aim at having some particular effect on their hearers who are consequently implicated in the ritual process. As a genre, the sermon is always audience-oriented or even audience-dependent and may be regarded as an instance of performance-centred rather than liturgy-centred ritual such as the Eucharist (Humphrey/Laidlaw, 1994: 8).

These two types of ritual differ further in that the latter is concerned with 'getting it right' whereas the former's efficacy rather depends on 'making it work' by whichever strategy is viable. Performance-centred ritual relies much more on subjective and idiosyncratic convictions and is consequently far less rigorously ritualised than liturgy-centred acts such as the Eucharist (Humphrey/Laidlaw, 1994: 8–11). Nor is performance-centred ritual as much concerned with the search for a prototype (cf. Jonathan Smith, 1987: 103; Lukken, 2005: 55); whereas liturgy-centred ritual aims at as close a re-staging as possible of its founding moment, in the case of the Eucharist that of Christ's last supper with his disciples,[3] the sermon aims at making meaning present at the very moment of listening. This does not entail that the sermon would rid itself of ritualistic strategies such as 'formality, fixity, and repetition' (Catherine Bell, 1992: 91–2) – but it certainly employs them less rigorously (cf. Lukken, 2005: 66). Whereas 'routinized' liturgy-centred ritual underwent critical scrutiny during the Reformation, performance-centred ritual such as a sermon presupposed that each actor must submit to '"ritual commitment", a particular stance with respect to his or her own action' (Humphrey/Laidlaw, 1994: 12; 88).

No less than the distributor of bread and wine, whose words, before the Reformation, had been believed to effect the transubstantiation, was the preacher, too, expected 'to do', and not merely say, 'things with words', both to and together with the people before him. The sermon was to alter people's lives, just as the consecrated host had always been (and still was) considered to have a conversional effect on those who received it. It would be wrong to assume that a preacher like Donne, although he attributed great significance to the sermon, would be negligent in the celebration of the Eucharist (cf. Dawson/Yachnin, 2001: 28). Nevertheless preachers 'saw the end of their eloquence as nothing less than salvation' (Crockett, 2000: 61), the salvation which was to be brought about by each congregation member's individual conversion. As Donne himself puts it: 'It hath alwaies beene the Lords way to glorifie himselfe in the conversion of Men, by the ministery of Men' (VI, 10, 205). The traditional conclusion of each sermon – the word 'Amen' (from the Hebrew, meaning 'So be it'/'Truly') – attests to the performative potential with which the sermon was believed to be endowed. The preacher was eager to exploit the sermon's performative power, for example when he urges his listeners to dedicate themselves to Christ at the very moment of hearing him preach: 'Yet if we have omitted our first early [i.e. the earliest occasion for converting ourselves to Christ], our youth, there is one early left for us; this minute; seek Christ early, now, now, as soon as his Spirit begins to shine upon your hearts' (I, 5, 250; cf. Chuilleanáin, 1984: 198). Similarly, in *Essays in Divinity*, the speaker admonishes himself: '*so, though this soul of mine, by which I partake thee, begin not now, yet let this minute, O God, this happy minute of thy visitation, be the beginning of her conversion*' (*Essays* 37). According to Pfister's scale of performativity, the relevance of an audience together with the effect which an utterance is meant to have on it are typical markers of performativity (Pfister, 2001; Crockett, 1995: 8). Moreover, Donne's sermons frequently employ questions and exclamations rather than statements, and make use not only of the third but also of the first and second person; and the 'hic et nunc' of their original performance context becomes obvious both in their argumentative urgency and the numerous dialogues they imagine. In repeatedly insisting on the individual's conversion to God which must precede salvation, they focus much less on what is given than on that which is to happen, to be done, to be undergone and to be experienced: the current process matters more than the eventual product, which is why one may even think of conversion as a rite of passage, resembling baptism or marriage.

Most importantly, however, Donne's sermons are performative because they perform what they are speaking of (Pfister, 2001: 302). As a preacher, Donne 'does not reduce the sense from the verbal medium but lets the meaning of the sacred words realize itself' (Chamberlin, 1976: 157). The 'sacred words' are, after all, already performative, and the preacher's task consists in interpreting and translating the words and decrees of God as found in the Scriptures:

> Our Regeneration is by his Word; that is, by faith, which comes by hearing; *The seed is the word of God*, sayes Christ himselfe; Even the seed of faith. Carry it higher, the Creation was by the word of God; *Dixit, & facta sunt*, God spoke, and all things were made. [...] the second Person in the Trinity, was so much by the Word, as that he is the Word; *Verbum caro*, It was that *Word*, that was made *Flesh*. So that God, who cannot enter into bands to us, hath given us security enough; He hath given us his Word; His written Word, his Scriptures; His Essentiall Word, his Son. [...] there was not onely a word, the Word, Christ himselfe, a Son of God in heaven, but a Voyce, the word uttered, and preached; Christ manifested in his Ordinance: *He heard a voice'*
>
> (IV, 10, 216–17)

When acknowledging the performative potential of the Biblical word, the preacher is faced with a dilemma: performatives are in principle not translatable. Each sermon faces the threefold challenge of translating historical specificities of Christianity into a present reality, of realising eternal Christian truths in the here and now, and of making generalities applicable to each individual listener (Ueding, 1992–2005: 47). This task is much more complex than it sounds in Rom. 10.17, which comprises rather a prominent Biblical definition for preaching: 'So then faith *cometh* by hearing, and hearing by the word of God'. The hearing necessitates the co-operation of those who are meant to hear, and the sermon herein echoes the sacrament of the Eucharist: 'In the same way [...] as each Christian participates in the activity which is the Lord's Supper, taking and eating the Bread, receiving and drinking the Wine, so also in the audible Sacrament which is the sermon he actively hears and takes into himself the Word of God' (Parker, 1992: 48; Targoff, 2008: 158) – the Christian, so to speak, has to swallow that for himself which the preacher brings before him, the 'preacher should be heard by a communicant somewhat *as* he receives the Eucharist' (Carrithers, 1972: 125; Johnson, 1999: 144). In the context of the Reformation, the sacred began to be less related to material objects than to transcendent, internal and, we may add, personally individualised experience (Pfister/von Rosador, 1991: 21). As Donne argues in a sermon on one of the Psalms:

> But these *Psalmes* were made, not onely to vent *David's* present holy passion, but to serve the Church of God, to the worlds end. And therefore, change the person, and we shall finde a whole quiver of arrows. Extend this *Man*, to all *Mankind*; carry *Davids* History up to *Adams* History, and consider us in that state, which wee inherit from *him*, and we shall see *arrows* fly about our ears, *A Deo prosequente*, the anger of God hanging over our heads, in a cloud of arrows; and *à conscientia remordente*, our own consciences shooting *poisoned arrows* of desperation into our souls (II, 1, 55)

How then do Donne's sermons manage to '[e]xtend this *Man*, to all *Mankind*', in order to turn the hearing of a transforming voice into a transformation of their audience (Esterhammer, 1994: xiiv)? If Donne's translations of the Biblical performatives are to be crowned with success, their communicative strategies must owe something to the processes of ritual, for 'ritual communication is not just an alternative way of expressing something but the expression of things that cannot be expressed in any other way' (Catherine Bell, 1992: 111).

God and self

In turning to the sermons themselves, we should start by asking what exactly the primary interest is and what consequently has to be translated. Most basically, they engage in a characterisation of one's relation to God and/or Christ, and they ponder how one's conversion to God can be effected. Consider the following passage, which distances itself very literally from the Calvinist doctrine of the 'irrestibility of grace' (cf. Cummings, 2002: 389): 'Christ promises to come to the door, and to knock at the door, and to stand at the door, and to enter if any man open; but he does not say, he will break open the door: it was not his pleasure to express such an earnestness, such an Irresistibility in his grace, so' (I, 6, 255–6). Humankind has not yet opened its door to God and, unless it does so, it cannot be reconciled to him. As another sermon makes clear, the term reconciliation implies 'a present enmity' with God, as well as 'a former friendship' (X, 5, 134). Attention is drawn to the (dangerous) miracle of humankind being 'allowed so high a sinne, as enmity with God' (X, 5, 135). So appalled is the speaker at this idea that his metaphors begin to become slightly confused as he marvels at that 'confounding honour, to be the enemy of God, of God who is not merely a multiplied Elephant, millions of Elephants multiplied into one, but a multiplied World' (X, 5, 135).[4] Yet there is hope, and the speaker encourages his listeners: 'You see what you had, and how you lost it. If it might not bee recovered, God would not call you to it' (X, 5, 136).

God's knock and call must be heard, humankind's union with Christ cannot be effected by Christ's agency alone but relies on the individual's adequate response: it is the result of a reciprocal process. After all, if God was happy to redeem people even against their will, preaching, the act of advertising for voluntary consent to be united with God, would be altogether unnecessary. Such a view explains Donne's reluctance to get too involved with Calvinist theories of predestination (Ferrell, 1992: 61; DiPasquale, 2008: 2), and it contradicts Shuger's notion of Donne's attitude towards God as exclusively 'a spirituality based on awe and subjection' (Shuger, 2000: 118). Although it is true that Donne's God is as little bound by law as any absolutist monarch, the relationship between God and humankind in Donne is less distant and more intimate than Shuger would have it. In their characterisations of God, his speakers focus not only on 'the total concentration of power into a single figure' (Shuger, 2000: 119) but as much on God's dependency on each believer's personal acceptance of his (self-)invitation as he knocks at the door.[5] 'For Donne, the grandeur of the human condition could be found in the fact that, by accepting or denying God's grace, individuals might elect to change their natures' (Harland, 1986: 710). The self becomes and remains self and human through its ability to change, its potential to convert or refuse to do so – a concept which corresponds to a notion of self as performative. In an earlier publication, Shuger seems to share such a view when she describes the early modern self 'not as self-awareness but as love or the response of the soul to God's pull' (Shuger, 1989: 11). She even argues that, in the early modern period, '[t]he self is an activity not a thing' (Shuger, 1989: 234) – and God, one might add, depends on each individual to become active in either accepting or refusing to let him enter.

Sweeping as this statement on the early modern self as 'an activity not a thing' may sound, it has some heuristic value for Donne, in whose sermons a concept of the self as coming into being through its response to certain 'pulls' holds not only for the 'pulls' of God but also for those of temptation: 'A woman of tentation, *Tendit arcum in incertum*, as that story speaks; shee paints, she curls, she sings, she gazes, and is gazed upon; There's an arrow shot *at random*; she aim'd at no particular mark; And thou puttest thy self within shot, and meetest the arrow; Thou soughtest the tentation, the tentation sought not thee' (II, 1, 57). Just as temptation depends on meeting or hitting the self, so does God depend on being encountered by it. Such a notion of the self goes back to Augustine, who regarded emotions and passions as the fundamental link to God. Rhetoric aiming at a stimulation of such passions was therefore not a deception but sacred, since it prepared the way to salvation (Shuger, 1989: 248). It is not by coincidence that the subject of obstinacy triggers Donne's most tempestuous outbursts, as in a sermon preached in December 1617 where he rails against '[t]hat stupid inconsideration, which passes on drowsily, and negligently upon Gods creatures, that sullen indifference in ones disposition, to love one thing no more than another, not to value, not to chuse, not to prefer, that stoniness, that inhumanity, not to be affected, not to be entendred' (I, 5, 241–2).[6]

'Obstruction rather than flow is cause and evidence of illness' (Schoenfeldt, 1999: 13), and this supports Selleck's view of Donne's body as humoral, which 'suggests a material embeddedness of self and surround' (Selleck, 2001: 150). Yet the self does not passively fall victim to its humoral make-up. Galenic physiology allows for a kind of 'self-control that authorizes individuality' (Schoenfeldt, 1999: 11; Selleck, 2001: 168), indeed that kind of individuality which, when it comes to conversion, is exercised in one's personal willingness or reluctance to convert oneself to God. In the context of Donne's above condemnation of 'indifferency', one may even suspect that inevitable disaster announces itself as soon as a person is no longer vulnerable. A notion of the self as inherently, but also ideally unstable and thus open to conversion, either to God or to temptation, is at the heart of Donne's sermons (cf. Sloane, 1985: 153). For Donne, there is some virtue even in infirmity, since it still leaves room for conversion: as the speaker of an early sermon argues, 'not to sin out of infirmity, or tentation, or heat of blood, but to sin in cold blood, and upon just reason, and mature considerations, and so deliberately and advisedly to continue to sin' (I, 2, 171) certainly comprises the worst one can come to. No help is available any more once 'the sin arises merely and immediately from my self: it is, when the heart hath usurp'd upon the devil, and upon the world too, and is able and apt to sin of it self, if there were no devil, and if there were no outward objects of tentation' (I, 2, 179). Such a self is no longer convertible as it can no longer be tempted either by the devil or by salvation. Sinning out of one's self implies an essentially stable and independent self – and this is the greatest corruption of all.

On the semantic level, Donne's sermons are concerned with promoting faith and conversion, but they never fail to present faith – opening the door to Christ and thus enabling him to save us – as anything but co-operative.[7] God's performative agency needs humankind not only as an object to act upon but also as a subject. While this need endows listeners with an active agency which they are to express individually by consent or resistance to their salvation, their consent is to become manifest in their submission to God as the supreme principle. This relationship between God and humanity reflects what Humphrey and Laidlaw term the paradox of intentionality with regard to the ritual act: 'Under ritualization the relation which normally exists between intention and act is transformed. We should make clear, however, that this transformation is itself the result of a deliberate act: the adoption of a ritual stance. It may seem to be a paradox, but it is a result of the actor having adopted this stance that ritual acts are non-intentional' (Humphrey/Laidlaw, 1994: 94). Although believers are required to renounce their own intentions once they have become converted Christians, this renunciation is preceded by their agreement to do so: as regards conversion, an instance of ritual initiated or even performed through the sermon, 'one both is, and is not, the author of one's acts' (Humphrey/Laidlaw, 1994: 106).

Without entering into any detailed discussion of Donne's religious allegiances, one could argue that such a concept of conversion combines and reconciles Roman Catholic and reformed approaches to salvation. Reformation theology considered itself different from Catholicism by arguing that salvation can be reached neither through good deeds, nor through ritual processes, but through the grace of God and the individual's faith. Calvinism even maintained that God had predestined each individual for either eternal life or damnation. For Catholics, by contrast, good actions, regular celebration of the Eucharist and observance of all sacraments played a significant role in improving one's chances for the afterlife. Considerable emphasis was put on each person's own responsibility to be preserved from purgatory and hell. Conversion, 'not a matter of conviction or works, though the first may produce and the second result from it' (Gosse, 1899: 99), opens up a third and new road towards salvation. Potentially initiated through the sermon and the result of performance-centred ritual, it may have appealed to early modern contemporaries since it reconciles aspects of Catholic and reformed doctrines. As it demands some activity from each believer in opening the door to Christ, it attributes partial responsibility to each man and woman. On the other hand, God's offer of salvation, which applies to everyone, notably precedes each individual's acceptance of it.

Their idea of conversion as a mutual process places Donne's sermons in some ways in between Roman Catholicism, which attributes more agency to the individual's free will and actions, and stricter forms of Calvinism, whose insistence on the doctrine of predestination and the irresistibility of grace denies free will (William Mueller, 1962: 179). God's promise of salvation is performed in the preacher's invitations to identify with the sermon – but both offers equally rely on being taken up by the audience. An inability or unwillingness to identify is tantamount to declining God's offer of salvation. Likewise, faith, the reformers' proclaimed road to salvation, is a conscious process which necessitates each believer's active employment of reason: 'For let no man thinke that *God* hath given him so much ease here, as to save him by believing he knoweth not what, or why. *Knowledge* cannot save us, but we cannot be saved without Knowledge; Faith is not on this side of Knowledge, but beyond it; we must necessarily come to *Knowledge* first, though we must not stay at it, when we are come thither' (III, 17, 359). God will not be satisfied with a faith that is, in the literal sense of the word, un-reflected. Each individual has to reflect upon and rationally engage with the Scriptures before God will condescend to ennoble his reason to faith (cf. Lowe, 1961; Sherwood, 1972).

How is this co-operation to be effected through the sermon? If the central agenda of the Biblical word is to move and invite individuals to consent willingly to their conversion, the difficulty of translating the Biblical word in all its performative might can be brought about solely by way of performing what is said in the Bible as immediately as possible in each sermon. The 'histoire' of the Bible, which is reflected on the semantic level of each sermon, is not only supposed to be narrated but also performed through its discourse. Harland (1986) reads Donne performatively by suggesting that the development of each sermon towards salvation (a process promoted by Luther, who suggested that each sermon move from 'Gesetz' to 'Evangelium', from law to gospel, from throwing down to raising up its listener) discursively mirrors the desirable development each congregation member should undergo, namely from a recognition of his or her sins and just damnation to an appreciation of salvation in Christ.[8] But although Harland quotes several critics to support this view, there are numerous Donne sermons in which the ideal of a characteristically 'rising action' fails to fully account for their general complexity. The dramatic tableau created at the end of Donne's last sermon *Death's Duel*, for example, in which he seemed 'not to preach mortification by a living voice, but mortality by a decayed body, and a dying face' (Walton, 1928: 49), leaves us in a precariously ambiguous position in between death and resurrection: 'There we leave you in that *blessed dependancy,* to *hang* upon *him* that *hangs* upon the *Crosse,* there *bath* in his *teares,* there *suck* at his *woundes,* and *lye downe in peace* in his *grave,* till hee vouchsafe you a *resurrection*, and an *ascension* into that *Kingdome*, which hee *hath purchas'd for you*, with the *inestimable price* of his *incorruptible blood*. AMEN' (X, 11, 248). Harland draws attention to another performative dimension in the sermons when claiming that the speaker's frequent assumption of the voice of Christ effects the reincarnation and resurrection of Christ in its discourse. He generally stresses the importance of identification and example and acknowledges that the variety of dramatic personae Donne employs consciously takes into account the congregation members' autonomy in choosing or refusing to identify. Eventually, however, Harland stops short of extending this recognition into a full-scale argument. The sermons' strong reliance on example is the result of the duality inherent in any kind of performance: performance is always for an audience, and frequently listeners are required to contribute actively to the performance via some kind of 'uptake'. This is exactly what is at stake on the semantic level of Donne's sermons: they present the (performative) power of the divine will as reliant on a co-operative willingness on the part of each individual, the willingness to be converted that they strive to promote and provoke.

The co-operation with God promoted on the level of story is to be effected by conversion into one or several of the dramatic personae presented there. Although Donne's sermons aim at motivating listeners to court God, this courting goes hand in hand with the preacher's courting of his listeners, as he attempts to coax them into an agreement with and an acceptance of God's offer: listeners are thus 'courted' to 'court' God.[9] As 'ritualization is first and foremost a strategy for the construction of certain types of power relationships effective within particular social organizations' (Catherine Bell, 1992: 197), the sermon's dependency on its listeners' identification with examples illustrates and reconstructs God's dependency on each individual's acceptance of God's coming to their door. The listeners' receptivity on the level of the sermon entails receptivity with regard to the relationship between God and humankind. 'The sun hath no benefit by his own light, nor the fire by his own heat, nor a perfume by the sweetness thereof, but only they who make their use, and enjoy this heat and fragrancy' we read in one of Donne's sermons (I, 5, 244). An inability to make use, an unwillingness to identify is equivalent to declining God's offer of salvation. By contrast,

> This is an impropriation without sacriledge, and an enclosure of a common without damage, to make God mine owne, to finde that all that God sayes is spoken to me, and all that Christ suffered was suffered for me. [...] it is indeed an incorrigible height of pride, when a man will not believe that he is meant in a libel, if he be not named in that libel. It is a fearfull obduration, to be Sermon-proofe, or not to take knowledge, that a judgement is denounced against him, because he is not named in the denouncing of that judgement. (VI, 10, 219)

Listeners are expected to make the link between their selves in their ordinary lives and the examples as presented in the text of the sermon, a connection characteristic of all ritual (Lukken, 2005: 69). Particularly a 'sense of *Christ's* relation to the individual soul is for Donne the essence of faith itself' (Quinn, 1962: 327, my emphasis). The 'story' about the choice each human being faces, of either accepting or refusing God's offer of salvation, is performed in the discourse of each sermon, which invites identification without ever being able to force it. Of course, there is some difficulty in providing a part for every listener in a sermon: 'If we would goe about to expresse, by what customes of sin this dominion is established, we should be put to a necessity of entring into every profession, and every conscience' (II, 3, 117). The individualisation of sinning does not contradict a Galenic concept of self: although human beings are all alike in being composed of the same four fluids, the unique mixture of these elements in every single person at the same time also allows for differences (Schoenfeldt, 1999: 20). Still, Donne trusts in the merits of identification: '*David* in his humble spirit feels in himselfe, but much more in his propheticall spirit, foresees, and foretells in others, the infectious *nature* of sin' (II, 3, 118). The infectiousness of sin enables identification.

Rather than identifying individual speech acts within the text of individual sermons, we ought to read the whole text of each sermon 'as Speech Act' (Esterhammer, 1994: 16). Any sermon may fail, at least with regard to its effect on the audience. The illocutionary force of each sermon comes down to an encouragement and promotion of conversion on the part of the speaker, so that the sermon's felicitousness would be limited merely to the audience's recognition of its illocutionary force as an invitation to identify with its examples. The sermon's perlocutionary effect (cf.

Austin, 1975: 102), by contrast, would consist in the actual conversion of the respective listener(s). This, however, is ultimately not within the power of the preacher because faith is not involuntarily effected by hearing. Alternatively, the speech act of a sermon can be interpreted similarly to that of a bet which depends on the audience's uptake (cf. Austin, 1975: 9) of the exempla offered by the preacher, whereas a refusal to identify would render the speech act of the sermon infelicitous, as incomplete. Depending on how likely one takes it to be that conversion may be effected through the speech act of a sermon, one may prefer to imagine the audience's (positive) reaction by identifying with the sermon's examples as an uptake and thus part of the sermon's illocutionary force, or merely as its perlocutionary effect which is less easily controlled and beyond the preacher's reach. As Donne puts it, 'He came to save by calling us, as an eloquent and a perswasive man draws his Auditory, but yet imprints no necessity upon the faculty of the will; so works Gods calling of us in his word' (I, 9, 313). Donne was aware 'that the invitation to share and participate could be rejected, as by a parishioner or communicant present in body only, or by half-hearted conformists' (Carrithers, 1972: 9). In order to 'draw[] his Auditory' in the service of God, the speaker would employ all the rhetorical strategies at his disposal (cf. Vickers, 1988: 270; Mitchell, 1962: 47ff.).

Although particularly Roman Catholic ritual was often denounced as outward show without any need for active co-operation on the individual's part, generally speaking, 'ritualization necessitates and engenders both consent and resistance' (Catherine Bell, 1992: 218) and relies on mutuality – which is why it easily lends itself to the idea of God's dependence on each individual believer's consent. The conversions that are to be brought about in the sermon further resemble ritual in their need for repetition (cf. Lukken, 2005: 39), as no conversion is once and for all effective and sufficient. Religion and ritual may only be recognised for what they are by the iterative processes they entail, and conversion relies even more on repetition than other rites of passage such as marriage or baptism, since these two rituals need (or ought) only be performed once in an individual's life. But because sin is to humankind like a tyrant that may even include as pious a man as St Paul, one ought to be aware that '[a] man is not presently learned, because he hath a good desire to be learned;

nor hath he that hath begun a conversion, presently accomplished his regeneration' (II, 3, 116). Conversion has to be undergone continuously and repeatedly, and this is why it constitutes the dominant and constantly rehearsed subject of all of Donne's sermons. Just as, according to Butler, the accumulative repetition of specific acts gradually shape one's gender (Butler, 1990), so does the self's faith in and salvation through God realise itself by repeated conversions. Such repetitive processes of conversion are typical not only of the sermon but also, as we shall see with Donne's *Devotions*, of meditative practice. By performing on the level of discourse that which is at issue on the level of the story, the listening to or reading of Donne's sermons reproduces the preacher's reading experience of the Biblical text (Chamberlin, 1976: 31; Davis, 1986: 179). The reader's own activity is consequently called upon: in their own post-sermonic meditations, triggered by the hearing of the sermon, all listeners are meant to re-enact the preacher's sermon-production for themselves (Ueding, 1992–2005: 70).

Moreover, listeners are to take on roles which are presented in the sermon. Such performance is not to be conceived of as an act of dissembling the self. A humoral concept of identity allows for an 'outside-in process of behavioral change'. Only by subscribing to a view of 'acting-as-becoming' (Selleck, 2001: 155) does the relevance of enacting the roles of dramatic exempla make sense. What is true of ritual, that serious content and theatrical form need by no means contradict each other (Althoff, 2003: 13), also applies for the medium of the sermon. Inward and outward spheres may be in contrast with one another – but what is inside may very likely also manifest itself externally, and, conversely, outward performance can shape one's inner core. With Donne, the 'separation' into inward and outward spheres is not as pervasive as Ferry suggests, nor is it plausible to claim that Donne is 'therefore defending a notion of what is in the heart which is closer to what a modern writer would call a *real self* or an *inner life*' (Ferry, 1983: 249–50; Sloane, 1985: 179). On the contrary, early moderns had not lived to embrace Descartes's 'pronounced dissociation of essential self from body' (Schoenfeldt, 1999: 11).

That *Bodies and Selves* (cf. Schoenfeldt, 1999) should be closely or even inseparably connected for Donne is illustrated by the way in which one of his sermons tackles the heaviness of the burden of sin. In taking the concept of 'burden' literally, the speaker vividly conjures up the sinner's dilemma: as 'the nature, and inconvenience of a Burden is, first to *Crooken*, and bend us downward from our naturall posture' (II, 3, 97), the individual is forced into a posture that directs the senses and affections more towards earthly and hence ungodly things – being bent down, one has difficulty in lifting one's eyes up to heaven. Furthermore, the speaker observes that the carrying of a heavy burden will '[t]*yre* us', thus slackening our zeal for godliness. Finally, if we are no longer able to walk upright, this 'makes us still apt and ready to stumble, and to fall under it [i.e. the burden]' (II, 3, 97). The oscillations between literal and metaphorical levels are striking: whereas the Biblical text uses the term 'heavy burden' primarily in a metaphorical sense, the preacher takes the text at its word and imagines one particular sinner under a physical burden, together with all the complications that may ensue from this predicament. Almost immediately, however, these concrete images once again become pregnant with metaphorical meaning, as with the reference to stumbling and falling – both of which here mean the act of sinning. The processes of the outer physical body and the inner soul keep blending over and into one another so that a separation into outer and inner spheres is difficult to maintain.

Once the above sermon turns to the plurality of sins one is subjected to, its language again begins to amalgamate concrete physical images with spiritual and psychological concepts, suggesting humankind 'will come to think it [. . .] a sordid, a *yeomanly* thing, still to be plowing, and weeding, and worming a conscience' (II, 3, 107). The overwhelming dimension of sin is pictured as a voice, '*sicut clamor*' that may be so loud as to outsound one's – spiritual – prayers to God (II, 3, 113). Conversely, if one were to imagine oneself as overwhelmed by the floods of sin, the physical effect of such water masses will not only blind oneself to the sight of him. God, too, will no longer be able to recognise the sinner as a creature shaped in his own image (II, 3, 114). The notion of water triggers another host of symbols, and even hopeful ones: the dove may return to the Ark with an olive leaf, and all water may eventually be turned into wine. Like a theatrical (re)production, this sermon realises and puts into physical terms the words of a text – and like many a staging, the actual realisations in turn often point beyond what is physically present on stage.

A similar strategy is at work once this sermon turns to a definition of sin. Although there have been attempts to explain away sin philosophically as nothing, 'for, whatsoever is any thing, was made by God, and ill, sin, is no creature of his making', and although Donne's speaker concedes that 'This is true', he has a counter-argument. If one were to apply these philosophical arguments to one's own body, one's physical life and sensations, one would necessarily discover that the concept of sin's being nothing 'will not ease my soul, no more then it will ease my body, that *sicknesse* is nothing, and *death* is nothing' (II, 3, 99). Only by applying theories to one's own body, i.e. through practical and physical identification, will one arrive at the gist of what sin is and what God's message consists of – the body, far from being rendered irrelevant in the face of a new *'real self* or an *inner life'* as argued by Ferry (1983: 250), serves as an indicator of the adequacy of theological doctrine.

The speaker insists that '[s]in is so far from being nothing, as that there is nothing else but sin in us' (II, 3, 100). More than anything else, '[o]ur sins are our *own*' (II, 3, 100). Interestingly, however, rather than retain the association of sin with each individual's inner core, the speaker employs metaphors of outward appearance when he laments how one cannot help even being born into the *role* and *costume* of sin: 'How naked soever we came out of our mothers wombe, otherwise, thus we came all apparel'd, apparell'd and invested in sin; And we multiply this wardrobe, with new *habits*, habits of customary sins, every day' (II, 3, 101). Sin does not differentiate between what is inside and outside, just as there is nothing but 'sin in us', each person's outward appearance and clothing is wholly permeated with sin, too.

Reading Donne's sermons, one ought to avoid a dichotomy of thinking and doing (Catherine Bell, 1992: 39), a separation between inner self and outer performance that has long been at the heart of (post-)Enlightenment thought. It was only after the 1650s that '[p]sychology developed as a separate discipline, breaking intrinsic correspondences that had been in place for millennia' (Lange, 1996: 246). Ritual comprises both thought and action (Grimes, 1990), which is why its theory constitutes a suitable approach to the early modern period in general and to Christian sacrament in particular (cf. Buc, 2001: 193; Summers/Pebworth, 1986: xii). In Donne's sermons, the self is changed through acting and performing. Phrases such as 'This is for you' or 'Here you are', which one might imagine to accompany God's offer of salvation, are reflected by the preacher's invitation to identify and re-(en)-act: 'this example/this imagined scenario is for you', 'Here, in this sermon, in this example, are you'. The '*Pro me*' of every salvational event (Engemann, 2002: 98) refers not only to the fact that Christ has died and risen *pro me*, but also to the notion that the sermon treating of his death is preached *pro me*. Donne makes it his habit to employ example extensively. At Paul's Cross, where he delivered a number of his sermons, preachers would occasionally have shared their 'stage' with an exemplary sinner which was to effect the audience's engagement 'in an individual's dramatic predicament' (Crockett, 1995: 39). Most of the time, however, Donne's use of example is typological, as listeners are encouraged to identify with Biblical personages (Frontain, 2004: 128; Lewalski, 1979: 282; Young, 2000: 175). This strategy harks back to Martin Luther's homiletics. Luther considered the mere preaching of doctrine and exhortation as insufficient if it was not supported by 'genus illustrans' or 'genus praedicandi'. Just as in Donne's sermons, this mode is intended to further the hearers' obedience to the content of the sermon (Rössler, 2002: 13). Somewhat less sophisticatedly, in Luther's own words: 'Wenn man articulum iustificationis predigt, so schläft das Volk und hustet. Wenn man aber anfängt, Historien und Exempel zu erzählen, da recht es beide Ohren auf und hört fleißig zu' (BoA 7: 26, quoted by Rössler, 1994: 355) (Whenever you preach on a certain aspect of the Law, people fall asleep and keep coughing. But as soon as you start telling stories and present them with exempla, they prick up their ears and listen attentively).

Donne's practice of employing example has both Catholic and Protestant roots: 'the appeal from the precedent of church tradition itself is strongly Roman Catholic in nature, but the fact that his precedents are drawn primarily from Scripture rather than tradition is Protestant' (Masselink, 1992: 90).[10] The manner in which the Protestant reformer Luther intends his listeners to dwell on Biblical example differs strikingly from Donne's: Luther has his audience meditate on how Christ 'sey unser gerechtfertiger und Heiland, thuen die augen zu, sehen und hoeren, fuelen und dencken nichts, sondern bleiben allein an dem wortte kleben' (quoted in Rössler, 2002: 15) (is our justification and our Saviour;

closing our eyes, neither seeing or hearing, feeling or thinking anything, we stick solely to the word). Donne by contrast encourages seeing, feeling and imagining in his hearers – rather than meditating on the word, he performs and stages it. Aware as Donne is of the significance of the senses, his sermons cater to their needs (Harland, 1987: 36). We may quite plausibly interpret this as a recompense for the loss of so much that once had been there to be seen, felt and imagined before the Reformation. Although Protestants condemned the supposedly superficial theatricalities of Catholicism, this did not prevent them from developing 'their own dramatic forms to replace the "idolatrous" spectacle and theatricality of the Roman Church' (Diehl, 1997: 5; Crockett, 1995: 32–3; Sugg, 2006).

Donne's religious allegiances have long been the subject of critical debate: According to Shami, Donne distinguished himself by a tolerant religious attitude which avoided controversy (Shami, 2000: 139, 151), and T. S. Healy even reads the whole of Donne's *Ignatius His Conclave* as 'the mockery of controversy itself' (*Ignatius* xxxix). Sullivan, by contrast, insists that 'Donne considered debate and comparison of contradictions important tools in the search for truth' (*Biathanatos* xxi). Donne's attitude is more adequately described as ambiguous rather than straightforwardly tolerant: in one of his letters, rather enigmatically, he says of himself: 'My Tenets are always, for the preservation of the Religion I was born in, and the peace of the State, and the rectifying of the Conscience' (*Letters* 306–7). Commenting on this passage, Goldberg suspects that 'Donne did not consider he had been born as himself until he entered the Church of England' (Goldberg, 1983: 210) – a view which Flynn, for whom Donne's Roman Catholic background 'never ceased to dominate *his* outlook' (Flynn, 1995: 176), would surely not share. Nevertheless, Donne had an integrative approach to diverse opinions in so far as the strategies employed in his sermons compensated for the relative drabness of reformed services – and the Church of England, after all, 'lay ecclesiologically midway between Rome and Geneva' (Horton Davies, 1986: 4; Doerksen, 1997: 102). If Crockett identifies 'logolatry' in the preaching of Thomas Playfere (Crockett, 2000: 71), a similar diagnosis also applies to Donne, as the vivid word-by-word illustrations of many of his sermons indicate. A similar preference for logocentrism and punning is familiar in Donne's poetry, as many of his metaphysical conceits originate from an overly literal exploration of certain expressions. In a homiletic context, however, this strategy appears self-contradictory, as the role of preaching had been strengthened in reformed services precisely to avoid too visual and dramatic a spectacle. Early modern sermons like Donne's simultaneously constituted 'a continuation of the perennial Christian tradition of preaching, a substitute for a medieval ritual rejected by Protestantism and a commentary on the reasons for rejection or acceptance of medieval practices' (Chuilleanáin, 1984: 199).

Theatrical rhetoric/rhetorical theatre

Donne's sermons are theatrical, not only in as far as they strive for sensual vividness, or as concerns their supposedly 'rising action' (Harland, 1986). More significantly, they employ the theatre's communicative situation. As they do not present their audiences with actual characters on a stage, they are theatrical in a more rhetorical sense. Rhetorics and theatre are not that far apart from each other. Both theatrical figures and orators share an interest in changing a current situation through words, and a play's typical division into three or five parts corresponds to the equally classical *divisio* of a speech (Pfister, 2000: 212–14) or indeed a sermon of Donne's, whose frequently tripartite structure also conveniently reflects the Holy Trinity. Donne combines both rhetorical and dialectic elements in his preaching (cf. Chamberlin, 1976: 83), but, if we concede that his sermons are predominantly concerned with converting their listeners, it is rhetoric rather than dialectic that 'reaches not only the intellect but the heart'. As people in general do know what is right and wrong, there is less need to persuade them rationally than there is emotionally (Shuger 1989, 132; Mitchell, 1962: 63). Donne is well aware of the necessity for playing on his hearer's affections and warns congregations never to 'call that *passion* in the Preacher, in which the Preacher is but *Sagittarius Dei*, the deliverer of Gods arrows; for Gods arrows, are *sagittae Compunctionis*, arrows that draw bloud from the eyes; Tears of repentance from *Mary Magdalen*, and from *Peter*; And when from thee?' (II, 1, 68). In sermons, the tears of the minister or his listeners indicate 'absolute, gender-independent powerlessness before God'. They are to be welcomed and appreciated as they signify emotional responsiveness and mark the sinner as malleable material for the Holy Ghost, although there had been (and was to come) a time when tears turned suspect for their potential hypocrisy. As a preacher, Donne valued affective expression very highly (Lange, 1996: 3, 11, 181, 173; Nelson, 2005: 5), and was more interested in moving than in teaching his listeners, whereas medieval preachers had traditionally favoured the aspect of 'docere' over 'movere' (Vickers, 1988: 291). Just as ritual 'is designed to do what it does without bringing what it is doing across the threshold of discourse or systematic thinking' (Catherine Bell, 1992: 93), so does the sermon attempt less to convince a congregation intellectually than emotionally and passionately.

Sacred rhetoric has great significance for the Christian grand style of preaching, as it 'moves the emotions, whether the harsher forensic impulses of pity and fear or the numinous feelings of wonder and mystery' (Shuger, 1989: 6–7) – and the potential evoking of impulses such as pity and fear once again harks back to the, albeit not necessarily Aristotelian, practices of early modern theatre. Some early modern preachers were indeed 'able to use the pulpit (as the best Elizabethan and Jacobean playwrights were able to use the stage) to bring [their] audiences to a point of catharsis' (Crockett, 2000: 75). As the Renaissance placed great emphasis on the importance of speech for human relations, 'good' men were allowed and even expected to employ rhetoric in order to move 'bad' men – as is typically supposed to happen in sermons (Vickers, 1988: 274).

In order to conjoin *magnitudo* and *praesentia*, to make vivid God himself and everything that pertains to him, early modern preaching cannot possibly do without stirring its hearers' emotions (Shuger, 1989: 196–9). *Enargia*, that is the presentation of evidence, the bringing before our eyes that which we are to recognise, goes hand in hand with *energia*, the passionate vigour which is to support the evidence. '[R]hetorical enargia is less like a painting than a play' (Shuger, 1989: 219), and implicitly theatrical strategies such as *exclamatio, apostrophe, imprecatio, aposiopesis* and *prosopopeia* were recommended first and foremost by Renaissance rhetoric (Vickers, 1988: 284).

Vividness is far more effective in dynamic processes than in visual stills. In one of Donne's sermons on Ps. 38.2, the arrows which stand for sin and temptation are repeatedly and variously considered 'in action', hence producing a sensual drama for the hearer's benefit:

> And he that does in some measure, soberly and religiously, goe about to draw out these arrows, yet never consummates, never perfects his own work; He pulls back the arrow a little way, and he sees *blood*, and he feels *spirit* to goe out with it, and he feels a *melancholy* take hold of him, the spirit and life of his life decays, and he falls to those companions again. Perchance he rushes out the arrow with a sudden, and a resolved vehemence, and he leaves the head in his body (II, 1, 64–5)

Having thus established before the members of his audience the incredible difficulties in ridding oneself from sin, Donne individually addresses each listener, inviting him and her to imagine themselves in this palpable and graphic (re)production of God's word, being pierced by the arrows as the speaker of the Psalm, 'For thine arrows stick fast in me, and thy hand presseth me sore' (Ps. 38.2): 'Now, how much hast thou to doe, that hast not pull'd at this arrow at all yet? Thou must pull thrice and more, before thou get it out; Thou must *doe*, and *leave undone* many things, before thou deliver thy selfe of that arrow, that sinne that transports thee' (II, 1, 64–5). As Donne succinctly argues himself, 'Rhetorique will make absent and remote things present to your understanding' (IV, 2, 87). The Christian grand style's general preference for visual over phonetic literary devices may be explained by the 'Renaissance's sense of the superiority of the eye to the ear' (Shuger, 1989: 127). And yet, seeing may be effected through hearing, specifically the hearing of a sermon: 'Man hath a natural way to come to God, by the eie, by the creature; So *Visible things* shew the *Invisible God*: But then, God hath super-induced a supernaturall way, by the eare. For, though hearing be naturall, yet that faith in God should come by hearing a man preach, is supernatural' (VI, 10, 217). Donne's speaker reiterates an important credo of Renaissance rhetoric, namely that 'tropes have to proceed via the ear to the mind's eye in vivid language' (Vickers, 1988: 322; Crockett, 1995: 54).

They do so most successfully wherever Donne does not only narrate the Biblical word but engages his audience in a multi-layered dialogue, as in a sermon preached at Whitehall in 1618 where he challenges his listeners thus: 'He [i.e. Christ] hath been in a pilgrimage towards thee long, coming towards thee, perchance 50, perchance 60 years; and how far is he got into thee yet? Is he yet come to thine eyes? Have they made *Jobs* Covenant, that they will not look upon a Maid' (I, 9, 308). If Christ is here personified as coming towards and into each listener, this entails that, ideally, each congregation member eventually ought to some extent embody Christ. Moreover, Donne introduces Job to encourage his audience to imitate the latter's exemplary oath not to 'look upon a Maid'. Each congregation member is implicated in a dialogue with both Job and Christ himself – and this involving confrontation is reflected by the three insistent questions which the preacher forces upon his listeners.

Hearing a sermon may help people to see God. However, when it came to visual enticement, the theatre was the sermon's most serious competitor – often better, and more voluntarily frequented than the church, although both provided 'a great measure of entertainment' (Stanwood, 2002: 140). There were many attempts at reforming the early modern sermon, most of them aimed at 'ridding England's pulpits of the "dumb dogs" who could do little more than read prepared services'. Preachers were encouraged to take a 'more theatrical [. . .] approach to their calling', and, during the reigns of Elizabeth, James and Charles, play-acting was often part of a preacher's qualification for the pulpit (Knapp, 2002: 117–18, 2; Crockett, 1995: 7, 65). Protestants were not in general opposed to the theatre. They were simply against its being open on Sundays because this turned stage-play and sermon into immediate rivals – for 'nothing was closer literary kin to the drama that flourished in early modern England than the sermon' (Ferrell/McCullough, 2000a: 8). As the following comparison from Richard Baker's 1662 refutation of Prynne's *Histrio-mastix* illustrates, theatrical and homiletic performances were regularly paralleled with one another: 'He [i.e. Prynne] tells us of some *Players*, and some *Spectatours* of *Plays*, that have died at the very *Play*, both suddenly, and strangely [. . .] Have not the like happened to some *Preachers* in the *Pulpit*; and to some devout persons, even at their *prayers*?' (Baker, 1972: 73). Both the space of the theatre and that of the church were consecrated to one particular purpose. The communicative processes that took place within either were structurally very similar: within the context of both church and theatre, a large crowd (of listeners or spectators) was encountered by and confronted with (a) single actor(s) who occupied stage and altar respectively (Höfele, 1991: 49–50; Chuilleanáin, 1984: 202–3). Church and theatre both engaged in the practice of structuring an otherwise amorphous world of space and time (Höfele, 1991: 58) – and, although the roundness of that world was reflected more obviously by the architecture of the early modern playhouse, Martin Bucer's mid-sixteenth-century suggestions for building a round church are highly suggestive (Crockett, 1995: 1–26), and many Reformation plays actually took place in a church setting (P. W. White, 1993). Just like actors' lines in the theatres, sermons, most contemporaries agreed, should not be read, but performed by heart, and polemical speech was a commonly accepted register both of theatrical performances and of religious dispute. Nor was there any general disapproval of acting in the pulpit, but simply an argument concerning the measure of theatricality appropriate for homiletic contexts (Crockett, 1995: 15, 13). Hence it seems no coincidence 'that the height of English theatrical preaching was also the heyday of the stage' (Crockett, 2000: 64; Diehl, 1997: 2), and one may even claim that 'Paul's Cross was an open theatre of the streets in a way which makes the Globe Theatre seem like a private club in comparison' (Cummings, 2002: 366).

Donne clearly was aware of the significant parallels between church service, or indeed sermon, and theatre. One of his sermons comments on the practice of applauding the preacher that had been common in the primitive church, thus implicitly corroborating Crockett's claim that sermon audiences were hardly less noisy than playgoers (Crockett, 1995: 39). Although Donne's speaker would not want to reinstate that practice,

> yet we cannot deny, but that though it were accompanied with many inconveniences, it testified a vehement devotion, and sense of that that was said, by the preacher, in the hearer; for, all that had been formerly used in Theaters, *Acclamations* and *Plaudites*, was brought into the *Church*, and not onely the vulgar people, but learned hearers were as loud, and as profuse in those declarations, those vocall acclamations, and those plaudits in the passages, and transitions, in Sermons, as ever they had been at the Stage, or other recitations *of their Poets, or Orators*. (X, 5, 132)

Crockett encourages us to 'think of the texts of sermons [...] in the way literary scholars have come to regard the texts of

Renaissance plays: as fascinating specimens of literary achievement on one hand, and as mere blueprints for performance on the other' (Crockett, 2000: 64). What is more, the sermon texts themselves ought to be considered performances as performative structures are already ingrained in them. 'Elizabethans not only listened to sermons but increasingly read them for their pleasure and edification' (Horton Davies, 1996: I, 232), as sermons managed to involve their audiences not only through their performative delivery but also as mere texts.

If we are to transfer the theatre's communicative situation to the sermon, the Biblical text each sermon relies on is the dramatic script, written by God as the 'Author'. The sermon constitutes an adaptation and actualisation of this text as frequently happens in theatre productions whose particular form, it is hoped, will even today have something to say to its audience. The preacher engages in explication and application, employing strategies similar to those used by Jesus in his parables to illustrate the relationship between God and humankind, as in the parable of the vineyard or the prodigal son. Donne's preacher, for example, uses the Biblical event of Mary and Joseph accidentally leaving their son Jesus behind at the temple in Jerusalem as an occasion to warn his listeners lest they lose Christ in a metaphorical and much more fundamental sense. The preacher functions as the master of revels, the 'director' of a new production of God's word, and the congregation comprises the audience that has assembled to watch and listen.[11] The only position which still remains to be filled is that of the actors. As we have seen, '[s]ometimes Donne [...] equates a Scriptural speaker or one of the Fathers with members of the congregation, giving his people, like actors, their scripts' (Webber, 1963: 199). If the realisation of the Biblical text takes place with the help of exempla which listeners are to imagine themselves in, the congregation, apart from being audience, also provides the (surrogate) actors for the sermon's performance.

'God sends humble and laborious Pastors, to souple and *appliable* Congregations' (X, 5, 139, my emphasis). Listeners are invited individually to apply the sermon's discourse and examples to themselves, in order to stage and perform the conversion to and reconciliation with God that is at issue on the level of the Biblical text. Donne's sermons frequently employ the first person plural in these passages, in order to avoid merely illustrating something *to* their congregations who are thus exclusively addressed as an audience, but also to enlist them as (en)actors of the Biblical text. 'First then, all these things are *literally* spoken of *David*; By *application*, of us; and by *figure*, of Christ. *Historically*, David; *morally*, we; *Typically*, Christ is the subject of this text' (II, 3, 97). The words of the Biblical text are not only addressed *to* the listeners. They are about, 'spoken *of*' them, they, the listeners, are *in* the sermon, 'on stage', and a mere witnessing of events will consequently not suffice. Attention is then paid to David's particular sin in committing adultery with Bathsheba, the wife of David's servant Uriah, whom he had murdered in order to be able to marry his widow. The speaker is careful to include his audience, for example through rhetorical questions, concerning not only the sin of adultery but also other trespasses: 'he did wrong to a loyall and a faithfull servant; and who can hope to be well served, that does so?' (II, 3, 98). The hint cannot go unnoticed, for, only a few lines later, the speaker expressly alerts his listeners: 'to us [. . .] the exaltation of those miseries [. . .] are intended', and 'to that second part, these considerations in our selves, we make thus much hast' (II, 3, 99).

Congregation members occupy a double function: the fact that they are expected to listen passively and at the same time invited to contribute actively to the sermon's performance aptly illustrates the 'quasi-sacramental theory of the reciprocal operations of preaching' (Ferrell, 1992: 67). It is 'quasi-sacramental', because, although both sermon and Eucharist significantly depend on the use of deictics, in the sacrament of the Eucharist, the announcement of transubstantiation, 'this is my body', was an attempt to employ deictics objectively, for this utterance was to mean the same thing regardless of who the individual speaker or audience might be. Donne's sermons, by contrast, employ deictics not only more frequently but also less determinately, as he liked to preach particularly on such verses as 'We pray yee in Christ's stead, be ye reconciled to God' (2 Cor. 5.20) where each personal pronoun could be interpreted variously, and more subjectively. A generous accumulation of deictics is 'only for discourses which can stand the intrusion of subjectivity' (Esterhammer, 1994: 23) – and Donne's sermons are not only able to stand subjectivity, they even depend on it, namely the theatrical subjectivity of listeners to imagine themselves in the roles offered by the sermon. Since the sermon's discursive system is theatrical, and 'all the world's a stage', too, this should allow for a rather smooth transition from sermon to real life.

The obligation of each sermon to the Biblical script is most manifest in the *divisio*, the introduction of the sermon's individual sections. After shortly contextualising the Biblical verse in question, the speaker typically explains, for example, how David's sins 'are all contracted in this *Text*, into two kinds, which will be our two parts, in handling these words; first, the *supergressae super, Mine iniquities are gone over my head*, there's the *multiplicity*, the number, the succession, and so the continuation of his sin: and then, the *Gravatae super, My sins are as a heavy burden, too heavy for me*, there's the greatenesse, the weight, the insupportablenesse of his sin' (II, 3, 95).

The sermon's general outline corresponds exactly to that of the Biblical script, the two acts or arguments in the Biblical text will determine the form of the sermon (cf. Schleiner, 1970: 166). David's 'two kinds' of sins are to make 'our two parts' in the sermon, so that the parallel between King David and us as sinners is established early on. Drawing on St Augustine, a simile between the overwhelming effect of sin and drowning in the sea is introduced, which allows the speaker to introduce yet another Biblical example, namely that of the '*Egyptians* submersion, *The Depths have covered them*, (there's the *supergressae super*, their iniquities, in that punishment of their iniquities, were gone over their heads)' (II, 3, 96). The next paragraph clarifies the reason for this additional example: 'The *Egyptians* had, *David* had, we have too many sins, to swim above water, and too great sins to get above water again, when we are sunk' (II, 3, 96). The employment of example serves to alert listeners to the necessity of applying what is said of or to Biblical figures to themselves, to encourage them to put themselves in the Biblical context of these examples.

Beginning as planned with the first major section of the Biblical text, the speaker explains how 'that first part, *supergressae Caput*, they are gone over my head' is to be taken:

> In which exaltation, is intimated all this; first, *sicut tectum, sicut fornix*, they are over his head, as a roofe, as a ceiling, as an Arch, they have made a wall of separation, betwixt God and us, so they are above our head; And then *sicut clamor*, they are ascended as a noise, they are got up to heaven, and cry to God for vengeance, so they are above our head; And again *sicut aquae*, they are risen and

> swollen as waters, they compass us, they smother us, they blinde us, they stupefie us, so they are above our head; But lastly and principally, *sicut Dominus*, they are got above us, as a Tyran, and an usurper, for so they are above our head too (II, 3, 97)

Different backdrops, different sceneries for the first part of the verse at hand are introduced and offered here, and, as the sermon develops, one finds that Donne decides in favour not of one but of all these staging possibilities of the Biblical text. Such *compositio loci* (the mental recreation of a place or scene) is reminiscent of Ignatius of Loyola's *Spiritual Exercises*, which similarly recommend an identification with Biblical example that would involve all the senses (Martz, 1954). In Donne's sermons, however, these sceneries aim less primarily at a realisation of the Biblical verse in as far as it may mirror David's experience than at constituting various backgrounds against which the text at hand encourages contemporary listeners to immerse themselves in the sermon (cf. William Mueller, 1962: 242). All four possibilities are concerned with the way in which sins can be seen to be 'above *our* head' (my emphasis), as is indicated by the repetition of this phrase at the end of each possible staging. The speaker presents his audience with different ways in which one may read, picture and realise God's word through his strategies of enargia, of bringing before each listener's eyes that which is otherwise difficult to grasp.

What this example also alerts us to are the ways in which the sermon's drama differs from that more straightforward theatricality of the stage. Once again, the relatedness of the sermon to ritual becomes relevant here: ritual differs from theatre so far as the acts of ritual, although they are non-intentional, as the participant in ritual allows personal intentions to be overruled by the regulations of ritual, are nevertheless carried out by each individual himself or herself – a participant's own decision to take part in the ritual precedes the temporary renunciation of intentionality during the ritual performance (Humphrey/Laidlaw, 1994: 94).

Similarly, in the sermon, listeners are expected to combine their own real-life personality with that of the role models offered in the exempla, whereas, in the case of theatre proper, the role usually overrules the actor's personality. In the sermon, as in ritual, by contrast, '[i]t is still we, as ourselves, who enact it and are conscious of it' (Humphrey/Laidlaw, 1994: 260), and so we should be, for, although the sermon is preached to the whole congregation, each listener should place himself or herself in those situations where the sermon most closely applies to him or her. Sermons strongly resemble ritualised acts as both 'are there for the self-interpreting self, and not some person-in-a-role, to enact' (Humphrey/Laidlaw, 1994: 247). In Donne's preaching, role and reality belong together – listeners are expected to take an active part in both fields: 'Hath God made this World his Theatre, *ut exhibeatur ludus deorum*, that man may represent God in his conversation; and wilt thou play no part? But think that thou only wast made to pass thy time merrily, and to be the only spectator upon this Theatre?' (I, 3, 207). Not only with regard to the world but also with respect to his sermons does the speaker expect listeners to do more than merely pass their 'time merrily', instead, they should be 'fit to be inserted' (I, 3, 208). Depending on how well the individual example is judged to apply to one's own situation, each listener will oscillate between the position of role-committed actor and fairly uninvolved spectator. The early modern recognition that '[e]very human being is constantly on stage in the theatre of the world' (Crockett, 2000: 77) should, ideally, always be linked to the plot and the characters that are negotiated in the sermons, for only then will one be able to recognise 'the true and lively theater of the transcendent manifest here'. This latter prospect is obviously more desirable than the alternative view also offered by some of Donne's sermons, namely a view which depicts *'civitas terrena* as meretricious mummery, essentially going nowhere' (Carrithers/Hardy, 1992: 51). While the latter concept expresses dissatisfaction with the multiplicity and indeterminacy of theatrical discourse, the former seems to respond to a need for faith as a matter of one's subjective identity and confidence (Mahler, 1991). There certainly are instances where Donne's writing articulates a distaste for theatricality as 'not only illusion but deception', but I doubt that Donne has nothing but contempt for the image of the 'theatre of the world, or the world as theatre' (Harris, 1962: 266–7). What is typical of Donne's writings, rather, is an awareness of both the potential and the risk inherent in theatre and theatricality.

If it is true that the community aspect of religion is more strongly emphasised by Catholicism whereas Protestant theology privileges the bond between each individual believer and his or her God, the theatrical strategies employed by Donne's sermons are representative of the English Church's much-debated *'via media'* between Catholicism and Protestantism. Ritual is not only important in so far as it allows us to realise ourselves, but should ideally also induce its participants to communication with others. Such community is another important element of what the preacher's calls for 'insertion' also aim at: by taking up the role models offered in Donne's sermons, listeners do more than merely establish an immediate relationship with God: not only are they potentially not alone in taking the role of a particular example – entering the stage of the sermon also entails an encounter with other actors taking part in the performance. Dialogue as such, which implies growth and development (Harland, 1986), and empathy that may eventually result in the taking on of another's personality, of converting oneself into someone else, cannot but involve us in an extremely close companionship with an Other – a recognition that is central also to Donne's *Devotions*. Likewise, in the Eucharist, it is not only an individual's communion with God but also its communion with all other Christians that is celebrated. Dissent and separation among humans also separates them from God: *'Zeal* is directed upon God, and charity upon our brethren; but God will not be seen, but by that spectacle; nor accept any thing for an act of zeal to himself, that violates charity towards our brethren, by the way' (II, 3, 111). It is through the theatrical 'spectacle' of *'Zeal'*, inherent in Donne's preaching, that God will be seen, and this spectacle is not only concerned with the individual's relationship towards the play into which the preacher expects his listener to insert himself but also necessitates 'charity towards our brethren', each man and woman's fellow actors on stage, 'by the way'. Although each individual's destiny is at stake, that same destiny is assumed to originate within and from the context of a community (cf. Chuilleanáin, 1984: 206).

As we know, acting serves both a representative and a performative function, by the actor's both having and being a body. It is this duality which illustrates the fundamental connectedness between the representative framework of the exempla provided by the preacher and their potential performance and en-actment if individual listeners are ready to join in by lending their bodies to the role. Listeners inhabited their own bodies while at the same time witnessing and undergoing the 'insertion' of themselves into the discourse of the sermon, the experience of which consequently amounted to 'a mode of expression that crosses modern boundaries between religion and literature, as well as text and performance' (Crockett, 2000: 62). Sermons were deemed important less for their informational potential than for their emotional merit. The awareness of Christ's death and resurrection was doubtless deeply engrained in the consciousness of congregations, and yet the dramatic irony of knowing the plot developments in advance was not likely to delimit the sermon's dynamics. Knowing something is not the same as trusting in something, and although both the audience at a play and the hearers of sermons may know what's coming, both still want to actually feel it by seeing it happen on stage, or even by experiencing it in their own bodies.

Listeners are encouraged to 'insert' themselves into the example of St Paul by re-enacting the dialogue between God and the Apostle-to-be at his conversion: 'Him that can resolve thee, scatter thee, annihilate thee with a word, and yet afford so many words, so many houres conferences, so many Sermons to reclaime thee, why persecutest Thou Him? Answer this question, with *Sauls* answer to this question, by another question, *Domine quid me vis facere? Lord what wilt thou have me do?*' (VI, 10, 222). In another sermon, listeners are asked not to take the part of the Apostle St Paul himself but to enter into immediate dialogue with him on the stage of a sermon. This time, the speaker takes the part of the Apostle, and in answering St Paul's question '*What hast thou, that thou hast not received from God?*', none of the listeners should be long in remembering that, clearly, their faults and sins are the only things that truly belong to themselves alone. It is not good works that will help men and women to get rid of their sins but a speech act that comprises a performative contradiction, during the articulation of which speakers oscillate between including themselves in their statements by using the first person plural and by setting themselves as examples for others wherever they employ the first person singular: 'Nothing can make them none of ours, but the avowing of them, the confessing of them to be ours. [...] for, if I say my sins are mine own, they are none of mine, but, by that confessing and appropriating of those sins to my selfe, they are made the sins of him, who hath suffered enough for all, my blessed Lord and Saviour, *Christ Jesus*' (II, 3, 102). The utterance of confession, vehemently recommended to all listeners, not only says but does something, even if it effects the very opposite of what it says – and it includes both listeners ('confessing of them to be *ours*', my emphasis) and the speaker ('if I say *my* sins are *mine own*', my emphasis). In the end, 'we are all *Adams, terrestres*, and *lutosi*, earth, and durty earth' (II, 3, 101).

As they are one's own, no blaming of sins on others will do, one should not 'come to say [. . .] [m]y father was of this Religion, why should not I continue in it?' (II, 3, 102). Instead, one ought to shed the old costumes of sin, convert to the correct religion and (thus) to God in general as it is 'him we must put on' (II, 3, 103). There is the challenge not only of acting by example but also of abandoning wrong-headed ways and choosing virtuous roles, as, in the following, various popular examples for blaming one's sin upon something other than oneself are called up. The speaker generously employs rhetorical questions and imagines what the exact lines of each self-defensive sinner may be, so that, eventually, each of these numerous excuses, such as blaming one's sin upon the times, one's age, one's profession, one's superior or even Adam or the Devil, is undermined.

The preacher's persona

The en-actment or acting out of the sermon is the result of a co-operation between the preacher's persona as 'director' and the congregation members as surrogate actors and simultaneous audience, which turns the sermon into 'a form of drama akin to masque, wherein cast and audience may share or exchange roles' (Carrithers, 1972: 18). The division of labour between speaker and audience sometimes becomes rather blurred. Reading Donne's sermons, one is struck by the frequent conflations and overlaps between the 'dramatic personae' created by the exempla and the speaker's position. Not infrequently does the preacher's persona feature both as director and as (en)actor: rather than simply pronouncing an invitation to the listeners to identify, the speaker, through his own example, illustrates to his listeners what it is that they are expected to do with the exempla he has provided (cf. Clark, 1982: 71) – as when he appears to be making his own confession while interspersing it with the fate of Jeremiah: 'I impute nothing to another, that I confesse not of my selfe, I call none of you to confession to me, I doe but confesse my self to God, and you' (II, 1, 53). This 'vitality and resourcefulness in styling and restyling *himself* as a variety of typical-yet-individualized characters' constitutes the counterpart to the sermon speakers' characterization of the '*congregation* as a variety of corporate identities' (Carrithers, 1972: 17). In order to illustrate how sins may function as a roof which prevents one from having immediate contact with God, the speaker introduces an anecdote of his own, an example that at the same time also places him in the tradition of famous Biblical predecessors. 'Lying at *Aix*, at *Aquisgrane*, a well known Town in *Germany*', the speaker is to spend the night in a house that is inhabited by Anabaptists who, although all related to one another by way of their religion and some of them by blood, 'detested one another', so much so that 'the son would excommunicate the father, in the room above him, and the Nephew the Uncle' (II, 3, 112). For the speaker, far too 'many floores of separation, were made between God and my prayers in that house' (II, 3, 113). He proceeds to explain that, '[a]s S. *John* is said to have quitted that *Bath*, into which *Cerinthus* the Heretique came, so did I this house;' (II, 3, 112) and illustrates how one ought to allow Biblical example to dominate and shape the actions of one's own life. Although the above quotation seems to recreate a personal experience of Donne's, one still ought to refrain from interpreting the preacher's persona biographically. The roles which Donne's homiletic speakers take serve, after all, to increase the efficacy of his sermons rather than portray the preacher's own life and normally lack the biographical detail of the above example (Sloane, 2006: 191–3).

The subjective role played by the speaker functions as an important rhetorical device which allows him to dramatise his own predicaments and emotional turmoil in order to better persuade his audience. '[T]he channel through which persuasion worked, was the *affectus*, [. . .] that power to feel which the orator, poet, painter, or musician aroused in himself' (Vickers, 1988: 277) before he turned to his audience. Donne was used to 'preaching the Word so, as shewed his own heart was possessed with those very thoughts and joys that he laboured to distil into others' (Walton, 1928: 27; Crockett, 2000: 63). Thomas Wright argued in 1601 that a Christian orator would be well advised to be familiar with his own passions: 'and the reason was, because he himselfe being extreamely passionate, knowing moreouer, the arte of moouing the affections of those auditors' (Wright, 1973: 5). That the speaker of Donne's sermons was not limited to the tasks of a director but also featured as an actor is an indication of the vital links between rhetoric and acting: 'All rhetoricians are at bottom actors, who adopt personae and act out the roles prescribed'. Like good acting, the 'credibility of rhetorical effect' (Vickers, 1988: 309) depended on how true to life the rhetorician's performance managed to be.

The fact that the preacher's persona, who, as director and producer of the word of God, is clearly in a position superior to his congregation, also deigns to feature as an actor in the dramatisation of the exempla he is producing and directing suggests that, although he is superior, he is nevertheless also thoroughly implicated in the common state of humankind. He is both a preacher and ordinary sinner in need of redemption at one and the same time. The preacher is a liminal figure as he is situated between the divine and the secular, God and humanity: 'In between pulpit and pew, heaven and earth, God's presence is given, received, and by its reception returned to the giver – thereby multiplying to a triple presence of preacher, sinner, and God in a holy interchange of selves' (Nardo, 1986: 162; Ferrell, 1992: 64–5). The most exemplary figure for such a 'triple presence of preacher, sinner, and God', is, of course, Christ.

By employing this discursive strategy, Donne's preacher not only imitates but actually performs, re-enacts and brings to life the most important dogma of Christian doctrine, namely that of God stooping so low as to become man and taking on a physical body in Christ, in whose person God and man are one. Just as God did not consider it beneath himself to become human, so Donne's preacher does not hesitate to figure simultaneously as director and (en)actor, lending his body to his own examples.[12] The Christian minister functions as an intermediary between God, the 'Author', and humankind, the actors, a position in which he once again parallels Christ. Christ is both God and man, that is author and actor, and, likewise, the part of director or, in the early modern period, 'master of revels' was usually taken by the author of the play or one of the actors or, indeed, someone who was both the author of and an actor in the respective play. Donne notably emphasised Christ's humanity much more than his contemporaries, especially when it came to analysing the Son of God's emotional make-up: 'Christ, says Donne, always came nearer to an excess than to an insufficiency of passion' (Lange, 1996: 176), and this assumption in turn encouraged Donne's preaching personae to generously exhibit their own emotions. As we read in one of his sermons, whereas an exaggeration of feeling may, admittedly, sometimes turn people into 'beasts', a lack of passion would always and inevitably associate them with the insensitiveness of 'dirt', a much less acceptable condition (IV, 13, 330).

In various sermons, the preacher's duties blend with what Christ himself has done: '*Obsecramus*, we have no other commission but to pray, and to intreat, and that we doe, in his words, in his tears, in his blood, and in his bowels who sent us' (X, 5, 125). The reincarnation of Christ through the assumption of his voice and persona (Harland, 1986) becomes possible through a repetition of the act of God becoming human, through the preacher's persona assuming both authority, by directing God's word, and humanity, by being subject to an example of that word. That it is far from easy to disentangle the various personal pronouns and adjectives in the preceding quotation further strengthens this point: whereas the third-person singular evidently refers to Christ, the first-person plural references deliberately oscillate between the 'we' of a community of preachers and a 'we' that includes Christ himself. Preachers are, by the nature of their office, images and intimate companions of Christ. This has consequences for the way in which the congregation should receive their preacher: they should simply 'say to us, we acknowledge that you do your duties, and we do receive you in Christs stead; what is it that you would have us doe?' (X, 5, 134). The final part of this advice harks back to the question the Apostle Paul asked of no less an authority than Christ himself – congregation members are thus encouraged to turn to their preacher in the same way as St Paul, at the very moment of his conversion, is said to have encountered the Lord himself.

Just as, in the beginning, God's word created the world and, through the person of Christ, not only communicated salvation, but actually brought it about, so is the sermon a continuation of these salvational events in our own present (Engemann, 2002: 96). For Donne, 'the spoken word [. . .] is a [. . .] sacramental event in which the work of God is palpable' (Stanwood/Asals, 1986: 6), palpable in the figure of Christ, of God become man, in the preacher. In a very literal sense, 'the preacher preaching the word re-enact[s] Christ's action on earth' (Hall, 1983: 214). Donne's sermons are concerned with the conversion of congregation members through 'insertion' into the sermons' exempla and, by implication, a conversion to God by accepting his offer of salvation. These processes are in turn effected through the speaker's conversion of his self, namely through his performance of Christ in the sermon. The sermon constitutes a ritual act that is 'waiting for, and apt for, the achievement of self-interpretation' (Humphrey/Laidlaw, 1994: 160), both on the part of churchgoers and that of the preacher himself.

The passion of Christ

The performative imitation of Christ is by no means the exclusive prerogative of the speaker. On the contrary, the imaginative performance of Christ, in particular of Christ's passion, plays an important role also for listeners: 'as Christ feels all the afflictions of his children, so his children will feel all the wounds that are inflicted upon him' (II, 3, 121), or, as another sermon points out, the promises of justification and sanctification 'are written in those reverend and sacred Records, and Rolles, and Parchments, even the skinne and flesh of our Blessed Saviour; written in those his stripes, and those his wounds, with that bloud, that can admit no *Index expurgationis*, no expunction, no satisfaction; But the life of his death lies in thy acceptation, and though he be come to his, thou art not come to thy *Consummatum est*, till that be done' (X, 5, 137). Donne's sermons are concerned on two levels with the project of live re-enactment. On the level of discourse, they employ rhetorical and theatrical strategies to revive and actualise the Biblical text, and, on the level of story, their primary thematic focus is on the passion and resurrection, the coming (back) to life of Christ which is considered pertinent to each person's life and death (Harland, 1987: 34; Johnson, 1999: 140). Each listener's performance and enactment of Christ's final line at the cross, his or her personal '*consummatum est*' not only entails the sinner's reconciliation with Christ, it also coincides with the sermon's success, as both listener and preacher meet and merge in the figure of Christ and his passion (cf. Nelson, 2005: 10; Crockett, 2000: 60; Masselink, 1992: 92).[13] The most accessible way for humankind to come to God is through the mediation of Christ, for, if God has become human in Christ, it follows quite naturally that each man and woman should aspire to retrace this motion in inverted form by taking on and performing the role of Christ, by slipping out of his or her own role and garment and putting on Christ. It is these processes that constitute the conversion of St Paul and also the *divisio* of one of Donne's sermons preached on that occasion: 'first, The Person, *Saul*, He, *He fell to the earth*; and then, his humiliation, his exinanition of himselfe, his devesting, putting off of himselfe, *He fell to the earth*; and lastly, his investing of Christ, his putting on of Christ, his rising againe by the power of a new inanimation, a new soule breathed into him from Christ, *He heard a voice, saying, Saul, Saul, why persecutest thou me?*' (VI, 10, 205–22).

In *Death's Duel*, Donne re-stages the passion of Christ over two pages and invites the congregation to '[t]ake in the *whole day* from the *houre* that *Christ received* the *passeover* upon *Thursday*, *unto* the *houre* in which hee *dyed* the *next day*. Make *this* present *day* that *day* in thy *devotion*, and consider what *hee did*, and remember what *you have done*' (X, 11, 245). This spiritual penance is to bring about salvation for those who follow Donne's guidance as 'spiritual director' (Davis, 1986: 176), for example when he volunteers theatrically to remind his listeners that they, like Peter, have betrayed the Lord: 'let me be thy *Cock*' (X, 11, 246). Again, this strategy of re-staging achieves a compromise between Protestant and Catholic concepts of ritual. A Protestant approach 'tends to constitute ritual as merely commemorative', with the death of Christ being 'utterly unlike any subsequent ritual commemoration or enactment' (Humphrey/Laidlaw, 1994: 157), and one is tempted to conclude that Donne's use of the terms 'consider' and 'remember' indicate that his imitation of Christ's passion is, in good Protestant fashion, merely commemorative. But if we look again, the past of Christ's passion and the present of our sins are brought together as closely as simple past and present perfect and are thus almost on the same time level: 'consider what *hee did*, and remember what *you have done*'. Christ's action even appears to be closer to the present, for whereas the verb 'consider' may be used with events both past and present, the term 'remember' predominantly refers to things past. Moreover, the phrasing of Donne's exhortation to '[m]ake *this* present *day* that *day* in thy *devotion*' makes it next to impossible to decide whether the day of Christ's passion or the present day is referred to as more or less remote than the other. While the speaker is certainly aware of the commemorative character of his meditation, he deliberately foregrounds the dominance of the speaker's and congregation's re-enactment of the crucifixion in the present of the sermon (cf. Targoff, 2008: 174–5).

In an earlier sermon, the speaker likewise encourages identification with Christ as the only viable way out of sin – but simultaneously warns his listeners to beware of (Catholic) idolatry, one example of which would have been any too extensive or detailed *imitatio Christi* (a re-enactment of Christ's passion): 'And as in his own person he admitted nails in his feet, as wel as in his hands, so crucifie thy hands, abstain from unjust actions, but crucifie thy feet too, make not one step towards the way of Idolaters, or other sinners' (II, 3, 109). One suspects that what the speaker encourages is less an actual revival of Catholic penitential practice than a mental re-staging of the crucifixion which features each individual sinner in the leading part. Moreover, in spite of all their efforts at creating Christ's presence, the sermons make no secret of the fact that, as long as one is still stuck in this life, salvation, which would consist in immediate identification with Christ, can never fully be perfected. Man's relationship towards God in the here and now is incommensurable with that of the life to come. As we read in 1 Cor. 13.12, a verse Donne also preached on: 'For now we see through a glass darkly, but then face to face'. Only after death may one potentially enjoy complete reconciliation and (re-)union with God. What Crockett says of Playfere once more also holds true for Donne: 'For the present it can only be prefigured in the ravishing performance of Playfere's [Donne's] sermon' (Crockett, 2000: 78). Donne certainly does his best to make his listeners experience as thorough as possible an identification with Christ as may be experienced in this world, and is, contrary to what Fish's reading of *Death's Duel* suggests, quite successful in doing so (Fish, 1972: 67).

Very actively do Donne's sermons endeavour to 'stir the hearts of his listeners to a fervent and active realization of Christ' (Chamberlin, 1976: 83). Presuming to take on the role of Jesus Christ constitutes a rather uncanny if not blasphemous act – albeit not that unusual a guise with Donne, whose poetic speakers, too, at times seem to be quite happy, even eager to play the part of Christian celebrities. In 'The Canonization', the speaker presumes to perform an auto-canonisation through his verse, planning to 'build in sonnets pretty roomes' (ll. 32) and suggesting that 'by these hymns, all shall approve / Us *Canoniz'd* for Love' (ll. 35–6). In one of the 'Holy Sonnets', he even usurps Christ's place at the cross: 'Spit in my face, yee Jewes, and pierce my side, / Buffet, and scoffe, scourge and crucifie mee' (ll. 1–2) – lines which, almost to the very letter, are echoed by one of the sermons Donne preached on the conversion of St Paul, where the speaker expounds on how all sinners 'scourge him, and scoffe him, and spit in his face, and crucifie him, and practise every day all the Jews did to him once' (X, 5, 122). In order to explore the daringness and potential drawbacks of identification with Biblical example, let us now consider in some detail two of Donne's conversion sermons.

The problem of St Paul's example

In the sermon he preached at St Paul's, '*The Sunday after the Conversion of S. Paul*', in 1625, Donne chooses the very moment of Paul's conversion as his textual basis: 'And he fell to the earth, and heard a voyce, saying, Saul, Saul, why persecutest thou me?', words that, according to the speaker, 'will reach to all the Story of S. *Pauls* Conversion, embrace all, involve and enwrap all' (VI, 10, 205). Being commemorative of the conversion of Paul, the sermon begins with the announcement: 'LET US NOW *praise famous Men, and our Fathers that begat us,* (saies the Wiseman) that is, that assisted our second generation, our spirituall Regeneration' (VI, 10, 205). The speaker does not take long to introduce the concept of conversion: 'It hath alwaies beene the Lords way to glorifie himselfe in the conversion of Men, by the ministry of Men' (VI, 10, 205). Significantly, this sentence has a double meaning: on the one hand, God glorifies himself in the conversion of (ordinary) men as it is effected by other men, namely divines; on the other hand, God glorifies himself to an even greater degree when those men, in whose conversion he glorified himself in the first place, turn into men who then contribute to the conversion of others. The latter certainly may be said to apply for St Paul – and also to John Donne, a convert from Roman Catholicism, who, as a preacher, consecutively engaged in contributing to the spiritual conversion of other men and women.

As the concept of conversion is at the heart of Donne's sermons, one expects that the biography of St Paul will prove a particularly useful example for converting congregation members. Notably, however, Paul is found to be rather an exceptional case, as becomes obvious in the first part of the sermon, concerned with the person of the Apostle: 'S. *Paul* was borne a man, an Apostle, not carved out, as the rest in time; but a fusil Apostle, an Apostle powered out, and cast in a Mold' (VI, 10, 207). His conversion should not be taken as representative by average churchgoers. 'Damascus', as Cummings has argued, 'is as much anti-type as archetype', since the 'Pauline experience is cited for its sheer untypicality' (Cummings, 2002: 370–1). While the ordinary individual conversion takes place 'in time', implying that one has to be subjected to conversional processes over and over again, Saul's conversion was different in that it took place once and for all, and quite dramatically: '[t]hen when he was in the height of his fury, Christ laid hold upon him' (VI, 10, 206).

Such a procedure is not an unusual manifestation of divine intervention: Christ also calmed the sea, exorcised unclean spirits and made the sun stand still, and one could say this was in general 'Christs method of curing' (VI, 10, 206). But while the performance of extraordinary actions may not be unusual for Christ, the performance of such extraordinary conversions upon one single human being is declared extremely rare. The speaker warns his brethren: 'Now, Beloved, wilt thou make this perverse use of this proceeding, God is rich in Mercy, Therefore I cannot misse Mercy?' (VI, 10, 207). Numerous examples follow which, phrased as rhetorical questions, are to dissuade listeners from identifying too immediately with Paul. The speaker asks his listeners if they would be '[s]o ill a Musician as to say, God is all Concord, therefore He and I can never disagree? So ill a Historian as to say, God hath called *Saul*, a Persecutor, then when he breathed threatnings and slaughter, then when he sued to the State for a Commission to persecute Christ, God hath called a theife, then when he was at the last gaspe'. The answer ought to be obvious: 'God forbid. It is not safe concluding out of single Instances' (VI, 10, 208). The sermon explicitly addresses the practice of 'inserting' oneself into examples offered by Bible or sermon – but not without drawing attention to the dangers inherent in doing so. For example, the conversion of the thief hanging next to Christ at his crucifixion 'was not converted at last, but at first; As soone as God afforded him any Call, he came' (VI, 10, 208). The congregation members' situation is very different, as God has kept and keeps calling them in each sermon. Accordingly, the speaker moves on to sternly interrogate his listeners: 'And at how many lights hast thou winked? And to how many Cals hast thou stopped thine eares, that deferrest thy repentance?' (VI, 10, 208).

The strategy of employing example is not without its dangers, the major risk being 'the danger of sinning by precedent, and presuming of mercy by example' (VI, 10, 209). It is due to the very exceptionality of the event that Paul's conversion is celebrated by the church, i.e. the conversion of him who 'tooke a delight in tearing the bowels of Christians' and was nevertheless miraculously 'received into the bowels of Christ Jesus' (VI, 10, 209). Much as it deserves ecclesiastic commemoration, the event of Saul's conversion would be dangerously mistaken if listeners assumed that this was how conversion was generally effected. Whereas, usually, listeners could not have done anything more appropriate than identify with the examples offered by the sermon, this time, the speaker paradoxically does his utmost to prevent them from doing so.

With martyrs, it is their death that is celebrated as their true birth, whereas with Paul it is his conversion, as '[h]ere was a true Transubstantiation, and a new Sacrament [. . .] These few words, *Saul, Saul, why persecutest thou me*, are words of Consecration; After these words, *Saul* was no longer *Saul*, but he was Christ: *Vivit in me Christus*, says he, *It is not I that live*, not I that do any thing, *but Christ in me*' (VI, 10, 209). The sacrament of the Eucharist is replaced by that of conversion, the turning of bread and wine into the body and blood of Christ is superseded by Paul himself becoming Christ, and not only spiritually, for, 'As he was made *Idem spiritus cum Domino*, The same spirit with the Lord, so in his very body, he had *Stigmata*, the very marks of the Lord Jesus' (VI, 10, 210). Rather than being present on the altar, Christ is present within St Paul, as he was, according to the English Church's reformed doctrine, said to be present in each communicant after communion (cf. McNees, 1987: 99).

At the very height of stressing the similarities between Paul and Christ, the speaker turns to considering Paul as a preacher. The effect he claims for Paul's epistles is evidently something his own preaching also aspires to: 'Wheresoever I open S. *Pauls* Epistles, I meet not words, but thunder, and universall thunder,

thunder that passes through all the world' (VI, 10, 210). Paul resembles Christ as he was '[s]o universall a Priest, [...] as that he sacrificed, not sheep and goats, *sed seipsum*, but himselfe' (VI, 10, 210). Like Donne himself, Paul exemplifies God's glorification in the conversion of humanity through the ministry of people who have themselves been converted, for, as a preacher, Paul 'as himself was, so he transubstantiates all them' (VI, 10, 210). Paul's similarity to Christ as a priest provides the subtext for the remainder of the sermon's argument. Moving on to the second part of the *divisio*, Paul's humiliation in falling upon the earth, the sermon begins to oscillate between literal and metaphorical meanings. Paul's falling to the ground is complemented by metaphorical concepts of falling, those of falling sick, poor, mad, desperate and into sin (VI, 10, 211). Falling is necessary, as God's way with 'the Nations' is 'first to cast them downe, before he can raise them up, first to breake them before he can make them in his fashion' (VI, 10, 212) – a view which presupposes a flexible, indeed performative concept of self.

Although God's working upon us is described in rather vehement terms, the speaker emphasises that, 'till the season for the fruit, till the assent of the soule come, all is not done' (VI, 10, 213). Each listener must convert himself or herself to God, and this is brought about through the sermon whose speaking persona frequently figures as Christ – hence, so long as listeners refuse to identify, 'all is not Donne', either. Conversion cannot take place without the sinner's assent, it relies on mutuality. The speaker encourages listeners to 'lay hold upon that hand that strikes us, and kisse that hand that wounds us' (VI, 10, 212) – as in the case of Paul, blindness, the destruction of what had been seen before, must precede the prospect of the real light, or, in other words, 'not darknesse, but a greater light, must make us blinde' (VI, 10, 215).

Having done his best to vividly present to his audience God's proceedings with Paul, the speaker confidently assumes that, almost with their own eyes, they now 'have seen *Sauls* sicknesse, and the exaltation of the disease [...] And you have seen his death, The death of the righteous, His humiliation, *He fell to the earth*' (VI, 10, 215–16). Proceeding, the speaker once again conceives of Paul as another Christ: 'And there remaines yet his Resurrection', a resurrection effected by words, as '[t]he Angel of the great Counsell, Christ Jesus, with the Trumpet of his owne mouth, rayses him, with that, *Saul, Saul, why persecutest thou me?'* (VI, 10, 216). The preacher stages and realises the Biblical words in such a way that the internal communication system, in which Christ's voice is heard to address Saul, overlaps with the sermon's external communicative situation, because the question *'Cur me?'* cannot but be felt to be directed also at the sermon audience:

> that that the voyce said to him, was, *Saul, Saul, why persecutest thou me?* We are unequall enemies, Thou seest I am too hard for thee, *Cur tu me?* Why wilt thou, thou in this weakenesse oppose me? And then, we might be good friends, Thou seest I offer parly, I offer treaty, *Cur tu me?* Why wilt thou oppose me, me that declare such a disposition to be reconciled to thee? In this so great a disadvantage on thy part, why wilt thou stirre at all? In this so great a peaceablenesse on my part, why wilt thou stirre against me? *Cur tu me? Why persecutest thou me?* (VI, 10, 216)

Christ is here seen to speak through the preacher, not only to Paul but to the congregation, and those who hear these words are not meant to remain uninvolved, as mere audience. Only a few pages earlier, the speaker had been quite severe in admonishing his listeners not to presume for themselves the example of Paul's radical conversion, but now they are almost forced to identify with the Apostle. They ought 'to consider God, not as he is in himselfe, but as he works upon us: The first thing that we can consider in our way to God, is his Word. Our Regeneration is by his Word; that is, by faith, which comes by hearing' (VI, 10, 216).

The word is something which Christ not only is but also has: 'It is not onely, Thou art the word of eternall life; (Christ is so) But thou hast it' (VI, 10, 216–17). Obviously, 'there was not onely a word, the Word, Christ himselfe, a Son of God in heaven, but a Voyce, the word uttered, and preached' (VI, 10, 217). If we recall that the preacher resembles Christ in being both superior to and yet implicated in the common sinful state of humankind, the conclusion of this section has an enormous impact if taken literally. The words 'Christ manifested in his Ordinance' (VI, 10, 217) come to betray an almost blasphemically close (self-)identification of the preacher with the figure of Christ – and this in a sermon that began by explicitly warning its audience against too immediate an identification with those Biblical examples that are rather singular. Donne's sermons are hardly ever of one mind on one and the same thing (Oliver, 1997: 242), not even on the usefulness of employing example. Whereas, on the one hand, this dramatic strategy may positively influence a believer's inner core, there is no certain evidence as to whether it actually does so: 'theater itself, including appearance, all the *seems* of costume, gesture, and spectacle, must be accepted' (Michael O'Connell, 1985: 303) in the bargain. Within the space of only eight pages, the speaker has moved from admonishing his listeners to beware of identifying with the prominent example of St Paul's conversion and ends up equating his own person with a no less exceptional figure than Christ himself. Evidently, this speaker fails to practise what he preaches.

In what follows, the preacher admonishes his listeners to recognise God's finger and his judgement in all that befalls them and to beware of ascribing it to circumstance. Just as Paul distinctly understood what God was saying to him, so should they, too, understand God's actions: 'Never thinke it a weakenesse, to call that a judgement of God, which others determine in Nature' (VI, 10, 219). Understanding someone entails that one should identify what is said as directed to oneself – and in this regard, one is allowed and indeed invited to follow Paul's example, as he explicitly understood that the voice of Christ was directed to him, and him alone. Listeners must by all means avoid 'not to take knowledge, that a judgement is denounced against him, because he is not named in the denouncing of that judgement' (VI, 10, 219). Each listener's roles are quite explicitly named in the Bible: 'Is not thy name *Cain*, if thou rise up against thy brother? And is not thy name *Zacheus*, if thou multiply thy wealth by oppression?' (VI, 10, 220). A modernised performance of the Biblical text should leave congregations unable to believe themselves exempted from God's addresses: 'Postdate the whole Bible, and whatsoever thou hearest spoken of such, as thou art, before, beleeve all that to be spoken but now, and spoken to thee' (VI, 10, 220).

The sermon ends on the re-enactment of the Biblical verse in which congregation members are challenged to take Paul's part in the dialogue, and answer Christ's question *'Cur me?'* with the Apostle's words, namely *'Domine quid me vis facere? Lord what wilt thou have me do?'* (VI, 10, 222). God is one 'to afford so many words, so many hours conferences, so many Sermons to reclaime thee' (VI, 10, 222) – again, the voice of Christ, who calls to Paul, is aligned with the preacher's voice who calls to the people. If one accepts this identification of preacher and Christ, the following takes on an interesting double meaning: 'Till he [Christ] be weary, we should not be weary, nor faint, nor murmur under our burdens; [...] for he, though he cannot suffer paine, may suffer dishonour in our sufferings; therefore attend his leisure' (VI, 10, 221). Listeners should become weary neither of their afflictions, as these are emblematic of Christ's passion, nor of the exhaustions a sermon may face them with – nor should preachers, emblems of Christ, in their turn ever weary of exhausting their congregations thus.

The reading of this sermon on the conversion of St Paul not only reveals quite unmistakably how much Donne's sermons rely upon example and their listener's voluntary self-insertion into these dramatised situations; it also draws attention to the dangerous potential of living, sinning and presuming forgiveness by example, a danger which even the preacher's persona itself seems to fall prey to when identifying himself overly with Jesus Christ. The insertion into Biblical examples needs careful controlling: whereas listeners are warned against identifying with Paul as regards his conversion, they are strongly encouraged to practise the same humility as he did when struck by the light of Christ. One wonders whether it is altogether from humility that Donne, as he writes in a letter, hopes that he 'might die in the pulpit' (*Letters* 243). After all, this would mean that he would die in the role of Christ. The preacher is very eager to monitor and guide the ways in which his brethren identify with Biblical example – but only God seems to be monitoring him.

The same dilemma is apparent in Donne's sermon on 2 Cor. 5.20, with which I began this chapter. There the speaker says of himself that, 'in what manner soever we come, we come *in Christs stead*, and though dimly, yet represent *him*' (X, 5, 120–1). Only a few lines later, he insists that, even as concerns the authority of Jeremiah, 'we claime not *that*, we distinguish between the extraordinary Commission of the *Prophet*, and the ordinary Commission of the *Priest*, we admit a great difference between them, and are farre from taking upon us, all that the Prophet might have done' (X, 5, 121). One feels the speaker doth protest too much. The reason this may be so follows without delay, as he explains that such over-identification with Biblical authority would be 'an errour, of which the *Church of Rome*, and some other over-zealous

Congregations have been equally guilty, and equally opposed Monarchy and Soveraignty' (X, 5, 121). Any reformed preacher would have been careful to avoid such charges being brought against him – yet the speaker meanders rather uneasily between assuming and denying the authority or even reincarnation of Christ for his preaching office. Reclaiming the title of Christ, he recalls that '[t]he Saviour of the world communicates to us the name of Saviours of the world too' (X, 5, 121), only to undermine this concept by pointing out that 'we are led by a low way' (X, 5, 122). This low way, however, preachers are to follow 'by the example of our blessed Saviour himself', and, as a consequence, 'since he bled, we may well sweat in his service, for the salvation of your souls' (X, 5, 122). Suddenly, the preacher once more seems to merge with Christ, especially as he begins to imagine how the congregation may crucify Christ all over again in the figure of the priest:

> Yea, if he that sent us suffer in us, [. . .] when you scourge him, and scoffe him, and spit in his face, and crucifie him, and practise every day all the Jews did to him once [. . .], by tearing and mangling his body, now glorified, by your blasphemous oaths, [. . .] when we see all this, *Arma nostra preces & fletus*, we can defend our selves, nor him, no other way, we present to you our tears, and our prayers, his tears, and his prayers that sent us, and if you will not be reduced with these, our Commission is at an end (X, 5, 122)

The sermon then proceeds to a closer analysis of this 'Christ-ian' humility by analysing the various potential interpretations of the verb that has been translated as 'pray', the first of which implies dejection in a drastic degree: 'as Physicians must consider excrements, so we must consider sin, the leprosie, the pestilence, the ordure of the soul' (X, 5, 123). This is a very fitting comparison for the business of a divine, for, '[j]ust as the self is always producing sins that need confession, so it is always manifesting noxious humors that demand evacuation' (Schoenfeldt, 1999: 33).

Another meaning for 'pray' is that of grieving 'within our selves, for the affliction of another' (X, 5, 123). However, 'pray' may also be understood as 'wound, and afflict another' (X, 5, 123), or making others grieve, and the combination of grieving both self-reflexively and transitively at the same time can be said to illustrate the rhetorical strategy whereby the speaker's performance of one particular emotion is to arouse that same feeling in his hearers. Such infectious grieving moreover illustrates the working mechanism of preaching where the preacher enters into a kind of contract with his hearers, 'by being beholden to *you* for your application, or making *you* beholden to us, for our ministration' (X, 5, 124). The preacher's calling, like Christ's, exposes him to various humiliating charges, and the speaker warns his listeners to beware of ascribing 'our zeale to the glory of God, and the good of your souls, to any inordinate passion, or sinister purpose in us' (X, 5, 124). Preachers have been accused of being mad, and so they are, 'mad for love of this soul, and ready to doe any act of danger [. . .], to *stand at her doore*, and *pray*, and begge, that *she would be reconciled to God*' (X, 5, 125) – words which echo precisely the terms Donne had used in an earlier sermon to describe Christ's relationship to humanity. Hence preachers may end up as *'fools for Christ'*: 'Lower then this, we cannot be cast, and higher then this we offer not to climbe' (X, 5, 125) – the paradox of this remark being easily resolved in the figure of Christ, who excelled in humility. The office of preaching is typically performed by praying 'in his tears, in his blood, and in his bowels who sent us [. . .] *in Christs stead*' (X, 5, 125).

As ambassadors of Christ, preachers differ from ordinary ambassadors because they must be heard in any case, even if their message should be disagreeable: 'But if you beleeve us to come in Christs stead, what ever our message be, you must heare us' (X, 5, 131). Modestly, the speaker does not expect '[t]hat vehemence of *zeale* which the Apostle found' (X, 5, 134). It is rather ironic that he should then expound on the enthusiastic ways in which congregations have continued to articulate their participation in sermons over no less than two pages. Since he acknowledges that the Apostle himself met with great zeal in the age of the early church, his own concluding judgement on such customs, that 'truly wee come too neare re-inducing this vain glorious fashion' (X, 5, 133) is not altogether convincing. At least one may wonder if it is the vainglory of the audience in commenting on the sermon that he is critical of here or the potential vainglory that may develop in a preacher who is too excessively applauded. The congregation, the speaker suggests, should simply respond to the preacher in the same way as Saul did to Christ. Once again, the relationship between God and human beings overlaps with that of preacher and listener. As pointed out at the very beginning of this chapter, the reconciliation, or, in my words, conversion to God, constitutes 'that to which all that we have said of a good Pastor and a good people, (which is the blessedest union of this world) bendeth, and driveth, what, and how blessed a thing it is to be reconciled to God' (X, 5, 134). The 'blessedest union of this world' attempts to bring about the 'blessedest union of this world and another world', the union between the human 'world' and the 'world' of God.

Judging from the precarious position which preachers are placed in, and elaborating still a bit further on the multiple meanings of 'pray', one suspects that the preacher's business is not only to 'pray' but also to accept the ever-present danger of becoming the 'prey' of his audience. And herein, again, preachers resemble Christ, who, although engaged in the business of someone else, namely his Father, and in the very best interest of humanity, eventually fell prey to the sinful outrageousness of his contemporaries, who accused him of being mad and eventually crucified him. The effect of this undercurrent is to suggest that, even in denouncing and condemning their preacher, each congregation would still be treating him as Christ – but, at the same time, the preacher also acknowledges that all his efforts may be in vain as he is as powerless against the potential reluctance and aggression of his listeners as any mediator or ambassador in the service of a higher power.[14] Finally, however, one wonders whether the speaker of these passages may not also be said to have fallen prey to his own pride – if only the pride he has in his own humility.

In Donne's sermons, preaching features as a 'gloriously' humble task, and is herein reminiscent of the mission the Son of God himself had been sent into the world to fulfil. The more the preacher succeeds in humbling himself, the more does he make himself resemble Christ – and the more he must beware of making a virtue and proud confidence of that humility since this would place him on the verge of 'the danger of sinning by precedent, and presuming of mercy by example' (VI, 10, 209). As has been argued with regard to some of Donne's devotional poems (Healy, 2005), readers and listeners should become wary whenever the preacher 'doth protest too much' about his own humility, as his role-play is ever 'paradoxical, simultaneously self-effacing and bold' (Crockett, 1995: 148; Webber, 1963: 117). The preacher's calling is 'essentially theatrical' (Crockett, 1995: 8) – all the essence it has derives from acting and dramatised representation. Whereas the majority of Donne's sermons confidently trust in the ways in which both saying and playing may effect faithful conversion to God, the two presently discussed pulpit performances draw both directly and unwittingly attention to the temptations of role-play and theatrical performance. Regardless of or indeed owing to their professed humility, their speakers come across not 'by a low way' but rather as 'over the top'.

Notes

1 This discussion of the minister's duties is typical of Donne's sermons (Oliver, 1997: 242; William Mueller, 1962: 78).
2 Raymond Frontain alerted me to the fact that, whereas Donne's preoccupation with the ladies has been notoriously speculated upon, his predilection for the theatre has not been treated as thoroughly. Exceptions are Harris's 1962 essay, which argues that Donne did not much appreciate the theatre at all, and Richmond's account (1973) of 'The Young Shakespeare' functioning as 'Donne's [by far superior] Master'.
3 Even the 'original' last supper is, however, re-enacted by the Biblical text itself, when the disciples recognise the resurrected Christ by the way in which he breaks the bread at Emmaus.
4 Donne does not 'stickle at the more unconventional and daring metaphors', as the Bible itself was hardly less innovative in its imagery (Mitchell, 1962: 156).
5 Another image Donne uses to characterise this reciprocal process of conversion is that of 'putting on Christ': 'This process of apparelling is not one which man can accomplish in his own strength, but neither is it one which God thrusts upon him: God enables man to put on Christ, but man's heart must be responsively willing to do so' (William Mueller, 1962: 131–2).
6 I am grateful to Matthias Bauer for pointing out to me that Donne's insistence on the relevance of emotionally moving one's audience may be linked to Sidney's *Apology for Poetry*: 'what so much good doth that teaching bring forth [. . .] as that it moveth one to do that which it doth teach?' The poet 'doth not only show the way, but giveth so sweet a prospect into the way as will entice any man to enter into it' (Sidney, 1595: 21) – and such enticement must be the declared goal also of a preacher.
7 This is also a defining characteristic of inter-confessional conversion (Marotti, 2005: 98).

8 This suggested 'plot' aligns sermon and ritual, as 'social drama' likewise proceeds through the four phases of '(1) breach, (2) crisis, (3) redress, (4) reintegration' (Grimes, 1990: 174).
9 In his reading of Donne's sermons as attempts to persuade the audience 'to "court" the divine' (Nelson, 2005: 26), Nelson fails to recognise that these persuasions are, in the first place, based on God's courting of human beings by knockings on their doors. The courting at stake in Donne's sermons is inherently mutual, as are relations of courtship and patronage in general (cf. Chapter 4).
10 Donne's habit of interspersing his sermons with Latin quotations (frequently from the Vulgate) similarly indicates both a linguistic and a religious hybridisation in the Bakhtinian sense, 'a mixture of two social languages within the limits of a single utterance' (Bakhtin, 1981: 358). There is no point in assigning religious labels to Donne's sermons, as Papazian does (cf. Papazian, 2003). Instead, Donne's religious thinking should be considered 'constantly hybrid in nature' (Oliver, 1997: 5; Shami, 2003: 144; Marotti, 2002: 361; Sloane, 1985: 3).
11 Although the term director was not common in the early modern period, the concept as such would have been familiar. Even medieval ritual relied on some director for negotiating between the general outlines of the respective ritual and its particular realisation (Althoff, 2003: 192). In the following, I shall use the term director to refer to the minister's function in the preaching process.
12 Harland sees Donne's frequent appropriations of the voice of Christ as so many instances of the resurrection, but the sermons' strategies of restoring Christ in their discourse are more complex and further-reaching than he grants (Harland, 1986). Nor would I agree that 'the Reformation preacher is asked to stand in for each person of the Trinity' (Crockett, 1995: 10). Donne's preaching personae identify much more frequently with the figure of Christ than with any other Trinitarian or Biblical personage.
13 Through their emphasis on Christ's passion, Donne's sermons once again recall the English reformed doctrine of the sacrificial Eucharist: 'Donne stresses individual identification with Christ's crucifixion as a prerequisite for union with Christ's body in the Eucharist' (McNees, 1987: 94). No fewer than 101 of Donne's 160 surviving sermons 'make in their concluding moments historical or liturgical reference to the Crucifixion' (Carrithers, 1972: 16). Sloane, by contrast, claims that only twenty of Donne's sermons directly feature Christ, but he notably fails to explain precisely what he means by 'directly' (Sloane, 2006: 195).
14 For the political implications of the trope of ambassadorship in Donne, cf. Adlington, 2008.

2

Promethean and protean performances – Worldly poems

> And by these hymnes, all shall approve
> Us *Canoniz'd* for Love.
> ('The Canonization', ll. 35–6)

Despite almost two hundred years of critical neglect, Donne is nowadays thoroughly '*Canoniz'd*'. His popularity results from his erotic and devotional poetry, but it is the interrelationship between the two genres that makes for Donne's idiosyncrasy. Hence 'hymnes' are to bring about 'The Canonization' of two not merely spiritual lovers, who 'dye and rise the same' (l. 26). While this may be read as a reference to Christ's death and resurrection, its orgasmic and phallic allusions would have been lost neither on early modern audiences (Carey, 1990: 29) nor on modern-day readers. Donne's provocative ambiguity remains one of the most extensively debated fields in Donne studies (Frontain, 1995: 5; Stevie Davies, 1994: 51).

Whereas Chapter 3 addresses the passionate links between Donne's worldly and divine poetry, the following pages are concerned with another characteristic of his oeuvre which the above lines also illustrate: they display an intriguing sense of knowing 'how to do things with words'. Hymns are to improve the singer's chances for salvation and to prepare him or her for communion with God. The poem's speaker transfers this type of speech act to the genre of poetry, and, not content with the prospect of salvation, aims at canonisation as well. This daring attempt is of significance since it rehearses a poetological statement that articulates Austin's speech act theory *avant la lettre*. Austin discovers that some utterances not only say but actually bring about something, merely by being uttered. More specifically, Austin's focus is on utterances which bring about a situational change for one or more persons, like the utterance 'I hereby pronounce you husband and wife'. While words first helped to effect a transformation, words also indicate that a shift has actually taken place: the two individuals in question are no longer (only) man and woman but husband and wife.

Donne's poem does not merely mention 'The Canonization', a passage from profane to sacred, nor simply anticipate it as an event that is to take place in the future. Instead, the above lines make up part of 'The Canonization' as both poem and process.[1] Although the fourth stanza employs the future tense ('And if no peece of Chronicle wee prove, / We'll build in sonnets pretty roomes', ll. 31–2), we are taken into the here and now of the poem: by the time that they arrive at these lines, readers have already read through three other 'pretty roomes', stanzas of a poem from Donne's *Songs and Sonets*. Since this collection does not include even one poem which strictly corresponds to the form of the sonnet, the meaning of 'sonnets' in 'The Canonization' may be paraphrased as 'little songs' – a notion of 'sonnet' which would include a hymnic song like 'The Canonization' itself. The deictic adjective in the phrase 'these hymnes', instead of 'those hymnes', which would be plausible if the speaker was referring to texts situated outside the poem, further hints that the reader will not have to look far for 'these hymnes', not even as far as a different poem. 'The poet has actually before our eyes built within the song the "pretty room"' (Brooks, 1968: 12) – and he has done so less by way of paradox, as Brooks argues, than by employing the power of language to do what it says.

'The Canonization' begins *in medias res* and makes us feel as if we are stumbling upon something already in process, happening at this very moment in the poem in front of us. Donne's poetry is highly involving in its use of personal pronouns and deictics, and the effect of these strategies becomes fully manifest only in reading. Hence this chapter will focus not primarily on what is said but on how what is said is transmitted and brought about, how the speaker's self manifests itself in and through a poem, which entails a 'shifting [of] our critical attention from texts to acts, from products to processes, and from codes and structures to modes and dynamic strategies' (Döring, 2005: 17; Greenblatt, 1990: 5). Most of Donne's work proves similarly astonishing as this self-made canonisation, and it is the frequent discomfort of performative contradiction, camouflaged and enhanced by ingenious metaphysical conceits, that lends his work its unmistakable vigour and (social) energy. An awareness of the performative potential of the poetic word, but also of the risks that attend it, lies at the heart of Donne's poetry.

'The Canonization' constitutes an instance 'in which to *say* something is to *do* something; or in which *by* saying or *in* saying something we are doing something' (Austin, 1975: 12). As is well known, Austin deliberately excludes literary utterances from his analysis, as performatives must be uttered 'seriously': 'I must not be joking, for example, nor writing a poem' (Austin, 1975: 9). However, he does not exclude literary utterances as misfires or abuses, and only once more does he return to the case of literature: 'a performative utterance will, for example, be *in a peculiar way* hollow or void if said by an actor on the stage, or if introduced in a poem, or spoken in soliloquy. [. . .] Language in such circumstances is in special ways – intelligibly – used not seriously, but in ways *parasitic* upon its normal use' (Austin, 1975: 22). Austin's characterisation of literary utterances as '*in a peculiar way* hollow or void' remains strangely vague itself. In admitting that literary contexts can produce intelligible utterances, he acknowledges that parallels exist between seriously performative and literary utterances – even if this connection is dubbed '*parasitic*'. Austin considered literary utterances only as imitative of serious performatives, ignoring that without 'a general iterability [. . .] there would not even be a "successful" performative' (Derrida, 1986: 325). 'For me to be able to make a promise in "real life," there must be iterable procedures or formulas, such as are used on stage' (Culler, 1994: 119) – or in the marriage service, a context Austin himself introduces. Just as Austin had begun his lecture by proving false the exclusion of performative utterances from linguistic analysis, so may we in turn 'reverse Austin's opposition between the serious and the parasitic' (Culler, 1994: 120). Literary utterances as significantly conditioned by social context as Donne's coterie poems certainly do not stand 'perversely outside the social and material circuit in which ordinary language works' (Haugen, 2002: 126). Although whatever is acted is not real, it is nevertheless really acted and may hence be socially relevant (Goffman, 2002: 192).

This chapter will explore the ways in which Donne's poems employ language performatively and begins by analysing their Promethean dimension. Their confidence in their own verbally creative might is supported by early modern poetics. Donne's poetry is Promethean in how it engages in the creation of world, truth and self. Metaphor and metaphysical conceit play an important role in the creation of poetic worlds – the relationship between world and word, of making the world fit the words and vice versa, is one of the most decisive criteria for the classification of speech acts (Searle, 1979: 1–29). Performative utterances are not necessarily concerned with factual truths, especially where they verge on the metaphorical: 'How can one answer this question, whether it is true or false that France is hexagonal?' (Austin, 1975: 143). Neither is poetry bound by truths that are prior to its utterance, as truth is redefined or deconstructed through poetic language and metaphor. These Promethean processes of world-creating and truth-creating are all undertaken by a speaker's voice, whose self comes into being through poetry, evolving through what it is saying and, by implication, doing.

Donne's poetic performances are not only Promethean but also protean: their speakers change shape by taking on ever new parts and roles (Post, 1999: 9) – and this explains why Donne's poetry has often been labelled 'dramatic'. The idea that a self comes into being through certain repeated acts is exemplified by 'Satyre I' and 'Satyre IV', where Elizabethan society and the court feature as hotbeds of theatricality. Moreover, Donne's poems function as (performative) 'utterance[s] in a speech situation' (Austin, 1975: 139). A commendatory poem like the 'Obsequies to the Lord Harrington' inevitably bears the marks of the social context in which it was uttered. The speaker frequently identifies with the soul of the deceased Lord, less for the deceased's sake than for his own, in order to impress the poem's audience. Just as an indirect speech act performs one illocutionary act by way of performing another, so does the writing of commendatory poetry indirectly perform a plea for patronage (Searle, 1979: 30–57). In order for the primary (and only indirectly communicated) illocutionary force to be acknowledged, indirect speech acts must be to some extent conventionalised – and Donne's audience would have had little difficulty in recognising the writing of encomiastic poetry as a common mode of pleading patronage.

Audience plays an important role in Donne's non-encomiastic poetry, too. Most of it was written and sometimes also performed for a coterie, so that the poems' contemporary speech situation resembles that of the theatre. Coteries provided an environment in which social upstarts were able to measure their talents against those of others – one important area of competition being poetry. Although what is happening within a poem may be fictional, each text itself has a social purpose (cf. Searle, 1979: 58–75). A comparative reading of 'The Canonization' and 'The Curse' exemplifies the ways in which what is at stake within a text is linked to a poem's contemporary speech situation. Whereas both 'The Canonization' and 'The Curse' have recourse to conventionalised practices of using language performatively, namely to sanctifying or cursing someone through words, the effect of these two poems themselves is more difficult to account for. According to Austin, 'the illocutionary act [...] has a certain *force* in saying something' and is 'conventional', whereas 'the perlocutionary act [...] is the *achieving of* certain *effects* by saying something' and is '*not* conventional' (Austin, 1975: 121). Although these two categories are hard to distinguish from one another, they correspond to what, with reference to the communicative situation of the theatre, I would like to describe as the internal and external communication system of a Donne poem (cf. Pinka, 1982: x). For example, if the speaker manages to win his (female) addressee's love, this success may also procure him the respect of his audience, but straightforwardly misogynist poems may likewise meet with the applause of a male coterie. The interplay between internal and external communicative system can be quite complex, as the illocutionary force of the speaker's words can, but need not, coincide with the poem's perlocutionary effect. The poetic speakers' attempts to persuade their various addressees may have worked to convince these poems' audiences, and since this double function recalls the different performative levels of Donne's sermons, this chapter concludes with a short comparison of these two genres' communicative strategies.

Promethean poetic power

'A poet is as much to say as a maker' (Puttenham, 1959: 3) – thus runs the first sentence of George Puttenham's *The Arte of English*

Poesie, a tract to defend poetry against common popular assaults. The reference to the 'maker' brings in God as 'the poet's best model' (Frontain, 1995: 15) – or Prometheus, who is associated with human skills and sciences and the creation of humankind from clay. The powerful likeness between the divine maker and the poetic creator of worlds is significantly verbal: Puttenham does not say, 'A poet is as much as a maker', but 'A poet is *as much to say* as a maker'. It is 'the creating power of religious *language*' that aligns the poet creator with his divine counterpart, as 'speaking the word bespeaks the world into existence' (Frontain, 1995: 16–17, my emphasis; cf. Lewalski, 1979; Rupp, 2005: 120). The official religion of England, albeit reformed, still remained strongly indebted to Catholicism and its concepts of language. In claiming that 'Protestantism seeks no less than to deconstruct the linguistic theology of Roman Catholicism' (Baumlin, 1991: 169), Baumlin introduces too radical an opposition (cf. DiPasquale, 1999). Poetry's world-creating powers were acknowledged not only by the former Catholic John Donne but by a majority of early modern poets – as the dedication of Puttenham's seminal tract to the Protestant Queen Elizabeth illustrates.

Not least in their employment of metaphysical conceits, i.e. metaphors which take their vehicle from the real world to connect it in a very literal way to a less concrete tenor (cf. Deubel, 1971: 77–8; Müller, 1992), Donne's poems insinuate that what is at stake in them is just (like) the real world – while, at the same time, these metaphors develop new ways of seeing that same world. They are world-creating and performative in that they do not simply reiterate what exists out there. While this may be true of metaphor in general, the effect is particularly striking in metaphysical conceits like Donne's: we are more aware of their world-creating dimension since they make us 'concede likeness while being strongly conscious of unlikeness' (Gardner, 1985: 19), they create new worlds not only in co-operation with but even against a reader's intuition or better judgement. Poetry is not tied to the laws of nature, and metaphysical conceits in particular, as Francis Bacon puts it, 'at pleasure join that which Nature hath severed, and sever that which Nature hath joined, and so make unlawful matches and divorces of things' (Bacon, 1947: 89). As Bacon further argues, poetry 'ever thought to have some participation of divineness, because it doth raise and erect the mind, by submitting the shows of things to the desires of the mind' (Bacon, 1947: 90). The poetic mind engages in its own truth-creating. A quotation from a sermon of Donne's suggests that he shared Bacon's view of poetry: 'How weak a thing is Poetry? (and yet poetry is a counterfait Creation and makes things that are not, as though they were)' (IV, 2, 87). A view of truth as linguistically relative goes far beyond poetic play: the literal and Scriptural truth which early reformers protested to was significantly complicated by the recognition that truth was not only literal but also literary (Cummings, 2002: 5; Doerksen, 1997: 15). Since it is the poetic speakers' utterances which create new worlds and reconstruct or deconstruct truths, these speakers' identities are likewise verbally self-fashioned and self-made. Not infrequently, Donne's speakers equate themselves with words, often those of the poem they are at that moment articulating.

Creating the world

Donne's poems engage in the creation of worlds wherever poetic language makes one stanza, 'one little roome, an every where' ('The good-morrow', l. 11; cf. Belsey, 1994: 143). In 'The good-morrow', the speaker does not bother to compete with real-world explorers: 'Let sea-discoverers to new worlds have gone, / Let Maps to others, worlds on worlds have showne' (ll. 12–13). The third anaphora, which concludes this climactic enumeration, marks the lovers' own world not only as distinct from but also as superior to that real world: 'Let us possess one world, each hath one, and is one' (l. 14). The poem's final stanza, or, for that matter 'roome', realises and elaborates the lovers' 'every where' as much more accommodating than the real world: 'Where can we finde two better hemispheares / Without sharpe North, without declining West?' (ll. 17–18).[2]

The world of lovers may also be less serene, as in 'A Valediction of weeping': tears, round and watery as they are, resemble the earth's 'round ball' (l. 10), on which '[a] workeman that hath copies by, can lay / An Europe, Afrique, and an Asia, / And quickly make that, which was nothing, *All*' (ll. 11–13). The poetic speaker resembles this 'workeman', for his words likewise turn the nothing of a tear into '*All*', once he claims that 'So doth each teare, / Which thee doth weare, / A globe, yea world by that impression grow' (ll. 14–16). Tears are turned into worlds, and, if we consider the poem's beginning, these tears appear to be the product of poetry: 'Let me powre forth / My teares before thy face' (ll. 1–2). The poetic world-creations of 'The good-morrow', or also of 'The Sunne Rising', where the 'walls' of the lovers' bedroom, and, by implication, those of the poem's rooms or stanzas, had been declared the sun's sole 'spheare' (l. 30), were nothing but exuberant. 'A Valediction of weeping', by contrast, points out how tears may not only amount to globes, but also threaten to flood and drown the world, as they are abundantly shed by the speaker and his beloved on the occasion of their separation. Hence the speaker tries to dissuade his addressee from further crying, as her tears are bound to encourage even further tears with him. He himself, however, had been the one to initiate this water cycle, and since he did so through the words of poetry, the final stanza reads as a veiled request that the addressee refrain not only from crying and drowning further earth balls, but especially from creating such verbal tears through the medium of poetry.

Whereas the ways in which metaphysical conceit contributes to the making and un-making of worlds have been widely recognised (cf. Holmes, 2001: 2), some less discussed poems like 'The Apparition', 'The Dreame' or 'Image of her whom I love' also, if more subtly, debate the relationship of truth and fancy, of reality as opposed to a dream, and the three poems resemble each other in as far as they all blur the opposition between such binaries. 'The Apparition' introduces a ghost as an uncanny link between the living and the dead, between this (real) world and the next. Such an 'Apparition' would have been religiously incorrect in post-Reformation England and could never have made it into a public genre as seriously concerned with religious truth like the English sermon. But in this poem, the ghastly speaker transfers the realms of purgatory even to this world where the addressee, 'Bath'd in a cold quicksilver sweat wil[l] lye / A veryer ghost than I' (ll. 12–13).

In 'The Dreame', the relationship between what is real and what is not is even more complicated (cf. Roston, 1974: 143–7; Pritchard, 1994). The speaker expresses his gratitude to his 'Deare love' for having woken him from a 'happy dreame', whose subject had not been suitable for a dream, it being 'a theame / For reason, much too strong for phantasie' (ll. 3–4). The speaker then changes his mind, arguing that the addressee has not actually broken his dream, but rather continued it: 'Thou art so truth, that thoughts of thee suffice, / To make dreames truths; and fables histories' (ll. 7–8). Thoughts, dreams and fables, all three of which are metaphors for poetry, are infused with a truth and non-dreaminess of their own. Much as dreams and reality are connected, the speaker is determined 'Not to dreame all my dreame', but to 'act the rest' (l. 10) – the notion of the speaker's dream as a wet dream exemplifies the intense connection between physical reality and dream world yet more graphically (Marotti, 1986: 92). The female addressee, knowing the speaker's thoughts and dreams better than an angel could, must be thought of as more than an angel and not considered 'any thing but thee' (l. 20), anything but that which she really and in truth is. Her real character is, however, determined by the speaker's 'Dreame': 'Comming and staying show'd thee, thee, / But rising makes me doubt, that now, / Thou art not thou' (ll. 21–3). When the addressee refuses to respond to and satisfy the speaker's desires, she cannot well be her own true self. Having first established the addressee's truth through phrases such as 'Thou art so truth' (l. 7) or 'For thou lovest truth' (l. 14), the speaker seizes upon her true character as something which is his to judge. Having made her true through his words, he may just as easily deny her truthfulness.

In 'Image of her whom I love', the speaker initially favours dream over reality. Only in the poem's final six lines does he change his mind in favour of being 'Mad with much *heart*, than *ideott* with none' (l. 26). The speaker's reasons for preferring dream to reality are the same as those given in 'The Dreame': if he manages to rid himself of the real imprint which the woman has left in his heart, i.e. if the 'Image of her whom I love' obeys the speaker's encouragement to 'goe, and take my heart from hence' (l. 5), he will be altogether free to create his own truth of her, a truth free of all that may oppose his desires. As soon as his heart is removed and, with it, reason, reality and his mistress as she is,

> Then *Fantasie* is Queene and soule, and all;
> She can present joyes meaner than you do;
> Convenient, and more proportionall.

> So, if I dreame I have you, I have you,
> For, all our joys are but fantasticall.
>
> (ll. 10–14)

Reality, and all the pains attendant to it, are firmly shut out. But, as is inevitable with dreams, one wakes up from them at some point. It is highly significant that the first thing the speaker turns to on waking is the writing of poetry:

> After a such fruition I shall wake,
> And, but the waking, nothing shall repent;
> And shall to love more thankfull Sonnets make
> Than if more *honour*, *teares*, and *paines* were spent.
>
> (ll. 17–20)

The words of poetry are to recreate and prolong the reality of a dream unimpeded by the intrusion of a real woman's coyness. There are strong parallels between dreams and the woman-, world- and truth-creating powers of making sonnets.[3]

Let us turn back to 'The Dreame': the poem tells the story of the speaker's dream of his 'Dear love' (l. 1) being interrupted by her presence as she really is. Initially delighted to be woken up and hoping 'To make dreames truths' (l. 8) with her, the speaker tries to integrate real world and dream – on the cusp of waking, he strives to accommodate empiric reality within the virtual scene of his dream. On facing a reality so little disposed to comply with his wishful dreaming, the speaker goes back to sleep again. When he decides to 'dreame that hope againe' (l. 30), his intention of turning over once more in his bed may be read as a turn to poetry where he is similarly able to make and unmake truths as suits him best. His final plan to 'dreame that hope againe' (l. 30) is most easily effected by returning to that very 'Dreame' which constitutes the poem at hand: after all, the speaker keeps on dreaming for over twenty lines before his hopes for the consummation of his dream in the real world begin to waver. The return to dreaming is thus 'poetic' rather than, as Roston maintains, 'prosaic' (Roston, 1974: 147). At the 'rising' (l. 22) – either the no longer dreamed but actual rising of his penis, or his rising from his bed, both of which may put the woman off, or indeed the woman's own rising in order to leave the speaker – the speaker begins to suspect that 'Thou art not thou' (l. 23), for the she from his dream clearly does not correspond to the woman now in front of him.[4]

So why not again and again go back to 'The Dreame', or at least the first two stanzas of it where the speaker's words and fancy still govern the real world?

In 'Image of her whom I love', however, the speaker decides against the pre-eminence of dreams and fancy over the heart which he had disposed of in the first stanza as it had 'growne too great and good' (l. 6) for him, and in 'The Dreame' there are likewise hints that he would be ready to renounce his erotic dream in favour of its actual realisation and orgasmic consumption: 'I / Will dreame that hope againe, but else would die' ('The Dreame', ll. 29–30). Despite the pain and frustration that may come with being 'Mad with much *heart*' ('Image of her whom I love', l. 26), even that madness would still offer enough to dream and write poems about, albeit such verse might be rather nightmarish and result in some of those less 'thankfull Sonnets' ('Image of her whom I love', l. 19) as, for example, 'The Apparition'. And even those cases where the speaker in fact 'would die' ('The Dreame', l. 30) provide food for poetry. 'Alas, true joyes at best are *dreame* enough' ('Image of her whom I love', l. 22), 'true joyes' still depend on the image, the dream or the poetry one has got in one's head to be fully realised – for example in the half-dreamy world of 'The good-morrow' where two lovers have just awakened from their slumber to the realisation of their mutual love.

Creating truth

In the dedicatory letter to 'An hymne to the Saints, and to Marquesse Hamylton', Donne openly acknowledges his averseness to write an obsequy. The only reason to accept this task is that it demonstrates his subservience to the addressee's will: 'I thanke you that you would command me that which I was loather to do, for, even that hath given a tincture of merit to the obedience of Your poor friend and servant in Christ Jesus I. D.' He explains his reluctance in the following terms: 'you know my uttermost when it was best, and even then I did best when I had least truth for my subjects. In this present case there is so much truth as it defeats all Poetry'. Donne's poetry wants to 'argue truth into existence' (Baumlin, 1991: 65), an over-abundance of actual truth hence constitutes a constraint. The obsequy itself is dedicated not solely to the deceased himself: the title 'An hymne to the Saints, and to

Marquesse Hamilton' already indicates the poem's more general character. It begins conventionally by mourning the loss of the deceased's soul, which, although it may have increased the heavens, has bereft this world: 'The *Chappell* wants an eare, *Councell* a tongue; / *Story*, a theame; and *Musicke* lacks a song' (ll. 15–16). The speaker's plea to the deceased for the purification of the living, 'Wish *him* a *David, her* a *Magdalen*' (l. 42), is similarly traditional.

Although Donne was not happy to address the subject in poetry, he was not reluctant to deal with the Marquesse's death altogether: 'If you had commanded mee to have waited on his body to Scotland and preached there, I would have embraced your obligation with much alacrity'. Whereas the sermon constitutes the appropriate genre for dealing with matters of truth, poetry, as Puttenham would have us know, is 'without any subiect of veritie' (Puttenham, 1959: 4). As fictional and aesthetic artefacts, poems are not accountable to divine truth or even the real world in the same way as sermons or theological treatises. In fact, the major focus of many Donne poems is on the very instability of reality and truth: in questioning the reliability of these categories, they contribute to the deconstruction of what is supposedly real and true.

If the discussion of 'The Dreame' and 'Image of her whom I love' has established external reality as something that can be reconstructed through poetry, it is all the more notable that a number of Donne's poems are nevertheless almost obsessively preoccupied with concepts of truth, particularly as they relate to woman's constancy. Just as the distinction between dream and reality is not easily maintained, so is the opposition of truth and falseness, of woman's constancy and inconstancy, of what's good and bad in woman, frequently blurred. Truth here implies less a woman's ready granting of male desire than a constancy in denying it – at least to those men who are not the speaker. A woman may be praised as true either for granting male desire or, by contrast, for firmly denying it. Depending on the particular partner and poem, truth may refer to one thing or its very opposite (cf. Meg Brown, 1995: 141).

Woman's being true and truth as such are considered positive values both in 'The Dreame', where they coincide with the granting of male desire, and also in 'Goe, and catche a falling starre', which articulates the speaker's supposedly unrealistic yearning for 'a woman true, and faire' (l. 17) who will not be 'False, ere I come, to two, or three' (l. 26) by granting herself to just everyone. But there are some notorious exceptions to this positive estimation of truth as female constancy. 'The Indifferent' begins with the speaker's boast of loving any kind of woman, no matter whether 'faire' or 'browne' (l. 1), voluptuous or thin (l. 2), introverted or outgoing (l. 3), and so forth. The one characteristic the speaker cannot endure in woman is truth: 'I can love any, so she be not true' (l. 9). In the second stanza, such a 'true' addressee is challenged by the speaker: 'Will no other vice content you?' (l. 10). The virtue of being true turns into vice here, and the speaker even suspects that the woman, having profited from his openness to and tolerance of all kinds of female whims, now deliberately seeks to strain his patience: 'have you all old vices spent, and now would finde out others?' (l. 12). By radically distancing himself from truth and constancy, the speaker fashions himself as playing the game of love according to the rules. In the third stanza, Venus, the playmaster of love, fines any of the woman addressee's attempts at 'dangerous constancie' (l. 25): "Since you will be true, / You shall be true to them, who'are false to you" (ll. 26–7).[5]

Once again, truth is denied any inherent essence and comes across as altogether relative to and dependent on the speaker's point of view, who, by allowing both men and women to love promiscuously, even aims to evade the 'essential' difference between male and female (Saunders, 2006: 128–31). The relativity of truth is at stake also in 'Twicknam garden' where the speaker likewise denigrates truth, albeit for different reasons. In 'Twicknam garden', he is anything but indifferent as to whom he loves, nor does he present himself as untrue. Quite the contrary: he invites other lovers to make use of his tears and test them against their mistresses' tears at home, 'For all are false, that tast not just like mine' (l. 22). One would expect that the truth of his beloved, who distinguishes herself before all other women 'where none is true but shee' (l. 26), would correspond nicely with his attitude towards her. But as the speaker complains, 'her truth kills mee' (l. 27), because it is relative in the literal sense of the word, that is relative to another man. Depending on who you are and whose truth you are talking about, truth may be highly desirable or fiercely regrettable. As 'Womans Constancy' hints, being true or not is not beyond our own control: although the speaker has to rely on vague speculations as to whether his mistress will still be true to him in the morning, and if not, what her excuses are likely to be, he decides to refrain from any attempts to convince her otherwise. For 'by to morrow, I may thinke so too' (l. 17), the 'may' hinting that his being true is subject to a consciously made decision, partly dependent on his mistress's remarks and her possible 'falsehood' (l. 13) the morning after.[6]

If truth is relative and may be consciously manipulated, the recognition of what's good or bad becomes more complex. 'Communitie' debates the difficulty of telling a good from a bad woman, concluding that, as nature 'did [women] so create, / That we may neither love, nor hate, / Onely this rests, All, all may use' (ll. 10–12). Yet the poem insists that it is, at least in principle, if not with regard to woman, possible to distinguish good from bad:

> Good wee must love, and must hate ill
> For ill is ill, and good good still
>
> (ll. 1–2)

Only 'things indifferent' (l. 3) such as women have to be handled differently. Them,

> wee may neither hate, nor love,
> But one, and then another prove,
> As wee shall finde our fancy bent.
>
> (ll. 4–6)

There is quite a broad field in life where 'fancy' determines what or who is good or bad at this moment or another. 'Fancy' is closely related to poetry, and indeed, this poem itself also engages in bending these categories:

> If then at first wise Nature had
> Made women either good or bad,
> Then some wee might hate, and some chuse.
>
> (ll. 7–9)

Instead of associating those fictitiously purely good or bad women with those females men might love or hate respectively, the word order aligns 'good' with those women 'wee might hate' and 'bad' with those to 'chuse'. Moreover, the whole of the third stanza inverts the link between what's good with what is praiseworthy and of what's bad with what is to be blamed:

If they were good it would be seene,
Good is as visible as greene,
And to all eyes itself betrayes:
If they were bad, they could not last,
Bad doth it selfe, and others wast,
So, they deserve nor blame, nor praise.

(ll. 13–18)

Although these lines contemplate the possibility of a clear-cut opposition between women good and bad, they simultaneously subvert this distinction by a chiasm that goes unexplained: the description of good comes before that of bad, but the final line puts blame before praise, implying that good women are to be blamed whereas bad women deserve praise.

In Donne's *Songs and Sonets* there is little good or bad, true or false, real or dreamed but the individual poem makes it so (cf. Baumlin, 1991: 242–4; Sloane, 1985: 63). Whereas 'The Expostulation' begins by mourning female falseness, 'Variety' introduces a speaker who wonders why, if 'The heavens rejoyce in motion, why should I / Abjure my so much lov'd variety' (ll. 1–2). Donne's Elegy 'Change' alternatively argues for the compromise of loving 'not any one, nor every one. / To live in one land, is captivitie, / To runne all countries, a wild roguery' (ll. 28–30), a solution the speaker accepts, at least by the time he will have reached a 'firmer age' (l. 76). By contrast, the exclusive ever-lastingness of the love constellations portrayed in 'The Canonization' or 'The good-morrow' testify to a faith in true love quite incompatible with the pessimist view of 'Goe and catche a falling starre' or the rakish celebration of polygamy advocated by 'Confined Love'.

Donne's poems distinguish themselves by their inconstancy towards constancy and truth: they question the possibility of truth as such, and, where they accept its potential existence, they often present it as relative, dependent on the speaker's and addressee's point of view. Not infrequently, truth is presented as something to be bent according to one's fancy or the fanciful words of poetry. Truth and constancy may be valued highly, as in the case of the 'true plain hearts' (l. 16) of 'The good-morrow' or harshly denigrated, as in 'The Indifferent'. The ensemble of Donne's poems questions the stability of truth that is often already undermined in individual poems on a larger scale. Not only are many of the poems (performatively) self-contradictory – they also contradict one another and are 'constantly aware of contradictory points of view, and this awareness gives the poetry extraordinary resilience as well as restlessness' (Summers/Pebworth, 1986b: xii).[7] The relative value of truth in Donne's poetry might easily be accounted for or excused by Sidney's famous dictum that the poet, in contrast to the astronomer or physician, 'nothing affirms, and therefore never lieth' (Sidney, 1947: 33). Poems herein resemble performatives, as either constitute '*not* utterances which could be "true" or "false"' (Austin, 1975: 12, italics original). Poetic truth is less affirmative or objective than Promethean, but, as 'The Indifferent' shows, it need not always be in the service of virtue, although this is what Sidney advocates.

This attitude towards truth constitutes a crucial difference between Donne's poetic work and his sermons: the latter present us with a truth that insists on its reliability and ever-current validity, as it is intrinsically connected to the divine truth of the Biblical word. So do most of Donne's religious poems, but, being poems, their truths are torn between thematic obligations and generic liberties. In 'Satyre III', the speaker is driven to both pity and scorn for the attempts of a Mirreus, a Crants, a Graius, a Phrygius and a Crassus to seek truth in the true religion. His advice:

>   doubt wisely, in strange way
> To stand inquiring right, is not to stray;
> To sleepe, or runne wrong is: on a huge hill,
> Cragged, and steep, Truth stands, and hee that will
> Reach her, about must, and about must goe;
> And what the'hills suddennes resists, winne so
>   ('Satyre III', ll. 77–82)

Truth is less an essence finally to be retrieved and discovered than a way of life, and the image of truth on a hill echoes Bacon (Bacon, 1972: 4). By his encouragement of constant doubting, probing and questioning, the long effort of which is reflected by the forced run-on line 80–1, the speaker distances himself from all those who already believe themselves to be in possession of truth. Any immediate attacks on truth are bound to fail, whereas an oscillating movement gradually leads uphill. A patient engagement with truth is also at the heart of 'A Litanie' where the Trinity is praised both for its power to promote faith and its resistance to human logical capacity:

> O Blessed glorious Trinity,
> Bones to philosophy, but milke to faith,
> Which, as wise serpents, diversly
> Most slipperinesse, yet most entanglings hath,
> As you distinguish'd undistinct
> By power, love, knowledge bee,
> Give mee a such selfe different instinct,
> Of these let all mee elemented bee,
> Of power, to love, to know, you'unnumbred three.
> (ll. 28–36)

The speaker asks to be granted the grace of appreciating the Trinity's inconceivable 'slipperinesse' in itself and himself: 'Give me a such selfe different instinct'. In the process, the Trinity must lose none of its 'distinguish'd undistinct' aspect, constituted as it is of 'you'unnumbred three'. Truth resides in paradox, for, while I may marry myself to truth, this does not mean that truth needs to be married to me only: the true church, at least, 'is most trew, and pleasing to thee [Christ], then / When she'is embrac'd and open to most men' ('Show me deare Christ', ll. 13–14).

The ways in which truth is debated in Donne's religious poetry differ both from the sermons and from his erotic poetry. Whereas the sermons' emphasis is less on the complexity of religious truth than on the moral imperative to act upon a (supposedly fairly certain) reality of religious truth, Donne's 'Satyre III' does not refrain from thematising the difficulties one may encounter in seeking 'true religion' ('Satyre III', l. 43). His religious differs from his erotic poetry as it never goes so far as to question or undermine the existence of truth as such or to disparage it as something not worth aspiring to. In Donne, truth is relative with regard to speaker, (poetic) genre and individual poem.

Creating the self

Being greatly concerned with the body, Donne's poetry is not merely metaphysical but indeed physical. In 'Aire and Angels' and 'The Extasie', Donne addresses the complex interconnections between the physical and the spiritual, as he does too in *Pseudo-Martyr*, in order to illustrate the relation between secular and spiritual authorities (*Pseudo-Martyr* 47). This preoccupation with the body moreover explains the interest in physical reincarnation in a poem like 'The Relique', where the speaker suggests that he wears a 'bracelet of bright haire about the bone' (l. 6) so that his and his beloved's soul 'at the last busie day, / Meet at this grave, and make a little stay' (ll. 10–11). In 'Aire and Angels', the speaker explains that, as his soul has to take 'limmes of flesh' (l. 8), his love for the addressee had to 'fixe it selfe in thy lip, eye, and brow' (l. 14). The second stanza questions this move as such love would over-emphasise physical things. Realising that 'nor in nothing, nor in things / Extreme, and scattring bright, can love inhere' (ll. 21–2), the speaker creates the image of the angel as pure spirit surrounded by the (though lesser) purity of air and concludes with the following misogynist twist: 'Just such disparitie / As is 'twixt Aire and Angells puritie, / 'Twixt womens love, and mens will ever bee' (ll. 26–8).

However, as the preceding lines reported the speaker's own struggle in arriving at the correct conception of love, this self-confident conclusiveness is dubious. 'The Extasie' debates the pros and cons of spiritual against physical love, and here, too, the speaker insists that the two are intrinsically linked: 'Soe soule into the soule may flow, / Though it to body first repaire' (ll. 59–60). This connection is so central that the speaker refers to it as 'That subtile knot, which makes us man' (l. 64). In a poem such as 'The Dreame', it is precisely the addressee's physicality which makes the speaker prefer her profaneness to any angel-like qualities. 'Loves Progress' goes even further, admonishing all men who love a woman from the wrong, that is spiritual motives: 'Can men more injure women then to say / They love them for that, by which they're not they?' (ll. 19–20). That by which they are 'they' is 'The right true end of love' (l. 2), women's naked sex. Depending on the poem, self and identity are conceived of differently, each poem alternatively preferring either the spiritual or the physical dimension.

The speaker of 'The Extasie' points out that 'Love's mysteries in souls doe grow, / But yet the body is his booke' ('The Extasie', ll. 71–2). The mysteries of love depend on their manifestation in a book, their realisation in language. The transference from soul to body, of the love mystery to the book progresses smoothly: any potential bystander observing the lovers as they move to their bodies or the writing of the book or indeed the poem of their love's mystery 'shall see / Small change, when we'are to bodies gone' (ll. 75–6, cf. Shullenberger, 1993: 59). The medium of language is trusted both for articulating love spiritually and for realising it physically. Language combines the two aspects of love and lends itself to the staging of physical and spiritual aspects of identity and self, as in Donne's 'Holy Sonnets', whose speakers again and again draw on physical and even sexual experience to articulate their spiritual turmoil. The self, or rather, the various selves of Donne's poetry, are not only both physical and spiritual but also intrinsically linguistic in as far as they are created by the book of Donne's poetry. Puttenham's *Arte of English Poesie* corroborates this concept of poetic self and identity: 'But *what else is language*, and vtterance, and discourse, & persuasion, and argument in man, *then the vertues of a well constitute body and minde*, little lesse naturall then his very sensuall actions, sauing that the one is perfited by nature at once, the other not without exercise and iteration?' (Puttenham, 1959: 190, my emphasis). As much as the worlds and truths they are in the process of creating, Donne's speakers themselves are poetically in the making, to be established in the here and now of each text, as in 'Going to Bed', where the speaker fashions himself and his addressee as two subjects on the brink of sexual union. Very much as in 'Loves Progress', where the speaker imagines himself travelling through 'the streight *Hellespont* between / The *Sestos* and *Abydos* of her breasts' (ll. 60–1), the speaker presents the woman as an object that has yet to be discovered and colonised by him in all its nakedness. Woman has to be made, cultivated and created first by being put to use, most gruesomely so 'Like an appointed lambe, when tenderly / The priest comes on his knees t'embowell her' ('Epithalamion made at Lincoln's Inne', ll. 89–90). Her being used in such ways is to effect a change in her identity as it is only thus that she *'puts on perfection, and a womans name'* (l. 96).

Whereas the words of some poems explore selfhood and identity as always in a process of becoming, there are other instances where Donne's speakers insist on the firmness of words and the stable personality behind them – even if this identity is one of nothingness, as in 'A nocturnall upon S.Lucies day, Being the shortest day'. The poem goes to great lengths to characterise 'the yeares midnight' (l. 1) in all its gloominess, but only to make the final stanza's shift of perspective from the general atmosphere to the speaker's self more effective: depressing and gloomy as sun, earth and life may be, 'all these seeme to laugh, / Compar'd with mee, who am their Epitaph' (ll. 8–9). Firstly, by his choice of the epitaph genre, the speaker presents himself as on the verge of death and decay. Secondly, he conceives of his identity as essential and stable. Just as an epitaph sums up one's life and is written on to a tomb as the corpse is stowed away into the nutshell of its coffin, so does this speaker's self comprise 'every dead thing' (l. 12), love has created him 'A quintessence even from nothingnesse' (l. 15), he is 'Of the first nothing, the Elixer grown' (l. 29). Finally, by picturing himself as an 'epitaph', the speaker conceives of his self as linguistic.[8] When he addresses them 'who shall lovers bee / At the next world, that is, at the next Spring:' (ll. 10–11) to 'Study me then' (l. 10), he is pointing not to himself but to his epitaph as an object worthy of their study. As the colon after line 11 indicates, what follows is just this epitaph which sums up the speaker's personality of non-being as opposed to 'All others' (l. 19), who 'from all things, draw all that's good, / Life, soule, forme, spirit, whence they beeing have' (ll. 19–20). Albeit a nothing, the speaker is at least not 'an ordinary nothing' (l. 35), which sets him off not only from humans but also from such common material things as plants or stones (l. 33). Unusual in its insistence on the speaker's nothingness rather than his long-lasting fame, the poem nevertheless conforms to the epitaph genre as it emphasises the speaker's exceptionality in his non-ordinary qualities of nothingness.

In 'Epitaph on Himselfe', Donne likewise employs the genre to write a poem and, by implication, to write himself. This poem is less concerned with the speaker's nothingness than with the refining powers of death and death poetry. The dedicatory letter informs us not only that what follows is the speaker's 'last funerall Scrowle' (l. 4) but also that it constitutes the speaker himself: he entreats the Countess of Bedford to place 'this last funerall Scrowle' (l. 4) in her cabinet 'That *I* might make your Cabinet my tombe' (l. 1, my emphasis). On opening the cabinet, the addressee will be confronted with his 'graves inside' (l. 10), the speaker himself, or rather, his corpse, but what she will find there will not, as in the 'Nocturnall', be less than her and more nothing than she could ever be. Rather, 'here', in our graves, 'to grow gold we lie' (l. 14). Like 'Nocturnall', 'Epitaph on Himselfe' hopes to instruct (cf. Scodel, 1991: 122): 'Heare this, and mend thy selfe, and thou mendst me, / By making me being dead, doe good to thee' (ll.

21–2). These lines indicate the significance of the reader's contribution to the poetic and self-creating or rather self-negating process performed in this poem: by hearing the epitaph, the addressee contributes to the 'making [...] dead' of the speaker, his death being the effect not merely of being uttered, but also of being heard and read.

Language (un)makes the selves of men and women, but in both poems the speaker strives hard to create a kind of selfhood that is essential rather than performative. Although the speaker's self-presentation as 'Of the first nothing, the Elixer grown' ('Nocturnall', l. 29) implicitly admits to the development which had to precede the manifestation of this essence – the speaker had to *grow* into this elixir first – these processes are located in a period prior to the poem. Likewise, in 'Epitaph on Himselfe', the speaker admits that the golden shade of death will only gradually manifest itself: 'here to *grow* gold we lie' (l. 14, my emphasis), but characterises himself as more refined than his addressee, who is still alive and thus, inevitably, 'not yet so good' (l. 11). The attempts of locating the performative and unstable dimensions of self and identity outside of the poem's space depend on the rhetoric of a speaker, a speaker, who is dying or dead, but whose very death is only enabled by those performative strategies of the poem which have to be taken up by the addressee to be fully realised. Both 'Nocturnall' and 'Epitaph on Himselfe' strive and perform very hard to create a kind of identity in death that is explicitly not performative but essential. This performance of essentialism is carried out by a supposedly dying and dead speaker, whose alleged death is just another performative effect. The poems' strategies of composition bring about the speaker's nihilist essence in 'Nocturnall' as well as the aural core of his being in 'Epitaph on Himselfe'. The speaker of 'Epitaph on Himselfe' truly ought to be thought 'well compos'd, that [he] could now / A last-sicke houre to syllables allow' (ll. 23–4), as well composed as the lines he has written, which describe and constitute him as he is (de-)composing into gold.

'Nocturnall' and 'Epitaph of Himselfe' present the dying/dead speaker as 'the grave / of all, that's nothing' (ll. 21–2) in one case and as the epitome of golden refinement in the other (l. 14). However, this power of language to create first one thing and then another draws attention to its fundamental evasiveness.

Language cannot create an essence, for essences are not created in the first place. Moreover, it is non-essential, but subject to its context, depending on the one who uses it and on the end which this speaker has in mind. In equating themselves with the linguistic products of their own poems, the speakers of 'Nocturnall' and 'Epitaph on Himselfe' imply that their identities resemble language, are at bottom linguistic, thereby inherently performative and not essential. No matter what an epitaph may have to say either about the epitaphee's essential nothingness or goldenness, it is still made up of words. The self, aligned with language as it is here, is subject to linguistic performance and the volatility that accompanies it, which is why, even in death, it may choose to perform in a variety of costumes, either of nothingness or of goldenness. The subject of near death elevates a poem such as 'Nocturnall' or 'Epitaph on Himselfe'. As both are spoken by the subject of the epitaph himself, they are the last words of a (supposedly) dying man. The truth of either of these suppositions is far less relevant than the speaker's ability to fashion himself thus – to perform as a dying man addressing his impending death in his own epitaph. Let us therefore consider the workings of role-play and protean shape shifting in Donne's poetry in more detail.

Protean poetic power I – theatricality and role-play

Donne's poetry is theatrical. T. S. Eliot's proverbial praise, which describes the metaphysical poets' 'mechanism of sensibility which could devour any kind of experience', follows immediately upon his observation that they were 'the successors of the dramatists of the sixteenth [century]' (Eliot, 1939: 287). So far, little effort has been made to analyse in more detail precisely how and why readers experience Donne's poems as inherently dramatic. Their theatricality literally goes without saying. The few definitions offered to define the dramatic character of Donne's writing are often merely conjectural (cf. Bartenschlager, 1970: 17). Zunder considers Donne 'dramatic: characteristically indirect or ironical' (Zunder, 1982: 35), and Hunt is similarly imprecise when describing Donne's poetry as 'the work of a man whose imagination operates in dramatic terms' (Hunt, 1954: 7). Moloney links Donne's poetry to 'dramatic precedent' (Moloney, 1985: 215), reading his marked departure from strict patterns of metre and rhyme as an affinity to trends in contemporary drama.

My focus will be on the inherent theatricality of the communicative situation of Donne's poetry rather than on linguistic features.[9] If it is true that Donne's poems are particularly dramatic, such theatricality may be an important feature of early modern poetry or even the early modern period in general (cf. Maassen, 2001: 297–9; Muir, 1997: 52). Bacon observes that poetry functions 'as a visible History, and is an image of actions as if they were present, as History is of actions in nature as they are, that is past' (Bacon, 1947: 90). That poetry should thus engage in making experience 'present' links it to the theatre, which typically confronts its audiences with just such 'an image of actions as if they were present'. A line like 'Busie old foole, unruly Sunne' ('The Sunne Rising', l. 1) establishes the sun as the speaker's addressee simply by talking to it – reference here functions as a speech act (cf. Searle, 1969: 28). Through apostrophe, the speaker of 'Death be not proud' (l. 1) pretends to be on speaking terms with death itself.[10] This is how poetry transforms fundamental crisis into governable play (Eckhard Lobsien, 2004: 372; Nardo, 1986) – and the term play is noteworthy here. In the theatre, there is no need to describe anything or anyone which or who is already present on stage, and, if there is something which the stage fails to illustrate physically to the audience's eye, that location or atmosphere (as the fields of France represented by the wooden O in *Henry V* or the tempest on the heath in *King Lear*) is created verbally by being declared or addressed as such. On the stage as well as in many of Donne's poems, it is the mere mentioning of something that makes it present and that makes it so.

There are various instances where Donne's poems employ metaphors of the theatre. In 'Of the Progres of the Soule: the Second Anniversary', the speaker elaborates on how human learning includes historical knowledge as to 'How others on our stage their parts did Act' (l. 286). However, such historical awareness does not concern the essence of things and fails to answer questions such as 'Why grasse is greene, or why our blood is red' as these have to remain 'mysteries which none have reach'd unto' (ll. 288–9). If one is unable to understand even the essential being of grass or blood, it is altogether out of the question that our 'Poore soule' (l. 254) should ever hope to know itself: 'Thou art too narrow, wretch, to comprehend / Even thy selfe' (ll. 261–2). As Montaigne puts it, 'We are all framed of flaps and patches and of so shapelesse and diverse a contexture, that every peece and every moment playeth his part' (Montaigne, 1946: II, 14). Only after death will we be able to perceive the genuine essence of things: 'In Heaven thou straight know'st all, concerning it, / And what concernes it not, shall straight forget' (ll. 299–300). Only in heaven will we be able to share in the encompassing knowledge of the hitherto ascended Elizabeth Drury commemorated in this poem.

As long as 'our stage' is still the earth, the 'selfe', and all that pertains to it, are not easily known. Here, it is primarily through self-fashioning and role-play that one's self comes into existence (cf. Stevie Davies, 1994: 5). Donne's 'Satyre I' can be read as a speaker's dilemma in being torn between the various contradictory parts he might or might not play, and 'Satyre IV' exhibits and scorns the performances surrounding life at court. In spite of criticising the ever-changing protean self, these satires fail to offer any alternatives. Whereas my reading of these two texts is primarily concerned with the ways in which Donne's poems themselves thematise a concept of the self as engaged in protean shape-shifting, the final section of this chapter explores how the theatrical acts of Donne's various speakers are reflective of their contemporary listeners or readers and how audiences might have responded to them.

Theatricality disparaged? Two satires

Self and identity are debated especially in Donne's Satires. In 'Satyre I', the speaker labours to fend off a 'fondling motley humorist' (l. 1) whose changefulness contrasts with the 'constant company' (l. 11) of the speaker's learned books. Some of these contain the works of 'Giddie fantastique Poëts of each land' (l. 10) – and upon mentioning them, the speaker's scholarly steadfastness begins to waver, and he wonders: 'Shall I leave all this [supposedly] constant company, / And follow headlong, wild uncertain thee?' (ll. 11–12). Soon afterwards, the speaker has been persuaded, although he lists certain conditions which the addressee will have to observe if the speaker is to join him for a walk in the streets. He admonishes the 'fondling motley humorist'

(l. 1) not to be taken in by the appearances and costumes of men they might encounter in the street,

> Not though a Captaine do come in thy way
> Bright parcell gilt, with forty dead mens pay,
> Nor though a briske perfum'd piert Courtier
> Deigne with a nod, thy courtesie to answer.
>
> (ll. 17–20)

The addressee is to renounce his motleyness and stick to and by the speaker. He must refrain from adapting his behaviour to the various designs he may have upon the different company they may meet. The speaker knows that his addressee hates virtue not only '*though* shee be naked, and bare' (l. 41, my emphasis), but probably for that very reason: he seems to be far more interested in clothing and apparel than in what is underneath – even though the clothing of the soul in the body, just like the moment when Adam and Eve covered themselves in 'beasts skin' (l. 46) marked the Fall: the soul was no longer identical with itself and easily obscured by the dissembling of putting on bodies and clothes (cf. McRae, 2007: 224). Despite these misgivings, the speaker shuts the door of his study and yields to the addressee's enticements, although he should have known that anything would have been more likely 'Then thou, when thou depart'st from mee, canst show / Whither, why, when, or with whom thou wouldst go' (ll. 63–4). Soon the speaker regrets to have come along, debasing the addressee to the level of a performing elephant or ape (l. 81).

But why should he try to persuade him to move on with him rather than leave him at his leisure talking to some fop or other (ll. 89–90)? Instead, the speaker insists: 'I for my lost sheep stay' (l. 93), revealing, in spite of all his criticism, how closely he is associated with that 'fondling motley humorist' (l. 1) who spies ever 'More men of sort, of parts, and qualities' (l. 105) who are just as little of one piece as himself. Eventually, having altogether lost contact with the speaker, the addressee 'flings from mee / Violently ravish'd to his lechery' (ll. 107–8) – but later seeks refuge at the speaker's home of all places:

> Many were there, he could command no more;
> Hee quarrell'd, fought, bled; and turn'd out of dore,

> Directly came to mee hanging the head,
> And constantly a while must keepe his bed.
>
> (ll. 109–12)

The bed in question is not, as one would expect, the addressee's but the speaker's, as there is no mentioning of the addressee's departure from the speaker's place to his own. With this conclusion, the distinction between the speaker's and addressee's identity becomes significantly blurred. The speaker, who is ever so critical of the addressee's wilful and erratic performances, may in fact be the very same person as that 'fondling motley humorist' to whom the whole satire addresses itself (cf. Scodel, 2005: 367; Carey, 1990: 53; Wiggins, 2000: 33).[11]

This insight would also help to explain why the speaker fails to simply leave the addressee to his own devices in line 93: his claim of 'I for my lost sheep stay' implies that part of himself has departed from him and he can do nothing but wait for it to return; he will even have to follow it in order to track down and retrieve whatever or whoever has got out of hand. The speaker's identity is thus divided in itself, with lines 95–104 not engaging in any proper dialogue between speaker and addressee, but in a 'dialogue of one'. The speaker's being torn between as many parts and roles of himself as the addressee could possibly take on also explains why he should be so inconsistent and lacking in firmness towards this addressee that is supposedly an Other. He is very aware of the conflicts that may arise from performative selves, and he also knows that it is a widespread custom: the addressee, we are told, spies ever 'More men of sort, of parts, and qualities' (l. 105), more men who are not whole in themselves. One could even argue that his misfortune when allowing himself to be 'Violently ravish'd to his lechery' (l. 108) has less to do with the fact that there are too many competitors apart from himself: the line 'Many were there, he could command no more' (l. 109) may plausibly be read as an account of his lack in self-commandment, his eventual failure to control and effectively co-ordinate his various selves at that point. Small wonder then that the speaker should be relieved and consequently very generous in offering the addressee – his alter ego that has finally returned to him – his bed. After all, this is the only way for him to ensure that he who is both speaker and addressee at the same time will behave 'constantly a while' (l. 112). Sharing a bed, the two alter egos are brought together, and in the seclusion of that private space they are not in danger of witnessing other men's performances, let alone being tempted to engage in such performances themselves. Their common bed prevents that kind of (marital) unfaithfulness which the speaker had already alluded to in lines 25–6: 'For better or worse, take mee, or leave mee: / To take, and leave mee is adultery' and seems to offer at least some temporary resting place where the speaker's and the addressee's self are for once at one with one another and thus faithfully 'married'.[12]

'Satyre IV' likewise thematises theatricality as something the speaker distances himself from while he is simultaneously tempted and absorbed by it. Moreover, the speaker establishes many parallels between life at court, the theatrical stage and Catholic worship (cf. Hurley, 2005: 49). In the famous first lines he takes up the concept of purgatory to characterise his experience of a day spent at court, which, he expects, will be considered sufficient compensation for his sins, in particular his sin of attending court in the first place. Setting himself off from those courtiers firmly entrenched in the mechanisms of self-fashioning common at court, he declares: 'My minde, neither with prides itch, nor yet hath been / Poyson'd with love to see, or to bee seene' (l. 5–6). However, having gone to court at all, he will be punished no less severely than if he had secretly attended Catholic Mass, as both court life and Catholicism rely on pompous show and theatrical pretension. Yet, if one of the speaker's strategies in denigrating life at court consists in aligning it with the practices of Catholicism, it is odd that he should at the same time activate the Catholic concept of purgatory (l. 3) as a means of distancing himself from these very heresies.[13]

This is not the only incongruity. The speaker's attitude to the outer appearance and costume of the other courtiers is quite dubious: for about 30 lines, he ridicules the importance that courtiers attribute to their dress, suggesting that this obsession owes much to the theatre (cf. Hester, 1982: 86–7): once they have wasted all their possessions on their outfits, they might as well get some of their money back by selling their costumes to the theatre which will have much use for them (l. 183). The link between court and theatre applies generally: 'Me seemes they doe as well / At stage, as court; All are players' (ll. 184–5). Such theatricality is related to the religious concepts of Catholicism: before entering the altar and stage of the Queen's 'Presence' (l. 199), each courtier is busy sorting out his outfit, a process which is linked to the Catholic practice of confession as, in tidying themselves up, the courtiers' outfits '*confesse* not only *mortall* / Great staines and holes in them, but *veniall* / Feathers and dust, wherewith they fornicate' (l. 201–3, my emphasis). The 'enter' of a prototypical courtier proceeds even with 'such nicetie / As a young preacher at his first time goes / To preach' (l. 208–10). However, in spite of taunting the courtiers' theatrical obsession with external appearance, earlier on, the speaker allowed himself to be led by dress:

> His cloths were strange, though coarse; and black, though bare;
> Sleevelesse his jerkin was, and it had beene
> Velvet, but 'twas now (so much ground was seene)
> Become Tufftaffatie
>
> (ll. 30–3)

In the next line, the speaker refers to the courtier as 'This thing' (l. 35). His judgement is much influenced by his opponent's outer appearance, hence characterising the speaker as no less obsessed with costume and attire than the courtiers he is later to criticise. Dress was one of the most decisive factors in determining social status (Sugg, 2006: 49), and in betraying a man's passions (Wright, 1973: 219) – an early modern and theatrical convention from which one cannot exempt oneself.

Although professing to hate him, the speaker has to concede his opponent's power with words; in his tongue,

> he can win widdowes, and pay scores,
> Make men speak treason, cosen subtlest whores,
> Out-flatter favorites, or outlie either
> Jovius, or Surius, or both together.
>
> (ll. 45–8)

The speaker fails to dissociate himself from the ensuing spectacle of small talk, foul-mouthing and feigned politeness. He cannot avoid playing along with this performance, and his desperate aside at the beginning of the scene is part of the play that is to start from here: 'I whisper, God! / How have I sinn'd, that thy wraths furious rod, / This fellow, chuseth me?' (ll. 49–51). Much as he detests this cultivated theatricality, the speaker obeys Bacon's advice on 'Simulation and Dissimulation': 'The best composition and temperature is to have openness in fame and opinion;

secrecy in habit; dissimulation in seasonable use; and a power to feign, if there be no remedy' (Bacon, 1972: 19). There seems to be no remedy but to act along, for, whereas a play used to be praised for resembling court life, nowadays, 'Playes were not so like Courts, as Courts'are like playes' (111, 'To Sr. *Henry Wootton*', l. 21).

The following hundred lines comprise the partly direct, partly indirect rendering of this uncalled for conversation. The theatrical script allocates the courtier the part of the self-centred fool whose conceitedness the speaker crosses by witty repartee and deliberate misunderstanding. However, the speaker soon realises that 'Crossing hurt mee', and he prefers to keep quiet and opt for 'sullenness' (l. 91). As he strives to exempt himself from the courtly mode of encountering dumbness with witty repartee, the speaker introduces the topic of 'new plays' (l. 93) in response to the question 'what newes?' (l. 93). What follows is extensive, unqualified commentary on the courtier's part, which smoothly blends into a summary of the latest gossip in town and court. The speaker no longer actively engages in the conversation, but he still performs, albeit non-verbally: 'I belch, spue, spit, / Looke pale, and sickly, like a Patient [. . .] So I sigh, and sweat / To hear this Makeron talke in vaine' (ll. 109–10, 116–17). But the 'gentleman protests too much' (Dubrow, 1979: 80). Even in suppressing any commentary concerning the courtier's disclosures as to 'Who loves Whores, who boyes, and who goats' (l. 128), the speaker is caught up in the play which the courtier forced upon him by engaging him in conversation (cf. Wiggins, 2000: 52–3):

> I more amas'd than Circes prisoners, when
> They themselves turne beasts, felt myselfe then
> Becomming Traytor, and mee thought I saw
> One of our Giant Statutes ope his jaw
> To sucke me in; for hearing him, I found
> That as burnt venome Leachers do grow sound
> By giving others their soares, I might growe
> Guilty, and he free: Therefore I did shew
> All signes of loathing
>
> (ll. 129–37)

Upon entering the (stage of the) court, there is no avoidance of acting and performance: 'Courts are Theaters, where some men play / Princes, some slaves, all to one end, and of one clay' (112,

'To Sr. *Henry Wotton'*, l. 23–4). Even then the speaker's non-verbal articulations are still theatrical and unwittingly comical: he merely 'did *shew* / All *signes* of loathing' (l. 137, my emphasis) where actual loathing would have forced him to leave the court without ever returning to it again. There is the serious danger of 'moral contamination', as 'one cannot take one's free status for granted. The poet must *perform* his freedom' (Scodel, 2005: 371–2). Performance, however, is that kind of behaviour which is typical of the court – which is why 'Satyre IV' constitutes a 'self-conscious failure' (Scodel, 2005: 377; Baumlin, 1991: 115–18; Corthell, 1997: 50–1).

But even if the satire as a whole displays an awareness of its own futility, the same is not true for the satirist speaker. He does run away once he has managed to rid himself of the courtier and at home reflects upon the rottenness of court life. Yet he returns there later in the day and altogether fails to provide any explanation for the incongruity of this act with his professed loathing of courtly show.[14] This time, the speaker does not get involved in any conversations and occupies the far safer position of spectator, from which he observes and judges the courtiers' interactions: ''tis fit / That they each other plague, they merit it' (ll. 217–18). He even criticises Glorius for his insufficiencies in performing appropriately: he 'only doth / Call a rough carelessenesse, good fashion; / Whose cloak his spurres teare; whom he spits on / He cares not' (ll. 220–3). On leaving the court under the eyes of 'Those Askaparts' (l. 233), the Queen's bodyguards, the speaker feels 'like a spyed Spie' (l. 237), a mere observer and spectator who has decided to be no more involved in the play itself. Having reported on the rottenness of court life, the speaker looks forward to being heard by preachers whom he challenges to 'Drowne the sinnes of this place' (l. 239), and he ends on the hope that, some day, the moral wisdom of his satire will be appreciated: 'yet some wise man shall, / I hope, esteeme my writs canonical' (ll. 243–4).

The boundaries between the speaker's position as observant spectator and his personal and active involvement with the court theatre were not at all times clear. His credibility suffers from the conversation he was led into by the courtier, and his professed disgust becomes even more questionable considering that nowhere does he give a reason for attending court in the first place. Despite himself, the speaker was fascinated both by the theatrical and the Catholic celebratory aspects of court life, so much so that he even failed to restrain himself from returning there a second time. Moreover, the speaker himself claims that witnessing vice is highly unlikely to promote virtue:

> Aretines pictures have made few chast;
> No more can Princes Courts, though there be few
> Better pictures of vice, teach me virtue
>
> (ll. 70–2)

Or, as we read in the previously quoted verse letter on court life,

> Let no man say there, Virtues flintie wall
> Shall locke vice in mee, I'll do none, but know'all.
> Men are spunges, which to poure out, receive,
> Who know false play, rather then lose, deceive.
>
> (112, 'To Sr. *Henry Wotton*', ll. 35–8)

This, however, is exactly what 'Satyre IV' aspires to: by vividly staging the vices of the court before the eyes of his audience, the speaker hopes to be able to move others, the Preachers, to 'Drowne the sinnes of this place' (l. 239). In fact, this is the only point where the speaker's motive for attendance at court is hinted at: his poem, as a good picture of vice, intends to teach virtue. But as 'Satyre IV' testifies to the speaker's inability to remain uninvolved with what he professes to detest, it satirises not just court life but also the satirist himself (cf. Baumlin, 1991: 78; Kerins, 1984: 49; Sanders, 1971: 35; Hester, 1982: 11; Lauritsen, 1976: 120). Although the speaker realises that he is absorbed by the theatricality of court life, he still seems to consider himself superior to its vices. The satire's final lines indicate that he still has some trust in the reformatory potential of his 'writs', a hope which his earlier remark on Aretine discredits. Donne's speaker is 'guilty of many of the failings for which he attacks others' (Kernan, 1959: 247; Marotti, 1986: 88, 103; Patterson, 1994: 151).

At first glance, 'Satyre I' and 'IV' appear to severely criticise and condemn the falseness and pretence of a social life that excessively relies on how a man performs his self. Thomas Wright, however, suggests hat some people might reveal more of their real identities when engaged in games or play: in such contexts they are far more likely to be off their guard and give free rein to their actual passions than when involved in serious conversation or interaction with others. Protected by the contexts of game and playing, men and women will be less careful in shielding their real selves from the curious eyes of potential observers (Wright, 1973: 197; Nardo, 1986). Yet, as Wright himself concedes, judging someone's inner passions by his performance, or even non-performance in games was a challenging task: 'Not to play at all proceedeth, either from extreame holinessse, grauitie, hypocrisie, or insensibilitie' (Wright, 1973: 203). Still play-acting was exposed to severe criticism: there was, after all, at least some possibility that the role which an actor would take on would have an influence on the person itself and allow his or her potentially 'dark' self to come to the surface. And who could tell if spectators might not allow themselves to identify just a bit too closely with what was going on on stage or within some particular character? By declaring itself to be removed from real-life situations, early modern theatre licensed an emotional lack of guardedness that was very difficult to control and contain and that might at any point exert some considerable influence on those involved – be they actors or audience. As Donne's 'Satyre I' and 'IV' suggest, it was nearly impossible to stick to the role of innocent bystander when confronted with the encompassing theatricality of social and courtly life. People's passions are always moved by the senses – and the passions, in turn, affect each person's humoral make-up, which in turn may again produce further passions: 'passions ingender humors, and humours bred passions' (Wright, 1973: 109). The company one keeps is indicative not only of what kind of passion one is most prone to (Wright, 1973: 114), but may further enhance this particular passion, which is why one ought to avoid such social environments (Wright, 1973: 122). Keeping company with courtiers, the speaker of Donne's 'Satyre IV' is not immune to their whims, and that he should return to their society instead of staying away from them is suggestive of the inclination of his passions.

Protean poetic power II – Worldly poetry and its audience

Donne's poems distinguish themselves by their protean speakers' 'restless succession of metamorphoses' (Sugg, 2006: 119), a type of role-play which affects both the poems' addressees and listeners. Speech acts constitute a social phenomenon, and Donne's poetic speech acts likewise display a high degree both of addressee and audience awareness. Donne's epicedes and obsequies are directed at the bereaved family of the deceased, and, as is also true for many of Donne's verse letters, the motive of these performances is that of persuading a patron or patroness to support him financially and morally (cf. Stevie Davies, 1994: 13). A process of 'mutual self-constitution' (Shullenberger, 1993: 53) takes place between the poem's subject and the subject of the audience, as in the dedicatory letter to the Countess of Bedford accompanying the 'Obsequies to the Lord Harrington', which Bald considers to be 'scarcely in the best of taste' (Bald, 1970: 76), and where the writer makes it clear that what follows has as much to do with the Countess herself as with her deceased brother. The 'Obsequies' are much concerned with the poetic speaker himself, who identifies with the deceased's soul. The concept of commendatory poetry as a plea for patronage was firmly established and therefore was recognised as an indirect speech act, whose primary illocutionary force, the original communicative purpose, is expressed indirectly.

The speech situation of Donne's non-commendatory worldly poems is often more complex and intricate. '[R]eaders were not only to identify with the speaker of a discourse, but to admire the ways in which identification was achieved' (Sloane, 1985: 279). The praise which Donne's poems may have met with is effected by the speaker's successful enactment of a role in which he has to be as convincing as possible – whether he features as devoted monogamous lover or raucous misogynist. Sanders's warning that the notion of poetic persona 'implies a relationship between the self that creates the poem, and the self that is created in the poem, which comes perilously close to being an imaginative dislocation – a collapse of psychic integrity' (Sanders, 1971: 24) is perhaps exaggerated. But it is true that, whereas the illocutionary force of what the speaker is saying may be straightforward, the effect which the poem as a whole may have on its audience, and the question as to how this may or may not parallel the illocutionary force of the speaker's utterances is more difficult to predict, and herein it resembles what Austin calls perlocutionary effect.

Many of Donne's poems display a tendency to blur the external and internal communication system (cf. Pfister, 2005; Schalkwyk, 2002), and the ensuing collisions between actor and role may be considered one of the major treats of such theatrical art (cf. Booth, 1998: 259). If we imagine a poem such as 'The Canonization' being read out to a group of young men at the Inns of Court, its beginning 'For Godsake, hold your tongue' (l. 1) may have been experienced as a theatrical aside – while it also refers to the speaker's opponent on the stage established by the poem's discourse. That Leech should develop a comparison between poetry and drama seems to indicate that an approach to poetry as a dramatic medium may be of general heuristic value (Leech, 1969: 190–1). After an analysis of an example of Donne's commendatory poetry, a comparative reading of 'The Canonization' and 'The Curse' is to illustrate the ways in which the Promethean and protean powers of Donne's poetry interact and how these poems reflect the relationship between Donne's coterie poetry and its audience.

The motivation for role-play in 'Obsequies to the Lord Harrington'

Donne's poetry betrays a considerable awareness of the ways in which devotion to a patron may be manipulated by one's motives in enacting or not enacting it. This recognition is present also in the last lines of Donne's 'A Letter to the Lady Carey, and Mrs. Essex Riche, from Amyens', where the speaker refers to the preceding lines in the hope that 'this be'enough to testifie / My true devotion, free from flattery: / He that beleeves himself, doth never lie' (ll. 61–3). As in those poems concerned with truth in women, truth and lies are presented as relative and subjective: if the speaker manages to make himself believe in the excessive praise of the two lady addressees that preceded this conclusion, he will not have lied. As instances of commendatory poetry, Donne's verse letters had quite a clear agenda: they were written in order to gain and maintain patronage and financial aid. They functioned as commodities, in that they not only served as an official plea for support but also constituted the compensation for that same support.

No matter whether one wishes to emphasise the manipulative potential over the creative might of poetic performance, what remains is that poetic performance makes or mars both speaker and addressee. With Donne's celebratory and commemorative poems in particular, the internal communication system of speaker and addressee and the external communication system between poet and reader frequently overlap. Thus Donne's 'La Corona', a series of devotional sonnets dedicated to Mrs Magdalen Herbert, begins with the line *'Deigne at my hands this crown of prayer and praise'* (l. 1, italics original), and only in line 7, when the addressee's 'thorny crowne' is mentioned, do we realise that the first line was not (primarily or exclusively) addressed to the dedicatee of these sonnets Mrs Herbert, but to Christ (cf. Patrick O'Connell, 1986). In establishing and perpetuating the fame of the dead person, Donne's obsequies serve both the deceased and the bereaved family members as well as the speaker and poet himself. Memorial verse inherits its quality both from the subject it addresses and from the degree to which the poetry manages to live up to the elevated subject of its discourse, the degree to which the speaker's soul manages to identify itself with that of the deceased. As Joseph Hall, addressing Donne, writes in his introductory poem to 'The Second Anniversary':

> So while thou mak'st her soules Hy progresse knowne
> Thou mak'st a noble progresse of thine owne,
> From this worlds carcasse having mounted hie
> To that pure life of Immortalitie
>   ('The Harbinger to the Progres', ll. 27–30)

Although Donne, in the dedicatory letter to the Countess of Bedford, which accompanies his 'Obsequies to the Lord Harrington' professes that 'hee which bestowes any cost upon the dead, obliges him which is dead, but not the heire' (ll. 2–3), he corrects himself straightaway. Given the Countess's closeness to her deceased brother, any praise dedicated to him should be taken as applying to her:

> But, Madam, since your noble brothers fortune being yours, the evidences also concerning it are yours, so his vertue being yours, the evidence concerning it, belong also to you, of which by your acceptance this may be one peece, in which quality I humbly present it, and as a testimony how intirely your family possesseth
>   Your Ladyships most humble
>   and thankfull servant
>   John Donne. (ll. 8–13)

The writer attempts to turn something abstract, an obligation towards the dead, into a concrete commodity in the here and now, a written testimony of his loyalty towards his major patroness the Countess of Bedford. If pleased with Donne's obsequy, the Countess would generously recompense the poet for his pains – especially because she was heir to the deceased's estate (Cedric Brown, 2008: 79). The dedicatory letter plays upon the possibilities of how poetry may do several things at once and how identities, here the identity of the Countess with her lately deceased brother, may merge and be taken as one.

The obsequy begins with an apostrophe to the deceased soul, who is expected to be in heaven. Although the speaker's addressing of the deceased as something other than himself, who is still living an earthly existence, emphasises the distance between them, he immediately focuses on the potential links that may yet be established between them with the addressee's help:

> If looking up to God; or downe to us,
> Thou finde that any way is pervious,
> Twixt heav'n and earth, and that mans actions doe
> Come to your knowledge, and affections too,
> See, and with joy, mee to that good degree
> Of goodnesse growne, that I can studie thee,
> And, by these meditations refin'd,
> Can unapparell and enlarge my minde,
> And so can make by this soft extasie,
> This place a map of heav'n, my selfe of thee.
>
> (ll. 5–14)

In a vein that recalls Roman Catholic emulations of saints, the speaker of the obsequy fashions himself as the student and examiner of the deceased, who is eager to 'unapparell and enlarge' his mind and work himself into such a 'soft extasie' as will enable him to identify with his subject ('my selfe of thee', l. 14). Rather than being subservient to the elevated personage mourned in this elegy, the speaker prefers to elevate himself to that great height which Lord Harrington's soul has reached. It is less the ennobling of Lord Harrington's soul that is at stake here than the ennobling effect which the speaker's unique meditation upon this subject has upon himself. Like Elizabeth Drury, Lord Harrington functions as '"occasion" rather than subject' (Lewalski, 1973; 13):

> I see
> Through all, both Church and State, in seeing thee;

> And I discerne by favour of this light,
> My selfe, the hardest object of the sight.
>
> (ll. 27–30)

The speaker's soul not only leaves his own body in his 'soft extasie' (l. 13), but it does so to be refined by amalgamating with the soul of another person. The 'soft extasie' is concerned not only with the speaker's putting off of himself but with the putting on of Lord Harrington's identity. The speaker engages in souls' role-play here, and that he should assume that this is possible is easily explained by the concept of human identity he proclaims in lines 45–51 where he establishes a parallel between the fluidity of his own personality and the deceased's multiple virtues:

> As bodies change, and as I do not weare
> Those spirits, humors, blood I did last yeare,
> And, as if on a streame I fixe mine eye,
> That drop, which I looked on, is presently
> Pusht with more waters from my sight, and gone,
> So in this sea of vertues, can no one
> Bee'insisted on
>
> (ll. 45–51)[15]

The poetic strategy by which the speaker likens the instability of his own self with the moving sea of virtues that distinguish Lord Harrington's soul effects the speaker's elevation to and identification with the addressee's position in heaven. What the speaker does here is reminiscent of the resurrection in the body: 'And as if man feed on mans flesh, and so / Part of his body to another owe' (ll. 53–4), so does the speaker here feed upon the virtuousness of Lord Harrington's soul, thus gaining, rather than, as Hurley suggests, losing in self-confidence (Hurley, 2005: 129).

The speaker elaborates why the deceased's numerous virtues cannot all be mentioned individually and concludes with a comparison which once again aligns him with the deceased's soul:

> Just as a perfect reader doth not dwell,
> On every syllable, nor stay to spell,
> Yet without doubt, hee doth distinctly see
> And lay together every A, and B;
> So, in short liv'd good men, is'not understood
> Each severall vertue, but the compound good.

> For, they all vertues paths in that pace tread,
> As Angells goe, and know, and as men read.
>
> (ll. 93–100)

This time, it is no longer the speaker's self whose fluidity is likened to the wide sea of Lord Harrington's virtues: instead, the sum of the latter's virtues is deemed good just as readers should not analyse a text word for word, but with regard to its effect as a whole – and, of course, not only judge it but judge it good and virtuous. This comparison occurs in a textual medium that is itself subject to reading and exposed to judgement. In reading 'Obsequies to the Lord Harrington', we should treat the text in the same way as we ought to approach the virtues of the deceased: accept it as something unquestionably good which needs no further dissection whatsoever. If one recalls the previous link between the fluidity of Lord Harrington's virtue and the fluidity of the speaker's self (l. 45–51) and reads it alongside the present comparison, one finds that, in combination, these two connections liken Lord Harrington's soul both to the speaker's self and to the text in front of us.[16] Whatever happens to the text also happens to the speaker and Lord Harrington, and whatever has happened to Lord Harrington has immediate consequences for the speaker and the text of the obsequy.

The speaker proceeds to mourn the young age at which Harrington passed away, especially since the shortness of his life means that he can serve as a model of virtue only for adolescents. The only way to profit from his example is through close identification with his death: 'Now I grow sure, that if a man would have / Good companie, his entry is a grave' (l. 165–6), and the speaker immediately focuses on that entry: 'Church-yards are our cities, unto which / The most repaire, that are in goodnesse rich' (ll. 171–2). The speaker imagines Lord Harrington's soul at the head of a triumphant pageantry in the streets of such a city, a conceit continued for the next 70 lines (ll. 177–246).

Traditionally, all citizens were free to comment on the triumpher, so the speaker claims that right, too: 'Let me here use that freedome, and expresse / My griefe, though not to make thy Triumph lesse' (ll. 181–2). Despite this claim, he departs from the fashion of eulogising the deceased and questions the deceased's right to a triumph on various accounts: triumphs are only a magistrate's due, and, since Lord Harrington's soul had not yet risen to that rank, 'Thou could'st no title, to this triumph have, / Thou didst intrude on death, usurp'dst a grave' (ll. 191–2). Moreover, the youthful Lord had not yet been a public figure exposed to the vices of other men, but had succeeded merely in overcoming his own desires and thus engaged in nothing but a civil war, 'For which to triumph, none admitted are' (ll. 202). And while Harrington preserved himself in the virtuous state which God originally placed him, he failed to enlarge his realm by recruiting new subjects and territories – although, 'Before men triumph, the dominion / Must be *enlarg'd* and not *preserv'd* alone' (ll. 205–6).[17] Lastly, a triumph can be granted only once peace has been installed in the territory of which the triumpher was in charge – and, since 'the Diocis / Of ev'ry'exemplar man, the whole world is' (ll. 225–6), neither has this criterion been met.

By the time the speaker has made a clean breast of all the arguments against the deceased soul's triumph in death, he cuts short his criticism and reminds himself that, much as the ordinary people may complain about the triumpher himself, 'it might never reference have / Unto the Senate, who this triumph gave' (ll. 231–2):

> And I (though with paine)
> Lessen our losse, to magnifie thy gaine
> Of triumph, when I say, It was more fit,
> That all men should lacke thee, then thou lack it.
>
> (l. 243–6)

Through the words of this elegy, the speaker may not only foster the memory of the deceased and his greatness ('to magnifie thy gaine / Of triumph') but at the same time also 'Lessen our losse' (l. 244), relieve himself and his addressees of their grief by arguing for the greater relevance of the deceased's triumph over the losses this entails for them. The deceased's triumph, precarious as its justification may be, is not only debated within the poem but performed by it. As lines 165–6 have already suggested 'that if a man would have / Good companie, his entry is a grave', the poem's conclusion takes up that same desire once again as the speaker regrets that

> in our time, be not suffered
> That testimonie of love, unto the dead,

> To die with them, and in their graves be hid,
> As Saxon wives, and French soldarii did
>
> (ll. 247–50)

Although the speaker may not go so far in his identification with the deceased as to die with him, the text of his poetry, which, as we have seen, has been likened to Lord Harrington's soul (ll. 93–100), which, in turn, had earlier on been compared to the speaker's self (ll. 45–51), is to perform the same death as Lord Harrington's soul:

> Doe not, faire soule, this sacrifice refuse,
> That in thy grave I doe interre my Muse,
> Who, by my griefe, great as thy worth, being cast
> Behind hand, yet hath spoke, and spoke her last.
>
> (ll. 255–8)

These being the last words of the poem, the elegy performs its own death here, in immediate reflection upon the death of Lord Harrington, as the elegy, 'by [the speaker's] griefe', is 'great as thy worth' (ll. 257). The speaker's muse moreover coincides with Lord Harrington's soul, for from the start, all the speaker's endeavour had been to 'make by this soft extasie, / This place [i.e. the poem] a map of heav'n, my selfe of thee' (ll. 13–14). Finally, the poem also performs the speaker's/poet's own death, as Lord Harrington's personality had earlier on been associated both with the speaker and with a text to be read. These last lines thus perform the death of the poem, the speaker, and his muse, all of which are in complicated ways entangled with the deceased Lord Harrington's soul.

It follows that the triumph death constituted for Lord Harrington has consequences for the poem and its speaker: Lord Harrington's triumph, questionable as it may be in various regards, may nevertheless not as such be questioned. Like all death triumphs, it has been authorised by the highest authority of the Senate, God himself. Similarly, doubtful as some of the speaker's strategies may be, they share in a parallel kind of triumph – having authorised themselves through the subject with which they closely identify, Lord Harrington's virtuous soul. The fame of the subject, the virtue of Lord Harrington's soul, is transferred to the speaker, the actor taking on that role. In enacting Lord Harrington's fame in the poem and ennobling his personage, the speaker heaps that same fame upon himself. The more the speaker extols his subject, the greater the praise he himself inherits. The poetic grandeur of the obsequy memorialises the grandeur of the deceased while simultaneously replacing it with the speaker's glory. '[A]nalogies between the literary status of the epitaph and the social status of the deceased' (Scodel, 1991: 5) are typical not only of the epitaph genre but also of longer commemorative poems.[18] The triumph of the poet comes close to superseding that of the deceased and manipulates the reader to forget and commemorate Lord Harrington's triumph at the same time (cf. Marotti, 1986: 207).

In his elegy 'On the untimely Death of the incomparable Prince, Henry', Donne's speaker even goes so far as to say that, since Prince Henry was the epitome of reason and took it all with him in his death,

> Wee
> May safelier say, that Wee are dead, then *Hee*.
> So, if our *Griefs* wee doo not well declare,
> W'have double Excuse; *Hee* is not *dead*; Wee are.
>
> (ll. 79–82)

Once again, the speaker foregrounds his own death to have a share in the deceased's claim to the fame of death. In spite of its alleged concern with another person, the speaker does not submit to the mask and role of the deceased subject, but actively makes it his own. Like any convincing actor, the speaker allows his own identity to merge with that of his role model and thus manifests himself as the particular self of that obsequy.

'The Canonization' and 'The Curse' as performative stakes of competition

At the end of 'The Canonization', the speaker imagines 'The Canonization' by quoting in direct speech the prayers that will be addressed to him and his lover as saints. Faithful supplicants are urging them to negotiate with God to grant them a love similar to theirs: 'Beg from above / A patterne of your love!' (l. 45). No more mentioning of the disturbances of the world, or warding off of some intruding busybody who would not leave the speaker to love in peace. 'The Canonization' has taken place right in front of us, while reading 'these hymnes': through the poem itself, the lovers have become '*Canoniz'd* for love'.[19] 'The Canonization' thus completed, one is left with a slightly disturbing after-effect. The speaker has just canonised himself and his lover, without waiting for the authorisation of this sanctification either by God or by the church. In sanctifying himself and his beloved, he takes Neoplatonist convention at its word (Hadfield, 2007: 213). The poem performs a canonisation that verges on blasphemy, a fact the speaker blissfully ignores while revelling in his newly gained saintliness. By presenting canonisation as something to be effected merely through words, the processes involved in this act are exposed. The ritual of canonisation is taken up in two contradictory ways: it is at the same time demystified as it is made present in and through the words of the poem. In only 45 lines, the speaker moves from using the Lord's name in vain ('For Godsake hold your tongue', l. 1) through anti-Petrarchism (ll. 10–18), celebrations of physical love (ll. 26–7) and poetological reflections (l. 36) to canonisation. Initially, the speaker aggressively turns against an addressee whom he suspects of criticising his love; his love soon becomes 'this love' (l. 27) as the speaker turns towards his beloved, no longer challenging the annoying meddler of the first two stanzas. He soon seems to have forgotten all about him, revelling in the exceptionality and perfect mutuality of his love, finally even bringing about his and her canonisation.[20]

Beginning by using the Lord's name in vain and finishing not only with the hope but with the realisation of his own canonisation, the speaker employs performative strategies typical of many Biblical psalms whose speakers similarly move from accusations of God towards a new confidence in his mercy within some 'pretty roomes' of hymnist song. Many of Donne's poems illustrate all that which words can do, but their linguistic force is not always in the service of such a benign purpose as amorous canonisation – and, even there, one may have some misgivings (cf. Sanders, 1971: 23). '[L]anguage can act in ways that parallel the infliction of physical pain and injury' (Butler, 1997: 4), and it is certainly used thus in 'The Curse'. This poem does not merely say something but aspires to having an effect, namely to have all evil and shame come down on 'Whoever guesses, thinks, or dreames he knowes / Who is my mistris' (ll. 1–2). These commencing lines rouse the reader's curiosity, and, since it is this very curiosity that the poem sets out to disparage, readers, by allowing themselves to become interested in the poem, have unwittingly placed themselves in the position of the cursed person. Whoever wants to know the lady or the poem is to 'wither by this curse' (l. 2) which makes up the remainder of the poem. Such powerful beginnings were popular since, in early modern poetry, 'readers' or listeners' responses are part of the measure of the success of a text' (Aughterson, 1998: 274; Deubel, 1971).

'The Curse' consists of four stanzas whose rhyme scheme (abbaaccc) is strikingly similar to that of 'The Canonization' (abbacccaa). Each stanza of 'The Canonization' ends on 'love' (cf. Deubel, 1971: 36–7), and, except for the final one, there is always an alliteration of the first two lines of each stanza in 'The Curse'. Owing to this regularity of rhyme and refrain, both poems share a song-like quality associated with performative genres like the hymn, but also with the curse or magical spell. The use of triads throughout 'The Curse' reflects the assumption that 'three was the number of superstition' (Shawcross in *Complete Poetry*, 1967: 128) – the same number being representative also of the Holy Trinity. In both poems, the speaker establishes his love as unique, albeit by different strategies. In 'The Canonization', the emphasis is on the speaker's love as a positive value of its own which, by the end of the poem, is safely isolated from all the world, whereas 'The Curse' strives to maintain that same isolation by repeatedly warding off anyone who dare discover his secret relationship. The strength of the curse heightens the exclusiveness of the speaker's love, whereas the only exclusiveness granted the object of the curse is that of 'His only,' and only 'his purse' (l. 3) as the sole enticement which may 'some dull heart to love dispose' (l. 4). Nor is the cursed person granted the seclusion which family and hereditary succession may offer, as it is insinuated that he 'incestuously an heire begot' (l. 16) and that his sons 'none of his may bee' (l. 20).

The speaker curses his victim thoroughly, wishing upon him sexual humiliation (l. 6), illness (l. 9), poverty (ll. 14, 22–4) and the ruin of his reputation (ll. 11–13). Finally, he adds not only 'What Tyrans, and their subjects interwish' (l. 26), but 'all ill which all / Prophets, or Poets spake' (l. 29), which he intends to 'Be'annex'd in schedules unto this [poem]' (l. 30) – making sure that no ill wish whatsoever escapes him. After an enumeration of particular disgraces, the last stanza moves toward a climax by recalling all evil that was ever bespoken by professional performers of the word, whose verbal efficacy the speaker evokes to supplement his own cursing capacities. The previous sub-curses were likewise predominantly based on the destructive power of words: the words the cursed victim might have said to the woman scorned by all, who, however, scorns him, will come back to him as he will have to distance himself from those embarrassing vows before others (ll. 7–8) – and scorning in itself, of course, signifies a verbal activity, too. Yet the 'fame [. . .] that 'twas shee' (ll. 12–13) is already established, and once again, it is words, words of gossip, that come down upon the head of the cursed person. Further evil may come through words which do not disclose anything true: 'May he dreame Treason, and beleeve, that hee / Meant to performe it, and confesse, and die' (ll. 17–18). The absence of words to explain his innocence and erroneous death ('And no record tell why', l. 19) will be filled with utterances constituting 'his infamie' (l. 21). 'The Curse' appropriates the strength of verbal expression on various levels: it uses the performative genre of the curse to do and not merely say something to the object of the speaker's wrath, specialising in those particular kinds of nastiness where evil is evoked through language, before it culminates in appropriating the ill-speaking resourcefulness of professional word-performers such as 'Tyrans' (l. 26), 'Prophets, or Poets' (l. 29).

But the impact of verbal articulation is even more encompassing than this reading insinuates: its might not only lends itself to the speaker but is available also to the cursed subject. Verbal power is 'borrowed from a storehouse of verbal formulas that belong to no one and precede everyone' (Fish, 1999: 163). Indeed, the accursed person's ability to appropriate verbal force by speculating on or telling all the world 'Who is [the speaker's] mistris' (l. 2) motivates the whole poem. 'The Curse' is to silence whoever knows the words that may ruin the speaker. The particular instances of verbal destruction mentioned by the poem suggest how the speaker himself may be beaten with his own weapons. The speaker cannot exercise the power of words without involuntarily revealing it as something that the accursed person himself may seize upon for his own ends. He can never hope to deprive his victim of the power to speak – and to speak against him.

The power hierarchies which the speaker strives to establish are anything but stable. In fact, the victim is in a better position, for, whereas the speaker's curse may not bear out, the likeliness that the victim's disclosure of the identity of the speaker's mistress will have damaging effects is high – the speaker's own words betray his nervousness at the thought of such disclosure. The tortures he thinks up to intimidate the accursed are oddly reminiscent of what might happen if the vilified victim did actually speak. In that case, it may actually be the speaker who will have to 'Forsweare to others, what to her he'hath sworne, / With feare of missing, shame of getting, torne' (ll. 7–8); he, and not his accursed opponent, may turn out to be 'Anguish'd, not 'twas sinne, but that 'twas shee' (l. 13). The strength of verbal articulation cuts both ways, as 'the curser often finds his curses turned back upon himself' (Ilona Bell, 1996: 120; Butler, 1997: 15; 39). Since 'dream' in Donne often refers to the production of poetry, the 'Whoever dreames', with which 'The Curse' begins, may hint at and strive to ward off a prospective poem to be composed on the speaker's mistress.

No reading of 'The Curse' is complete without an interpretation of its ending: 'if it be a shee / Nature before hand hath outcursed mee' (ll. 31–2). Traditionally, these lines are taken as one of Donne's many misogynist outbursts: no matter how harsh the cruelties the speaker thought up, nature would have outdone him in cursing had she made the accursed person a woman (cf. Ilona Bell, 1996: 108). If the accursed person is male, the speaker may safely rely on the workings of his curse, as for it being a female, he need worry even less as nature would already, and better, have taken care of the cursing. But there is also a different way of understanding these final lines: Whereas the previous reading takes the speaker and Nature to be fighting for the same cause, one could also imagine these lines to suggest that, in the case of the accursed being a woman, Nature would have 'out-cursed' the speaker by turning him into the object of a curse far more powerful than the one he produced (cf. Klawitter, 1994: 184).

Bell solves 'The Riddle of Donne's "Curse"' biographically, arguing that 'If *there* be a shee', that 'shee' would have been Ann More, thus a 'shee' whose identity would indeed lead to Donne's being 'outcursed' (Ilona Bell, 1996: 121). But the speaker's being 'outcursed by nature', 'if it be a shee' may also be interpreted differently. Firstly, much of the preceding curse would be inapplicable with regard to a woman: apart from the third-person male pronouns which the speaker uses to refer to his victim, the image of a woman buying love from a man (l. 3–4) is not convincing. Neither did an early modern woman normally own land which she could lose if she 'incestuously an heire begot' (ll. 15–16), and finally, a woman can always be certain about being the mother of her children (l. 20). Thus, if the victim of this curse was indeed a woman, 'Nature' would have 'out-cursed' the speaker by making his curse largely ineffective and irrelevant.

Secondly, the speaker would have suffered a severe blow if the accursed person were female because women were considered more talkative than men. Women, as opposed to men, were characterised as cold and humid, and even subject to leaking, as their monthly period confirmed (cf. Paster, 2004: 14). This recognition led to the belief that women were worse at 'keeping themselves together', at keeping things to themselves. If 'The Curse' is about a competition between curser and accursed in terms of verbal power, the curser threatening the accursed to beware of inquiring into, let alone articulating, the identity of his mistress, things would look rather bleak if the accursed were female and hence both more nosy and gossipy than the average male, and less able (or willing) to control herself and her tongue. No words whatsoever would be sufficient to contain the verbal power of a female mouth which, presumably, not even the woman herself would be able to control, even if she tried.[21]

Both 'The Canonization' and 'The Curse' show an awareness of the inevitable waywardness of words. No matter how confident their speakers appear, the language they exploit so effectively may just as easily be turned against them. Although 'The Canonization' ends on a far more serene note than 'The Curse', one should not forget that it starts off with the oath 'For Godsake' (l. 1). If God's name may be thus used in vain, the same may happen to the name of the poem's '*Canoniz'd*' Saints. By illustrating how words bring about a canonisation, the speaker reminds us also of how easily it may be undone again: it would take only a few words for the greatest curse of all, the performative act of excommunication, to fall upon these lovers. Small wonder that the speaker should continue the first line with the words 'hold your tongue' (l. 1), for who knows what might happen if the addressee actually spoke. Quite possibly, the consequences would resemble those of 'The Curse', a poem whose origin may actually lie with 'the excommunication rites of the Roman Catholic Church' (Bryan, 1962: 306).

Heteroglossia, the many voices included in cursing and discourses of Roman Catholic ritual and lovemaking respectively, dominates these two poems. In that 'The Canonization' ends on the supplicants' plea for intercession with 'above', it is not only made up of the celebration of a special kind of love but also incorporates the response to its own monument. The poem constitutes less 'a self-contained urn', as Brooks (1968) argues, than 'a chain of discourses and representations'. Its final lines constitute an attempt to monitor, to absorb in itself, all future reactions to the lovers' poetic monument, and in choosing 'The Canonization' as 'canonical example' Brooks 'responds much as the poem predicts' (Culler, 1994: 203–4). Even though the singling out of but one voice (or loving couple) for (literary) sainthood 'is that process that blurs heteroglossia, that is, that facilitates a naïve, single-voiced reading' (Bakhtin, 1981: 425), many different discourses articulate themselves in Donne's 'Canonization'.

Moreover, the poem is haunted not only by other voices but also by those of others. In all likelihood, it was conceived for a verbally competitive coterie, hence not only its text but also its contemporary social context made 'heteroglossia' inevitable. The strong tradition of reading it biographically (cf. Haskin, 1993; Kelly, 1995/96), as Donne's defiant farewell to the public world, pronounced at his socially suicidal marriage, ignores the linguistic competitiveness that is at stake here. In 'The Canonization' and 'The Curse', the performative effect of language is both intensified and delimited. The demonstration of one's rhetorical skill serves as a reminder that such abilities may also be used against him who speaks at that moment. In 'A Valediction of my name, in the window', the power of words is questioned even by the speaker himself: after ten stanzas of elaborating on the manifold effects of the name in the window, he revokes his previous earnestness about the strength of 'glasse, and lines' (l. 61) and encourages the addressee to 'Impute this idle talke, to that I goe, / For dying men talke often so' (l. 66, cf. Baumlin, 1991: 183–4). As the poem itself also ends and dies on these lines, this creates an ambiguity that is not easily dissolved: 'dying men' may refer to men bidding farewell, an interpretation strengthened by the reference to the speaker's long absence equating just so many daily deaths ('Since I die daily, daily mourne', l. 42), and an impending goodbye may trigger melancholic fantasies both inappropriate and unrealistic. On the other hand, if the speaker fashions himself as on the verge of dying, these his last words, coinciding with the final lines of this poem, are instilled with great authority, for who would not take seriously the last words of a dying man? In the phrase 'dying men talke often so' (l. 66), does the 'so' refer to the relevance of the first ten stanzas and their insistence on what a 'name in the window' can do? Or does it also include recognition of the irrationality of these previous stanzas, the final insight that 'glasse, and lines must bee / No meanes our firme substantiall love to keepe' (ll. 61–2)? It is impossible to decide whether the wisdom of this supposedly dying man speaks from his professed trust in language (stanzas 1–10) or from the disclaimer of that same faith (stanza 11).

Role-play and coterie

If it is true that love is 'kept by art' ('The Expostulation', l. 70), parallels hold between the mechanisms of the internal and those of the external communication system of many Donne poems – the story presented on the poem's internal level and the external communicative situation of its original discourse are intrinsically connected. Not only does the speaker of various *Songs and Sonets* employ much art in order to persuade a woman to (make) love (to) him (cf. Pfister, 2005: 219; Puttenham, 1959: 190) – by the very same art, the poet may gain the love of his respective audience, which, as concerns Donne's worldly poetry, consisted predominantly of a male coterie. It is the art of the speaker's persuasive strategies that makes his performance and, by implication, the poem as a whole convincing, hence gaining him the respect of a group of males that is best 'kept by art'. Both women addressees and male fellow poets may be wooed by good poetry (cf. Saunders, 2006: 183). The thematic relation between male friendship and what today is called heterosexual love is noteworthy here: a 'resemblance to male friendship was the pinnacle that the love relationship between a man and a woman could barely hope to attain' (Bach, 2005: 281). The concerns of the internal communicative systems of Donne's erotic poetry are subordinate to the external communicative situation not only structurally but also thematically and categorically.

'[N]eat formalist distinctions between poet and persona, fictive listener and real reader break down in interesting ways' (Marotti, 1986: xiii) – but the phrase 'interesting ways' already hints that parallels between speaker and addressee, poet and reader are creatively exploited rather than altogether broken. Intricate correspondences appear in 'The Dreame', where the woman's knowledge of the speaker's secret desires reflects the poet's sharing of his thoughts and poems with his coterie. In 'The Canonization' the speaker aggressively chides an imagined observer who may or may not have formed part of the poem's contemporary audience, hence parallels hold between what is at issue on the poem's internal level and what we may suspect to have been its effect on an audience. If, on the internal level, the speaker achieves an auto-canonisation, this success within the internal communication system also gains the poet some respect with his listeners. The (auto-)canonisation of the lovers may effect the canonisation of the poet. Just as the initially private lovers turn into socially available icons of worship, so is the poem as a whole implicated in contexts both personal and social (Holmes, 2001: 128).[22]

Owing to the poetic rivalry to which the context of performance and male coterie subjects the poem, there are two objects of desire at stake here, both of which are to be impressed by one and the same poem: the speaker's beloved is to be moved into returning the love which the speaker bears her, and the poet's competitors are to be impressed (cf. Pfister, 2005: 210). Especially Donne's love poetry was 'properly a social activity', since it had the important function of negotiating relationships between men rather than what may or may not pass between man and woman (Marotti, 1986: 9, 35).[23] Donne was firmly established in that 'still powerful traditional culture based on the spoken word, spectacle, and manuscript' (Bristol/Marotti, 2000b: 6). The term 'spectacle' alludes to the performative nature of Donne's poetry, and one may even consider his coterie poems 'as scripts for performances' (Pebworth, 1989: 62; Wollman, 1993: 89). Whereas a printed poem constitutes a 'thing', a poem in manuscript functions as 'an utterance' (Pebworth, 1989: 65) – the term 'utterance', of course, being a familiar one in Austin's theory of performatives.[24]

The majority of Donne's worldly poems were written for those predominantly male domains of '(1) aristocratic households; (2) the universities; and (3) the Inns of Court (and City)' (Marotti, 1995: 149).[25] The male bonding occasioned by such encounters depends on a general equality among all members in employing language, which of course also enables competition and verbal rivalry in terms of who gets the best or last word. Moreover, considering the socially precarious position of Donne and his coterie, 'the topic of wit' could be understood as a shared 'cultural practice *of* resistance, a symptom of energies and ideals that the system repressed or marginalized – in short, of linguistic grace under pressure' (Patterson, 1990: 42). A certain competitiveness among friends need not necessarily weaken, but may indeed further strengthen male–male bonds. Both of these aspects are, as we have seen, quite obviously present in 'The Curse'. At poetry sessions, various poets might present and perform their poems or even those of others for the benefit of their fellow members, and some poems were in fact created in response to others. Such interactivity is reminiscent of the situation of the early modern theatre where actors and audience would likewise interact with one another, and it accounts for the instability not only of early modern play texts but also of contemporary manuscript poems (cf. Marotti, 1995: 135–43). As twenty-first-century readers of the printed poems by the canonised author John Donne, we are always in the danger of neglecting the performative dimension of their original context.

Having said that parallels exist between the love which a poem's speaker hopes to engender with his female addressee and the respect which the poet attempts to gain from his male poetic and potentially also sexual rivals, one confronts the dilemma of those Donne poems that are not very loving at all but straightforwardly misogynistic. Yet since '[t]he person who was expected to be impressed was not the lady, but other men' (Hobby, 1993: 47), one can see how many men might be even more convinced by the sexual voracity of 'The Indifferent' than by the cloistered monogamy of 'The good-morrow'. There is considerable power involved in the actor's 'threat of instability, the threat of Proteus' (Crockett, 1995: 16). Using Donne's less monogamous poetry as a source of biographical evidence for the poet's love life is beside the point – as it would have been difficult for him to embody each and every one of his poetic speakers in real life, it is more likely that all of his speakers are, to some degree, fictional. Poetry in general and dramatic monologue proper differ only in so far as the poetic personae employed by the former constitute fictionalisations of the poet's own self, whereas dramatic monologue creates fictions of a person other than the poet (Höfele, 1985: 194). Whether the man John Donne was closer to the devoted monogamous lover of 'The Canonization' or rather resembled the rampant rake of the elegies will have to remain a matter of biographical conjecture, but it is fairly certain that '[h]e liked to be among lively, intelligent males' (Carey, 1990: 61) – and the writing and presenting of poetry constituted an important skill in accessing that milieu (Hobby, 1993: 47).

Various as the topics addressed by way of poetry in such coterie circles used to be, most of them centred on the theme of courtly love. Neoplatonist and Petrarchist modes of poetry reflect what Luce Irigaray has termed the 'patriarchal utilization of woman as a mirror of the masculine ego' (Berry, 1989: 8). But it was not only chaste women who functioned as reflectors for male (social) identity. Under the threat of censorship, obscene topics were ideally suited for enhancing social bonding and mutual solidarity, as 'libertine attitudes are the social defense of the emotionally vulnerable' (Marotti, 1986: 78). In distancing themselves from Petrarchism and rehearsing an Ovidian desire for male mastery instead, Donne's elegies are 'the product of, and a reaction to, the historical situation of England's rule by a woman' (Guibbory, 1999; Hadfield, 2007: 215). Whether virtuous or libertine, Donne's coterie poetry confronts us with two communicative levels: the speaker's utterances on the poem's internal level determine illocutionary force, whereas the relevance of a poem as a whole can be identified with the perlocutionary effect it may have (had) on its audience. Of all three literary genres, those two levels of communication are most clearly present and distinct from one another in drama. Any play is obviously made up of various illocutionary acts while it is, at the same time, possibly more immediately than prose or poetry, implicated in social and historical contexts on which it may or may not have some perlocutionary effect. Donne's poetry is also significantly theatrical, both in terms of the speech acts that are at stake on the level of the text itself and with regard to the poetic texts as speech acts in themselves. In order to avoid under-estimating the social function of Donne's coterie poems, one is well advised to read them theatrically.

If we conceive of Donne's poems as poems written for and presented in front of a coterie of men who presumably knew each other fairly well (cf. Marotti, 1986: 19, 37), it is worthwhile to take into account Francis Bacon's concept 'Of Friendship'. Bacon values friendship highly as he considers the possibility of opening one's mind to a friend the only remedy of fending off any illnesses of obstruction (Bacon, 1972: 80). He also makes clear why only a friend can serve that function: as all men are included in relationships which assign them certain roles in accordance with which they have to behave (a man has to speak as a father to his son and as a husband to his wife), only 'a friend may speak as the case requires, and not as it sorteth with the person.[26] But to enumerate these things were endless: I have given the rule, where a man cannot fitly play his own part: if he have not a friend, he may quit the stage' (Bacon, 1973: 86, cf. Korhonen, 2006: 300–1). Only as and with a friend can one truly be oneself – but since speaking as a self depends on 'as the case requires', it follows that, depending on the individual situation, one may speak differently and take on various roles. Bacon's metaphors of the theatre are noteworthy: 'if he have not a friend, he may quit the stage' – friendship has to do with theatre, and with the adoption of different roles for oneself; there is more than one way to be yourself with your friends. If the self is less essential than theatrical, then surely the variety of roles which an audience of friends allows for gives one more liberty than those narrowly fixed roles one has to play with other people.[27]

The interaction between speaker and addressee may be as explicitly playful as in 'The undertaking'. The poem's speaker refuses to give away any details about his love relationship, and 'The undertaking' thus debates how one should not undertake to tell about the undertaking itself. Depending on whether they know of the undertaking which is going on between the speaker and some woman or not, listeners may either bond with the speaker in sharing his secret and agree that it not be shared with others so that it exclusively belongs to the poet and some select listener(s) – or they may enjoy and allow themselves to be teased in the same way as the poem's addressee. 'The Relique' similarly prevents the addressee from knowing the speaker's beloved, but this time this significant gap is blamed on the incapacities of language itself: 'All measure, and all language, I should passe, / Should I tell what a miracle shee was' (ll. 32–3). Likewise, 'Negative Love' argues that language is often insufficient, at least if we demand that it express that which 'be simply perfectest' (l. 10), for that 'can by no way be exprest / But *Negatives*' (ll. 11–12).

Although language does not always meet the demands of illustrating a 'miracle' or that which is 'perfectest', the same does not apply for performance. The poet speaker of 'The triple Foole' had counted on just that limiting and curtailing quality of words when he decided to confine his overpowering grief in the prison of poetic diction:

> I thought, if I could draw my paines
> Through Rimes vexation, I should them allay,
> Griefe brought to numbers cannot be so fierce,
> For, he tames it, that fetters it in verse.
>
> (ll. 8–11)

However, what the speaker had not taken into account was the effect which a performance of these lines might have: it brings to life again, even effects the triumph of those very emotions which he had meant to banish and ban into poetic language:

> Some man, his art and voice to show,
> Doth Set and sing my paine,
> And, by delighting many, frees againe
> Griefe, which verse did restraine.
>
> (ll. 12–15)

The performance of the speakers' lines makes his love and grief vivid once again not only to him but also to others, 'For both their triumphs [i.e. those of love and grief] so are published' (l. 20; cf. Saunders, 2006: 11–16). However, even as this poem discourages the publicity and vividness which poetic performance entails, it is still highly likely that this poem, too, was read aloud and performed to others. 'The triple Foole' is thus not only a meta-poetic, but indeed a meta-theatrical poem in so far as it comments on performative practices while being in itself implicated in that same system of performance. It constitutes, so to speak, Donne's way of saying on-stage that 'All the World's a Stage, and all the men and women merely players'. Interpreting the self-reflexive moves in Donne's poetry as meta-theatrical rather than (merely) meta-poetic acquires further plausibility from Sidney's view of all human arts and activities as *'actors and players,* as it were, of what nature will have set forth' (Sidney, 1947: 6).

Another meta-theatrical element which some of Donne's poems employ is the idea of the play within the play: while a large number of Donne's *Songs and Sonets* are directly addressed to a female as the speaker's desired object, there are also poems where the literal addressee does not coincide with the speaker's beloved: in 'The Sunne Rising', it is the sun who is aggressively approached as 'Busie old foole, unruly Sunne' (l. 1). Although the sun here functions as grammatical addressee, this theatrical move in effect constitutes a rhetorical strategy by way of which the speaker compliments the lady and celebrates the encompassing dimension of their mutual love: 'She'is all States, and all Princes, I' (l. 21, cf. Dyson/Lovelock, 1985: 185). In transferring the communicative system of the theatre to this poem, one finds that it effectively creates a play within a play which consists of the speaker's imagined dispute with the sun. This staged dialogue is imagined as being witnessed by the desired woman who will hopefully be persuaded by the vehemence with which the speaker here celebrates the excessiveness of their love that may not even be outshone by the sun (cf. Malzahn, 2003: 66). The woman watching this play within the play is in turn watched by the readers and listeners of this poem. Although she is not explicitly mentioned, the poem's actual audience is likely to add her imaginatively, and to picture her as being successfully persuaded by the play which the speaker has set up for her. If the woman is imagined as being impressed with the speaker's move, the poem's actual and empirical readers are similarly likely to be impressed by the cunning dramatic expertise behind 'The Sunne Rising' and with the poem (and its poet) as such (cf. Klawitter, 1994: 129; Altizer, 1973: 94–5). The staging and performance of a speaker's success with his beloved offers a promising avenue for also convincing his listeners and readers into appreciating the artist for his poetic, dramatic and finally sexual prowess.

The successful wooing of a woman is not the only method of convincing the actual reader or listener: male bonding is effected also by the poetic staging and sharing of sexual fantasies. One common example is that of picturing one's lover having sex with someone else, and, in threatening the woman with vengeance as in 'The Apparition', the speaker knows himself to be in league with the equally jealous listeners to his poetry. Moreover, role-playing, as well as looking on, certainly adds some spice to one's sex life, and the speakers of 'Breake of Day' or 'Selfe Love' do not hesitate even to convert themselves into female characters. Apart from realising a male fantasy of entering a woman's body more thoroughly than physically possible, these speakers' femaleness is bound to attract the desire of the poems' male audience, so that, while the male poet may ensure his listeners' loyalty towards him by enacting a typically male fantasy, the female speaker directs the (male) audience's desire for the female object towards herself. While 'Selfe Love' stages the spectacle of a woman masturbating, 'Sapho to Philaenis' not only enacts the notorious fantasy of two women together but also imagines the thoughts a woman may have while masturbating – another play within the play of male speculation about an intrusion into all-female spheres (cf. Saunders, 2006: 139).

Donne's poetry displays a strong awareness both of addressee and audience. Whether they will applaud a poetic performance is up to the listeners themselves: what happens on stage, i.e. within the internal communication system, has to be credited and corroborated by the audience. Many dramatic characters have some goal they want to achieve – and the more they succeed in this, the greater are their chances of gaining both the respect (or fear) of other dramatic characters and the auditors at the same time. Schemers and villains are the most rewarding parts for an actor: they are convincing by the way in which they manage to manipulate and persuade others. If the character has achieved his goal, so has the actor, as he not only inhabits, but also inherits the role.

Although generally of great relevance for poetry, the visual potential of language is fairly insignificant in Donne. Most of the time, his poems imply a high degree of physical closeness between speaker and addressee, poet and listener. Such physical intimacy is reminiscent of the theatre where the different actors, as well as the audience, are in close proximity to one another, hence making any exaggerated efforts at visualisation unnecessary. As soon as the actor's performance suggests that something is there, it is there indeed. Rather than rely on visualisation or descriptive strategies, Donne's speakers are aware of 'the superior effectiveness of performing an emotion rather than speaking about it', of the greater potential of showing as opposed to telling (Pfister, 2005: 216) – although, of course, at least in poetry, all showing still remains within the realm of telling.

The theatricality of Donne's coterie poems, their being situated in the context of both an internal and an external communicative system, enable the many roles which their poetic speakers take. Many speakers of the *Songs and Sonets* and elegies fashion themselves as innovative in their ways of getting a woman into bed: since most of these poems were written for an exclusive all-male audience, a poetic demonstration of male creativity in making a woman consent to making love would cause listeners to respond to the man behind these performances in such a way as would not be altogether different from the women addressees who allowed themselves to be impressed and persuaded by the poems' speakers. On the other hand, although many a woman addressee would have no tolerance whatsoever for the promiscuity and sexual voraciousness of some of Donne's speakers and would certainly never be enticed to make love to any of these frank misogynists, these same roles may nevertheless have been convincing to Donne's coterie, who would, again, have applauded the poet behind those speech acts for the general speech act of his poem.

Donne's poems are concerned as much with the love of his various addressees as with the love of his empirical audience, which accounts for the ambiguous references of many personal pronouns and adjectives in them. Separate as these two communication systems are, one can never be quite sure when the speaker is addressing an addressee within the poem, when an actual listener and when both of them simultaneously. The role-plays of Donne's poetic speakers bring about similar transformations in the addressees' and listeners' attitudes towards both the speaker and the poet. The success the speaker has with his addressee (no matter if by legitimate or politically incorrect means) gains the poet the respect of his audience.

The dramatic strategies employed by Donne's poetry are in many ways similar to the theatrical practice of his sermons. However, since the drama of the Biblical script supposedly really did implicate and include each and every listener, the sermons encouraged listeners to insert themselves directly into the roles the preacher created for them. The play staged in the sermons was 'for real' and rather serious at that. The objective of Donne's homiletic performances was to point out to their listeners that what they performed was indeed about them and of immediate relevance for them. The various mini-dramas performed in Donne's erotic poems, by contrast, are largely fictional: the poems' speakers take on roles and interact with other fictional characters created by them. Concerning Donne's elegy 'Going to Bed', listeners were hardly expected to insert themselves into the poetic persuasive process by filling in the part of the lady being wooed and thus start undressing at the command of the speaker – rather, as Marotti puts it, '[a]lthough the mistress in the poem is technically the addressee, the speaker seems to look beyond her to an audience of understanding males' (Marotti, 1986, 55; C. G. Martin, 1995: 80). While a number of Donne's poems delight in an occasional blurring of internal and external communication system by employing second-person singular pronouns referring to either or both addressee and listener, these instances come across as a theatrical aside which hardly amounts to the challenge of actually joining the speaker on the stage of the poetic text – an encouragement, which, by contrast, is common in Donne's sermons.[28]

There frequently is a connection between the fictional artefact of a poem and the world of the listener, in as far as the actor/speaker's persuasive success on the internal level is to convince empirical listeners on the external level. If the speaker is able to convert the addressee of his poems at his will, this movement is mirrored by what the poem as a whole manages to do with its listener, namely to allow himself to be convinced by the poem's artistic and rhetorical achievement and success. But the connection between the kind of play we experience in the poems and between the poem as a whole and its listeners is far more indirect than the link between the religious drama enacted in the sermons where Biblical stories of conversion are presented for each congregation member to literally transfer to his or her own person. The poems' speakers depend far more on their listeners' good will than those of the sermons, who know God's authority is behind them.

Particularly in commendatory poetry, speakers find themselves in a position inferior to that of addressee and listener, hence they cannot possibly expect their listeners to condescend to sharing the stage with them, let alone direct them to do so. The theatrical conversions of the poems are concerned far more with the speaker himself than are the sermons, which are devoted to the one drama of a person's conversion to God, a plot which is ulterior to the speaker's personal and private motivations and allows for little variety in terms of the characters involved in it. The poems, by contrast, include a considerable variety of theatrical transformations and role-play, and depending on genre and audience, the rhetorical and theatrical goals of individual poems may differ. The thematic focus of Donne's divine poetry is more limited – but, as we shall see, theatricality takes on yet another, more 'dramatically problematic' dimension there than it does in Donne's sermons.

Notes

1 Although Greene believes that speech act theory fails to account for the quasi-magical character of most ritual (Greene, 1996: 27), Austin himself uses rituals to introduce his thesis of language as performative. The ritual of canonisation is therefore well in line with Austin's own examples.
2 Donne often favours microcosm over macrocosm, such as in 'The Canonization', a preference which contributes to this poem's 'agoraphobic nature' (Kawasaki, 1971: 33). 'The Sunne Rising', by contrast, is couched in a language of state and empire (Goldberg, 1983: 111).
3 Through relocating a few lines, the poem consists of two 14-line Shakespearean sonnets (Pritchard, 1994).
4 Wiggins, by contrast, reads 'The Dreame' as a poem of physical consummation, with the woman 'rising' only after the speaker and she have made love (Wiggins, 2000).
5 Carey interprets Donne's speakers' preoccupation with fidelity and falseness as indirect articulations of the poet's own betrayal of his religion, a biographical reading I do not share, nor would I agree that, for Donne, sexuality inevitably entails betrayal (cf. Carey, 1990: 24).
6 This poem may be one of Donne's rare female-persona poems, hence suggesting that truth-creating power lends itself to any speaker, whether male or female.
7 Cf. Wiggins, 2000: 18; Meg Brown, 1995: 12; Holmes, 2001: 117, as well as Aers/Kress (1981b) for the 'Vexatious Contraries' of Donne's poetry, which readers and critics alike have often preferred to ignore (cf. Docherty, 1986: 4; Herz, 1986: 3; Baumlin, 1991).

8 A similar notion of identity as linguistic is alluded to in *Essays in Divinity*, where the speaker apostrophises 'man, which art said to be the Epilogue, and *compendium* of all this world' (*Essays* 30).
9 Shullenberger is alone in identifying a theatrical situation in a few Donne poems (Shullenberger, 1993: 46).
10 In order to defeat the power of death, 'let us remove her strangenesse from her, let us *converse*, frequent, and acquaint our selves with her' (Montaigne, 1946: 79, my emphasis; Hadfield, 2007: 208).
11 The humorist's inability to hear the speaker indicates a 'perilous adulteration of discourse itself' (Baumlin, 1991: 75), whereas the humorist's rueful return to the marriage bed announces a reconciliation of signifier and signified.
12 Joan Hartwig interprets the addressee and the speaker of Donne's 'Satyre I' as body and soul respectively – a view which, however, appears too simplistic, since the performances of the addressee are by no means exclusively triggered by physical needs (Hartwig, 1995: 263–7).
13 The court alluded to here is that of Elizabeth I, a social context to which the former Catholic Donne was never fully to belong. If one were to read 'Satyre IV' biographically, its critical attitude may betray the poet's thwarted ambitions (cf. Dubrow, 1979: 80). Since the speaker's alleged Catholicism appears more moderate than the pompous show at court, he is apparently prevented from becoming a suitor because he is too little, rather than too much, engaging in Popish ceremony.
14 The remainder of the satire has often been considered part of that Dantesque 'trance' which descends upon the speaker in line 157. However, in lines 175–80, the speaker explicitly points out that the courtiers now return to court for the second time that day, so that what follows is not a mere nightmarish recapitulation of the speaker's morning visit.
15 The characteristic instability of self in Donne's poetry has been variously commented upon. Cf. Corthell, 1997: 18; David Baker, 2004; Müller, 1983: 60; Baumlin, 1991: 245; Carey, 1981: 172; Ellrodt, 2000: 32; Norbrook, 1990: 16; more generally also see Martin/Barresi, 2006: 121; Paster, 2004: 19.
16 A similar equation occurs in the dedicatory poem to 'La Corona', where Mrs Herbert is likened to St Mary Magdalen, and, since the latter 'did harbour *Christ* himselfe, a Guest', Mrs Herbert ought to 'Harbour these *Hymns*, to his dear name addrest' (ll. 12–14).
17 The *Obsequies* themselves, by contrast, 'testif[y] to [the speaker's] own advance in goodness through contemplating Harrington, who thereby is shown to be able after death to enlarge God's kingdom' (Lewalski, 1973: 69).

18 I do not share Marotti's reading of this poem as Donne's professed farewell to poetry – although it is true that the speaker at the poem's end abandons his muse, he does so by allowing it to share a grave and identify with Lord Harrington, who is clearly granted eternal life – the blessing of which the speaker's muse would also share (cf. Marotti, 1986: 233, 274).

19 The question of whether 'The Canonization' enforces or rather satirises Roman Catholicism is difficult to answer: cf. Labriola, 1995: 120; Baumlin, 1991: 227–8; Hunt, 1954: 72ff.

20 Despite the poem's anti-Petrarchan stance, the woman in 'The Canonization' remains just as silent as her Petrarchan predecessors. Cf. Docherty, 1986: 44; differently Müller, 1983: 69.

21 Aggressive female talkativeness is discussed also by Juvenal's satires. Cf. Juvenal, 2004: 255–7, 273.

22 A recognition of potential correspondences between internal and external communicative systems does not entail a biographical approach. In their readings of 'The Canonization', Marotti and Low come to diametrically opposed conclusions, which reveals the fallacies attendant upon biographical criticism (cf. Marotti, 1986: 157–60; Low, 1993: 48–9).

23 In the Lothian portrait, Donne appears to be holding a book of poetry, hence 'not simply posturing as a gallant, but as a lover who writes amorous verse' (Marotti, 1986: 68). Since such portraits were normally commissioned for public self-presentation, this further stresses the social dimension of love poetry in the early modern period – even if Mousley suggests that at least some of Donne's poems may be exempt from such 'public operations of power' (Mousley, 2005: 7).

24 For the exclusive and elitist character of manuscript circles as opposed to print culture, cf. Marotti, 1993: 61, and 1995: 210.

25 It has been suggested that Donne's readership occasionally included women, like the poet's wife Ann (Flynn, 1989), a claim that has been refuted on various counts (cf. Halley, 1989). Moreover, even what Donne wrote for female patrons may have been presented to a male coterie before or after its dedication to the patroness.

26 In discussing the doctrine of the Eucharist in a sermon, Donne's speaker argues that the state of the bread involved in Holy Communion changes in ways that are similar to humankind's ever protean identity: 'It is other Bread, so, as a Judge is another man, upon the bench, then he is at home, in his owne house' (VII, 11, 294). This comparison illustrates how closely the debates surrounding the Eucharist were bound up with early modern concepts of identity.

27 Bacon's essay 'Of Friendship' appears more adequate for describing the relations between the members of Donne's coterie(s) than his tract 'Of Followers and Friends', where the possibility of friendship

between equals is questioned since competition prevailed particularly amongst men of similar degree (cf. Marotti, 1986). As I have argued above, and even with reference to Marotti's work, competition and friendship need not necessarily outrule one another.
28 Moreover, whereas Donne's sermons, and, as we shall see, his *Devotions*, correspond more to Dawson's view of theatre as the re-creation of Eucharistic presence, his worldly poetry engages in playfully competitive negotiations of rank and hence epitomises what Yachnin takes to be the predominant characteristic of Elizabethan theatre (Dawson/Yachnin, 2001: 3).

3

Passionate performances – Poems erotic and divine

> for I
> Except you'enthrall mee, never shall be free,
> Nor ever chast, except you ravish mee.
> ('Batter my heart', ll. 12–14)

Whereas Donne's erotic poems are much indebted to religious metaphor, his nineteen 'Holy Sonnets' strongly rely on erotic imagery. After an analysis of Donne's religiously erotic poems, these are now to be compared to his erotically religious poetry. As it engages in a histrionics of love making, Donne's erotic poetry conceives of love as a matter of (artful) performance, hence subscribing to a concept of love as passion as defined by Niklas Luhmann (Halpern, 1999), but also Roland Barthes. Passion does not denote a state of fulfilment here, but rather desire, the absence of sexual gratification (Stanwood et al., 1993: 272). Theatricality and role-play feature abundantly in both Donne's erotic and devotional writings. Whereas the speaker of 'Going to Bed' is passionate in his part of would-be lover, the speaker of 'Spit in my face' identifies himself with the passion of the suffering Christ who awaits his death, on which salvation is to follow, a performance which, at least as official ritual, would no longer have been an option in post-Reformation England. Passion constitutes the link between what Donne's contemporaries – and even critics nowadays – used to consider two altogether distinct kinds of poetry. It is the common denominator of the various roles Donne's speakers assume.

Roland Barthes's *A Lover's Discourse: Fragments* and Niklas Luhmann's *Liebe als Passion* may initially appear incompatible in their approach. A seminal text of post-structuralist theory, Barthes's *Fragments* may be expected to question the existence of the communicative codes which system theorist Luhmann is at pains to identify. The code of love, however, is untypical in that it keeps outgrowing and deconstructing itself. When it comes to love, post-structuralism and system theory blend more harmoniously than otherwise. Both Barthes and Luhmann perceive of self and identity as socially and culturally conditioned and agree that the performance of love only produces that love in the first place.

Much as the insights generated by Barthes's and Luhmann's theories are applicable also to Donne's divine poetry, when it comes to religion, the poetic empowerment to do things with words does not entail arbitrary articulation, but expressing the right thing with words. Thus the speaker in 'A Litanie' prays: 'When wee are mov'd to seeme religious / Only to vent wit, Lord deliver us' ('A Litanie', ll. 188–9; cf. Wilcox, 1995: 13–15). In 'Holy Sonnets', there is a somewhat desperate sense to whatever wit they may articulate – and their grief derives from the difficulties of translating a code of love as passion into divine contexts. Functioning as dramas of their own, these poems are different not only from Donne's erotic but also from his homiletic theatricality.

Performing passion

According to Luhmann, love poses a communicational dilemma. On the one hand, any communication system must be accessible to all participants, otherwise it would fail to connect two persons by way of successful communication. Love, too, has to articulate itself. On the other hand, any intimate relationship is a private affair and distinguishes itself by its exclusiveness. This communicational dilemma has led to a specific code of passion which is distinctly performative: it is not preceded by a feeling of love which it subsequently encodes, but produces that emotion in the first place. Love has no being of its own and is but that code, that passion which men and women have to enact in order to be lovers at all. If I play the role of a passionate lover, I am already that self-same figure. The loving subject, as Barthes maintains, is made up of its own discourses, the lover is the *Lover's Discourse*. Since love does not exist unless it be performed, Barthes's *Fragments* employ a 'dramatic method' (Barthes, 1979: 3). Just as it would have been insufficient for Donne's sermons simply to retell the Biblical word, Barthes's text works 'not by description but by simulation, by writing in the first person' (Belsey, 1994: 18). *A Lover's Discourse* confronts us with 'someone speaking within himself, *amorously*, confronting the other (the loved object), who does not speak' (Barthes, 1979: 3).

Just as world, truth and self, so is love also dependent on its performative production in Donne's poetry. The majority of his erotic speakers enjoy the idea of lovemaking as the performance of certain roles, because such protean shape-changing allows them to manipulate both themselves and their lovers at will. Active engagement in performance proves empowering – and love depends on excessive, even histrionic performance to come into being at all. In 'The Expostulation', the speaker keeps complaining about his lady's lack of truth for over fifty lines, only to then suggest a reappraisal of their mutual love: 'Now have I curst, let us our love revive' (l. 53). The remaining lines make no secret of the performative strategies involved in reviving that love:

> I could beginne againe to court and praise,
> And in that pleasure lengthen the short dayes
> Of my lifes lease; like Painters that do take
> Delight, not in made worke, but whiles they make;
> I could renew those times, when first I saw
> Love in your eyes, that gave my tongue the law
> To like what you lik'd; and at maskes and playes
> Commend the selfe same Actors, the same wayes;
> [...]
> All which were such soft pastimes, as in these
> Love was as subtilly catch'd, as a disease;
> But being got it is a treasure sweet,
> Which to defend is harder then to get:
> And ought not be prophan'd on either part,
> For though 'tis got by *chance*, 'tis kept by *art*.
>
> (ll. 55–70)

Love may be revived through the performative powers of play-acting: the poem's speaker 'could beginne againe to court and praise' and be confident of the success of his verbal performance, no matter if his tongue would have followed 'the law / To like' what she liked of its own accord or whether it performed but in accordance with that kind of art which is necessary to create and keep his or rather her love. Thus it was that 'Love was as subtilly catch'd, as a disease', and the speaker does well to 'Commend the selfe same Actors, the same wayes' as his lady. The ambiguity of 'selfe same' is telling: not only should the speaker praise the same actors as his lady, he ought to recommend also to his own 'selfe' his lady's preferred acting style, as this most likely ensures his success with her. The lovers' single-mindedness in theatrical performance and courtship is decisive for both the initiation and preservation of their love. The kind of art thus called for is intrinsically theatrical. The love created by this art 'ought not be prophan'd on either part', which implies that both speaker and addressee are actors on the same stage and must take care to play their parts well: the addressee must not remain a mere spectator who passively looks on. Whereas 'Satyre IV' ostentatiously denigrates performance, the speaker of 'The Expostulation' not only openly admits to the performative artfulness of love but even reveals that one may be fascinated more by the performance leading up to than by the final achievement of a relationship: 'like painters that do take / Delight, not in made work, but whiles they make'. Although love is 'got by chance', the speaker's own initiative is highly relevant: through his performances, he takes his luck into his own hands.

If love is all about performance, his resistance to enact it will enable a lover to remove himself rather easily from its grasp. Feeding it 'upon / That which love worst endures, *discretion*' (ll. 5–6), the speaker of 'Loves diet' abstains from any excessive performances of love: 'Above one sigh a day I'allow'd him not' (l. 7), and since this is a sigh 'Of which my fortune, and my faults had part' (l. 8), even that is not exclusively directed at any woman but functions more as an aside. Moreover, the speaker refuses to consider the lady as a fellow actor on the stage of love performances:

> And if sometimes by stealth he got
> A she sigh from my mistresse heart,
> And thought to feast on that, I let him see
> 'Twas neither very sound, nor meant to mee.
>
> (ll. 9–12)

By the end of the poem, the speaker has come to a point where he can put his performances of love on and off at will:

> Now negligent of sport I lye,
> And now as other Fawkners use,

I spring a mistresse, sweare, write, sigh and weepe:
And the game kill'd, or lost, goe talke, and sleepe.

(ll. 27–30)

Excess

The code of love has to be both intimately individual and generally accessible: 'a difficult paradox: I can be understood by everyone (love comes from books, its dialect is a common one), but I can be heard (received "prophetically") only by subjects who have *exactly and right now* the same language I have' (Barthes, 1979: 212). This dilemma is reflected by the excessiveness of the love code, a contradiction in terms: whereas a 'code' denotes a set of rules which has to be observed, 'excess' indicates a violation of that code, a going beyond the limits prescribed by it. Passionate performances must be conventional and original simultaneously. As follows from Derrida's reinterpretation of Austin, like all language, performatives are to some degree citational and iterative – but passionate performances have to outgrow and exceed the original which they nevertheless quote. Donne's flouting of regular metre, for which, according to Ben Jonson, he 'deserved hanging', suggests just such a deliberate exceeding of a given poetic code. In 'The Canonization', but also in many 'Holy Sonnets', the conventional iambic pentameter can still be sensed – if only as a foil against which the individual lines' deliberate floutings, illustrative of their speakers' emotional excesses, are set off (cf. Nutt, 1999: 181; Stein, 1962: 24–9; Saunders, 2006: 108).

It is not always easy to observe and flout the code of love simultaneously: as Donne writes in one of his letters, 'I should be loath that in any thing of mine, composed of her, she should not appear much better then some of those of whom I have written. And yet I cannot hope for better expressings then I have given of them. So you see how much I should wrong her, by making her but equall to others. I would I could be beleeved, when I say that all that is written of them, is but prophecy of her' (*Letters* 260). Once one has reached the height of excess, like Donne in his Anniversaries, the production of more passionate poetry, e.g. for the Countess of Bedford, confronts the writer with an impasse.

The love code distinguishes itself by permanently exceeding itself, which accounts for the many paradoxical characterisations of love (Luhmann, 1994: 83), such as the idea of love as sweet martyrdom. In Donne's 'Loves Deitie', the speaker spends three stanzas moaning about love's cruelty in making him love a woman who scorns him – still he does not want his love to end. In the final stanza, he calls himself to order:

> Rebell and Atheist, too, why murmure I,
> As though I felt the worst that love could doe?
> Love might make me leave loving, or might trie
> A deeper plague, to make her love mee too
>
> (ll. 22–5)

Bad as it is to be unhappily in love, things could still be worse: no longer to be in love. Nor does the speaker want his desired female to love him back. This would entail the lady's inconstancy and falseness, but, more significantly, love may only ever exist in the 'not yet', as the moment of its fulfilment always threatens to announce its own end (Luhmann, 1994: 89). Regrettably, man is, for example, subject to post-coital sadness (cf. 'Farewell to Love'; Ricks, 1988). 'Love's Deitie' deals with the particularly painful case of the speaker's own love exceeding that of his beloved, of love unfulfilled and wasted on someone not wanting it. With the wide reception of Petrarch's Canzoniere, this sub-code of unrequited affection became the most typical manifestation of love.[1]

'Desire is by definition unfulfilled: you want what you don't have' (Belsey, 1994: 136; Barthes, 1979: 54). Gratification, rarely as it does occur in Donne, such as in 'The good-morrow' or 'The Canonization', is only for the moment. Isolated from any socially regulated environment, it typically does not take place in the context of long-term arrangements such as marriage (cf. Belsey, 1994: 148). The same holds true for the paradoxical pseudo-solutions of Donne's religious poetry: 'Donne's resolutions almost never represent more than momentary stability' (Lange, 1996: 188). Excess would not be excessive if it could be preserved for long (Luhmann, 1994: 89). 'Loves infinitenesse' or 'Loves growth' affirm that love neither can nor must be confined, as it tends continuously to outgrow itself. Role-play may be the one solution to the marital dilemma of eternal bondage. Once both partners act as if they had not yet secured their beloved's affection, both will be as attentive towards one another as when they were still courting.

Hate is much more closely related to the excessive code of love than a peacefully settled relationship (Luhmann, 1994: 86). In 'The Prohibition', the speaker encourages his addressee to 'love and hate mee too, / So, these extreames shall neythers office doe' (ll. 17–18). To be appropriately excessive, however, love and hate have to keep exceeding one another, so that the speaker is once again unlikely to end up in a comfortably settled relationship. Due to the excessiveness of both love and hate, Donne's lovingly passionate speakers can be just as passionately scornful and misogynist at other times and in other poems. In 'Loves Alchymie', the speaker warns: 'Hope not for minde in women; at their best / Sweetnesse, and wit they'are, but, *Mummy,* possesst' (ll. 23–4). As soon as the speaker's desire is gratified by possessing the woman, love threatens to turn into hate.

There is no need to scrutinise such texts for implicit hints of consideration and kindness. The link between poems as disparate as 'The Canonization' and 'Loves Alchymie' is 'passionate'. In most cases, it is the absence of fulfilment that is characteristic of passion, especially where this passion is articulated in language. '[W]hen I am fulfilled or remember having been so, language seems pusillanimous' (Barthes, 1979: 55). Or, more drastically: '[t]o speak amorously is to expend without an end in sight, without a *crisis;* it is to practice a relation without orgasm' (Barthes, 1979: 73).

'The Will' exemplifies this frustrated excessiveness of love: the 'Legacies' (l. 2) which the speaker bequeaths to posterity are neither appropriate nor adequate nor welcome. Deliberately, he grants all he has to those who are unable or unwilling to appreciate his offerings, having too much of what is given them in the first place. Love itself has taught the speaker this mode of distribution: not to give sensibly or wisely, but excessively, and without being asked to do so:

> Thou, Love, hast taught me heretofore
> By making mee serve her who'had twenty more,
> That I should give to none, but such, as had too much before.
>
> (ll. 7–9)

At the speaker's death, love, a phenomenon which depends on its performers to come into being, is likewise bound to die:

Therefore I'll give no more; but I'll undoe
The world by dying; because love dies too.
Then all you beauties will bee no more worth
Than gold in Mines, where none doth draw it forth

(ll. 46–9)

The speaker is associated with the figure of a poet whose work specialised in excavating and verbalising the excesses of love.

Love and literature

Literature plays an important part in forming and perpetuating the code of love as passion; Barthes in particular encourages the lover's abandonment 'to the literal expression, the lyrical utterance of my "passion"' (Barthes, 1979: 42; Luhmann, 1994: 50). In 'Valediction of the booke', the speaker informs his addressee, whom he is about to leave, 'How I shall stay, though she [destiny] Esloygne me thus, / And how posterity shall know it too' (ll. 3–4). The addressee's glory is to outlast that of her most famous predecessors, and the medium by which the speaker's presence and thus the couple's togetherness will be ensured is literary (Baumlin, 1991: 189). The addressee is advised to

Study our manuscripts, those Myriades
Of letters, which have past twixt thee and mee,
Thence write our Annals, and in them will bee
To all whom loves subliming fire invades,
Rule and example found

(ll. 10–14)

These writings are no mere records of their past love. Instead, everybody will be astonished to see 'how Love this grace to us affords, / To make, to keep, to use, to be these his Records' (ll. 17–18). The lovers produce and preserve these records in themselves, but they are at the same time also made by them, in as far as they use them – constituted by their discourses, as Barthes puts it. Love is imagined as a code that is, on the one hand, generally accessible 'To all whom loves subliming fire invades' (l. 13), and may even offer information to 'Loves Divines' (l. 28), 'Lawyers' (l. 37) or 'Statesmen' (l. 46). On the other hand, as the first stanza points out, love is unique to each individual couple and cannot be equated with other literary or loving examples on a one-to-one basis.

The love code relies on recognition effects, although this endangers its exclusiveness. Donne's elegy 'Natures lay Ideot' straightforwardly discusses love as a code whose exclusiveness is far from reliable (cf. Fish, 1990). The speaker insists that it was him who 'taught thee to love' (l. 1):

> Foole, thou didst not understand
> The mystique language of the eye nor hand:
> Nor couldst thou judge the difference of the aire
> Of sighes, and say, this lies, this sounds despaire
>
> (ll. 3–6)

Lovemaking relies on codes, codes for the articulation of that which normally escapes articulation, of what is 'mystique' or of 'despaire', codes which have to be acquired first, by learning and being 'taught' (l. 1). For better or worse, the general code of love much resembles the individual subcode of

> the Alphabet
> Of flowers, how they devisefully being set
> And bound up, might with speechlesse secrecie
> Deliver arrands mutely, 'and mutually.
>
> (ll. 9–12)

Like 'the Alphabet / Of flowers', the code of love expresses what exceeds the mere signifier. An arrangement of flowers communicates something that goes beyond itself, and it does so secretly and understandably at the same time, its message is individual and yet coded, as each flower is imbued with symbolic meaning (cf. Baumlin, 1991: 251). This double-edged nature of love, that its code is also accessible to his male competitors, pains the speaker – his intention had been to acquaint his female addressee with the love code exclusively as it concerns the relationship between the two of them. Now, although '[t]hy graces and good words my creatures bee' (l. 25), 'strangers [are now to] taste' (l. 27) and enjoy all that which the speaker had meant only for himself.

Whereas, in 'Natures lay Ideot', the speaker is angry at how the love code, once practised, enables a woman to cheat on her teacher in love, the publicity of the love code's performativity poses a general problem for all illegitimate love affairs. A lover's performance is not easily confined to the audience of one addressee only, which is why the speaker of 'A Valediction forbidding mourning' entreats his beloved to refrain from open manifestations of her love for him by forbidding her to express her love in such a conventional way as will immediately communicate it to the public:

> So let us melt, and make no noise,
> No teare-floods, nor sigh-tempests move,
> T'were prophanation of our joyes
> To tell the layetie our love.
>
> (ll. 5–8)

The love code relies on conventional and public mechanisms of courtship, yet the 'art' of keeping love (cf. 'The Expostulation') must simultaneously ensure a relationship's uniqueness. The metaphysical conceits in 'A Valediction forbidding mourning', the 'expansion' of the lovers' souls '[l]ike gold to ayery thinnesse beate' (ll. 23–4) and the notorious image of the 'stiffe twin compasses' (l. 26) are an attempt to do just that. Because they are so unusual, they create a unique, less conventional and more abstract realm within which the two lovers preserve their 'sacred' love from the gaze of the uninitiated public, here referred to as 'the layetie' (l. 8). By taking refuge in the exclusiveness of these conceits, the speaker creates a private stage upon which the lovers may enact the uniqueness of their love. Although the writing of poetry and metaphorical language constitute conventional strategies of wooing and winning a lady, to employ metaphor as innovatively as Donne supersedes convention. Metaphysical conceits reflect the paradox of desire, which, 'even when it is profoundly conventional, is at the same time the location of a resistance to convention' (Belsey, 1994: 7).

The early modern love code

Apart from being both commonly available and yet exclusive, the love code is socially and historically determined (Luhmann, 1994: 23–4). Luhmann identifies two major developments, the first of which, from ideal to paradox, he locates in the early modern period. Paradox occurs once sexual consummation becomes a real possibility (Luhmann, 1994: 53–9). No longer a perfect and rather ephemeral object, the lady becomes accessible to the speaker's actively appropriating imagination (Luhmann, 1994: 62).

> This flea is you and I, and this
> Our mariage bed, and mariage temple is;
> Though parents grudge, and you, w'are met,
> And cloysterd in these living walls of Jet.
>
> (ll. 12–15)

The lady may do what she will – although the speaker does not yet possess her physically, he does so in his imagination, trapping her within as narrow a space as the insides of a flea (cf. Altizer, 1973: xi). The lady has come a great distance from her Petrarchan predecessor (cf. DiPasquale, 1995), as she is imaginatively and sexually captured by a literary strategy that works less through an elevation of ideals than through a metaphor that 'yokes' together what is altogether disparate and, by its being 'surprisingly self-contradictory', is closely related to paradox (Baldick, 1996: 159). It may be impractical to address the desired object as the sole representative of one's entire world since this may result in a problematic paradox (Luhmann, 1994: 218), yet this is precisely what metaphysical conceits do. Whereas 'The Flea' transposes the lovers to a microcosmic level, 'The Sun Rising' pictures their union as the macrocosm on which the sun may comfortably centre: 'Shine here to us, and thou art every where; / This bed thy center is, these walls, thy spheare' (ll. 29–30). In their apparent insouciance as to what may or may not constitute paradox, both poems exemplify what Luhmann considers the second historical stage of love as passion.

The third stage, of the code's self-reflexiveness, Luhmann locates around 1800. This date, and Luhmann's historical chart in general, appear questionable since the distinctions implied by them are too sweeping. If ideal is replaced by paradox in early modern discourses of love, this simultaneously entails self-reflexiveness. By way of its excessiveness, the love code itself is by definition paradoxical: for, as we have seen, it is marked by rules that exist only to be exceeded and outdone.

Passion, post-medieval

Whereas the Middle Ages saw passion as a serious illness that was difficult, if not impossible to cure, because it turned the lover into an object of his own suffering, the early modern period develops a different attitude. Passion becomes an excuse not for passive suffering but for action, it creates a kind of activity that presents itself as passive, and, since it cannot be helped, it allows a paradoxical liberty that is at the same time (supposedly) subject to an external force (Luhmann, 1994: 73).

Thomas Wright's 1601 treatise seems to contradict such an ambiguous notion of passion, or, rather, the passions. Wright locates the passions in between what is external and internal, in between the senses and reason, body and mind: 'because when these affections [i.e. the passions] are stirring in our mindes, they alter the humours of our bodies, causing some passion or alteration in them' (Wright, 1973: 13). The passions exert an influence on our physical state (a constantly sad spirit may dry the bones, for example) (Wright, 1973: 102). Likewise, 'men, in great pain, or exceeding pleasure, can scarce speake, see, heare or think of any thing which concerneth not their passion' (Wright, 1973: 94) and are herein hardly able to help themselves. One may therefore conclude that people are as passively subjected to their passions as to physical illness. At the same time, the largest part of Wright's tract contains suggestions as to how to control one's passions. Men and women are thus both subjected to, and, at least theoretically, able to manipulate their passions at will (cf. Paster, 1993: 14; Baumbach, 2007: 32). Moreover, Wright identifies desire as the root of all other passions (Wright, 1973: 220), and informs his reader that one may at least sometimes successfully decipher the actions of others by paying attention to their outward behaviour (Wright, 1973: 162). The passions articulate themselves according to a certain code.

Wright's account of the *Passions of the Minde* largely corroborates Luhmann's concept of early modern passion. Both agree that passion, or the passions, constitute the guiding principle for actions that imply both activity and passiveness. The lover tries to conquer the desired other through articulating his utter submission to the other's will and is not easily tamed by opposition (Luhmann, 1994: 77). 'Love-as-passion is therefore a force, a strength ("this violence, this stubborn, indomitable passion")' (Barthes, 1979: 84). The concept of passion as sickness, as in the final lines of 'Oh, to vex me', perseveres, but takes on an altogether different dimension for early moderns, since both love parties recognise its metaphorical character, or the action ruling the passion (Luhmann, 1994: 63).

Passion's double-edged character is epitomised in the Petrarchan model (cf. Guibbory, 1993a: 206; Guss, 1966). The poetic speaker desires a woman whom he can never attain and who therefore appears to be in a higher and more active position. At the same time, the speaker actively fashions himself in the role of passive and subservient admirer. He is passionate concerning the vehemence with which he insists upon his inferiority, but also because he is in pain and forced to endure his suffering passively. The male lover normally plays the part of an active, self-determined sufferer, but there is the occasional 'anxiety that the beloved's passive power might suddenly seek active expression' (Philippa Berry, 1989: 2–4), hence the male lover's active passion retains some traces of actual subjection.

Passionate common features

Passion constitutes the most striking connection between Donne's religiously erotic poetry and his erotically religious verse. A male speaker's communication with his desired female and a sinner's address to God distinguish themselves by a similar kind of 'disequilibrium' (Barthes, 1979: 86) caused by the absence or unattainability of the desired object, whether female or divine (cf. Rupp, 2001: 34). Moreover, in the 'Holy Sonnets', as much as in Donne's erotic poetry, passion is no longer something one succumbs to passively (cf. Guibbory, 1993b: 141).

The recognition that subject–object relations should be ambiguous or even inverted in a state of passion is, after all, a Christian notion: 'for us the "subject" (since Christianity) is *the one who suffers*' (Barthes, 1979: 188–9) – and the speaker of 'Batter my heart' is highly active, even domineering as he yearns to suffer and challenges God to save him (cf. Cummings, 2002: 398; Stevie Davies, 1994: 64). Donne's erotic and devotional speakers are passionate in the double sense of the word: they are assertive, forceful and determined – and most so when it comes to insisting upon their humility, dejection and suffering. They are object of the pain they undergo, but also subjects in that they perform that pain in poetry. A Donnean religious speaker oscillates between subject and object, activity and passivity, autonomy and dependence and conflates aggression and humility into aggressive humility and humble aggression, as he 'brags his worthlessness like a scoundrel's trophy' (Stevie Davies, 1994: 65). Moreover, both Donne's erotic and religious speakers describe their passionate state as paradoxical. Just as the speaker of 'Loves Deitie' would rather go on suffering than no longer be in love, so, according to 'A Litanie', 'Not to be Martyrs, is a martyrdome' (l. 90). This parallel between erotic and religious passion again echoes early modern religious doctrine, according to which suffering was an integral part of Christian life and a justification in itself (cf. Luhmann, 1994: 80).

Just as Donne's lovers insist that their love exceeds all that went before, so does each sinner strive to picture his suffering as altogether exceptional. The amorous speech act is distinct from speech acts in Austin's sense which, at least initially, he defines as reliant on the repetition of a generally accepted formula. In that they have recourse to a certain code, passionate speech acts also have to meet a set of felicity conditions. But since passion, both religious and erotic, defines itself by its excessiveness, any of its actual performances can only be successful if it has not been performed in quite that way before. The successful performance of verbal passion relies on being its own first time – or on convincing its addressees and audiences that this is the case.

If both ardent love and religious fervour rely on the performative contradictoriness of a code of excess, Donne's idiosyncratic appropriation of the sonnet for religious themes is symptomatic. The sonnet constitutes a code that is exceeded and personalised by its application to religious themes which in turn sublimate the theme of erotic love. Moreover, Donne's sonnets conflate Petrarchan and Shakespearean rhyme schemes: whereas the octave almost always rhymes abbaabba, observing the Petrarchan rather than the English pattern, the sestet does not continue the Petrarchan scheme of two tercets. All sonnets end on a concluding couplet, the distinguishing feature of the Shakespearean form. Donne's use of the sonnet pays tribute to a well-established poetic code but simultaneously flouts its established patterns both formally and with regard to his thematic choice.

The technique of foregrounding one's own passion against a background of other, more established conventions works also on a semantic level in poems as different as 'The broken heart' and 'O Might those sighes'. Both speakers refer to other lovers or sinners in order to mark their passion as exceeding that of their predecessors. 'The broken heart' begins by pointing out that

> He is starke mad, who ever sayes,
> That he hath beene in love an houre,
> Yet not that love so soone decayes,
> But that it can tenne in lesse space devour
>
> (ll. 1–4)

The speaker's experience of love is more intense and more excessive than that of others: his passion is so violent that he can sustain it for only a tenth of the time.

The strategies of 'O Might those sighes' are more complex. The speaker recalls passionate but misdirected performances which he wasted on some erotic aspiration or other:

> O Might those sighes and teares returne againe
> Into my breast and eyes, which I have spent,
> That I might in this holy discontent
> Mourne with some fruit, as I have mourn'd in vaine
>
> (ll. 1–4)

The speaker does not doubt the efficacy of performances of mourning as such. If he is denied those fruits which a mournful performance should have given him, this is merely due to his previous waste of the necessary passionate ingredients of sighs and tears: 'In mine Idolatry what showres of raine / Mine eyes did waste? What griefs my heart did rent?' (ll. 5–6). The recognition of wasted passion is so painful that it effects yet another bout of mourning, not because of past grievances, but in remembrance of the lacking justification for that grief: 'That sufferance was my sinne, now I repent; / 'Cause I did suffer I must suffer paine' (ll. 7–8). With the sonnet's octave finishing on that line, the speaker moves on to perform that meta-pain. Passion necessitates that its performance exceed anything previous, and the speaker, despite his unfortunate shortage of sighs and tears, finds a way to fashion his own contrition and pain as more intense than that of any other sinner:

> Th'hydroptique drunkard, and night-scouting thiefe,
> The itchy Lecher, and selfe tickling proud
> Have the remembrance of past joyes, for reliefe
> Of comming ills. To (poore) me is allow'd

> No ease; for, long, yet vehement griefe hath beene
> Th'effect and cause, the punishment and sinne.
>
> (ll. 9–14)

Whereas others indulged in forbidden pleasures, the speaker's sin does not even offer him the consolation of enjoyable memories. The speaker manages to fashion his own suffering as exceeding that of other sinners and thus heightens his chances to be mourning 'with some fruit' (l. 4) this time. The excessiveness of his grief undoes the speaker's initial fear that he may once and for all have wasted his chance of getting any reward for his mourning performances.

Although poems such as 'Valediction of the booke' and 'O Might those sighes' betray an awareness that '[t]his "affective contagion," this induction, proceeds from others, from the language, from books, from friends', their speakers will not acquiesce in the fact that 'no love is original' (Barthes, 1979: 136). As lacking in originality as any love may ever be – Donne's speakers take great pains to make their passion appear unique and are thus altogether in accordance with a code of love as excessive passion.

Passion problems

The parallels between Donne's erotic and religious poems are overwhelming (cf. Martz, 1962: 215; Hester, 1996a). Donne's speakers are passionate, and, in enacting a code of love as passion, they all perform a role. Yet there are striking differences between these two major kinds of Donne's poetry. Although Marotti seems to argue as much, neither Donne's divine nor his erotic poems are sufficiently accounted for by the 'frustrated ambition' he identifies as their central subtext. Oddly enough, although he acknowledges that 'the circumstances of their original composition' might perhaps have been those of 'an exercise in private devotion' (Marotti, 1986: 252), Marotti insists on treating Donne's divine poetry as coterie literature – even though he is otherwise so interested in biographical contexts. To Donne, man's relationship to woman would have been inferior not only to male–male friendship but far more so to man's relationship to God (Bach, 2005: 263). A reading of his devotional poetry in the same vein as all his other writing would hence be inadequate. Let us therefore consider the various 'passion problems' of Donne's divine poetry, since this is where it differs most significantly from his erotic poems.

Self-interest

Someone who performs a part may eventually inherit that role. This does not mean that, initially, these roles were not adopted for a certain purpose, for winning a lady's or a coterie's favour, or gaining divine benevolence. But whereas a good actor, especially a practised man who knows the 'ways of women', may be fairly certain that most females will be taken in by his performance and grant him his request, when the addressee is God we should be wary of the ulterior and potentially selfish motives behind a performance of passionate suffering.

In the amorous constellation between a passionately suffering speaker and God, the role of Christ, the archetypal sufferer, naturally suggests itself. Turning to Christ is altogether legitimate and even advisable whenever one finds oneself overwhelmed by an abundance of passion: 'humble thy self before him, open thy sores and wounds vnto him, and the good Samritane will powre in both wine and oyle; and then thou shalt see thy passions melt, and fall away as clowdes are consumed by the Sunne' (Wright, 1973: 131). Wright's pun on 'Sunne' and 'son' is familiar from Donne's poetry, much of which is indebted to 'the dramatic assertion that Christ's death is not limited and fixed to a point in time and space but an omnipresent, continuing reality accessible to humanity' (Malpezzi, 1995: 152).[2] As is the case with erotic relationships, '[t]he subject painfully identifies himself with some person (or character) who occupies the same position as himself in the amorous structure [. . .] I am the one who has the same place I have' (Barthes, 1979: 129). Christ is an ideal role model: his life is emblematic of the Christian credo '[t]herefore that he may raise the Lord throws down' ('Hymne to God my God, in my sicknesse', l. 30), the alleged plot of much of Donne's divine poetry. Not only does Christ's model allow Donne's speakers to make sense of their lives – by enacting the suffering of Jesus, they also improve their own chances for the next life (cf. Carey, 1990: 82; Frontain, 2004: 140–1; Docherty, 1986: 239; Martz, 1962). As Kempis writes in *The Imitation of Christ*: 'If thou bear the cross willingly it will bear thee and lead thee to the desired end, namely, where there shall be an end of suffering, though here there shall not be' (Kempis, 1934: 104). Donne would have been aware of the problematic implications of self-interest: as the speaker of *Biathanatos* recognises, 'to grant that we may wish death to be in heauen [...] is a larger scope, and somewhat more dangerous, and slippery a graunt, then we vrge towards, because herein onely the interest, and good of the party seeme to be considered' (*Biathanatos* 90).

A number of Donne's poetic speakers re-enact the Lord's passion: affliction constitutes 'a means of realizing Christ's presence' (McNees, 1987: 110). The speaker of 'A Hymne to God the Father', confronts God with ever more sins, hence taking upon himself the sins of the world in what is less a Christian than a Christ-like fashion and expostulates with God: 'Sweare by thy selfe, that at my death thy Sunne / shall shine as it shines now, and heretofore' (ll. 15–16). Taking into account Donne's predilection for punning, 'thy Sunne' also reads 'thy Son'. God is asked to swear by himself that part of himself, his son, who is both divine and human, must not be diminished at the speaker's death. The speaker's implicit assumption that his death may have an influence upon Christ's glorification appears presumptuous (cf. Clements, 1990: 77), but if we recall how, like Christ, he heaped more and more sins upon himself, this passage appears to equate the speaker with the Son of God – all faithful Christians may consider themselves God's children. This also explains the self-assertiveness with which the speaker challenges God to swear by himself – 'thy selfe' includes the speaker, whose self, through his theatrical conversion into the character of Christ, is coherent with God's own self. Only if God swears that his son will shine at the speaker's death will he have 'done' (l. 17) – son and Donne are equivalent to each other. This punning cleverness indicates how much linguistic artistry is needed to identify the speaker with Christ, with all the salvational grace this implies. Wright has no patience with such obscurity: 'Who of purpose writeth obscurely, peruerteth the naturall communication of men, because we write to declare our mindes, and he that affecteth obscuritie, seemeth, not to be willing that men should conceiue his meaning' (Wright, 1973: 211–12). This may be just the point also of Donne's obscurity: that the meaning, the potential self-interest of his writing, be camouflaged (cf. Oliver, 1997: 114).

'Spit in my face' meditatively re-stages Christ's passion (cf. Müller, 1986: 73–5; Sherwood, 1984: 14): 'Spit in my face yee Jewes, and pierce my side, / Buffet, and scoffe, scourge, and crucifie me' (ll. 1–2). His sins, the speaker claims, are worse than 'the Jewes impiety: / They kill'd once an inglorious man, but I / Crucifie him daily, being now glorified' (ll. 6–8). The ambiguity of what is subject to 'glorified' strengthens the speaker's identification with Christ – grammatically, the participle could refer either to the speaker's 'I' or to the 'him' of Christ which precedes it. Both Christ's and/or his own (presumed) glorification aggravate his case in comparison with the Jews who did not know whom they were crucifying and were certainly not glorified. But the speaker's insistence that he be worse than them effects a self-aggrandisement (cf. Saunders, 2006: 49) altogether out of place in a poem fashioning itself as a penitent *imitatio Christi*. Moreover, the speaker's sin may also consist in going on to crucify Christ in the present re-enactment of the Lord's passion. Replaying Christ's passion crucifies not only the speaker but also Christ himself all over again. The poem hence questions its own strategy of re-enacting Christ's passion (cf. Labriola, 2003: 54; Patrick O'Connell, 1986: 123). *Pseudo-Martyr* openly criticises the custom of imitating Christ through suffering, since this 'dooth not onely diminish CHRISTS Passion, by associating an Assistant to it, and determine his Priesthood [. . .] by usurping that office our selves, but it preferres our worke before his' (*Pseudo-Martyr* 87). A view of the self as performative destabilises the hierarchy between pattern and repetition (Krämer, 2001: 260, 267): any verbal *imitatio Christi* is as much about Jesus as about the speaker.

The sonnet's final four lines praise God's disinterestedness in taking on a human body in Christ (cf. Labriola, 2003: 53–4), whereas Jacob dressed up in a goat's skin as his brother Esau in order to deceive his father Isaac into blessing him before his elder brother:

> And *Jacob* came cloth'd in vile harsh attire
> But to supplant, and with gainfull intent:
> God cloth'd himself in vile mans flesh, that so
> Hee might be weake enough to suffer woe.
>
> (ll. 10–14)

These four lines comment on the sonnet's octave where the speaker inverted God's 'dressing down', God's becoming human in Christ, by 'dressing up' and playing the part of Christ who was both divine and human – in retrospect quite possibly a theatrical move motivated by 'gainfull intent'. The egoism behind Jacob's disguise is rewarded: he receives not only the blessing of Isaac, but, after some wrestling, even that of God Himself: 'for as a prince hast thou power with God and with men, and hast prevailed' (Gen. 32.28). This poem's speaker similarly attempts to 'trick God the father by assuming the external guise of another' (Labriola, 2003: 56). ''Twas much, that man was made like God before, / But, that God should be made like man, much more' ('Wilt thou love God', ll. 13–14): the two movements, of humankind being or becoming like God and God becoming like man, are interrelated. According to Kempis, Christ encourages his brethren to imitate him: 'Behold, I offered up myself wholly unto my Father for thee, and gave my whole body and blood for thy food, that I might be wholly thine and that thou mightest continue mine to the end. But if thou abide in self and do not offer thyself up freely unto my will, thine oblation is not entire, and there wil be no perfect union between us' (Kempis, 1934: 140). But whereas God sacrificed himself in taking on a human body, the speaker of 'Spit in my face' apparently replays Christ's passion more for the 'gainfull intent' to share Christ's redemption. Wright explicitly warns: 'Be not too credulous to men in their owne causes' (Wright, 1973: 150). To interpret the re-enactment of Christ's passion as a development from 'degenerate self-love into the regenerate variety' (Harland, 1995: 162) appears too smooth a reading.

Most of Donne's poems are more interested in the passion than in Christ's resurrection (cf. Bridge, 2001; Sessions, 1987: 7; Roston, 2007: 203), such as in 'The Crosse', written in defence of the sign of the cross in baptism against the Puritan view of crossing as a remnant of Papistry. The speaker insists on the significance of the cross as an essential theatrical prop: paradoxically, the lack of a cross entails a far more serious crucifixion: 'no affliction, / No Crosse is so extreme, as to have none' (ll. 13–14). Moreover, a renunciation of the cross would be unnatural as the cross is built into man's physical frame: 'Who can deny mee power, and liberty / To stretch mine arms, and mine owne Crosse to be?' (ll. 17–18). The whole world contains but crosses: 'All the Globes frame, and spheares, is nothing else / But the Meridians crossing Parallels' (ll. 23–4). Our spiritual crosses are buried within us and need to be freed from what obscures them, similarly to how 'Carvers do not faces make, / But that away, which hid them there, do take' (ll. 33–4). The cross of Christ and our identity with the crucified will thus be revealed: 'Let Crosses, soe, take what hid Christ in thee, / And be his image, or not his, but hee' (l. 35–6).

Whereas 'The Crosse' was completed, Donne's poem 'Resurrection' remained 'imperfect'. At the very height of his physical suffering, Christ appears most humanly vivid, whereas the resurrection foregrounds his divinity. Moreover, Christ's passion and death enables humanity to live – we (will) live because Christ has died for us. Donne's speakers take on the role of Christ because they hope to follow his example: Christ's resurrection is subsequent to his passion. Yet a thorough, convincing and lifelike performance of the passion must take place without the foreknowledge that he or she who suffers will be redeemed later on. The majority of Donne's sermons and devotional poems only mention in passing Christ's resurrection, re-enacting the Lord's passion instead. Donne's Christ figures must pretend that they are unaware of the redeeming potential of their passion – otherwise they would not only fail to perform convincingly but be criticised for their opportunism. 'If I would not serve God, except I might be saved for serving him, I shall not be saved though I serve him; My first end in serving God, must not be my self, but he and his glory' (II, 14, 309). Many 'Holy Sonnets' are explicitly addressed to God or Christ himself. Since God is watching, a substandard role-performance will not do. In order to succeed with one's audience, to convince God to ennoble one's performance through redemption, each speaker has to act ingeniously; to suffer convincingly, one must not disclose any foreknowledge of the happy ending.

Yet many devotional poems use passion as a means to an end whenever they confuse the speaker's attitude towards God with the model of erotic love where even 'my man, / Can be as happy'as I can; If he can / Endure the short scorne of a Bridegroomes play' ('Loves Alchymie', ll. 15–17). Clearly, speakers would forfeit their chances of salvation if they openly considered their enactment of Christ's passion as something akin to 'the short scorne of a Bridegroomes play' that will soon be crowned with success. But the many parallels between Donne's erotic and divine poetry hint that many speakers regard both gaining the love of God and of woman as a mere chain of cause and effect where a bit of suffering ultimately entails being heard. To be sure, quite a number of Donne's erotic and devotional poems confront cold unyielding mistresses or an apparently merciless God, and 'Batter my heart' deliberately obscures the parallels between worldly and religious wooing by casting the speaker in the role of the passive female who depends on the male aggressiveness of the divine: 'for I / Except you'enthrall mee, never shall be free, / Nor ever chast, except you ravish mee' (ll. 12–14). Yet the speaker of Donne's 'Hymne to God my God, in my sicknesse' finds great comfort in the insight that, 'As West and East / In all flatt Maps (and I am one) are one, / So death doth touch the Resurrection' (ll. 13–15; cf. Lewalski, 1979: 254). The poem ends on an *imitatio Christi*:[3]

> So, in his purple wrapp'd receive mee Lord,
> By these his thornes give me his other Crowne;
> And as to others soules I preach'd thy word,
> Be this my Text, my sermon to mine owne,
> Therefore that he may raise the Lord throws down.
>
> (ll. 26–30)

The speaker assumes a connection between Christ's thorny crown, symbolised by his sickness, and the reward for this passion as Christ's 'other Crowne', that is eternal life. A number of poetic speakers thus fall prey to the temptation Donne warns against in one of his sermons, 'the danger of sinning by precedent, and presuming of mercy by example' (VI, 10, 209), here the example of Christ. Listeners are cautioned against imitating Jesus out of some calculating hope for redemption.

Whereas the speakers of Donne's erotic poems appear fairly experienced in seducing women, those of the divine poems cannot know about the success of their passionate performance until their very end. Deliberate calculation, which encourages a speaker to act in a certain way in order to trigger the desired reaction, is highly problematic when the addressee is God: he will neither be tricked nor taken in as easily as the various mistresses for whom Donne's erotic speakers perform (cf. Bellette, 1975: 333), nor would he, once he discovers the speaker's motives in performing Christ, be impressed by the speaker's ingenuity in doing so. By contrast, many a female addressee was probably quite aware of a speaker's gainful intentions, and, in recognition of his performative prowess, may still have yielded to him. But God will not be reckoned with. Just as Augustine knows he ought to quit his 'post as a salesman of words in the markets of rhetoric' (Augustine, 1991: 155) once he approaches God, so does Donne's religious poetry become problematic wherever its speakers fail to shed the 'gainfull intent' familiar from much of his poetry of coterie and patronage.

Working problems

The recognition of God as a critical and knowing spectator on whose judgement Donne's religious speakers depend explains why many of them question the basis of theatrical conversion, the idea of 'acting-as-becoming' (Selleck, 2001: 155) – and they do so far more anxiously than Donne's erotic speakers. From a post-Enlightenment point of view, which distinguishes between a real core of self and merely external gestures, one would suppose that the insertion of oneself into a given role constituted nothing but mere play-acting, an act of dissembling which could never have any effect upon the individual (cf. Fischer-Lichte, 2002). For early modern contemporaries, by contrast, taking on the role of Christ was believed to have an effect on the man or woman who undertook the play-acting. Nor would the re-enactment of Christ's example have been considered hypocritical; rather, it indicated one's determination to improve oneself by way of (theatrical) imitation. Only on the basis of a concept of 'acting-as-becoming' does the theatrical incorporation of Biblical example make sense. The question of how what is inside translates itself into external appearances was, however, hotly debated. Montaigne warns that *'It is no part of a well grounded judgement, simply to judge our selves by our exteriour actions*: A man must thorowly sound himselfe, and dive into his heart, and there see by what wards or springs the motions stirre' (Montaigne, 1946: II, 15, italics original). In his essay on Physiognomy, however, he qualifies his statement that 'A mans looke or aire of his face, is but a weake warrant' by adding that 'notwithstanding it is of some consideration' (Montaigne, 1946: III, 316). Thomas Wright makes it his task to analyse how the passions manifest themselves physically. The knowledge of these processes he considers vital for knowing not only others but also ourselves. But such information is not easily obtained – there is art in discovering others' passions by closely attending to their 'words and deedes, speech and action'. Wise men and women may try to mortify their passions and crafty people dissemble them – and Wright himself advises his reader 'to conceale, as much as thou canst, thy inclinations' (Wright, 1973: 136; 161–2). 'In many externall actions may bee discouered internal passions, as in playing, feasting, going, drinking, praising, apparelling, conuersing, and writing' (Wright, 1973: 197) – but, as Wright well knows, external manifestations are not trustworthy indicators of internal inclinations, nor need that which is seen from the outside exert an influence on one's inner life.

The same ambiguity accounts for the inconsistencies and inefficacies of theatricality and role-play as they surface in Donne's divine poems. 'O my blacke Soule!' questions the direct link between what is outside and what is inside by indicating that the same colour of costume may indicate contradictory states of mind: its 'verbal games with colour-symbolism turn the drama of redemption into the antics of a moral chameleon' (Sanders, 1971: 128). Whereas the speaker began by exclaiming to his 'blacke Soule' (l. 1), black for all its sickness and sin, he encourages it in line 11 to stick to that black exterior, but with a different internal motivation:

> Oh make thy selfe with holy mourning blacke,
> And red with blushing, as thou art with sinne;
> Or wash thee in Christs blood, which hath this might
> That being red, it dyes red soules to white.
>
> (ll. 11–14)

One may be black with sickness as well as with mourning, red with blushing and regret as well as with sin. Christ's blood is no longer that element on which all performance centres, but instead puts an end to all outward colouring as it dyes (dies) everything the no-colour white. The insecurity concerning the relationship between inside and outside was the heritage of the Reformation: '[w]ith Luther, and earlier with Erasmus, we begin to find antitheses of inside and outside', but reformers also show 'a reluctance to dismiss the performative, efficacious sign' (Greene, 1996: 19).

Donne's 'Holy Sonnets' are similarly inconsistent as regards the trust they do and do not place in external features. Donne's speakers either trust the security of language's 'protective fiction' (Rajan, 1999: 54) or are appalled at the fictionality of their utterances. In 'What if this present', the speaker deduces from outside appearances internal states of mind (cf. Castiglione, 1966: 308–9; Aughterson, 1998: 272):

> Beauty, of pitty, foulnesse onely is
> A signe of rigour: so I say to thee,
> To wicked spirits are horrid shapes assign'd,
> This beauteous forme assures a pitious minde.
>
> (ll. 11–14)

Not only, however, is this reasoning related to what the speaker 'said to all my profane mistresses' (l. 10), so that the 'manipulative insincerity of the erotic analogy' transfers itself also to the speaker's 'desire for Christ' (Young, 2000: 26). It is also doubtful whether Christ's face actually is beauteous and thus pitiful:[4] 'Teares in his eyes quench the amasing light, / Blood fills his frownes, which from his pierc'd head fell' (ll. 5–6). The poem's reasoning is problematic because it interprets Christ's face as an immediate reflection of the Saviour's merciful state of mind, and because its conclusions rely upon debatable aesthetic categories – it is thus illustrative of the two major traps of physiognomic interpretation (cf. Baumbach, 2007: 16).

Since many of Donne's devotional poems employ erotic imagery to render the speaker's relationship towards God, parallels between the religious sincerity of 'If faithfull soules' and poems such as 'The Legacie' or 'The broken heart' inevitably arise. 'If faithfull soules' is quite explicit about the potential insufficiencies of performance and the lack of a natural link between that which is inside and outside:

> But if our mindes to these soules be descry'd
> By circumstances, and by signes that be
> Apparent in us not immediately,
> How shall my mindes white truth by them be try'd?
>
> (ll. 5–8)

Inward states do not necessarily manifest themselves in external 'signs' and may be at odds with what is seen on the outside – as when 'Pharisaicall / Dissemblers feigne devotion' (ll. 11–12). The poem recalls the two mutually contradictory meanings of 'perform' – to enact versus to pretend (Pfister, 2005: 220). Even its concluding couplet, where the speaker encourages his soul to turn 'to God, for he knowes best / Thy griefe, for he put it into my breast' (ll. 13–14), does not offer lasting consolation. Even for Donne, the rhythm of this last line is extremely stumbling and betrays the ambiguity of this final move: the speaker addresses his soul as something separate from and non-identical with himself ('Thy griefe' versus 'my breast'). Moreover, his breast implicates his heart, whose reliability as the supposed seat of one's true self is deconstructed by Donne's erotic poems. In 'The Legacie', the speaker, on looking for his heart, finds only 'something like a heart' (l. 17) which, seeming but '[a]s good as could be made by art' (l. 21), proves anything but authentic and finally turns out to be not even his own. In 'The broken heart', the speaker's heart has come to pieces and no longer fulfils the tasks of an intact heart: 'My ragges of heart can like, wish, and adore, / But after one such love, can love no more' (ll. 31–2; cf. Lange, 1996: 191, 201; Fish, 1990: 173).

Although many 'Holy Sonnets' question their own performative power, this does not mean that they would stop performing altogether. This is altogether in accordance with *A Lover's Discourse*: the dubiousness of language paradoxically encourages an even stronger reliance on the linguistic medium: 'Signs are not proofs, since anyone can produce false or ambiguous signs. Hence one falls back, paradoxically, on the omnipotence of language: since nothing assures language, I will regard it as the sole and final assurance' (Barthes, 1979: 215). The speaker of 'If poysonous mineralls' knows that challenging God will not get him any further and wonders how he 'dare dispute with thee? / O God, Oh!' (ll. 9–10) – yet the majority of Donne's divine poems argue with God. Such paradoxical behaviour is typical of the passionate state: 'to know that writing compensates for nothing, sublimates nothing, that it is precisely *there where you are not* – this is the beginning of writing' (Barthes, 1979: 100).

Gender trouble

The parallels between Donne's erotic and divine poems are undeniable (cf. Schoenfeldt, 1997a: 209). Yet there are differences: first, the recognition that a passionate performance may spring from egotistical motives is far more problematic when God is the one who should be convinced by it. Secondly, the acknowledgement of the performative character of love has serious consequences for the divine poems. Whereas this performative dimension enables the speaker of 'Loves diet' to be in and out of love at will, that same insight is shocking to the speaker of 'Oh, to vex me', who, trapped in a role-conflict, is haunted by the parallels between his erotic and religious love (cf. Franssen, 1996: 160; Janel Mueller, 1994: 43–4):

> As humorous is my contritione
> As my prophane Love, and as soone forgott:
> As ridlingly distempered, cold and hott,
> As praying, as mute; as infinite, as none.
>
> (ll. 5–8)

The 'As' anaphora illustrates how the speaker's religious devotion is ever too similar to his worldly way of love: his faith is just as unreliable as the vows he makes towards his beloved, as his 'devout fitts come and go away / Like a fantastique Ague' (ll. 12–13). The irregular number of syllables per line and the octave's imperfect rhymes underline the speaker's agitation. Only in the sonnet's concluding couplet does the speaker attempt to dissolve the unacceptable parallel between erotic and religious devotion: whereas the feverish fits attendant upon 'prophane Love' signify an insecure lover's worst days, with regard to the love of God the opposite holds true: 'Those are my best dayes, when I shake with feare' (l. 14).

But this final line may also be read differently. The speaker insinuates that, whereas the exposure to his mistress's waywardness would leave him devastated, in a religious context, such a crisis should be greeted as the appropriate state for facing God. But sonnets are notorious for being more concerned with the speaker's self-fashioning than with love or the beloved object – and the (poetic) performance of dejection allows for a grand display of the lover's self. The speaker's (love-)sickness (cf. Rollin, 1986) is empowering rather than disabling, and reflective of a passion that is post-medieval. The 'best dayes' of a love sonneteer thus awkwardly resemble those of a sinner who fears God's rod, and the speaker's self-fashioning grandeur fails to produce the humility which would be adequate for facing God (cf. Fish, 1990: 177; Selleck, 2001: 160).

Moreover, as soon as the parallels between the passionate performances of Donne's erotic and divine poems become obvious, we confront a gender dilemma (cf. DiPasquale, 2008: 1): the transference of the love code to the relationship between individual and God inevitably places God in the position of the female. The speaker of 'Oh, to vex me' woos and courts God as he would a worldly mistress, namely in the form of a sonnet (cf. Schoenfeldt, 1997a: 221; Low, 1993). In the erotic poems, the speaker's union with the woman is effected by dying, that is orgasm, and many religious poems likewise point to the speaker's prospective reconciliation with God by 'dying in Him' (cf. Stevie Davies, 1994: 54; Ricks, 1988: 48). In both cases, speakers often experience the impossibility of dying as martyrdom, but, much more than the erotic poems, the divine poems must insist upon their speakers' utter submission to God's will. The hierarchy between the menial sinner and God in all his glory is to be maintained at any cost – but this is not easily done if God is cast in a female part. The speaker of 'Batter my heart' fails to resolve this role-conflict. On the one hand, he fashions himself in the role of a woman who, 'Except you'enthrall me, never shall be free, / Nor ever chast, except you ravish mee' (ll. 13–4; cf. Bates, 2007: 1) and conceives of himself as an object (Selleck, 2008: 85). On the other hand, he employs the medium of the amatory sonnet in order to woo God with a passionate aggression that manifests itself in eight imperatives addressed to the 'three person'd God' (l. 1) himself. Although the speaker is here 'abdicating his male gender', he still retains his ' "virile" style' (Stevie Davies, 1994: 51; Hodgson, 1999: 104).

'Batter my heart' is divided between the passive and patient female and the active and assertive male poles of erotic and religious passion. In 'Going to Bed', the speaker had complained 'until I labour, I in labour lie' ('Going to Bed', l. 2), and this allusion to the pangs of labour had served to underline the unnaturalness of the speaker's being deprived of his sexual exertions. The speaker of 'Batter my heart', by contrast, 'Labour[s] to admit' God (l. 6, cf. Frontain, 1987), and hence exhibits just that kind of attitude which the speaker of 'Going to Bed' would have welcomed in his 'Madam' (l. 1), whom he addresses as 'O my America! my new-found-land' (l. 27). In 'Hymne to God, my God, in my sicknesse', the speaker himself takes the part of an intercontinental map and, no longer a coloniser of land, instead awaits colonisation. The poem's lyrical I, who would normally enjoy being as emphatically masculine and heterosexual as the vast majority of

Donne's poetic speakers, must no longer conceive of himself as a male.[5] This fundamental change of identity is necessary in order to leave behind all those 'prophane mistresses' ('What if this present', l. 10) and instead allow for God's 'tender jealousy' ('Since she whome I lovd', l. 13). Blasphemic as the result may occasionally be, Donne's speakers cannot but conceive of God in physical, even sexual terms, as sex constitutes one of the most intense experiences available to humankind (cf. Kerrigan, 1999: 211–13). Moreover, transsexual switches such as in 'Batter my heart' are common in mystical poems and function as attempts to overcome and defy nature, in particular sexual desire (Linsley, 1995: 209; Saunders, 2006: 57).

Although 'Since she whome I lovd' appears to renounce human love in favour of God, Donne's religious speakers have not forgotten that devotion which they were fortunate enough to find in women (cf. DiPasquale, 2008: 50). If man was initially like God, he still resembles him most in his power of creating men, vigorously defended by the speaker of 'Loves Warre', who cannot imagine any '[m]ore glorious service' for the military purpose than, together with his mistress, 'staying to make men' (l. 46). Whereas the erotic poems celebrate the divine reproductive power of humankind, their religious counterparts focus on the human form which God chose to take in Christ.

A minister should know both sides of the story, since he ought to be able to 'Bring man to heaven, and heaven againe to man' ('To Mr Tilman', l. 48) and preach both on 'Gods graces, mens offences' (l. 50). Male offences are often concerned with the earthly business of man-creating, while God's graces are only granted to reasonably humble and admitting feminine characters, which is why it would serve the newly ordained preacher Tilman well to now become 'a blest Hermaphrodite' (l. 54), as this will enable him to empathise with either sex. The hermaphroditism of Donne's divine speakers, however, complicates the transfer of love as passion to religious contexts, as this code was far more rigorously and differently gendered than would have been adequate for religious contexts. Yet Donne is not alone in his efforts to flout conventional gender patterns: 'When Elizabeth Tudor calls herself a king and James Stuart declares himself a wet nurse, we can see at the highest political levels the function of such cross-gendering' (Hodgson, 1999: 25).

Communication difficulties

The gender ambiguities of Donne's religious speakers draw attention to the differences between the communicative situations of Donne's erotic and religious poetry (cf. Bald, 1970: 10). Most of Donne's erotic poems were circulated in manuscript and performed for a male coterie which the poet hoped to impress by the way in which he persuaded his mistress to comply with his sexual desires. What takes place between speaker and addressee is thus transposed to the external communication system. Although the divine poetry uses a similar model of love as passion, their communicative situation is different. Not only do these poems conflate male and female identities: they do so because, contrary to the *Songs and Sonets*, the addressee and the audience of each poem are no longer distinct. Whereas Donne's erotic poetry is directed towards a female addressee in order to gain the respect of a male audience, addressee and audience, internal and external communication system collapse in the 'Holy Sonnets'. These address themselves to God ('Father, part of his double interest'), Christ ('Show me deare Christ, thy spouse, so bright and cleare') and the speaker himself ('O my blacke Soule!') alternatively, often switching between addressees within one sonnet. The poems' audience consists of the exact same subjects. Being meditations (the heading under which these poems were grouped in an early manuscript), they are to be heard again and again by the speaker and poet himself; being 'divine', they are also meant as prayers, to be heard by God and Christ. 'This is my playes last scene' (l. 1) constitutes a play which belongs to the speaker: he performs for himself. On the other hand, this poetic play is directed towards God: by elaborating upon its dramatic crisis (observe the accumulation of 'last', ll. 1–4, and 'latest', l. 4), it hopes to persuade and convince its divine audience to 'Impute me righteous' (l. 13). From a Calvinist perspective at least, once the speaker considered himself righteous, he could indeed trust in salvation. His attempts at convincing both God and himself to 'Impute me righteous' are intrinsically bound up with one another.

Although Donne sent 'sacred verse to such friends as Sir Henry Goodyer, George Garrard, and Magdalen Herbert', his religious poems are not in the same sense 'coterie literature' (Marotti, 1986:

245) as the *Songs and Sonets*. In Donne's divine poetry, listeners and readers are encouraged to imagine themselves in the role of the grieving speaker, for the roles of addressee and audience are occupied by God or Christ. Readers are invited to undergo the same processes as the speaker (and poet), and they are to do so repeatedly – that the first and final lines of 'La Corona' should be identical works as an 'invitation to read over again with deepened insight' (Patrick O'Connell, 1986: 121). Contrary to theatregoers, whose pleasure in watching other people's tragedy disgusts Augustine (Augustine, 1991: 36), readers are to experience the grieving unrest of the 'Holy Sonnets' in and as themselves, through entering the stage of such a 'playes last scene' (cf. Radzinowicz, 1987: 44).

If successfully engaged in, such a reading culminates in a much more intimate experience than Donne's sermons, where listeners are to identify with the roles offered by the preacher. No such hierarchy exists in the 'Holy Sonnets'. Readers must not consider themselves merely as their addressee, but, like the speaker, should treat them as 'my Text, my Sermon to mine owne' ('Hymne to God my God, in my sicknesse', l. 30). Each of Donne's divine poems can be taken as a '"Soliloquy [,]...a preaching to ones self," in Richard Baxter's succinct definition' (Benet, 2001: 167). There are differences between 'the parts and the purposes of sermon and meditation' (Lewalski, 1973: 90), between the audience as other and the audience as self. Congregation members are to 'preach over the Sermons which you heare, to your owne soules in your meditation' (VI, 347–8).

If addressee and audience coincide, the gap between speaker and poet, role and actor, is considerably reduced. For each poem to succeed as meditation, the speaker must be altogether at one with himself (cf. Martz, 1962: 322). Donne's 'Holy Sonnets' often only attempt to create selves that are at one with themselves, whereas the potential success of these endeavours is deferred to an unknown point beyond the poem's final lines: to the speakers' despair, 'they are pre-mystical rather than precisely mystical' (Clements, 1990: 77). 'Despair' does here not refer to that deadly sin which may, at its worst, entice a man to suicide, but ought to be understood as a great eagerness to please God (cf. *Biathanatos* 35), while at the same time doubting one's success in winning his mercy (Bald, 1970: 234).

Since, in Donne's divine poems, addressee and audience coalesce into one, the device of bonding with the audience by poking fun at the poem's addressee is no longer an option. In the first place, their divine omniscience will prevent addressees and audience from being taken in by the speaker's manoeuvres. And since addressee and audience coincide, the speaker cannot pretend one thing to the one and something different to the other. Instead, he must convince his illustrious audience by being nothing but – himself. That self, however, likewise functions as both addressee and audience of Donne's 'Divine Meditations' – a number of 'Holy Sonnets' are directed to the speaker's soul, so that his own self may prove the speaker's most challenging critic. Hard as it is to take in God, it may be yet more difficult to convince oneself by one's own performance. Whereas it is irrelevant if an individual is or is not taken in by his own performance in a social context – one may be convincing even if one is not convinced by one's own performance (Branaman, 1997: 95) – the situation of Donne's religious poems is different. Without any external reference which may serve as a guideline, the speaker is altogether thrown back upon himself (cf. Sugg, 2006: 111).

'[M]etaphysical style heightens and liberates personality' (Gardner, 1985: 28), but the speaker of Donne's 'A Litanie' certainly does not revel in this freedom. Such insecurity is quite common in Donne's divine poetry, which, unlike his sermons, is meant for those 'lesser Chappels, which are my friends' (*Letters* 33). In 'A Litanie', the speaker attempts to place the 'Lord' in the position of both speaker and listener, so that the speaker's own personality is backgrounded:

> Heare us, for till thou heare us, Lord
> We know not what to say.
> Thine ear to'our sighes, teares, thoughts gives voice and word.
> O Thou who Satan heard'st in Jobs sicke day,
> Hear thy selfe now, for thou in us dost pray.
>
> (ll. 203–7)

God's listening encourages and inspires the speaker's words. Sense relies on the interdependence of performing and being listened to. Once again, speaker and audience are not altogether distinct from one another, for, as the speaker argues, it is God who prays in himself. In the concluding lines of 'A Litanie', the speaker further elaborates this interconnectedness between his prayers and his divine audience's reactions: not only is his verbal plea dependent on God's listening but his hearing, too, depends on God's willingness to hear him as well: 'That we may heare, Lord heare us, when wee pray' (l. 216). The speaker's conduct corresponds very closely with the supposed reactions of the Lord himself (cf. Müller, 1986). The sinner's responsibility for his deeds is accordingly diminished as it cannot be separated from whatever the Lord does or does not grant him.

In 'Oh, to vex me', by contrast, the speaker is quite aware of his own responsibility in his approach to God – and, much to his regret, he also realises that his tactics owe much to his 'prophane' (l. 6) love performances. He is not concerned about his inconstant attitude in love matters, but worried to find that this same inconstancy now affects his relationship to God. The transfer of the concept of love as an excessive code of passion to religious and meditative contexts does not work all too smoothly. Declarations of love are always simultaneously a private and public or social event. 'No one wants to speak of love unless it is *for* someone' (Barthes, 1979: 74), and one particular someone at that. Yet each lover's discourse always and inevitably 'has a meaning (meanings) greatly in excess of its address; though I write your name on my work, it is for "them" that it has been written (the others, the readers)' (Barthes, 1979: 78) – with regard to the performance conditions of Donne's erotic poetry, a predominantly male coterie. Although, when in love, one is reluctant to speak of rather than to the beloved object and hesitates to use the third rather than the second person, all love matters are prone to become the subject of gossip, so that the beloved will eventually be talked about by others and not only by the lover (Barthes, 1979: 183). Such situations of male comradeship and gossip may be responsible for first lines like 'For Godsake hold your tongue, and let me love', or the beginning of 'The Curse' (l. 1).

In Donne's divine poems, however, addressee and audience are one and the same, which means that their counterparts also have to be identical: the actor has to be at one with his role. Whereas secular love is always a social affair which includes others, the devotion of Donne's religious poetry takes place more privately between God and the self: 'Churches are best for prayer, that have least light: / To see God only, I go out of sight' ('A Hymne to

Christ, at the Author's last going into Germany', ll. 29–30). In the annotations to his *Spiritual Exercises*, Ignatius likewise advocated seclusion as an important precondition for successful meditation: 'As a general rule in making the Exercises, the more one disengages oneself from all friends and acquaintances, and from all worldly preoccupations, the more profit will there be' (Ignatius, 2004: 288).

Since worldly love is always also a social affair, erotic fulfilment may stand in the way of divine meditation. 'Since she whome I lovd' suggests as much: once the beloved addressee (here Donne's wife Ann) has died, the speaker is able to dedicate himself exclusively to God: 'Wholy in heavenly things my mind is sett' (l. 4). To be sure, the speaker's adoration of his wife had not dissuaded him from turning to God. In Neoplatonic fashion, 'Here the admyring her my mind did whett / To seeke thee God; so streames do shew the head' (ll. 5–6, cf. Schwartz, 2008: 95, 102). Yet the speaker shows some understanding for God's motives in robbing him of his wife. God's jealousy is not only accounted for by the fleshly sins which the speaker is now no longer able to indulge in: 'But in thy tender jealosy dost doubt / Least the World, fleshe, yea Devill putt thee out' (ll. 13–14). 'The World', the social context from which love cannot free itself, is suspected of being the first reason for God's 'ravishment' of Anne's soul. Only outside of that social frame, one may conclude, is religious devotion possible – which is why even today Catholic clerics are expected to remain celibates.

The 'Holy Sonnets' as theatres of their own

Through an interpretation of Donne's 'Holy Sonnets' as 'autotheatrical', I would like to suggest a denominationally neutral reading of these poems. Although Donne refused to elevate theologically controversial points to the status of religious dogma (Roston, 2007: 176), there is no end of attempts to identify the religious affiliation of Donne's divine poems.[6] In drawing some parallels between Donne's 'Holy Sonnets' and Ignatian spiritual exercises, I am, like Louis Martz, less interested in classifying these poems as Roman Catholic than in pointing out their closeness to ritual. Ritual has been identified with Catholicism rather than Protestantism, but, especially in the English Church, its significance must not be underestimated and ought to be considered a human constant rather than a matter of religious denomination.

How can religious devotion be realised if it is closely linked to a notion of erotic love as passion while, at the same time, it differs significantly from that model with regard to its communicative situation? If, in religious devotion, addressee and audience are one and the same, the pattern of worldly love can be transferred to devotional contexts only if it is isolated from the social network in which it normally takes place. In a state of devotion, the speaker has to adopt an autistic frame of mind: just as 'the autistic child frequently watches his own fingers touching objects (but does not watch the objects themselves)' (Barthes, 1979: 160–1), so would everything other than the speaker's self have to be excluded from focus once he is engaged in divine meditation. Rather than playing a part on the stage of a theatre and being judged for the performance of a particular role, the religious self has to be his own theatre and audience at the same time (cf. Korhonen, 2006: 71): 'I take a role: I am *the one who is going to cry*; and I play this role for myself, and *it makes me cry*: I am my own theater. And seeing me cry this way makes me cry all the more; and if the tears tend to decrease, I quickly repeat to myself the lacerating phrase that will set them flowing again. I have two speakers in myself, busy *raising the tone*, from one utterance to the next, as in the old stichomythias' (Barthes, 1979: 161). Strikingly similar insights are already found in Montaigne:

> An Orator (saith Rhetorick) in the play of his pleading, shall be moved at the sound of his owne voice, and by his fained agitations: and suffer himselfe to be cozoned by the passion he representeth: imprinting a lively and essentiall sorrow, by the jugling he acteth, to transferre it into the judges, whom of the two it concerneth lesse: As the persons hired at our funerals who to aide the ceremony of mourning, make sale of their teares by measure, and of their sorrow by waight. For although they strive to act it in a borrowed forme, yet by habituating and ordering their countenance, it is certaine they are often wholly transported into it, and entertaine the impression of a true and unfained melancholly. (Montaigne, 1946: III, 59–60)

Barthes borrows a term from an author still older than Montaigne, namely Ignatius of Loyola, and uses it as the heading of the chapter I have just quoted from: *'The* Loquela [. . .] designates the flux of language through which the subject tirelessly rehashes the effects of a wound or the consequences of an action: an emphatic form of the lover's discourse' (Barthes, 1979: 160; Bates, 2007: 1). In Ignatius's own words, it designates the '"recapitulation" [. . .] that the intellect, carefully and without digressing onto any other subject, should range over the memory of matters contemplated in the previous exercises, and make the same three colloquies' (Ignatius, 2004: 298). Such behaviour is characteristically antisocial: an injured lover's autistic *'twiddling'* is 'marked by stereotyped and compulsive features'. '[T]he lover suffering from the *loquela'* cannot stop twiddling 'his wound' (Barthes, 1979: 161), which is bound to bore and disgust his acquaintances and will eventually exclude him from his social environment. Being without an audience, apart from one's self and God or Christ, constitutes the desirable communicative situation for divine meditation as exemplified by Ignatius of Loyola, whose idea of diligent meditation necessitates solitude: 'Keeping one's eyes closed or fixed on one spot, without allowing the gaze to wander, one says the word "Father", staying with this word for as long as one finds meanings, comparisons, relish and consolation in considerations related to it' (Ignatius, 2004: 332). Whereas Protestant meditations tend to be set outside and in nature, the claustrophobic effect of the 'Holy Sonnets' is typically Ignatian (Roston, 2007: 187–90), although it must be said that Protestants and Catholics alike used meditation to cultivate the inner life (cf. Martz, 1962: 9; 1994: 121–2). Although Donne's 'Holy Sonnets' are far more ruptured than Ignatius's exercises (Targoff, 2008: 110), the sonnet form adds towards making them 'systematic and deliberate' (Low, 1978: 4).

Ignatius's concept of colloquy helps to grasp the communicative situation of Donne's 'Holy Sonnets'. A colloquy normally takes its cue from the life and passion of Christ: one may be '[i]magining Christ Our Lord before me on the cross [. . .] asking how it came about that the Creator made Himself man' and then proceed to focus on the self: 'Then, turning to myself I shall ask, what have I done for Christ? What am I doing for Christ? What ought I to do for Christ? Finally, seeing Him in that state hanging on the cross, talk over whatever comes to mind' (Ignatius, 2004: 296): exorbitant grief and repentance. A colloquy brings the meditator close to martyrdom, for *'he which honors a prophet in the name of a Prophet, shall haue a Prophets reward, So he shall haue a Martyrs reward, which honors vinctum Christi'* (*Biathanatos* 56). Both Donne's 'Holy Sonnets', and Ignatian Spiritual Exercises, aim at creating an appropriately grieving and repentant state of mind within the meditating self, one that is persuasive and convincing to both addressee and audience – God, Christ and the speaker's self. Ignatian exercises would have to be performed orally (Ignatius, 2004: 281). Once the words of a meditation are written down and no longer spoken, the performative mechanism is transferred to the text's internal level, rendered vivid through the meditator's 'tireless [. . .] rehash[ing]' (Barthes, 1979: 160). Through meditation, the self must bring itself to and remain in a state of grief, and it does so by a continual re-performance of its own sorrow for its own sake, such as through 'diminishing [it]self by means of comparison' (Ignatius, 2004: 297). It is this strategy which Donne employs in 'Why are wee by all creatures', where the speaker compares himself unfavourably to the greater purity of lower creatures such as 'horse' (l. 5), 'bull, and boar' (l. 6). Such self-abasement is not hypocritical (cf. Docherty, 1986). Whereas some of Donne's erotic speakers may deliberately decide to be what they are not, his religious speakers strive hard to become as one with themselves, to reach a second paradise where signifier and signified, actor and role, once again coincide (cf. Docherty, 1986: 89; Eckhard Lobsien, 2004: 365). 'I make myself cry, in order to prove to myself that my grief is not an illusion: tears are signs, not expressions' (Barthes, 1979: 182): once I become aware that I am indeed crying for all my grief, this is bound to encourage me to cry even more (cf. Lewalski, 1979: 20; Carlson, 1996: 197). Donne's devotional speakers take great pains to raise within themselves such emotions as may be sufficiently penitent and desperate to be acknowledged and eventually pitied by God.

According to Francis Bacon, it is 'The Nature of Poetry' to work 'by submitting the shows of things to the desires of the mind' (Bacon, 1947: 90). If, 'for Donne, the theatrical production of emotion was its sincerest expression' (Stevie Davies, 1994: 53), the term 'production' should be taken literally: theatrical production is as far as sincerity may go, but, at the same time, the repeated and autistic expression of one's despair indeed produces these same emotions (cf. Kaufman, 1996; Guibbory, 2007: 238) – which, ideally, leads to yet more vehement articulations of grief and so on. Donne's 'Holy Sonnets' strive to replace their supposed 'emotional poverty' (Hunt, 1954: 134) by performances of religious fervour. The self is to be shocked and grieved at its desperate state, while this same grief constitutes its own remedy, a mechanism symptomatic of religion in general. Only religion creates guilt in the first place – but it also provides the means for its alleviation (Rollin, 1986: 131–7; cf. McNees, 1992: 35): 'affliction is itself a sign of grace' (Sellin, 1996: 165). The primary communicative purpose behind Donne's 'Holy Sonnets' is to remind the self that 'Despaire behind, and death before doth cast / such terrour' ('Thou hast made me', ll. 6–7), to make 'those sighes and teares returne againe' ('O Might those sighes', l. 1), and to recreate 'new seas in mine eyes, that so I might / Drowne my world with my weeping earnestly' ('I am a little world', ll. 7–8).

The self is to make itself cry, yet this does not make Donne's 'Holy Sonnets' a discourse of 'feigned devotion' (cf. Oliver, 1997). Actor and audience coincide, as in Montaigne's example of the hired mourners. The communicative situation of the 'Holy Sonnets' herein differs from that of the sermons, where, although listeners function both as enactors of Biblical examples and as audience, they never do so simultaneously. The more tears a speaker produces, the louder he cries, the more likely is he to make himself cry even more and to succeed in being heard and obliged also by God and Christ. This kind of autosuggestion works well for the orator, and, by implication, for the poet. His 'imprinting a lively and essentiall sorrow, by the jugling he acteth' enables him 'to transferre it into the judges, whom of the two it concerneth lesse' (Montaigne, 1946: III, 59–60) – the judges, in the case of Donne's divine poetry, being God and Christ. Thus the speaker of 'The Lamentations of Jeremy' proclaims: 'Mine eye doth drop down teares incessantly, / Untill the Lord looke downe from heaven to see' (ll. 247–8). The constant 'autistic' 'rehashing' of tears and pain in actual fact effects tears and constitutes that same pain for himself and before God and Christ (cf. Frontain, 1992: 91): And indeed, just five lines later, the speaker of the 'Lamentations' has been proved correct in his hope: 'And thou my voice didst heare; / Oh from my sigh, and crye, stop not thine eare' (ll. 255–6, cf. Targoff, 2008: 106).

Tears are among the primary desired effects of the Ignatian spiritual exercises. Particularly when it comes to contemplating Christ's passion, 'I should start to draw upon all my powers to grieve, to feel sorrow and to weep', for it is 'proper to prayer on the Passion to ask for grief with Christ in grief, to be broken with Christ who is broken, and for tears and interior suffering on account of that great suffering that Christ has endured for me' – while all happy thoughts, regarding the resurrection, are to be excluded (Ignatius, 2004: 321–3). Whereas tears were generally considered an adequate means of furthering a congregation's devotion in listening to a sermon, weeping was seen far more critically or even considered hypocritical in the less controllable context of devotional poetry (cf. Lange, 1996: 17 and passim; Shell, 1999: 93).

Their particular type of theatricality places much of Donne's divine meditations in close proximity to ritual (cf. Young, 2000: 82; McNees, 1992: 61). Ritual differs from theatre in that it does not distinguish between audience and (en)actors (Turner, 1989: 178), whereas, in theatre – as in Donne's more straightforwardly theatrical erotic poems – actor and audience do not coincide: 'Theater comes into existence when a separation occurs between spectators and performance'. Ritual performances are much less oriented towards entertainment than efficacy (Schechner, 1988: 126) – as are Donne's religious poems in comparison with his worldly poetry. They aim to create a certain mindset in the articulating self, and by cultivating an adequate attitude of repentant grief, they hope to be efficacious in gaining the benevolence of the divine, that 'absent Other', the link to which is another characteristic of ritual performances.

Contrary to Donne's coterie performances, where various historical and biographical references may be identified (cf. Ilona Bell (1996) on 'The Curse', or Hester's (2000) reading of 'The Baite'), Donne's divine speakers are located in what Schechner calls 'symbolic time'. This is again typical of ritual rather than theatre. Such an 'out-of-the world' attitude can be achieved only if the performers manage to transport themselves into a 'trance' – a state closely approaching that of meditation, where speaker and poet, role and actor merge and become one. In order to profit from this trance, it is necessary that the audience – in the case of Donne's divine poems, the speaker's self, potential other readers, but also God and Christ – both 'participates' and 'believes'. For the ritual to be efficacious, undivided identification is necessary, identification of the speaker's self with itself, of other readers' selves with that same self, and of God and Christ with the speaker's performances.

The first kind of identification is brought about by the speaker's being at one with the poet and his belief in and conviction by what he is doing; no longer may he but know and watch 'what he's doing' (Schechner, 1988: 120) and be divided in his identity. The second identification must take place through each reader's insertion of himself into the speaker's position, to apply these divine meditations to himself. The third identification, that of God and Christ with the speaker/poet, is attempted in such poems where the speaker tries to take upon himself the role of Christ as sufferer, where his tears of compassion are to enact his identification with the passion of Christ (cf. Lange, 1996: 161).

No performance is ever simply ritual or theatre.[7] The entertainment value of Donne's 'Holy Sonnets' is considerable, and Donne's commendatory poetry in particular was meant to be efficacious in wheedling symbolic, as well as material support out of its audience of patrons. Such an intermingling of ritual and theatre, of efficacy and entertainment, may be typical especially of the Elizabethan–Jacobean period, for it was then that these two strands often intersected (Schechner, 1986: 122). All of Donne's poems can be read performatively, but there are different types of performances, in some of which the performer may 'be in a trance', while in others, he may 'be conscious'. Moreover, one may identify a 'move from ritual to theater [. . .] when a participating audience fragments into a collection of people who attend because the show is advertised, who pay admission, who evaluate what they are going to see before, during, and after seeing it' (Schechner, 1986: 142). Although members of Donne's coterie did not pay to witness the poet's worldly performances, they would have pronounced judgement on what he presented; and, quite probably, the payment Donne's patron(esse)s were willing to make for his encomiastic poetry would have depended on their evaluation of the poet's performance. Donne's divine poems, by contrast, are far less dependent on their readers' value judgements. Instead, their success lies rather in whether they manage to transform their audience 'from a collection of separate individuals into a group or congregation of participants' (Schechner, 1986: 142).

Another possible distinction between ritual and theatre consists in their different authority structures: 'ritual is an event upon which its participants depend; theater is an event which depends on its participants' (Schechner, 1986: 126). In his divine poems, Donne was able to treat his readers with more familiarity or even authority than in his commendatory writing: 'The only deference he needed to express was towards God' (Marotti, 1986: 260). Both in *Songs and Sonets* and in the 'Holy Sonnets', 'performing artists [. . .] work on themselves, trying to induce deep psychophysical transformations', yet the two groups of poems differ not only as regards the depth of their transformations but even more so as regards their being 'temporary or [. . .] permanent' (Schechner, 1986: 278). 'Oh, to vex me', for example, indicates that the desired metamorphoses which the speaker is to undergo at least ought to be more permanent than they have been so far.

To sum up: whereas the code of erotic love is characterised by a duplicity according to which love has a meaning both intimately and personally, that is to the lover and the beloved object who share the stage, as well as to the world which constitutes the general audience, this opposition does not equally apply for Donne's 'Divine Meditations'. Here, the internal and external communication system coincide, as addressee and audience collapse into one. Because the 'Holy Sonnets' are devoted to making the self cry at its own misery, and then continuously cry again at the sight of the crying, the 'fury in the[ir] words' is more relevant than 'the words themselves' (Blackmur, 1954: 12). They are meditations exclusively concerned with God and self, while an exhibition of grief to a more general public runs the danger of diminishing what the 'Holy Sonnets' endeavour to perpetuate and intensify: 'Griefe weares, and lessens, that tears breath affords' ('Death', l. 4). Because the speaker's self is both speaker and audience, the poems become the stage where it performs and watches itself perform simultaneously. The meditating self remains its own theatre. It cannot be one persona with his addressee and a different persona with his audience, as is possible in the erotic poems. This is why Donne's divine speakers become uncomfortable as soon as they notice a gap between the roles they are playing and their identity as an actor. Whereas Puttenham is willing to 'allow our Courtly Poet to be a dissembler only in the subtilties of his arte, that is, when he is most artificiall' (Puttenham, 1959: 186), pretence is out of the question when a poem's purpose is devotion to God. Both in Donne's erotic poetry and in the divine poems, there is an actor as well as a role – only that, in the divine poetry, the two must concur at any cost.

Despite their probing doubtfulness concerning the concurrence of external and internal, the 'Holy Sonnets' desperately insist on the performative power of words which, by way of repeated meditation, may bring about the necessary repentance for the self's encounter with God, Christ and itself (cf. Wilcox, 1995: 16). Their 'performance implies not just doing or even re-doing, but a self-consciousness about doing and re-doing, on the part of both performers and spectators' (Carlson, 1996: 195). Whereas, in the *Songs and Sonets*, this awareness of love as a performance which could be intensified, slackened and manipulated at will was part of the fun, such self-reflexiveness is far more serious in divine poetry, where the speaker has to perform and abandon himself to his grief simultaneously. A certain loss of performative control, in order to lose and dissolve oneself in one's own grief is inevitable. But just as Donne's erotic speakers are reluctant to quit their Petrarchan position in order to merge with their beloved, so the speakers of the 'Holy Sonnets' mostly fail to renounce their relative self-sufficiency for the sake of – ultimately – encountering the divine (cf. Kuchar, 2008; Fish, 1990).

Erotic versus divine versus homiletic theatres

Donne's poetry confronts us with different concepts of theatricality: in some instances, '[p]erformance kills belief: [...] acknowledging theatricality kills the credibility of the supernatural' (Greenblatt, 1990: 109) – whereas, at other times, performance is trusted to enforce sincerity (Döring, 2005: 22). Poetic self-reflexiveness is fairly unproblematic in Donne's erotic poems, where the performativity of a code of love as passion is openly acknowledged and often considered merely a matter of training. Many of them offer exhibitions of a speaker's performative abilities. In *Songs and Sonets*, the separateness of what is happening on the text's stage, or internally, from what goes on externally, between the poet or performer and his audience, is rarely questioned. This does not mean that there may not sometimes be strong parallels between the speaker–addressee and the performer–audience relationship, or that what goes on within the poem is less real or relevant than what goes on between the poem as a whole and its audience. To persuade a female addressee to engage in heterosexual lovemaking may gain one the respect of a male audience and thus result in homosocial bonding. Outrageous misogyny may be equally or even more effective in securing a male audience's good will. In Donne's erotic poetry, the poem's 'I' can be two things at one time: from the addressee's point of view, he is a passionate lover or misogynist, whereas the audience may regard him as an ingenious actor and clever schemer. The erotic poems are thus illustrative of how one may be another person when performing as and in front of different people.

In the 'Holy Sonnets', by contrast, self-reflexiveness becomes problematic: their speakers must maintain their roles not only before the addressee(s) but also in front of the audience. Although many *Songs and Sonets*, as well as numerous 'Divine Meditations', directly address their inherent performativity, the former may do so with little concern, whereas Donne's religious poems are much less at ease with regard to their reliance on performative strategies and frequently doubt these strategies' efficacy. The recognition that outward performance may not automatically be taken as proof for 'what is in the heart' (Ferry, 1983: 249) is not, as Ferry argues, advocated by the poems' speakers, but, if anything, earnestly feared. The suspicion that the 'arguing, reasoning, exclaiming and doubting that takes place in [this divine] poetry may be the performance of belief rather than the possession of belief' (Healy, 2005: 77), and not of performance as possession of faith, constitutes the most fundamental angst at the back of Donne's 'Divine Meditations'.

The precondition for successful meditation is that one's performance gets out of control, spiralling itself into a perpetuum mobile of its own. Not only should each meditation's speaker, in acknowledgement of the collapse of addressee and audience into one, become identical with his role – the speaker's self is also his own addressee and audience, which he has both to persuade and convince through his performance, which he himself is at the same time also observing. Donne's erotic speakers revel in their – albeit only imagined – control of their female addressees. In 'Going to

Bed', the speaker is in charge of every item of clothing of his mistress and minutely records how it has to be taken off, while 'Lecture upon the Shadow' places greater emphasis on monitoring the lady's spiritual improvement: 'Stand still, and I will read to thee / A Lecture, Love, in love's philosophy' (ll. 1–2). Likewise, the speaker of 'At the round earths' assumes an almost Godlike power when he commands: 'At the round earths imagin'd corners, blow / Your trumpets, Angells' (ll. 1–2). Such speakers are bound to have difficulty in yielding up all control to the spiralling circularity of meditative practice by allowing their various identities to merge, in subservience to their divine addressee and audience. 'If faithfull soules', in particular, alludes to the serious dangers which the speaker's inability to be at one with himself may entail: how indeed 'shall my mindes white truth [. . .] be try'd?' (l. 8) by redeemed souls if what is inside does not communicate itself adequately to the outside?

The potential conflict between internal and external spheres is frequently addressed by Donne's 'Holy Sonnets', but not necessarily solved. Rather too enthusiastically, Louis Martz describes this collection as 'intense, imaginative meditation that brings together the senses, the emotions, and the intellectual faculties of man; brings them together in a moment of dramatic, creative experience' (Martz, 1962: 1). Creative resolution is certainly what these sonnets aim at – but, more often than not, they reflect the failure of their own attempts at meditation. Early modern tracts took very seriously the risks of being distracted from one's meditation (Martz, 1962: 123), and were aware of the self's 'concentration' difficulties, that is the challenge of focusing on but one centre. What Augustine's *Confessions* complain about is true also of Donne's divine speakers: 'the self which willed to serve was identical with the self which was unwilling. It was I. I was neither wholly willing nor wholly unwilling. So I was in conflict with myself and was dissociated from myself. The dissociation came about against my will' (Augustine, 1991: 148).

In the absence of external guidelines or elements of control, the formal pattern of the sonnet functions as a compensation, or even as a straitjacket to prevent the speaker's inner turmoil from spinning not profitably and meditatively, but unredeemably out of control. The tripartite structure (4-4-6) of the Petrarchan sonnet reflects the three stages of Ignatian meditation, 'the acts of memory, understanding, and will – portions which we might call composition, analysis, and colloquy' (Martz, 1962: 38). But even this attempt at formal stability is doomed. Although respected for the artistic demands it places upon poets (cf. Pfister, 2005: 224), this lyrical form was reserved for love poetry, whose communicative situation would have been very different. Again, 'Oh, to vex me' is a case in point: the speaker reproaches himself for facing God in the same way as his 'prophane Love' (l. 6) – sometimes acting this, sometimes the opposite part: 'As praying, as mute; as infinite, as none' (l. 8). Like Augustine's speaker, he acknowledges how 'contraryes meete in one' (l. 1). But whereas such irresolute behaviour is excusable in a speaker of Petrarchan love poems, whose inconstancy will meet the approval of the male audience, if not of his female addressee, it is much less forgivable in a divine meditation, where the speaker is to persuade himself by his own performance in order to perform ever more convincingly. Although the speaker argues against worldly love as the model for his relationship to God, by using the sonnet, he does so in the form of (worldly) love poetry. That Donne should flout the structure of the sonnet by amalgamating Petrarchan with Shakespearean forms indicates how these poems' concerns can hardly be contained by as strict a pattern as the sonnet (cf. Targoff, 2008: 106; Cummings, 2002: 406; McNees, 1992; DiPasquale, 1999). The lyrical I's inadequacy is reflected by the way in which 'our expectations of the form are thwarted' (Bellette, 1975: 328).

In some ways, the *Songs and Sonets* are more similar to Donne's sermons than are his divine poems: both were written for (semi-)public performance, whereas the divine poems circulated much more privately (Marotti, 1986: 250; Klawitter, 1995). Whereas Donne's sermons and his erotic poetry are both functionally and structurally performative, the dimension of functional performativity is to some degree lost or at least shifted towards a divine audience in his 'Holy Sonnets' (cf. Maassen, 2001: 289). In the sermons, listeners were part of the theatrical set-up, as they were asked to conceive of themselves as Biblical characters who engaged in dramatic action on the level of the sermon, whereas the separation between audience and stage is more firmly established in the *Songs and Sonets*. Yet both genres depend on their different audiences' feedback. Like an actor, who acts independently, but nevertheless depends upon others for the success of his performance or even for his living, the speakers of Donne's erotic poetry, as well as his homiletic speakers, are fairly independent in their ways of performing, but the reasons for them to perform in the first place are beyond their authority. As we have seen with Donne's sermons, man and woman generally act on their own responsibilities and have various (theatrical) possibilities to convert themselves (in)to Christ and God, but they cannot possibly escape from their dependence on God's grace.

In the 'Holy Sonnets', no feedback to judge one's behaviour is available. There is no clear reaction from any force external to the speaker's self, neither from an imagined female nor an appreciative male audience, nor from a Biblical character or a congregation which would recognise the speaker in his role as preacher and priest. The acknowledgement by the 'Holy Sonnets' of God or Christ is always deferred to an uncertain point beyond the individual poem. Both Donne's sermons and devotional poetry employ theatrical strategies in order to vivify Christ's resurrection. But his pulpit performances are far more confident about the efficacy of this procedure than most 'Holy Sonnets'. Donne's divine poetry and his activities as a man of the church provided an outlet for two entirely different aspects of the same man (Targoff, 2001: 94) – and two kinds of self-confidence.

As public religious articulations, the sermons cannot but insist that, by and large, their listeners' participation in exempla and, by implication, in the mutual relationship between God and humanity, constitutes a fairly reliable strategy for reaching salvation. They are uttered with a preacher's Christlike authority, whereas, as concerns the private sinners of the devotional poems, more strident argumentative and linguistic efforts are needed, which betray these speakers' insecurity. The speaker of the sermons knows his place: as God's ambassador, he is justified in taking upon himself the role of St Paul or even Christ. What distinguishes the homiletic genre is the performance and restaging of the Biblical script. Protected by the role of the preacher, the speaker does not (primarily) feature as himself. While the public mode of the sermons is closely related to a prophetical rhetoric, the 'Holy Sonnets', as articulations of an individual soul's struggles, resemble the speech of the Psalmist (Lewalski, 1979: 4; Radzinowicz, 1987), recalling a mode of meditative prayer. Related as they both are to Biblical models, each of them uses language performatively. Donne's prose letters may be considered his most private documents – and yet, as we shall see in the last two chapters, their communicative strategies both echo and anticipate those of another religious and more public piece of Donne's, *Devotions Upon Emergent Occasions*.

Notes

1 For Donne's complicated relationship to Petrarchism, see Guss (1966) and Dubrow (1995).
2 For different opinions on the denominational roots of *imitatio Christi*, cf. Lewalski (1973: 77; 1979: 254) as opposed to Sloane (1985: 188).
3 For a discussion of Donne's meditative stance towards *imitatio Christi*, cf. Stevie Davies (1994: 25) and Frontain (1994: 40), as well as Ignatius of Loyola on *Anima Christi* (Ignatius, 2004: 359).
4 Harland (1995: 167) and Benet (2001: 171) go along with the speaker's argument, as do Sloane (1985: 204–6) and Targoff (2008: 129), who take 'beauteous form' to be referring to the poem itself, whereas Fish (1999: 175) and Low (1993: 79) emphasise the sonnet's argumentative inconsistency.
5 The alternative of reading the 'Holy Sonnets' homoerotically appears less convincing. Cf. Schoenfeldt (1997a: 222) and Saunders (2006: 82–91).
6 Carey classifies the 'Holy Sonnets' as 'documents of Protestant religious pain' (1981: 43; Stachniewski, 1991; Lewalski, 1979), whereas DiPasquale and Young tend to associate them with Roman Catholic modes of worship (DiPasquale, 1993: 78; Young: 2000, 8). Baumlin and Cummings warn against generalising Donne's religious leanings (Baumlin, 1991: 47; Cummings, 2002: 369).
7 In his characterisation of social life, Goffman 'oscillates between metaphors of drama, ritual, and game' (Branaman, 1997: xlvi): depending on its context and purpose, a performance may be as serious as ritual or as playful as game. The drama metaphor works as a compromise between the notions of social life as ritual versus social life as play.

4
Patronage performances – Letters

(for our Letters are our selves) and in them absent friends meet)
(*Letters* 240)

Donne's letters have aroused the interest of literary critics in so far as they may shed some biographical light on their author. Much as one may be wary of identifying the speaker of a literary text with its author, this is commonly done in the case of letters. The idea of the letter as a mirror of its writer's soul had great currency during the sixteenth and seventeenth centuries in England (Müller, 1980; Jagodzinski, 1999: 76). Influenced by Antiquity, much of early modern epistolary writing adopted Demetrius's theory of the letter and its style as emblematic of its author, and this identification of the letter with its writer frequently implied a close association of the epistolary genre with spoken dialogue (Müller, 1980: 139–41; 147). Humanists such as Erasmus, Juan Luis Vives and Justus Lipsius are important representatives of the 'epistolary topos' (Müller, 1980). Their theories of letters proved influential also for the early modern period.

If the primary purpose of a letter is the immediate and individual expression of oneself, the abundance of theoretical treatises on the art of letter writing seems paradoxical. However, owing to the letter's close relatedness to oral genres, the writer's self-expression is governed by numerous rhetorical strategies and retains much of the public character of classical oration (Müller, 1980: 141–3, 153). Even though early modern epistolary theory compares the letter to the less prescriptive form of dialogue, the idea of the epistle as 'speculum animi' or 'imago cordis' is supplemented by elaborate catalogues on the conventions of letter writing (Müller, 1980: 144).

Erasmus's *On the Writing of Letters* (1536) and Angel Day's *The English Secretary* (1599) exerted considerable influence on early modern letter writing. Day draws strongly on his predecessor, but the two tracts differ in the extent to which they emphasise the relevance of epistolary convention over the writer's individuality. Erasmus's treatise originated from its author's dissatisfaction with contemporary epistolary theory. Although he does not discard long-established conventions altogether (Sowards in Erasmus, 1985: liii) and retains the transference of *arts dictaminis*, the five parts of classical oration, to the writing of a letter, Erasmus makes a point of insisting on the writer's 'good judgment and adaptation of style to subject matter and person addressed' (Fantazzi in Erasmus, 1536: 7–8) before moving on to an extensive classification of letter types. Whereas these sub-genres are distinct primarily as regards their topic, Erasmus insists that this is not the only, nor even the most important factor in determining a letter's style:

> A letter's style will not only conform to the topic, but, as befits any good go-between (for a letter performs the function of a messenger), it will take account of times and persons: it will not speak of the same subject on all occasions or to all persons alike; it will present itself in one guise to the old, in another to the young; its aspect will vary according as the person addressed is stern and forbidding, or of a more jovial nature; a courtier or a philosopher, an intimate acquaintance or a total stranger, a man of leisure or one engaged in active pursuits; a faithful companion or a false friend and ill-wisher. At the same time the style will also keep in mind the writer and not merely the recipient or the purpose for which it was sent. (Erasmus, 1985: 19)

The particular form of each letter is determined by a complex interplay of topic, occasion and the character of both addressee and writer. The ensuing idiosyncrasies are to be applauded rather than criticised: 'variation and unevenness of style and subject-matter which would merit condemnation elsewhere here have a peculiar charm' (Erasmus, 1985: 20). Each letter constitutes an individual appropriation of convention. Although the writer's personality is granted some influence, this does not mean that letters simply function as reflectors of his inner soul. Erasmus's terminology is instructive: he talks of the letter's 'guise' and 'aspect' as variable and responsive to the character of both recipient and writer, and the nature of the relationship which may or may not (yet) exist between them. 'Therefore [the letter] will play the part of a Mercury [...], transforming itself into every shape required by the topic at hand' (Erasmus, 1985: 19).

If we combine Erasmus's definition with Müller's notion of the 'epistolary topos', it follows that letters, in as far as they are emblematic of their composers, constitute so many mercuric performances of their writers' selves. This does not mean that the writer's personality is obscured rather than revealed by epistolary performances. Angel Day encourages the art of letter writing according to certain rules over a laissez-faire attitude 'that euery one naturally can speake, or in some sort or other set down their meaning' and recommends '[c]omlines in deliuerance, concerning the person and cause, whereupon the direction is grounded' (Day, 1967: 1, 2). Day ignores the part the writer may play in a letter's composition, but according to Erasmus, the writer's personality does inform his or her epistolary art, even if, since all letters are performances, this does not entail a simple equation of the letter with the writer's soul. With prose non-fiction, 'one inevitably assumes that in this medium a writer is who he says he is' (Webber, 1968: 5). Both Donne's letters and *Devotions* have suffered from this predicament, which I hope to avoid by reading either as articulations by Donne's writing and speaking personae rather than John Donne himself (cf. Maurer, 1976; Cameron, 1976). In the following I shall therefore refer to Donne's (letter) writers rather than to John Donne as the voice of his epistolary art.

Yet although writers may put up a variety of epistolary performances as they don different theatrical costumes, a group of letters by the same author reflects their idiosyncratic performance style. In this chapter, I shall analyse what aspects the performances of Donne's prose letters share and in which ways their strategies may be typical of Donne. His letters are remarkable as regards both the frequency and the immediacy with which they refer to the materiality of language and of letters in particular, and herein they betray a considerable awareness of contemporary debates on letter writing. Not unlike his poetry, Donne's epistolary prose endeavours no less than all that words can do. Much of it is reminiscent of Donne's commendatory poetry, owing to the sometimes more, sometimes less indirect pleas for patronage, which seem to have occasioned their writing. A number of letters address themselves to friends, but, since Donne often found himself under pecuniary strain, any distinction between letters seeking financial support and those interested in the addressee for mere friendship is not easily ascertained. Serious friendship assumes the generosity of one's companion in times of monetary need, and, conversely, patron(esse)s would have been flattered by the letter writer's testimony of genuine personal interest.

In order to further his chances for secular preferment, a courtier should seek the favour of every potential 'friend', 'sponsor' or 'employer' (Brennan, 1988: 1). Donne's letters acknowledge that friendship and patronage are closely linked: a letter to his 'very much respected friend Mr George Garrard' praises the addressee's ability to 'distinguish between the voyces of my love, and of my necessity, if any thing in my Letters sound like an importunity' (*Letters* 283). A concept of '*amicitia utilis*' (Van Houdt/Papy, 2002: 6) appears more promising as a model for such epistolary relationships than Patricia Thomson's or also Arthur Marotti's (2006) attempts to establish rigorous oppositions between Donne's letters to his patron(esse)s and his friends. Whereas, today, one assumes that 'the best friends are purely disinterested and that friendship and influence, political, social, or financial, make a dirty mixture' (Hyatte, 1994: 5), Antiquity's notions of friendship not only permit but encourage self-interest, as the highest level of friendship is to increase both 'the friends' mutual pleasure and utility' (Hyatte, 1994: 6; Korhonen, 2006: 62). Letters of friendship may well 'contain a request', or even 'protest' (Erasmus, 1985: 203), as early modern private domains were imbued with interests of a more public nature (Robert Harding, 1981: 47), and the seeking of royal favour was significantly furthered by personal friendships. Donne's epistolary writings oscillate between material needs and the invaluable and 'immaterial' concerns of friendship.

As in the epitaph poems, Donne's letter writers frequently establish a close connection between their words and their own persons: they 'become' the word, become their own writing. If, as in Donne's sermons, rhetoric 'will make absent and remote things present to your understanding' (IV, 2, 87), as concerns his letters, this 'absent thing' is the writer, whose letter makes himself present to the addressee. Yet this is not enough: 'Sir, more then kisses, letters *mingle Soules*; / For, thus friends absent speake' ('To Sr.

Henry Wotton', 112, ll. 1–2, my emphasis). The (epistolary) union of writer and addressee is familiar from some poems addressed in the previous chapter, where it is, however, never alluded to as insistently, nor do the consequences of these attempts at identification of speaker and addressee ever become an issue for their own sake. 'Throughout his career as a poet, a correspondent, and a priest, Donne is concerned with the ways in which one person – human or Divine – conveys himself or herself to another' (DiPasquale, 1999: 249; Jagodzinski, 1999: 86; Targoff, 2008: 25–48). The seeking of patronage, as well as the cultivation of friendship, are delicate affairs. Donne's writers strive to evoke closeness and thus a sense of mutual obligation and dependency. His letters aim to proceed from communication towards communion. They are not only concerned with making 'friends absent speake' and communicate, but also with making 'friends absent' present to one another, and sometimes even as one another, to have them come together and commune.

Donne's letters, I suggest, ought to be read as performances and exercises in self-fashioning. *Letters to Severall Persons of Honour*, the major collection of Donne's epistolary writing, itself underwent considerable processes of 'fashioning', or, rather, of being made 'fashionable'. In preparing his father's letters for the press in 1651, John Donne Jr clearly recognised 'the increasing prestige of posthumous letters as adjuncts to literary immortality', and also their marketability. This caused him to modify 'the addressees of some of his father's letters for publication, likely for patronage purposes' (Schneider, 2005: 242, 285; Bennett, 1941: 120), so that we can never be sure to whom a letter was in fact addressed. The process through which the letter's '[p]ublication inserted two additional elements into the letter-writing dyad', namely 'the publisher, and the book-buying reader' (Jagodzinski, 1999: 86), multiplied the attempts at self-fashioning which had been characteristic of Donne's letters even before their publication. Printed publications of letters, especially as regards the emphasis they place on prefaces and dedications, on closings and farewells, rehearse and re-enact the conventions of the letter genre on another level (cf. Jagodzinksi, 1999: 92).

In entangling friendship with issues of patronage, Donne's letters appear to counteract Montaigne's dictum that, between friends, no ulterior motives must be involved: 'in friendship, there is no commerce or busines depending on the same, but it selfe' (Montaigne, 1946: I, 199) – and this distinguishes friendship from love and marriage, where both business and hierarchical power relations feature significantly. However, towards the end of 'Of Friendship', Montaigne suggests that the love of a friend is so profound '[b]ecause it was he, because it was my selfe' (Montaigne, 1946: I, 201), hence friends should experience it as a favour to themselves whenever they give something to each other (Montaigne, 1946, I: 204), '[a]ll things being by effect common betweene them' (Montaigne, 1946, I: 202–3). Although the position of Donne's letter writing personae is mostly inferior to that of their addressees, they strive to eliminate social hierarchies and to enable friendship on an equal basis precisely by bringing about an intimate identification of writer with addressee and therefore function as 'vehicles for communion' (Jagodzinksi, 1999: 89).

Once such communion has been established, the speaker no longer needs to humble himself quite as much. Any self-deprecation now also includes the honourable addressee, and any elevation of the writer is simultaneously to the honour of the letter's recipient. Although the social gap between a patronage-seeking writer of letters and his patron or patroness addressee may have been more considerable than with a friend writing to a friend, early modern patronage systems, too, were reciprocal: they furthered networks that were in the interest of both patron and patronage-seeker (cf. Parry, 2002: 124). However, although Donne worked to secure a reliable patron for over twenty years, he never succeeded in doing so long-term. Barred from any secular employment, he found security only when, at the instigation of King James, he took holy orders in 1615 (Parry, 2002: 130).[1] In recompense for this preferment, the King would have expected Donne to propagate religious orthodoxy. Apart from a patron's interest in being endowed with poetic fame by his client in return for material benefits, a worthy protégé was to shape public opinion in accordance with his patron's interests (cf. Brennan, 1988: 10). Donne's ill-fortune in seeking secular patronage resulted both from his Roman Catholic background and the infamous circumstances of his marriage. Moreover, particularly under James I, the number of those seeking favour generally exceeded the number of open government offices (Peck, 1981: 41–5).

The religious repercussions of Donne's epistolary communication as communion are noteworthy. Whereas Marotti interprets virtually all Donne has ever written, including such religious pieces as the 'Holy Sonnets', as testimonies of 'Donne's depression over his lack of worldly success' (Marotti, 1981: 227), I am more interested in the ways in which Donne's attempts at seeking secular favour by letters are imbued with religious concepts. As with the chapter on Donne's worldly poetry, this one on Donne's secular efforts also looks forward to the one following it. Donne's *Devotions* likewise rehearse a religion of communication as communion.

All that words can do – Material language

The first edition of Donne's poetry from 1631 also contained a number of letters, presumably meant 'as examples of "epistolary elegance"'. Conversely, some of Donne's letters in verse were published in John Gough's *The Academy of Complements* in 1645, a letter writing manual (Jagodzinski, 1999: 87). Important connections hold between Donne's poetic and epistolary writing, and, although space does not permit a detailed inquiry into all they share, one aspect which features prominently in both is their approach to language as material. 'A Valediction of my name, in the window' emphasises the concrete process of scratching a name into glass. The circumstantial details concerning the writing of the name in the window are taken literally and, in all their physicality, transferred to a non-literal, metaphysical level. The firmness of the diamond scratching the name is transferred to the speaker and his love (ll. 1–2): just as no 'showers and tempests can outwash' the engraved name, '[s]o shall all times finde mee the same' (ll. 15–16). The 'ragged'-ness of the inscribed name – a diamond does not glide on glass as smoothly as a pen on paper – is to represent the speaker's 'ruinous Anatomie' (ll. 23–4). Donne is at his most crudely material in the satire 'Upon Mr. Thomas Coryats Crudities', where the speaker elaborates upon the usefulness of the material, if not of the content of Coryat's book: apart from providing paper for stitching up and repairing other damaged volumes, of the book's pages 'Some shall wrap pils, and save a friends life so, / Some shall stop muskets, and so kill a fo'' (ll. 61–2).[2]

Whereas no one would feel flattered by sharing the fate of Coryat's pages, at times Donne's speakers appear quite willing to change places with their verse. Thus, in a letter *To Mr T. W.*, the speaker is jealous of his own lines for factually encountering their addressee:

> So, though I languish, prest with Melancholy,
> My verse, the strict Map of my misery,
> Shall live to see that, for whose want I dye.
>
> Therefore I envie them, and doe repent,
> That from unhappy mee, things happy'are sent
>
> (117: 'To Mr T. W.', ll. 7–11)

The speaker hopes that his lines at least function as a mediator for the love he bears the addressee and encourage him to return that love:

> Yet as a Picture, or bare Sacrament,
> Accept these lines, and if in them there be
> Merit of love, bestow that love on mee.
>
> (ll. 12–14)

Although the verse letters often mourn the absence of a beloved friend and/or patron, the transporting power of writing is sometimes estimated higher than physical contact: '*more* than kisses, letters mingle Soules' ('To Sr. Henry Wotton', 112, l. 1, my emphasis).

In the context of these remarks, the poem 'A Valediction of my name, in the window' itself appears as the window which bears the speaker's name and creates his presence. Consider the first four lines:

> My name engrav'd *herein*,
> Doth contribute *my* firmnesse to *this glasse*,
> Which, ever since that charme, hath beene
> As hard, as that which grav'd it, was
>
> (ll. 1–4, my emphasis)

The speaker's identity coincides with his name in the window, and, if this window is (also) the poem, we are not surprised to find that a mingling of speaker and addressee should take place in the second stanza as this window is looked through and as, by implication, this poem is being read:

'Tis much that Glass should bee
As all confessing, and through-shine as I,
'Tis more, that it shewes thee to thee,
And cleare reflects thee to thine eye.
But all such rules, love's magique can undoe,
Here you see mee, and I am you.

(ll. 7–12)

The words of poetry have the power not only to bridge the gap between absent lovers, but even function as an avatar of the speaker and addressee's identities.[3] These high-flown expectations are qualified at the end of the poem, not only, as noted earlier, by the speaker's presentation of the preceding poem as the words of 'dying men' but because 'glasse, and lines', including those of the present poem, 'must bee, / No meanes our firme substantiall love to keepe' (ll. 61–2).

Epistolary material and the cultivation of friendship

The indecision of 'A Valediction of my name, in the window' as to whether words do or do not have material power is even more central to Donne's prose letters, which debate their own material and spiritual dimensions no less explicitly (cf. Piers Brown, 2009: 70). Consider the letter '*To my honoured friend S. T. Lucey*': 'for as the greatest advantage which mans soul is thought to have beyond others, is that which they call *Actum reflexum*, and *iteratum*, (for Beasts do the same things as we do, but they do not consider nor remember the circumstances and inducements; and by what power, and faculty, it is that they do them) so of those which they call *Actum reflexum* the noblest is that which reflects upon the soul it self, and considers and meditates it' (*Letters* 12). The writer then devotes himself to that very 'noblest' reflection on the human soul – and in doing so raises the genre of the letter, since he endows it with this elevated theme. His writing simultaneously 'dignifies the praiser' – the writer, 'and the praised' – the soul (Milgate, 1967: xxxviii). Self-reflection is declared the distinguishing trademark of humanity over beasts also in the eighteenth meditation of Donne's *Devotions* (cf. Wilcox, 2000: 161). This dictum takes on particular significance if we consider that almost every single letter of Donne's betrays considerable self-awareness in commenting upon itself and the letter genre in general, so much so that they may be said to 'delineate a theory of epistolary communication that applies to much of Donne's other writing' (Marotti, 2006: 40; Guillén, 1986: 75).

Many of Donne's letters hardly communicate on anything other than themselves. In a letter *'To Sir* H. G.', the writer acknowledges that, since he has neither business nor pleasure to attend to, there is no reason why he should not write regularly. Still he has an excuse for the infrequency of his letters: 'no mans Letters might be better wanted then mine, since my whole Letter is nothing else but a confession that I should and would write' (*Letters* 87). Donne's letter writers did not always consider this excessive self-reflexiveness negatively. A letter *'To sir* H. G.' begins by explaining: 'this Letter shall but talke, not discourse; it shall but gossip, not consider, nor consult, so it is made halfe with a prejudice of being lost by the way' (*Letters* 143). Both letters are phatic, their purpose is less to communicate something than to communicate at all and to maintain communication (cf. Schneider, 2005: 55–66; Altman, 1982: 89) and perform an *Actum Reflexum* on their phatic dimension. Through this act of self-reflection, these two examples – and many more could be given – share the defining characteristic of the human soul (cf. Seigel, 2005: 12), in this case most likely that of the writer.

Donne was obsessed with maintaining the connection between the physical and the spiritual dimension (cf. Targoff, 2008: 1). His letters, too, strive to combine the soul with the body, the immaterial with the material. Although they appear to be concerned with 'delivering spirit rather than matter' (Targoff, 2008: 29; Goldberg, 1983: 211) since their actual content is often rather thin, they engage in issues both physical and spiritual[4] – 'Their nature is mixed, as that of human beings is' (Jagodzinski, 1999: 89). If the letter's relatedness to the soul manifests itself in reflections upon its own medium, its indebtedness to the physical body reveals itself by the ways in which it ponders its materiality. A letter's concrete facts and spiritual effects are as closely intermingled as body is with soul. Donne's *Letters* play on their epistolary (im)materiality and its contribution to the cultivation of friendship (cf. Guillén, 1986: 78).

Friendship is linked to material acts. As we read in a letter *'To sir* H. R.' (*Letters* 26–31), 'The first sphere onely which is resisted by nothing, absolves his course every day; and so doth true friendship well placed often iterate in act or purpose, the same offices' (*Letters* 26–7). Throughout his life, and especially during his years at Mitcham, from whence this particular letter was sent, Donne was unable to meet the majority of his friends on a face-to-face basis. The 'offices' which he was able to offer had to be epistolary. One of Donne's letters warns against that kind of friendship which merely obeys a certain fashion, or blindly adopts the example of a friend's religious views, for that 'may be some kinde of a second wisdome; but it is but writing by a copy' (*Letters* 28). The metaphor 'writing by a copy' indicates that writing as such is considered an acceptable medium for nurturing friendship, but insists on the genuine origin from which epistolary action should spring. Even if letter writing manuals were much in vogue in the early modern period and tempted some writers simply to reproduce their patterns, the above criticism indicates that, just as friendship should amount to more than a mere imitation of the other, so should the letters engaged in its service be originals (cf. Stewart/Wolfe, 2004: 79; Henderson, 1993: 152).

Sometimes, however, the relevance of a particular letter, and hence both its originality and materiality, are diminished. Paradoxically, such a devaluation of individual letters manages to preserve the significance of epistolary writing in general. In a letter '*To Sir G. F.*', the writer points out that 'any Pacquet from me into *England* should go, not only without just fraight, but without ballast, if it had not a letter to you' (*Letters* 73), thus implying each letter's material weight and relevance. Yet, acknowledging the hazardous circumstances of the transmission of both his letters and those from his addressee, the writer argues: '[b]ut Sir, if our Letters come not in due order, and so make not a certain and concurrent chain, yet if they come as Atomes, and so meet at last, by any crooked, and casuall application, they make up, and they nourish bodies of friendship' (*Letters* 73–4). This confidence is questioned again a few lines later when he explains that, owing to these communicational ruptures, he does not yet know 'whether I be increased by a childe, or diminished by the losse of a wife' (*Letters* 74).

There is more than one way to think and write of letter writing. Whereas above the idea of many atoms making up one whole was to console both writer and addressee regarding the probable loss of letters, a letter '*To the Honourable Lady Mrs. B. W.*' complains about the certainty with which this particular letter will arrive at its destination, for '[a]ll adventures towards you should be of more difficulty and hazard'. At least there is the 'comfort' that 'it may be so many of my letters are lost already that it is time that one should come [...] to bring word, that the rest were lost' (*Letters* 5). The writer would welcome it if some of his letters were lost and thus immaterial – but this loss ought to be communicated via letter and thus become material again.

In another letter, the writer insists that 'in Letters, by which we deliver over our affections, and assurances of friendship, and the best faculties of our souls, times and daies cannot have interest, nor be considerable, because that which passes by them, is eternall, and out of the measure of time' (*Letters* 23). However, the writer here has a clear motive for supporting the temporal immateriality of his communications. The present letter had been declared to exist before it was actually composed, as the Countess of Bedford's brother had reported Donne's promise to write as 'an act already done' (*Letters* 23). According to speech act theory, a promise constitutes an act, and the writer acknowledges the obligations this implies. In another letter, he wonders: 'How weak are my performances, when even my promises are defective?' (*Letters* 21). Since his letter to the Countess has been announced not only as promised but also as written, the writer is very eager to make the world fit the words of the Countess's brother, whose utterances 'provide me a means of doing him a service in this act, which is but doing right to my self: for by this performance of mine own word, I have also justified that part of his Letter which concerned me; and it had been a double guiltinesse in me, to have made him guilty towards you' (*Letters* 23). In order to belittle his guilt, the writer insists on the irrelevance of dates in letters and emphasises the encompassing immateriality of the values transmitted by this medium. Were one to insist on the where and when of each letter, his negligence would be more difficult to excuse. Elsewhere, the writer himself wonders about the date of a certain letter he received, but soon thinks better of his speculative efforts: 'in the offices of so spirituall a thing as friendship, so momentary a thing as time, must have no consideration' (*Letters* 246). Since, however, he yearns for an additional letter, he declares to keep that latest letter 'to read every day, as newly written: to which vexation it must be subject, till you relieve it with an other' (*Letters*

246). As irrelevant as time may be, he clearly would appreciate it if the addressee soon provided him with some more recent epistolary material.

Depending on context, addressee and the writer's purpose, Donne's letters either stress or diminish the concrete materiality of their medium. The writer always remains aware of both epistolary materiality and immateriality, the letter's physical properties and the spiritual affairs it engages in. Much as it stresses the cultivation of personal relationships as an epistolary purpose beyond materiality, Donne's epistolary writing often discusses the material size of individual letters. The assumption that greater length implies greater devotion on the writer's part is, however, countered by the estimation that one 'may hit better with this hail-shot of little Letters (because they may come thick) then with great bullets' (*Letters* 264). This letter may be too short if it was meant to contain all his thanks, but 'since it comes to begge more, perchance it may be long enough, because I know not how short you will be with an absent friend' (*Letters* 264). Normally, one would think that further requests necessitate an extraordinarily long letter. In the ways in which they deliberately flout and invert conventional expectations, Donne's letters recall the argumentative twists of poems such as 'Valediction of my name, in the window'.

Bold as they are, Donne's writers are quite aware that letter writing is a mutual activity. Although a letter's delivery was far from guaranteed, they keep writing – for writing enhances friendship even where a letter fails to reach its destination: 'When we thinke of a friend, we do not count that a lost thought, though that friend never knew of it. If we write to a friend, we must not call it a lost Letter, though it never finde him to whom it was addressed: for we owe our selves that office, to be mindefull of our friends' (*Letters* 286). The writing of letters is conducive to friendship not only through ingratiating the writer to the addressee. For Donne, each man ought to cultivate not only his own memory with his friend but also his friend's memory within himself.

A letter 'To Sir H. G.' notes not only the performative value of letters for friendship (hence suggesting a performative view of language in general), but also considers letter writing and friendship as mutual endeavours:

> In the History or style of friendship, which is best written both in deeds and words, a Letter which is of a mixed nature, and hath something of both, is a mixed Parenthesis: It may be left out, yet it contributes, though not to the being, yet to the verdure, and freshnesse thereof. Letters have truly the same office, as oaths. As these amongst light and empty men, are but fillings, and pauses, and interjections; but with weightier, they are sad attestations: So are Letters to some complement, and obligation to others. (*Letters* 114)

Friendship depends both on 'deeds and words', and a letter ought to be acknowledged as a medium of both word and deed. In addition, a letter's factual impact owes a lot to its reception. The weight of an individual letter is intrinsically linked to the metaphorical weight, the relevance of the communicants, who are part and parcel of its discourse.

Depending on the occasion, the genre of letters, the written as opposed to the spoken word, is considered with varying degrees of optimism. In the above-mentioned letter, letters are estimated highly, because they 'go from me more considerately, and because they are permanent; for in them I may speak to you in your chamber a year hence before I know not whom, and not hear myself' (*Letters* 114). In a different letter, the speaker by contrast acknowledges 'what dead carcasses things written are, in respect of things spoken' (*Letters* 25): their permanence distances them considerably from the occasion which originally initiated them. The longevity of the epistolary medium cuts both ways: apart from outliving their initial occasion, letters also draw attention to the transience of life and are always in danger of losing their immediate currency. 'As written dialogue, epistolary discourse is obsessed with its oral model. [...] epistolary language is preoccupied with immediacy, with presence, because it is a product of absence' (Altman, 1982: 135; Jagodzinski, 1999: 75). Yet the dictum that '*more* then kisses, letters mingle Soules' (112, ll. 1–2, my emphasis) implies that the written word is at times superior to oral and more physical kinds of communication. Donne's letters question the 'phonocentrism' of Western philosophy (cf. Culler, 1994: 92) even before the arrival of deconstruction – not only by paralleling epistolary discourse with oral communication but also in avoiding a general prioritisation of the latter over the former.

The written text cannot but outlast its original occasion, as is suggested also in *Devotions*: 'And that which you call *present*, is not *now* the same that it was, when you began to call it so in this Line, (before you found that word, *present*, or that *Monosyllable, now*, the present, & the *Now* is past,)' (*Devotions* 71). The gap between a writer's situation and that present which the addressee of his letter is able to access may prove considerable. In Donne's letters, the immaterial fleetingness of the spoken word is regularly contrasted with the material permanence of words written on a page, but in a letter 'To *Sr* G. M.' the writer attempts to justify the frequency of his letters by aligning it with oral customs of communication: 'If you were here, you would not think me importune, if I bid you good morrow every day; and such a patience will excuse my often Letters' (*Letters* 105).

Donne's epistolary writing keeps wavering between its trust in the performative potential of (written) language and a nagging suspicion of its insufficiencies. His letters are representative of the general ambiguity with which the Renaissance encountered the relationship between language written and spoken (cf. Van Houdt/Papy, 2002: 4). The recognition of the physical materiality of the written letter is countered by the greater, if more transient, pertinence of the spoken word as well as by the immaterial and spiritual values and concepts of friendship which letters are significantly meant to shape and cultivate (cf. Jagodzinski, 1999: 91). At the same time, Donne's letters strive to make the most of their own potential for having material effects and are thus illustrative of a performative concept of language that considers words as deeds.

The letter as commodity

The material dimension of Donne's letters regularly manifests itself in mercantile vocabulary. One letter describes the writer's ignorance as to how many letters he has received from the addressee as the 'ill Affection of a desperate debtor, that he dares not come to an account, nor take knowledge how much he owes' (*Letters* 253). Another expresses delight in writing to his addressee without having heard anything from him in return, 'because it hath in it so much more merit' (*Letters* 178). Donne's letter writers consider the letter as a recompense for received material support.

Letters serve as a medium for protesting the writer's loyalty to his benefactors. In the context of this 'Tudor mix of payment for civil service with personal loyalty' (Faust, 1993: 85), the degree of that (im-material) loyalty is very subtly declared to increase in proportion with the real and material efforts which the addressee had previously made in the writer's favour.

Donne's *Letters to severall Persons of Honour* abound in epistolary documents whose sole function is to reassure the addressee of the writer's loyalties: 'therefore, Sir, though I have no more to say, but to renew the obligations I have towards you, and to continue my place in your love, I would not forbear to tell you so' (*Letters* 41–2). Protesting his obligations is here ingeniously linked to the 'place in your love' which the writer hopes to cultivate – and which might ensure him of future benefits. This is a strategy the writer intends to keep practising: 'Howsoever with every commodity, I shall say something, though it be but a descant upon this plain song, that I am *Your affectionate servant* J. Donne' (*Letters* 42). The meaning of 'with every commodity' is ambiguous: is it merely referring to every practical opportunity which may henceforth arise for the writer to protest his loyalty? But 'commodity' may also mean all further benefits which the addressee will grant the writer, or every letter he will compose in recompense for such future favours. Like all forms of Renaissance art, letters, too, were 'increasingly unable to resist the commodity form' (Wayne, 1995: 144), as they became included in the exchange pattern of patronage systems.

The writer's readiness to declare his gratefulness for received favours indicates the client's worthiness to be so endowed by his sponsor. In a letter *'To the Honourable Knight Sir G. P.'*, the writer points out that the addressee made no mistake in presenting and recommending Donne to the Lady Huntington, for 'she never laid obligation upon any man, readier to express his acknowledgement of them, to any servant of her servants' (*Letters* 184). The writer fully acknowledges her favours, a recognition that keeps improving his character: 'And, at what time soever she thought best of me in her life, I am better than that, for my goodnesse is my thankfulnesse, and I am every day fuller of that then before, to her LaP' (*Letters* 185). The writer's greatly improving character would of course also justify all future benefits which the patroness may afford him.

Donne's letters present patronage as 'a mutually advantageous relationship', since the client offers his patron 'the intangible gift of prestige, depending on his own status, ability, or wealth' (Peck, 1981: 30). It is interesting how a letter *'To the Honourable Knight Sir H. Goodere'* openly acknowledges that, whereas the writer has received material and fairly substantial benefits from his addressee, he is able to repay these offices only through letters (cf. Schneider, 2005: 126) – and how he nevertheless manages to present his letters as something valuable and dignified: 'Because things be conserved by the same means, which established them, I nurse that friendship by Letters, which you began so: though you have since strengthened it by more solid aliment and real offices. In these Letters from the Country there is this merit, that I do otherwise unwillingly turn mine eye or thoughts from my books, companions in whom there is no falshood nor frowardnesse' (*Letters* 68). The writer begins by pointing out that his writing of letters is only consistent with how his addressee originally began this friendship. Then he notes that the addressee made some more substantial contribution to their bond than himself – yet he is quick to insist that his letters must not be underestimated: after all, he cuts down on his reading in order to make time for a letter to the addressee. That he should then praise his books as 'companions' without 'falshood nor frowardnesse' suggests that leaving them aside for a moment did not come easy to him: the addressee should feel all the more honoured that he actually did so.[5]

Elsewhere the writer greatly praises the long letter he has received from the addressee, claiming that he loves it 'as my mistresses face, every line and feature, but best altogether' (*Letters* 247). He acknowledges the debt that ensues from the addressee's epistolary generosity: 'All that I can do towards retribution, is, (as other bankrupts do in prison) to make means by Commissioners, that a great debt may be accepted by small summes weekly' (*Letters* 247). Swiftly, he devises an even better excuse for the comparative shortness of his present letter: 'You know that they say, those are the strongest, and the firmest, and most precious things, which are composed of the most, and smallest parts' (*Letters* 247). The ensemble of various shorter letters he intends to write will be worth more than one single long letter. This argument has a subtle edge to it: as regards the letter he has received, the writer wants to thank the addressee not only for 'every particular part of it' but especially 'for the length' (*Letters* 246). Yet his own plan of sending various short letters appears slightly superior to the addressee's long letter – or at least it works as a clever excuse for his laconism.

Apart from the writing of letters, there is one other way in which one may recompense one's benefactors: by praying for them. Taking note of his addressee's desire for more letters, the writer of 'To my good friend S H. G.' declares himself quite happy to write more often, for thus 'you give me means to pay some of my debts to you: the interest of which I pay in all my prayers for you, which, if it please not God to shew here, I hope we shall finde again together in heaven, whither they were sent' (*Letters* 194). The writing of letters and the act of praying for the addressee are closely aligned with one another. As the writing of more letters works to pay some of the writer's debt, so praying compensates for the interest he owes. Both letter and prayer depend on their being sent – the former to the addressee, the latter to heaven. The relationship of writer to addressee and of praying subject to God are thus paralleled, as will be suggested also by my reading of *Devotions*. If the writer stands in the addressee's debt, this creditor–debtor relationship ought to be placed in the larger context in which each stands in the debt of God. Hence a different letter promises to remember all of Lady Huntington's favours, 'nor leave them unrequited in my Exchequer, which is, the blessings of God upon my prayers' (*Letters* 237). Elsewhere, the winter urges his addressee to 'beleeve me that I shall ever with much affection, and much devotion joine both your fortune and your last best happinesse, with the desire of mine own in all my civill, and divine wishes, as the only retribution in the power of *Your affectionate servant* Jo. Donne' (*Letters* 127). The ostentatious servility of these lines suffers if we consider the easy opportunism with which clients forsook their patrons '[i]f a noble's fortunes were seen to be taking a downward turn' (Brennan, 1988: 3 4). The reciprocal entanglements of the patronage system granted the client considerable power over his patron – even though, just as the effectiveness of prayers depends on God's readiness to acknowledge them, so does the acceptability of letters depend on their addressees' benevolence.

As my discussion of the sermons has shown, Donne imagined the conferring of grace as mutual: the individual's consent and co-operation was an essential component. In the context of Donne's letters, it is noteworthy that the term 'grace' may not be used only with respect to a patron and God himself – it can refer also to a writer's elegance of expression (Müller, 1980: 143). Such a view questions Calvinist concepts of predestination and the irresistibility of grace, but it would not have been incompatible with the Thirty-Nine Articles (1563), for these 'present the Calvinist doctrine of predestination in such a way as to render it practicably ambiguous' (Cressy/Ferrell, 1996: 59). Article 17 even warns against too exaggerated a contemplation of the doctrine of predestination: while it may have a positive effect on godly people, for 'curious and carnal persons', it constitutes 'a most dangerous downfall, whereby the Devil doth thrust them either into desperation, or into wretchlessness of most unclean living, no less perilous than desperation' (Cressy/Ferrell, 1996: 64). Even those less endowed with the Christian spirit should not give themselves up. Donne's letter writers – and the same is true also of the speaker of *Devotions* – are not only far from giving up, they are also quite confident that their efforts will be gracefully received. A letter 'To Sir I. H.' encourages his addressee to think as well as possible of the writer's motives and to excuse any of the letter's potential shortcomings:

> We often excuse and advance mean Authors, by the age in which they lived, so will your love do this Letter; and you will tell your self, that if he which writ it knew wherein he might express his affection, or any thing which might have made his Letter welcommer, he would have done it. As it is, you may accept it so, as we do many *China* manufactures, of which when we know no use, yet we satisfie our curiosity in considering them, because we knew not how, nor of what matter they were made. (*Letters* 118)

Rather boldly, the writer does not only ask the addressee to accept his letter as the result of his best efforts but even assumes that this is what the addressee 'will' think it to be. Whereas the first part of his argument attributes any potential shortcomings to the writer's own insufficiencies, the second part likens his letter to '*China* manufactures'. Should the addressee find it deficient, this may be blamed on the addressee's ignorance and inability of judgement.

Another letter claims that even the absence of letters must not be criticised: just as one does not hold dear one's land only when it yields fruit, 'so is not friendship then onely to be esteemed, when she is delivered of a Letter, or any other reall office, but in her continuall propensnesse and inclination to do it' (*Letters* 238). Like land, friendship is a value of its own, which may manifest itself in commodities such as letters or prayers.

Many of Donne's letters openly present themselves as commodities, composed in return for material generosities. Yet they often elevate themselves to a status which amounts to more than modest and inevitably insufficient compensation, and initial gestures of humility and subservience appear, with hindsight, mere rhetorical convention (cf. Van Houdt/Papy, 2002: 8; Marotti, 2006: 42). Material benefits are countered by the material presence of written letters – whose business with concerns beyond the material realm, with prayers, suggests their implicit superiority over materialism.

Being the word and becoming as one

By and large, Donne's epistolary writing owes but little to medieval *ars dictaminis* (poetic or compositional art) and instead resembles the Ciceronian model of the familiar letter. Yet 'the Classical *topos* that the letter is the mirror of the soul should be read as describing self-presentation or self-fashioning rather than self-revelation or self-analysis' (Henderson, 2002: 23; Boutcher, 2002: 138, 163). It is no coincidence that whereas the first folio of Erasmus's *De conscribendis epistolis* is critical of 'theatrical apparatus and grandiloquence' in letter writing, this scepticism is missing in the later version of the treatise (Fantazzi in Erasmus, 1536: 4). Some theatricality must go into letter writing. Early modern letters may be read as 'a traditionally sincere portrayal of an essential self, but at the same time, as a possibly manipulated portrayal of a rhetorical self' (Faust, 1993: 82; Maurer, 1982: 184). The epistolary genre was congenial to Donne's preoccupation with 'being and seeming' (Milgate, 1967: xxxv). Such self-fashioning need not be equated with a 'capacity for deception and falsehood' (Schneider, 2005: 102). Instead, we may consider 'the written being and the writing being [as] coincident and differential' (Goldberg, 1990: 24): the one interacts with and influences the other. If, in the epistolary novel, 'fiction conventionally masquerades as a real-life product' (Altman, 1982: 6), Donne's letters conversely function as real-life products which exploit the possibilities of fiction. In addition, they do not only engage in fashioning the writer's persona but frequently also have him identify with the whole of his epistle.

Whenever Donne's writers deprecate their own letters, this negative verbal existence extends itself also to the writer's persona. Towards the end of a letter *'To Sir* H. G.', we read that 'as this Letter is nothing, so if ever it come to you, you will know it without a name, and therefore I may end it here' (*Letters* 146) – without a signature. By leaving out his name, the scribe fashions himself as no less nothing than his letter. The implication is that the sender of the letter will be known by the character of his epistle, which presupposes a high degree of intimacy between writer and addressee – and if the writer is both closely associated with the addressee and at the same time 'nothing', this nothingness transfers itself also to the recipient and the relevance of this epistolary correspondence in general.

Belittlement of self by way of epistolary deconstruction is not uncommon. A letter *'To my honoured friend* G. G. *Esquire'* assumes that 'our Letters are our selves [...] and in them absent friends meet' (*Letters* 240). The writer moves on to give two reasons for his reluctance to report upon himself, 'first, because it is not for my gravity, to write of feathers, and straws, and in good faith, I am no more, considered in my body, or fortune' (*Letters* 240). This reasoning is paradoxical: how plausible is the writer's gravity when he considers himself to be of no more weight than 'feathers, and straws' – or, conversely, how could we imagine him to be no more than that and still credit him on his 'gravity'? More significantly, his assumed humility is immediately betrayed when, in spite of the reasons he gives against it, he does elaborate upon his state of health. The letter's argumentative shiftiness and self-contradictory entanglement reflects the instability and inconsistency of the writer's illness as he finds himself suspended between his 'gravity' on the one hand and 'feathers, and strawes' on the other.

In another letter, the writer likewise cannot but make his letter resemble himself in spite of protesting that this is precisely what he hopes to avoid: 'Sir, you see what unconcerning things I am fain to write of, lest I should write of my self, who am so little a history or tale, that I should not hold out to make a Letter long enough to send over a Sea to you; for I should dispatch my self in this one word that I am *Your affectionate servant and lover* J. Donne' (*Letters* 190). Since these are the final words of his letter, the writer does in fact dispatch himself in this subscription: what he 'should' do becomes what he does, his words perform what they describe. Much as this may be true of most formulas of farewell, it has particular significance here: the subscription is preceded by many lines which treat of numerous 'unconcerning things' – and thus a letter which, owing to the writer's own claim to insignificance, is adequately representative of him. Moreover, this (supposedly) non-voluntary epistolary self-revelation does make up a letter 'long enough to send over a Sea to you', so that the writer's humble opinion of himself comes across as either simply mistaken or, alternatively, ingeniously fabricated.

A similar kind of self-contradiction is at work in a letter 'To S H. G.', although this time the writer does not deny the link between an epistle and its producer. The letter begins by declaring, 'I Send not my Letters as tribute, nor interest, nor recompense, nor for commerce, nor as testimonials of my love, nor provokers of yours, nor to justifie my custome of writing, nor for a vent and utterance of my meditations' (*Letters* 109). Instead, 'I desire that you might have in your hands Letters of mine of all kindes, as conveyances and deliverers of me to you, whether you accept me as a friend, or as a patient, or as a penitent, or as a beadsman, for I decline no jurisdiction, or refuse any tenure' (*Letters* 109). The purpose of these letters is precisely not to serve a certain function (How, 2003: 3) but to be and bear the writer, in some role or other (cf. Targoff, 2008). Particularly among friends, as Bacon notes, one does not have to stick to one social role only but 'may speak as the case requires, and not as it sorteth with the person' (Bacon, 1972: 86). However, since one takes on different roles on various occasions, the numerous purposes of letter writing, whose relevance the writer just disclaimed, are significant after all: they enable the writer to adopt different roles, each of which manifests itself in a respective letter, to communicate itself to the recipient. The variety of roles in which the writer wants to communicate himself is mirrored by the different and partly incongruous claims which make up this letter's argument, and by implication its writer.

Although the writer aims to communicate himself in as many roles as possible, he does not seem afraid that this variety of character may be misread as weakness or inconsistency. On the contrary, he intends to familiarise his addressee with all aspects of his rich personality. In a letter *'To the Countesse of* Bedford', the writer characterises the particular 'office of this Letter, to convey my best wishes, and all the effects of a noble love unto you (which are the best fruits that so poor a soil, as my poor soul is, can produce' (*Letters* 23–4). Again, the letter appears to turn into the writer's soul itself: 'And for my part, I shall make it so like my soul, that as that affection, of which it is the messenger, begun in me without my knowing when, any more then I know when my soul began; so it shall continue as long as that' (*Letters* 24). Once again, the announcement of the writer's intention seems to imply its own performance, but the future aspect of these the letter's last words still allows for some insecurity and openness as to whether the equation of the writer's soul with this letter and its project will be acknowledged. Its success, we may suspect, depends not only on the writer's own efforts but also on his addressee's willingness to co-operate with him on this count. Earlier on, the writer suggested that his addressee 'may be pleased to allow the Letter thus much of the souls privilege, as to exempt it from straitnesse of hours, or any measure of times, and so beleeve it came then' (*Letters* 24), i.e. before its actual date. The letter at hand, as discussed above, had been promised as composed before it actually was written, or indeed before any conceivable date, a prerequisite for establishing its equation with the writer's soul, whose date of origin can likewise never be known. In asking its addressee to accept that, like the writer's soul, it was conceived before the beginning of time, this letter illustrates how '[t]he epistolary form [...] [makes] the reader (narratee) almost as important an agent in the narrative as the writer (narrator)' (Altman, 1982: 88).

To facilitate the writer's identification with his own text, the addressee must co-operate – he functions as 'an accomplice' (Guillén, 1986: 100). Writers variously comment on the presence of welcome addressees in their own letters. Thus the writer of a letter addressed to Donne's sister Mrs Cokayne delightedly reports on how he 'this day met the acceptablest guest in the acceptablest manner, your Letter, walking in my chamber' (Simpson *Prose* 166). There are many instances where writers picture the reception of letters as truly life-saving (cf. 'To the worthiest Lady Mrs. Bridget White', *Letters* 1–2). In that many letters eagerly seek to evoke epistolary responses, they once more resemble their writers: letters are written out of a desire for company. A feeling of togetherness may be created not only by receiving an answer to one's own letter but also in the process of writing oneself. What the writer appreciates most about Mrs Martha Garet's brother's visit, is, as he says in a letter to her, 'that he brought you with him; which he doth, as well by letting me see how you do, as by giving me occasions, and leave to talk with you by this Letter' (*Letters* 40). He declares himself 'loth to leave [writing]; for as long as in any fashion, I can have your brother and you here, you make my house a kind of Dorvey; but since I cannot stay you here, I will come thither to you; which I do, by wrapping up in this paper, the heart of Your most affectionate servant J. Donne' (*Letters* 41). The writer may successfully conjure up his addressee not only upon receiving a letter from him but even as he is writing to him or her. Addressee and writer thus encounter each other, and, as they manifest themselves in the epistolary word, they may become as one. In writing, the writer's heart encounters that of his addressee – hence the instructive etymological error of epistolography, which assumed that 'correspondence' referred to the way in which two hearts talked with one another (Müller, 1980: 157).

Although they recognise that they depend on their addressees' co-operation, this does not make Donne's letter writers very humble. Instead, they conceive of their relationship towards their addressees as one of mutual obligation and give-and-take. Drawing on Erasmus's letter writing manual, Magnusson shows how these 'recommendations strongly confirm the theatricality and self-consciousness of humanist identity construction' (Magnusson, 1999: 66), and how relationships may be actively negotiated in the epistolary medium. Many of Donne's speakers engage in role-play in order to become one with their various and often socially superior addressees, which is altogether in keeping with Erasmus, who suggested role-play as a viable method in the teaching of letter writing: 'one may compose a letter from a wife to her husband who is tarrying abroad, telling him to hasten home; or a letter from the aged and eloquent Nestor urging Achilles to bear nobly Agamemnon's seizure of Briseis' (Erasmus, 1985:

24). Many of Donne's letter writers turn their own dependency into a source of self-confidence and virtue. Donne's letter '24. To a Friend' begins by acknowledging the writer's humble deference to his addressee: the writer knows the addressee but as the friend of a friend and 'can pretend no other title to your friendship, than that I am allowed some little interest in them, who have more in you' (Simpson *Prose* 140). Soon, however, he moves on to a more general statement which he takes to be valid also with regard to this particular relationship: 'But, as in Divine, so in Morall things, where the beginning is from others, the assistance, and co-operation, is in our selves' (Simpson *Prose* 140–1). On the one hand, this statement emphasizes the writer's obligation towards the addressee who, owing to his higher status, must have been the one to begin this friendship 'as formerly I had the honour to hold with you' (Simpson *Prose* 141). On the other hand, it simultaneously points out that, although the beginning may lie with the addressee, for their friendship's maintenance the recipient has to rely no less on the writer than vice versa. Since writer and addressee are geographically separated, this co-operation has to remain epistolary: For, 'If Letters be not able to do that office, they are yet able, at least to testifie, that he, who sends them, would be glad to do more, if he could' (Simpson *Prose* 141).

The letter proves well-planned: having addressed those 'Morall things' of friendship, the writer, after a wish that he and the addressee be reunited at least in heaven, smoothly moves on to matters 'Divine'. The writer hopes that their differences in terms of religion will be irrelevant; he assumes that his tolerance of the addressee's faith will entitle him to that tolerance also, and says so twice: 'That we differ in our wayes, I hope we pardon one another. [. . .] And this taste of mine towards you, makes me hope for, and claime the same disposition in you towards me' (Simpson *Prose* 141). The contrast between the letter's humble beginning and the writer's later 'claime' of tolerance is reminiscent of the ways in which Donne's religious writings oscillate between excessive humility and imperatives directed even at the Lord himself. In one's relationship towards both God and humanity, even if 'the beginning' may be the superior's, 'the assistance, and co-operation, is in our selves'. This insight encourages an exploration of Donne's religion of letters, one aspect of which becomes manifest whenever letter writers emphasise their utter dependence on their addressees' memory of them and the ensuing manifestations of their good will. In *'To the honourable Knight Sr Henry Goodere'*, the writer readily grants that he cannot think of any convincing arguments in his own favour: 'because I know no stronger argument to move you to love me, but because you have done so, doe so still, to make my reason better' (*Letters* 226). One could well imagine Donne's religious speakers approaching God in a similarly bold vein, making a virtue and strength even out of their very lack of argumentative consistency.

Towards a religion of letters

The writing personae of Donne's letters consider themselves altogether dependent on the benevolence of influential personages. Approaching these people is a delicate affair, and they cannot always be accessed directly. Donne's letter writers often use addressees they feel more closely associated with as intercessors and herein cite Catholic practices of Christian worship. A letter entitled *'To your selfe'* begins by protesting the writer's 'desire to serve you' (*Letters* 294), but later asks the addressee: 'Except you know reason to the contrary, I pray deliver this Letter according to the addresse' (*Letters* 294). Although he knows the second addressee's whereabouts, the writer considers it inappropriate to do so without the present addressee's intercession. The enclosed letter is to refresh his memory with the second addressee: 'as by our Law, a man may be *Felo de se*, if he kill himself, so I think a man may be *Fur de se*, if he steale himselfe out of the memory of them, which are content to harbour him' (*Letters* 295). Slipping from a patron's memory is social suicide (cf. Cedric Brown, 2008: 65). The esteem in which the writer holds himself is equivalent with the opinion in which he stands with his social superiors.

Only by the end of the letter does the writer recall his current addressee: 'I begin to be loath to be lost, since I have afforded my selfe some valuation and price, ever since I received the stampe and impression of being *Your very humble and affectionate servant* J. Donne' (*Letters* 295). By this move, he avoids devaluating the present addressee in favour of the socially superior addressee of the enclosed letter, but simultaneously betrays the reason for his deference: the present addressee's good connections to yet more influential personages. As the writing persona of another letter makes clear, one may well expect something in return for such deference: 'You forget me absolutely and intirely, whensoever you forget me to that noble Countesse' (*Letters* 176). Donne's letters reflect the actual complexity of the patronage system, which was shaped not only by the binary hierarchy of patron and client but also by 'the hierarchies among patrons considered as a social group' (Gundersheimer, 1981: 16). Artists, though inferior to their patrons, made a conscious decision as to whose patronage they sought.

Occasionally, letter writers directly communicate their subservience to a third person by articulating it in a letter to a closely related associate of the patron(ess) in question. A letter '*To Sir* H. G.' asks the addressee to present the writer's 'humble thanks' to the 'good Lady' (*Letters* 151). Surely, his explanation – 'for I have made her opinion of me, the ballance by which I weigh my self' (*Letters* 151) – is likewise destined for her ears. Such letters willingly take into account that they may be read also by that third party which – supposedly – cannot be approached directly. In a letter '*To the worthiest Knight Sir* Henry Goodere', the writer prescribes the words in which he wants his addressee to inform the 'Lady *Huntington*' about his well-being as coextensive with her favours: 'I beseech you, let her Lad: know, that she hath sowed her favours towards me, in such a ground, that if I be grown better (as I hope I am) her favours are grown with me, and though they were great when she conferred them, yet, (if I mend every day) they increase in me every day, and therefore every day multiply my thankfulnesse towards her Ladiship' (*Letters* 236–7). At the end of this eulogy (both on the Lady and, implicitly, himself), he allows the addressee to 'say what you will (if you like not this expression)' (*Letters* 237), but the implication is that the addressee will either use these exact words or allow the Lady Huntington to overhear this letter by reading it aloud in her presence – just as prayers to saints were uttered in the hope that God himself would deign to listen in. Moreover, 'some of the letters to Goodere were at least meant to be shown or alluded to by Goodere in his frequent transactions with the Countess of Bedford' (Maurer, 1976: 237; Cedric Brown, 2008: 71) – who functioned as just another intercessor in Donne's attempts to be, eventually, heard by King James himself.

Whenever a writer protests his dependence on her ladyship's generosity, he presents himself as 'all hers'. 'Being yours', the addressee's, is what many of Donne's letter writers aspire to, as in *'To my very much honoured friend* George Garrard *Esquire at* Sion': 'I Know not which of us wonne it by the hand, in the last charge of Letters. If you wonne, you wonne nothing, because I am nothing, or whatsoever I am, you wonne nothing, because I was all yours before' (*Letters* 281), and in *'To the Right Honourable the Lord Viscount of* Rochester', the writer claims that 'You may have many better bargaines in your purchases, but never a better title then to me, nor any thing which you may call yours more absolutely and intirely' (*Letters* 290). Even if 'being yours' is not quite the same as 'being you', it is significant that this letter concludes with the writer's own name and the title of his addressee 'on the same sheet of paper, thereby accomplishing a correspondence that he conceives of as prohibited by the time, space, or social order of the world' (Maurer, 1982: 193):

> I should never wish other station, then such as might make me still, and onely
> Your Lordships
> > *Most humble and devoted servant*
> > > J. Donne. (*Letters* 291)

The difference between being 'yours' and 'you', 'Your Lordships' and 'Your Lordship' is minute. As Derrida has shown, like all utterances, signatures rely on citationality: 'In order to function, that is, in order to be legible, a signature must have a repeatable, iterable, imitable form' (Derrida, 1986: 328). Signatures 'authorise' an utterance – and where their 'authors' identify with their respective addressees, so may signatures also engage in role-play.

The same letter alludes to a religion of letters when it points out that, just as 'it is easier for God to recollect the Principles, and Elements of our bodies, howsoever they be scattered, then it was at first to create them of nothing' (*Letters* 291), so will the addressee have less difficulty in removing any obstacles in the way of the writer's aspirations than in originally begetting these hopes. There often seems to be some grandeur behind the enthusiastic self-deprecation of such approaches to human or divine authorities, grandeur no less significant than that of the revered addressee. A letter *'To the gallant Knight Sir* Tho. Lucy' claims, 'Sir, your own soul cannot be more zealous of your peace, then I am' (*Letters* 210).

The addressee's soul is insinuated to be not just equivalent with but potentially inferior to that of the writer – at least as regards their concern for the addressee's peace.

Not only may the writer move from 'being yours' to 'being you' – the addressee, too, contributes to that process of identification, for example in the reading out of a letter: he then takes and speaks the writer's part. Quite a number of Donne's letters were probably written with the intention of being read aloud and overheard by patrons or patronesses who could not have been reached otherwise (cf. Marotti, 2006: 42; Earle, 1999a: 7). That such semi-public reading performances should have been common is hinted in a letter '*To Sir* H. G.': 'One thing more I must tell you; but so softly, that I am loath to hear my self: and so softly, that if that good Lady were in the room, with you and this Letter, she might not hear' (*Letters* 196). Writers usually would have taken into account that their letters were orally performed. Today's concepts of epistolary privacy do not hold for early modern times. Letters contributed to the gradual separation of public and private spheres, but, even if this does not apply for Donne's letters, there often was a secretary involved in their penning. Moreover, they depended on a bearer and were read by more people than their addressee (cf. Stewart/Wolfe, 2004: 181; Schneider, 2005: 22–7, 68–72).

In a letter entitled '*To the same*', the mutual dependence of the parties involved in an intercourse of letters is intimately explored. The writer is convinced that his sickness must also have affected the addressee: 'For nearer Contracts then generall Christianity, had made us so much towards one, that one part cannot escape the distemper of the other' (*Letters* 58).[6] Hence he became particularly eager to recover, both in order to reassure the addressee in his fears for him and to prove that the recipient's prayers had been heard. However, despite their close connectedness, it would be inappropriate for the writer to insist that his own sickness actually infected the addressee. Their bond is rather complex: 'Sir, though my fortune hath made me such as I am, rather a sicknesse and disease of the world then any part of it, yet I esteemed my self so far from being so to you, as I esteemed you to be far from being so of the world, as to measure men by fortune or events' (*Letters* 59). The addressee's prayers for the writer's health and his recent letter are paralleled in their medical effects: 'I am now gone so far towards health, as there is not infirmity enough left in me for an assurance of so much noblenesse and truth, as your last Letter is to work upon, that might cure a greater indisposition then I am now in' (*Letters* 59).

The writer's sickness continues to serve as a thematic and metaphorical source: firstly, it provides a context in which the writer's close, almost infectious bonding with the addressee was easily established. Secondly, by pointing out the curative effect which the addressee's letter had on his health, and by presenting his sickness as not quite cured, the writer asks for more of that potent medicine. He warns the addressee that he 'shall not be rid of this Ague of my Letters, though perchance the fit change daies' (*Letters* 60), but also makes plausible why he has to stop writing at this point: 'Sir, I dare sit no longer in my wastcoat, nor have any thing worth the danger of a relapse to write. I owe you so much of my health, as I would not mingle you in any occasion of repairing it' (*Letters* 60). The figuration of letters as intimate, potentially infectious but also curative intercourse is central also to a letter '*To Sir* H. R.', which the writer characterises as mutually advisory: 'This, Sir, I use to say to you, rather to have so good a witnesse and corrector of my meditations, then to advise; and yet to do that too, since it is pardonable in a friend' (*Letters* 30). Just like the writing of letters, the giving of advice is beneficial to both writer and addressee.

In a letter '*To Sr* G. M.', there is ample evidence as to why one ought to estimate letters as highly as Donne's writers do. Interactivity constitutes their major strength. The writer parallels the Biblical epistle with the familiar letter: 'The Evangiles and Acts, teach us what to believe, but the Epistles of the Apostles what to do' (*Letters* 106). It soon becomes clear that the telling of 'what to do' is by no means a mere transmission of information. Instead, letters make vivid whatever kind of knowledge is at stake: 'as some poisons, and some medicines, hurt not, nor profit, except the creature in which they reside, contribute their lively activitie, and vigor; so, much of the knowledge buried in Books perisheth, and becomes ineffectuall, if it be not applied, and refreshed by a companion, or friend' (*Letters* 107). The refreshment of such knowledge not only is the responsibility of the writer but also lies with the recipient. Letters encourage interactivity, since each of them begets further occasion for communication and debate. Consequently one tends to prefer 'the papers of any living now, (especially friends)' to the writings of deceased men, '[a]nd we do justly in it, for the writings and words of men present, we may examine, controll, and expostulate, and receive satisfaction from the authors; but the other we must beleeve, or discredit; they present no mean' (*Letters* 107). Communicating by letter makes present the authors of those 'writings and words', so that they become almost physically manifest. After his theoretical discourse on the nature of letters, the writer returns to the letter he is currently engaged in: 'Since then at this time, I am upon the stage, you may be content to hear me' (*Letters* 107). He then baffles his reader's expectations by confessing that 'now I have nothing to say' (*Letters* 108). Like the majority of Donne's letter writers, he is concerned less with communicating something than with conveying himself to his addressee.

Some of Donne's letters rid themselves of the burden of communicating anything apart from themselves by leaving it to their addressees to add whatever may be missing. In a letter *'To Sir G. F'*, we read: 'Therefore give me leave to end this, in which if you did not finde the remembrance of my humblest services to my Lady *Bedford*, your love and faith ought to try all the experiments of pouders, and dryings, and waterings to discover some lines which appeared not; because it is impossible that a Letter should come from me, with such an ungratefull silence' (*Letters* 76–7). Despite the ironic subtext, the implication that it is the addressee's fault if he fails to find what he expects recalls the mutually communicative and interactive relationship between writers and addressees. In *'To the Honourable Lady Mrs. B. W.'*, the writer fashions his letter as 'a bashfull servant, who though he have an extreme desire to put himself in your presence, yet hath not much to say when he is come' (*Letters* 6). He then encourages his addressee to continue the letter in his place:

> Yet hath it as much to say as you can think; because what degrees soever of honour, respect, and devotion, you can imagine or believe to be in any, this letter tells you, that all those are in me towards you. So that for this letter you are my Secretary; for your worthiness, and your opinion that I have a just estimation of them, write it: so that it is as long, and as good, as you think it; and nothing is left to me, but as a witness, to subscribe the name of
> *Your most humble servant*
>
> J. D. (*Letters* 6)

Once again, the writer's humility is dubious. By implying that the addressee is to play secretary to him, the writer undermines the social hierarchies of this master- (or rather mistress-)servant relationship (cf. Targoff, 2008: 38). According to Angel Day, the relationship between secretary and employer need not be strictly hierarchical: 'so each vertue kindled by the others Grace, maketh at last a coniunction, which by the multitude of fauors rising from the one, and a thankfull compensation alwayes procured in the other, groweth in the end to simpathie vnseparable, and therby by all intendiment concludeth a most perfect vniting' (Day, 1967: 113). The longer and more intimately they co-operate, the more will master and servant become as one, and it is only thus that a secretary can write letters which reflect and embody his employer's soul. Such playful exploitations and inversions of social hierarchies abound in Donne's letters. They are the immediate consequence of a concept of letter writing as mutually obliging, as a communication or communion of selves rather than a mere transmission of information. As I shall show, this interactive dimension of epistolary communication places it in close proximity to the communion that constitutes the purpose of Donne's *Devotions*.

Quite a number of Donne's writers presume that their addressees will not mind their impoliteness. As one letter to Sir Henry Wotton casually expects, '[i]n the meane tyme Sir have the honor of forgiving two faults together: my not writing last tyme and my abrupt ending now' (Simpson *Prose* 112). Another *'To Sir H. G.'* begins thus: 'I love to give you advantages upon me, therefore I put my self in need of another pardon from you, by not coming to you' (*Letters* 150). Such playfulness may be owing to the familiarity between Donne and Goodyer, but these strategies are also at work in other letters. The ambiguity of 'advantages' is significant: being excused for not coming to see the addressee would clearly be to the writer's advantage – but this benefit turns into the advantage of the addressee over the writer if he indeed forgave him. The bond between writer and addressee is supposedly so intimate that the interests of the one coincide with those of the other, a connectedness implied also by a formula of petition suggested by Erasmus: 'The matter is of such a nature that if you consider what I am asking of you, you should be asking it of me' (Erasmus, 1985: 180). Shortly after Donne's secret marriage to

George More's daughter Ann, the writer employs just this strategy to persuade his father-in-law to be generous, 'to take to your selfe the comfort of having saved from such destruction as your just anger might have layd upon him, a sorowfull and honest man' (Simpson *Prose* 118) – the comfort which More ought to grant Donne is to become a comfort to the addressee himself.

This time, the writer's endeavours were not blessed with quick success. Not always are strategies of role-play and identification successful in 'making social change thinkable' (Magnusson, 1999: 88). Yet many letter writers characterise their own desire as coinciding with that of their benefactors, even when those superiors cannot be approached directly. In one letter to Goodyer, there is reference to a 'Mr *Fowler*', to whom the writer and addressee conjointly offered 'a gift of me': '[i]f your leisure suffer it, I pray finde whether I be in him still, and conserve me in his love; and so perfect your own work, or doe it over again, and restore me to the place, which by your favour I had in him' (*Letters* 81). The writer's promotion is fashioned as the addressee's success. A letter '*To the Honourable Knight Sir* Robert Karre' even presents the writer's advantage not only as the addressee's but even as that of a second addressee who can be approached only through intercession: 'For, esteeming my selfe, by so good a title, as my Lords own words, to be under his providence, and care of my fortune, I make it the best part of my studies, how I might ease his Lordship by finding out something for my selfe. Which, because I thinke I have done, as though I had done him a service therein, I adventure to desire to speake with him' (*Letters* 292–3).

Another letter begins by stressing the writer's inadequacy as a friend for the addressee – although it simultaneously explains how he can still be useful for him: 'Though my friendship be good for nothing else, it may give you the profit of a tentation, or of an affliction: It may excuse your patience; and though it cannot allure, it shall importune you. Though I know you have many worthy friends of all rankes, yet I adde something, since I which am of none, would fain be your friend too. There is some of the honour and some of the degrees of a Creation, to make a friendship of nothing' (*Letters* 65). The writer then decides 'not to annihilate myself utterly (for though it seem humblenesse, yet it is a work of as much almightinesse, to bring a thing to nothing, as from nothing)' (*Letters* 65). Although his humility elevates the addressee, there appears to be almightiness even in such self-deprecation. Conversely, the act of making 'a friendship of nothing' (*Letters* 65) has something of 'a Creation' about it and would elevate the addressee to the level of a Creator – whose might, however, since it may become manifest also in utter destruction, simultaneously aligns itself with the writer's humble powers. The more the writer humbles himself, the greater the creational act of the addressee – on the other hand, the less the writer considers himself to be, the more do his annihilating powers approach the divine. The less he is, the more of an affliction will he be to the addressee, and, from a Calvinist point of view, one ought to consider one's afflictions as blessings. Writer and addressee are closely entangled with one other, approaching a state of becoming as one, a state of communion, however unstable and ambiguous, which is paradigmatic of the epistolary genre in which '[t]he letter writer simultaneously seeks to affect his reader and is affected by him' (Altman, 1982: 88).

A number of Donne's *Letters to severall Persons of Honour* served as accompanying letters to pieces of writing which Donne sent to his friends or patrons. His letter *'To the right honourable the Countess of* Montgomery' came together with a sermon she had asked for. The letter debates the differences between the sermon in oral performance and its written version:

> I know what dead carcasses things written are, in respect of things spoken. But in things of this kinde, that soul that inanimates them, receives debts from them: The Spirit of God that dictates them in the speaker or writer, and is present in his tongue or hand, meets himself again (as we meet our selves in a glass) in the eies and hearts of the hearers and readers: and that Spirit, which is ever the same to an equall devotion, makes a writing and a speaking equall means to edification. (*Letters* 25)

A sermon is meant for oral performance, but, with regard to religious texts, communication does not suffer by its transference into writing, because the divine spirit which inspires both speaker and writer is reflected by hearers and readers alike. Religious devotion is effected by 'that Spirit, which is ever the same', so that the experiences of producer and recipient are likely to be similar. This argument is very similar to what Donne's letters promote with regard to the epistolary genre. The present letter continues: 'In one circumstance, my preaching and my writing this sermon is too equall : that that your Ladiship heard in a hoarse voyce then, you read in a course hand now' (*Letters* 25–6). The 'now' may easily refer also to the present letter, presumably written in a similarly 'course hand' – 'that Spirit' which inspires sermons may be present also in letters (cf. Cormican, 1978: 24; Patrides, 1981).

Just as preaching was one of, if not the most essential element of early modern reformed services, so must the cultivation of friendship primarily depend on the practice of (regular) letter writing. In *'To my most worthy friend Sir* Henry Goodere', we read:

> Because evennesse conduces as much to strength and firmnesse as greatnesse doth, I would not discontinue my course of writing. It is a sacrifice, which though friends need not, friendship doth; which hath in it so much divinity, that as we must be ever equally disposed inwardly so to doe or suffer for it, so we must sepose some certain times for the outward service thereof, though it be but formall and testimonial; that time to me towards you is Tuesday, and my Temple, the Rose in Smith-field. (*Letters* 116)

In presenting the letter as 'the sacrifice offered at the temple of friendship' (Targoff, 2008: 32), the parallel between friendship and religion is treated rather playfully. But the recognition of a need for regularity with regard both to religion and friendship should be taken seriously. It explains once again why, in their newslessness, so many of Donne's letters seem to lack a purpose – they are their own purpose, because their writers consider them images or avatars of both receiver and sender. Donne's theology of letters is 'sacramental, Eucharistic, unashamedly iconophilic' (Jagodzinski, 1999: 75), and, wherever there is sacrament, there also lurks the danger of sacrilege. A letter to 'Lady Mrs B. W.' again accompanies an 'enclosed' (*Letters* 4) piece of writing: another letter to her, written quite a while ago, but the writer still feels she ought to have it: 'I durst not tear it, after it was yours: there is some sacriledge in defacing any thing consecrated to you, and some impiety to despair that any thing devoted to you should not be reserved to a good issue' (*Letters* 4–5).

The addressee is made to resemble God himself here – just as God ought to be approached regularly, so does the writer underline the constancy of his attachment, declaring himself 'very sure that I always think the same thoughts of you' (*Letters* 5), which is why he argues that there is no reason for this letter to continue much longer. The same goes for prayers, as we read in a letter 'To S H. G.': 'long prayers have more of the man, as ambition of eloquence, and a complacencie in the work, and more of the Devil by often distractions' (*Letters* 112). This letter considers the communicative processes of prayers and letters as closely interlinked: 'If at any time I seem to studie you more inquisitively, it is for no other end but to know how to present you to God in my prayers, and what to ask of him for you; for even that holy exercise may not be done inopportunely, no nor importunely' (*Letters* 110): the importuning of the addressee is prerequisite for enabling the writer to adequately importune God on his behalf.

The writer's insistence that 'that advantage of nearer familiarity with God, which the act of incarnation gave us, is grounded upon Gods assuming us, not our going to him' (*Letters* 110–11), is reminiscent of how letter writers consider themselves made and unmade, elevated and crushed by their socially superior addressees: 'Donne's dependence [. . .] is self-constitutive' (Goldberg, 1983: 211). The writer's preference for fixed hours and dates to be 'bestowed upon thanksgiving then petition, upon praise then prayer' (*Letters* 111) may have a lot to do with his recognition that, except for thanks, 'nothing doth so innocently provoke new graces, as gratitude' (*Letters* 111). The thankfulness of Donne's letter writers towards their patrons takes up a lot of space – 'letters and prayers both worked, to make a place for oneself in the world' (Goldberg, 1983: 218). Some writers do not make much of an effort to hide their hopes for 'new graces' behind the profuseness of their thanks. After all, 'there is some degree of thankfulnesse in asking more (for that confesses all former obligations, and a desire to be still in the same dependency)' (*Letters* 95). The desire for profit which prayers of thanks are expected to yield with God is no more veiled than this 'thankful' epistolary plea.

Neither prayers nor letters ought to be overly long: 'for, after in the beginning we have well intreated God to hearken, we speak no more to him. Even this Letter is some example of such infirmitie, which being intended for a Letter, is extended and strayed into a Homilie' (*Letters* 112). Since self-reflexiveness constitutes, as I have shown, the defining feature of that part of a person most profoundly involved in religious communication, i.e. the human soul, it works as another common feature of the friendship of letters and religion of the soul. The present letter draws an additional parallel between epistolary communication and the preparation for communion with the divine:

> I make account that this writing of letters, when it is with any seriousness, is a kind of extasie, and a departure and secession and suspension of the soul, which doth then communicate it self to two bodies: And as I would every day provide for my souls last convoy, though I know not when I shall die, and perchance I shall never die; so for these extasies in letters, I oftentimes deliver my self over in writing when I know not when those letters shall be sent to you, and many times they never are (*Letters* 11)

The 'departure and secession and suspension of the soul' takes place by letter with human addressees, and by prayer if the addressee is God. In both cases, the soul simultaneously remains with the writer and transfers itself to the addressee. As suggested by the word 'extasie[s]', both experiences are fleeting and ungovernable. The gratification to be gained from either can be only a momentary substitute. Fortunately, as we read in a letter *'To the Lady* G', 'since there is a Religion in friendship, and a death in absence, to make up an intire frame there must be a heaven too' (*Letters* 245). If there is 'death in absence', there must be life in companionship. Letters are written and prayers are uttered in order to bridge momentarily the distance between writer/speaker and addressee, but at some point these props will no longer be necessary. Writer and addressee gain new life and are resurrected from death by being reunited, when all human beings and God will be standing face to face – in heaven.

Nowhere is the link between the writing of letters and the utterance of prayers more prominent than in Donne's so-called marriage letters, when the addressees of his letters, Sir George More and Sir Thomas Egerton, as well as God himself, confronted him in their most terrible shapes. The practice of intercession which Donne had so long depended on worked against him when Sir George, after his own anger had been assuaged, approached Egerton with the request to reconsider his dismissal of Donne as his secretary. All the writer can do is to persuade his addressee More to intercede with Egerton, no longer against the writer's best interest but instead in his favour. His best argument is to remind him that, by having mercy follow upon justice, the addressee would imitate God's own pattern: 'I beseech yow also to undertake that charitable office of being my mediator to my Lord, whom as upon your just complainte yow found full of justice, I doubt not but yow shall also find full of mercy, for so ys the Almighty pattern of Justice and Mercy equally full of bothe' (Simpson *Prose* 117). Writing to Egerton, he similarly encourages his addressee to follow God's own example: 'I have therefore no way before me; but must turn back to your Lordship, who knowes that redemtion was no less worke than creation' (Simpson *Prose* 119–20).

God is the potential source of both justice and mercy. The writer laments that 'yt pleases God, from whom I acknowledge the punishment to be just, to accompany my other ylls with so much sicknes as I have no refuge but that of mercy, which I beg of him, my Lord, and yow' (*Letters* 115). The writer is here doing several things at once: except for it not being capitalised (and Donne uses capital and lower case rather inconsistently), 'him' could be referring both to God and to Donne's previous master Egerton, as could be claimed for 'my Lord', while the 'yow' is clearly addressing More: begging by letter and praying to God not only parallel each other, but occur simultaneously. Another letter similarly joins these two actions: 'since yt hath pleasd God to joyne with yow in punishing thereof with increasing my sicknes, and that he gives me now audience by prayer, yt emboldneth me also to address my humble request to your Lordship' (Simpson *Prose* 115). The 'now' may refer also to the present of the letter, so that, at the moment when he is beseeching his Lordship, God himself may also be lending his ear to the writer's epistolary pleas.

In the same letter, the writer acknowledges how he was improved by the addressee's severe punishment: 'Your justice hath been mercifull in making me know my offence, and yt hath much profited me that I am dejected' (Simpson *Prose* 116). In the sermons, speakers similarly praise God for the afflictions he heaps upon man for improving him. Yet the writer would welcome it even more if his addressees resembled God also in his infinite mercy: 'I hope that God (to whom for that I hartily direct many prayers) wyll informe yow to make that use, that as of evyll manners good lawes growe, so owt of disobedience and boldnes yow wyll take occasion to show mercy and tendernes' (Simpson *Prose* 117). In a sense God is here asked to intercede with Ann's father on the writer's behalf whereas, in other letters, it was the socially inferior person whom the writer approached in order to promote him to some higher personage. In Donne's marriage letters, God and addressee are interlinked so tightly that they almost coincide. There are good reasons for this strategy, since it not only flatters the addressees but also suggests that, in order to maintain their divine identities, they ought to imitate God's own pattern: 'The offence which was to God in this matter, his mercy hath assurd my conscience is pardoned' (Simpson *Prose* 119). Egerton, who was so like God in exercising justice, should follow him also in pardoning the writer, who hopes (less for his addressee's sake than for his own) that 'Allmighty God dwell ever in your Lordships hart, and fill yt with good desires, and graunt them' (Simpson *Prose* 121). Nevertheless, Egerton remained firm on the dismissal of his secretary, and it likewise took many years until Sir George More relented towards his son-in-law. As intricate and devoutly religious these epistolary performances undoubtedly are – in this case, no saying nor playing worked to achieve the desired outcome, as these two senior men may have been less flattered than offended at finding their identities convoluted with that of God himself.

In a letter 'To Sir Robert Ker' from 1623, the link between letter and religious homily returns once more:

> Sir, I took up this paper to write a Letter; but my imaginations were full of a Sermon before, for I write but a few hours before I am to Preach, and so instead of a Letter I send you a Homily. Let it have thus much of a Letter, That I am confident in your love, and deliver my self over to your service. And thus much of a Homily, That you and I shall accompanie one another to the possession of Heaven, in the same way wherein God put us at first. (Simpson *Prose* 155–6)

Letter and homily are presented as two genres that cohabitate peacefully as both are concerned with securing the communion of writer and addressee, either in this world or the next. The next world is relevant not only as it concerns one's reunion with one's friends but even more so with regard to one's reconciliation with God. The latter is central to a series of homilies Donne likewise composed in 1623: *Devotions Upon Emergent Occasions*. Since these were written with the intention of being published, they should not be read in the same way as Donne's letters – although, in a letter 'To Sir Edward Herbert', immediately after Donne's ordination, the writer protests that 'as I was ever, by my devotion, and your acceptance, your humble servant, so I ame become, by this addition, capable of the dignity, of beeinge Your very humble chapleyn J. DONNE' (Simpson *Prose* 146). Let us now turn to the *Devotions* that were written by the ordained priest and the public man, and see what parallels exist between the 'devotion' of a 'servant' and that of a 'chapleyn'.

Notes

1 Donne's motives for taking orders are much disputed: cf. Gosse, 1899: 161; Bald, 1970: 301; Stubbs, 2007: 267; 301–2.
2 For the concrete social functions of poetry, cf. Marotti, 1995: 2–3; Scarry, 1988a: 73.
3 A similar merging of identities through poetry is at stake in Donne's verse letter 'The Storme. To Mr. *Christopher Brooke*', which begins 'Thou which art I, ('tis nothing to be soe) / Thou which art still thy selfe, by these [lines] shalt know / Part of our passage' (ll. 1–3).
4 As regards eighteenth-century letters as featured in Richardson's *Pamela*, '[t]he physicality of the letter might stand for the body of the letter-writer in quasi-sexual textual encounters' (Earle, 1999a: 6). Moreover, much attention was paid to a letter's material appearance: 'The amount of unfilled space on a page, for example, well might imply respect in an era in which most paper was imported and expensive' (Steen, 2001: 66).
5 For the notion of books as friends, cf. Korhonen, 2006: 49, 269.
6 Sharing another's sickness is central also to Donne's *Devotions*.

5

(Inter)Personal performances – *Devotions*

therefore never send to know for whom the *bell* tolls; It tolls for *thee*.
(*Devotions* 87)

This chapter centres on *Devotions Upon Emergent Occasions*, a work originating from an illness during which Donne considered himself on the verge of death, and one of the few writings he published. There are important points of contact between epistolary and devotional modes: as the post-Reformation period witnessed shifts in devotional practices and a new interest in the self, these changes had consequences for early modern epistolary styles (Henderson, 2002: 27, 35; cf. Schneider, 2005: 37; How, 2003: 200). Moreover, just as most letter writers would have observed epistolary conventions at the same time as they adapted them for their individual purpose, so is the speaker of Donne's *Devotions* both exemplary and individualised (cf. Burke, 1997: 23). Just as a religion of letters and friendship is cultivated by continued correspondence, so do regular prayer and devotion prevent one from neglecting one's relationship to God. If letter writing 'is a sacrifice, which though friends need not, friendship doth' (*Letters* 116), prayer and devotion likewise are 'a sacrifice, which though God needs not, faith doth'. Relations of friendship and devotion may already be established – but both require careful attention. Moreover, the entanglements between the speaker's physical and spiritual sickness in *Devotions* (cf. Targoff, 2008: 130–53) have their counterpart in the (im)material contiguities of Donne's letters.

The *Devotions* focus primarily on the speaker's communication and communion with God. One of Donne's letters, however, desires that, in heaven, 'I hope you and all yours shall meet

Your poor friend, and affectionate servant J. Donne' (*Letters* 186) – a prospect which includes the addressee's and the writer's (comm)union with God and with each other. The most famous passage of *Devotions* refers less to the individual's union with God than to the interrelatedness of all people: 'No Man is an *Iland*, intire of it selfe [. . .] therefore never send to know for whom the *bell* tolls; It tolls for *thee*' (*Devotions* 87). As in Donne's letters, there is encouragement to identify, coincide and commune with him whom the tolling bell signifies instead of focusing but on oneself: 'I', after all, 'is the core of Island' (Beer, 1997: 43).

The *Devotions* were written as a religiously instructive piece of writing, yet their generating gesture is that of addressing God. In doing so, they rehearse practices of communication and communion similar to those of Donne's letters, one of which, by characterising itself as 'meditation[]' (*Letters* 78), in turn exhibits its proximity to devotional writing. Communication and communion, or *conversatio* and *conversio* (cf. Questier, 1996), are fundamental both to Donne's theology and his understanding of relationships between human beings. The sequence of each devotion's three parts – meditation, expostulation and prayer – indicates a gradual shift from communication towards communion, a communion closely associated with the figure of Christ. The 'Holy Communion' thus effected is far from stable and often comes across as highly ambiguous. In this life, no lasting communion with the divine can ever be achieved.[1] The *Devotions* may be read as so many attempts at communion, and encouragements to their readers to continuously repeat these efforts for life.

Another point Donne's *Devotions* share with his letters is that each of these prose writings has a poetic counterpart. His letters in verse have been analysed more thoroughly than his prose letters, but little has been said on the different implications of poetic and prose epistolary writing. Nor has much attention been paid to the generic differences between Donne's 'Holy Sonnets' and his *Devotions*, although these works' relatedness to one another has been recognised (cf. Rollin, 1994). Evidence of Donne's own attitude towards the merits of verse over prose and vice versa can be found in his prose letters, and I shall conclude this chapter with a tentative analysis of his employment of verse as opposed to prose.

The *Devotions'* interest in becoming the other

The fifth meditation of *Devotions* begins with the claim that 'As Sicknesse is the greatest misery, so the greatest misery of sicknes is *solitude*' (*Devotions* 24). Many of Donne's letters do not only complain of but even owe their very existence to the writer's solitude. No matter how sick he was, Donne would continue to write letters to alleviate his loneliness, informing his addressees on the progress of his various illnesses. Not even God himself, the above passage continues, likes to be without company, 'as there is a plurality of persons in *God*, though there bee but one *God*', and in the house of God, there are *'many mansions'* (*Devotions* 25). The society which God allowed himself he also granted to humankind: He 'came not so neer seeing a *defect* in any of his works, as when he saw that it was not good, for man to bee *alone*, therefore *hee made him a helper*; and one that should helpe him so, as to increase the *number*, and give him *her owne*, and *more societie'* (*Devotions* 25). Hence propagating marriage and reproduction as the fulfilment of the divine purpose, the speaker condemns the assumption that 'the way to the *Communion of Saints*, should be by such a *solitude*, as excludes all doing of good here' as a *'disease* of the *mind'* (*Devotions* 26) and promotes a concept of reformed, rather than Catholic celibate priesthood. In the expostulation, the focus shifts towards a more direct addressing of God: 'I am not able to passe this agony alone; not alone without *thee*; Thou art thy spirit; not alone without *thine*; spirituall and temporall *Phisicians*, are *thine*; not alone without *mine*; Thos whom the bands of *blood*, or *friendship*, hath made *mine*, are *mine*; And if *thou*, or *thine*, or *mine*, abandon me, I am *alone*; and wo unto me if I bee alone' (*Devotions* 27). These parallelisms indicate that it is not only *'thine'* that are coextensive with *'thee'*, i.e. God, but also *'mine'*. Despite the hierarchy between God, his servants (physicians) and the patient's family and friends, the absence of either entails the 'wo' of solitude the speaker fears.

Meditations 16 to 18 are most explicit in their analysis of how, in the solitude of sickness, the speaker is related to his fellow human beings. The tolling bells from the nearby steeple announce the burial of men and women from his near environment – both biblically and literally his neighbours. In recognition of God's commandment to love one's fellow human beings as oneself, the speaker interprets the tolling bells as an invitation to identify with his unknown neighbours: 'And when these *Bells* tell me, that now one, and now another is buried, must not I acknowledge, that they have the *correction* due to me, and paid the *debt* that I owe?' (*Devotions* 82). Since one would love to identify with people who are better off than oneself, one should embrace the example of this recently deceased neighbour with the same alacrity: 'We scarce heare of any man *preferred*, but wee thinke of our selves, that wee might very well have beene that *Man*; Why might not I have beene that *Man*, that is carried to his *grave* now?' (*Devotions* 82). The speaker then makes it seem as if that neighbour's death constitutes a 'preferment' rather than something to be eschewed, 'so when these hourely *Bells* tell me of so many *funerals* of men like me, it presents, if not a *desire* that it may, yet a *comfort* whensoever mine shall come' (*Devotions* 83). One's readiness to embrace death should come altogether voluntarily.

Since these death bells make the speaker positively aware of his own mortality, he dismisses all contemporary discussions of the potentially Papist '*Ceremony* of *Bells* at *funerals*' (*Devotions* 83) as irrelevant (cf. Levy-Navarro, 2003; Doerksen, 2004: 165; Strier, 1996: 107). The speaker's devout reaction implicitly confirms the bells' usefulness, for 'We cannot, wee cannot, O my *God*, take in too many *helps* for religious *duties*' (*Devotions* 84). Earlier on, the speaker valued the bells even as highly as the sermon: 'And this continuing of ringing after his *entring*, is to bring him to mee in the *application*. Where I lie, I could heare the *Psalme*, and did joine with the *Congregation* in it; but I could not heare the *Sermon*, and these latter *bells* are a *repetition Sermon* to mee' (*Devotions* 84). The idea of application, of identification with, of taking to oneself an other is the distinct characteristic of both the sermon and the tolling bells: 'I make account that I heare this dead brother of ours, who is now carried out to his *burial*, to speake to mee, and to *preach* my *funeral Sermon*, in the voice of these *Bells*' (*Devotions* 85).

The tolling bells are the only topic addressed over no fewer than three devotions. Meditation 17 offers an alternative interpretation of the bells, no less relevant for the speaker: 'perchance I may thinke my selfe so much better than I am, as that they who are about mee, and see my state, may have caused it to toll for mee, and I know not that' (*Devotions* 86). But even if the bells were not 'his' in this literal sense, it rests that '[t]he *Church* is *Catholike*, *universall*, so are all her *Actions*; *All* that she does, belongs to *all'* (*Devotions* 86). Just as each congregation member has to accept and apply each sermon to himself or herself in order for it to be efficacious, so 'The *Bell* doth toll for him that *thinkes* it doth' (*Devotions* 86). This concept is at the heart also of Donne's most-quoted words (cf. D. N. Smith, 1973: 5): 'No Man is an *Iland*, intire of it selfe; every man is a peece of the *Continent*, a part of the *maine*; if a *Clod* bee washed away by the *Sea*, *Europe* is the lesse, as well as if a *Promontorie* were, as well as if a *Mannor* of thy *friends*, or of thine owne were; Any Mans *death* diminishes *me*, because I am involved in *Mankinde*; And therefore never send to know for whom the *bell* tolls; It tolls for *thee'* (*Devotions* 87).[2]

Usually, one would expect that the connectedness of all people should make one particularly prone to inquire whose manor or ground has been diminished by the sea. Yet this passage advises against any inquiries whatsoever as the supposedly logical consequence of one's involvement in humankind: 'therefore never send to know for whom the *bell* tolls'. Any such communication would depend on a number of intermediaries. Since the person for whom the bells toll is dead, no first-hand answer can be obtained. Secondly, the speaker of the *Devotions* is bound to his bed and hence himself unable to contact the deceased's closest kin. All he can do is to 'send' a servant or friend to go and find out for whom the bell tolls – and who knows how many intermediaries that messenger will have to ask before receiving the desired answer, and how reliable his informers may be. Instead of venturing upon such a highly mediated communicational project, it is best not to communicate at all but to identify, to come together, to commune immediately with him for whom the bell tolls: 'It tolls for *thee'*. The term communion is appropriate here. Presumably, final communion with God and Christ is what the deceased is undergoing at this moment. In this sense, the 'brotherhood of men is communion in Christ' (Webber 1968, 13).[3]

As in the previous devotion, the speaker again encourages identification with the deceased: '*affliction* is a *treasure*, and scarce any Man hath *enough* of it. No Man hath *affliction* enough, that is not matured, and ripened by it, and made fit for *God* by that *affliction*' (*Devotions* 87). The point is to identify with the deceased not merely for the sake of general human sympathy and kindness but in order to make oneself more agreeable to God Himself, something doubtless in each person's own interest. This aspect is taken up again when the speaker envisions Biblical characters speaking to him through the ringing of the bells: 'I heare thy *Moses* telling mee, and all within the *compasse* of this *sound, This is the blessing wherewith I blesse you before my death*; This, that before your death, you would consider your owne in mine' (*Devotions* 88). So the speaker does in the prayer where he thanks God for the hint 'that this *bell* which *tolls* for another, before it come to *ring out*, may take in me too. As *death is the wages of sinne*, it is *due* to mee; As death is *the end of sicknesse*, it belongs to *mee*; And though so disobedient a *servant* as I, may be afraid to *die*, yet to so mercifull a *Master* as thou, I cannot be afraid to *come*' (*Devotions* 89). The speaker claims the death of the person who has just passed away. This recognition serves as a backdrop to the final lines of this prayer in which the speaker pleads with God in favour of the individual for whom the bells toll: 'In his behalfe, and in his name, heare thy *Sonne* crying to thee, *My God, my God, Why hast thou forsaken me*? and forsake him not; but with thy *left hand* lay his *body* in the *grave*, (if that bee thy *determination* upon him) and with thy *right hand* receive his *soule* into thy *Kingdome*, and unite *him & us* in one *Communion of Saints*. Amen' (*Devotions* 90). Since, a few lines earlier, the speaker had appropriated the death of his neighbour to himself, this passage expresses a recommendation not only of the deceased's cause but of the speaker's own interest that God may equate their lots through redemption.

The union of the speaker's course with that of the person commemorated by the bells is continued in the superscription of Devotion 18: 'At inde, Mortuus es, sonitu celeri, pulsuque agitato. *The bell rings out, and tells me in him, that I am dead*' (*Devotions* 91). The meditation then speculates on the possible whereabouts of the deceased. The speaker admits that he is not competent in that respect: not knowing who he was, 'I saw not his *way*, nor his *end*, nor can aske them, who did, thereby to *conclude*, or *argue*, whither he is *gone*' (*Devotions* 290). Communication, if it could at all take place, would be mediated — but the speaker soon recognises an authority to judge within himself: 'But yet I have one nearer mee than all these, mine owne *Charity*; I aske that; & that tels me, *He is gone to everlasting rest*, and *joy*, and *glory*: I owe him a good *opinion*; it is but *thankfull charity* in mee, because I received *benefit* and *instruction* from him when his *Bell* told' (*Devotions* 92). The expression 'mine owne charity' is noteworthy: it recalls how closely the speaker identifies with the deceased's situation, as witnessed by the devotion's superscription. The charity which he protests to on behalf of the deceased is but a *'thankfull charity in mee'* (my emphasis on 'mee'): in *'charitably'* believing that the deceased's soul has gone to heaven, the speaker exercises that same benevolence in his own favour (cf. Targoff, 2008: 148; D. N. Smith, 1973: 11). By wishing someone else well, he is praying also for himself – a common strategy also of Donne's letters.

In the expostulation, the speaker debates funeral rites and asks God: 'why wouldest thou not suffer those, that serve thee in *holy services*, to doe any *office* about the *dead*, nor *assist* at their *funeral*?' (*Devotions* 93). After all, with the help of the tolling bells, 'I, by the meditation of *his death*, produce a better *life* in my selfe' (*Devotions* 94). The speaker wonders whether 'the neglecting of this *sound* ministred to mee in this *mans death'* (*Devotions* 95) does not constitute a greater sin than its active application. Whatever service is done to the dead may, by way of identification, serve those still living – and the profit to be drawn from the dead is only one instance of a general principle articulated in an earlier meditation: 'and so, when we seeme to begin with others, in such assistances, indeed wee doe beginne with our selves, and wee our selves are principally in our contemplation; and so all these officious, and mutuall assistances, are but *complements* towards others, and our true end is *our selves*' (*Devotions* 57). As the writer of the letter *'To all my friends: Sir* H. Goodere' recognises, it is part of the human condition to profit from and depend on each others' examples: 'All these bands I willingly receive, for no man is lesse of himself than I: nor any man enough of himself. To be so, is all one with omnipotence' (*Letters* 44).[4] It may even be profitable to depend on the example of another. In the prayer of Devotion 18, the speaker profusely thanks God for 'the *ringing* of this *bell'* (*Devotions* 95), since it encourages him to hope that, as the deceased soul's fate is presumably concomitant with that of Christ (Johnson, 1999: 60), '*wee* with *it*, may soone enjoy the full *consummation* of all, in *body* and *soule'* (*Devotions* 96). Clearly, the speaker has come some way from his earlier claim that, since 'No Man is an *Iland* [. . .] [a]ny mans *death* diminishes *me'* (*Devotions* 87).

The prayer to Devotion 18 concludes the bell sequence on the tolling bells and makes it seem as if, in granting redemption and glorification to both the deceased and the speaker, God was doing a favour also to his son Jesus Christ, and thus, himself: 'I humbly beg at thy hand, O our most mercifull *God*, for thy Sonne *Christ Jesus sake*: That that blessed *Sonne* of thine, may have the *consummation* of his *dignitie*, by entring into his *last office*, the office of a *Judge*, and may have *societie* of humane *bodies* in *heaven*, as well as hee hath had ever of *soules*' (*Devotions* 96, cf. also *Essays* 100). The strategy of fashioning a favour which the speaker himself hopes for as an advantage on the giver's part is again reminiscent of Donne's letters. Moreover, the speaker implicitly asserts that he and God/Christ are so closely associated with each other, already in such a state of communion, that the speaker's good cannot but be in God's or Christ's interest, too, and hence their 'common' good. Not only humanity, but Christ, too, relies on being both with souls and bodies, so that our relationship to God is based on mutual dependency. In conclusion, as the speaker points out to God, in saving us, 'thou mayest receive *delight* from them, and they *glorie* from thee, for evermore. *Amen*' (*Devotions* 97).

The speaker's communion with him for whom the bell tolls is in no way disinterested. If the deceased is right there and then entering into communion with God, this places him or her in a situation which the speaker would clearly like to share. As my reading of the speaker's advice 'never send to know for whom the *bell* tolls; it tolls for *thee*' (*Devotions* 87) has shown, the *Devotions* tend to privilege communion, a becoming as one, over 'mere' communication. The speaker is quite aware that he will have to await his death in order to experience ultimate communion with the Lord and that any acts of communion effected in this life are but vicarious. Yet a development from communication towards communion is built into the structure of each individual devotion as it consists of the three parts of meditation, expostulation, and prayer.

From communication towards communion

Each of Donne's *Devotions* takes its beginning from the speaker's meditation upon himself or the general human condition. The expostulation focuses on the speaker's relationship to God – through communication, he experiments with the position he holds towards him. Finally, in the concluding prayer, the speaker has become so intimate with God that, especially towards the end, the two of them seem no longer to communicate but to commune, to come together, as one.[5] As it moves from meditation towards prayer, each devotion increases in performativity – not '[a]lthough', but because 'the Expostulations and the Prayers [. . .] depend upon an audience' (Conti, 2003: 152; Pfister, 2001: 302).

What it means to communicate, is, of course, not all that clearly distinguished from communion – and was even less so in Donne's time. For 'communicate, v.', the OED gives the general explanation 'to make common to many, share, impart, divide', and the explanation for 'commune, v.' is 'to make common, share'. Although these two interpretations are almost equivalent, it is significant that 'communicate, v.' seems to have a more public character than 'commune, v.'. Whereas 'communicate, v.', in a sense now obsolete, but common from the late sixteenth to the eighteenth century, was equivalent to 'To impart (as a share, portion, or specimen); to give, bestow (a material thing)', such acts of concrete and material transmission do not seem to have been associated with 'commune, v.'. In contrast with 'communicate, v.', 'commune, v.', during the sixteenth century, but also today may for example mean 'To hold intimate (chiefly mental or spiritual) intercourse (*with*)', with the limitation that this sense now applies only to the field of the 'literary, devotional and poetic'. The definitions given for the respective nouns, 'communication' and 'communion', likewise reflect these subtle differences. All the said verbs and nouns, however, suggest mutuality. 'Communion' is defined as 'mutual intercourse', and one sense of 'communication', now obsolete, is '[c]ommon participation'. From the late seventeenth century onwards, the idea of two entities becoming one is still present in 'communicate, v.' whenever reference is made to 'vessels, spaces, rooms, etc.', which 'open into each other by a common channel or aperture whereby the whole becomes as one space'. What the two terms further share, of course, is their connectedness to the reception of the Eucharist, the Holy Communion.

Precisely because in Donne's time 'communicate, v.' and 'commune, v.' were used almost interchangeably, we may assume that communication, whether epistolary or devotional, could be both material and spiritual. Depending on the genre or individual text, a piece of writing functions as an actual exchange between two more or less clearly demarcated entities, but also as a means of effecting a relationship between speaker and addressee that is better characterised as a coming together, a coincidence and becoming as one of the two 'communicants'. In acknowledgement of the slightly different but largely overlapping meanings of 'commune, *v.*' and 'communicate, *v.*', I shall use the former term wherever the spiritual intimacy and comm-union of speaker and addressee are foregrounded and the latter wherever the two entities involved remain separate from one another. Let us now turn to the various dimensions in which Donne's *Devotions* commu(nicat)e.

Their full title runs as follows:

DEVOTIONS
UPON
Emergent Occasions, and severall
steps in my Sicknes:
DIGESTED INTO
1. MEDITATIONS *upon our Humane Condition.*
2. EXPOSTULATIONS, *and Debatements with God.*
3. PRAYERS, *upon the severall Occasions, to him.*

After a consideration of *'our Humane Condition'*, each devotion opens up towards God by entering into *'Debatements'* with him, during which speaker and addressee still remain separate from one another – the Expostulations are those passages where the two are least of one mind. The third part diminishes that distance between speaker and addressee, aiming to effect their coming together. This can be achieved by ridding the speaker of himself, or, more generally, his human condition, the principal subject of each devotion's first section. In the prayer concluding Devotion 7, the speaker asks God to endow his corrections with 'thy two qualities, those two operations, that as they *scourge* us, they may scourge us into the way to thee: that when thy have shewed us, that we are nothing in our selves, they may also shew us, that thou art all things unto us' (*Devotions* 40). Before one can fully grasp God's absolute significance for oneself, it is vital to internalise one's human insignificance. This quotation reflects the structure of each individual devotion, suggesting that each potential recognition of God as 'all things unto us' that amounts to making us one with God must be preceded by human acknowledgement of utter inadequacy and nothingness normally treated in the meditation. Only then can that comm(union) with God and Christ be effected, which the speaker, at the end of this devotion's prayer, looks forward to as the prospect 'to die in *thee*, and by that death, to bee united to him, who died for me' (*Devotions* 40). Each devotion takes its cue from the patient's inner turmoil and concludes with a comparative reassurance on the speaker's part (cf. Targoff, 2008: 131; Partridge, 1978: 208; Webber, 1963: 184; Doerksen, 2004: 148). Herein they differ strikingly from Donne's 'Holy Sonnets' whose spiritual unrest is hardly ever stilled.

Meditating on (the end of all) human communication

In contemplating *'our Humane Condition'*, many meditations address the enormous gap between our superiority over the rest of the creation and our mortal nothingness. Walking upright, we are privileged over all other beings: '*Man* in his naturall forme, is carried to the con-contemplation [*sic*!] of that place, which is his *home*, *Heaven*' (*Devotions* 15). But his elevated position is always endangered: 'A fever can fillip him downe, a fever can depose him' (*Devotions* 15). The worst consequence of such illness is not the pain attendant upon it but the patient's inability to communicate any more, as even 'that hande that signed Pardons, is too weake to begge his owne, if hee might have it for lifting up that hand' (*Devotions* 15). Sickness may be worse even than death, for '[i]n the *Grave* I may speak thorough the stones, in the voice of my friends, and in the accents of those wordes, which their love may afford my memory; Here I am mine owne *Ghost*, and rather affright my beholders, then instruct them' (*Devotions* 15). Even before death, no communication with other human beings is possible as the speaker 'must practise [his] lying in the *grave*, by lying still' (*Devotions* 16). Other meditations likewise expound on humanity's greatness: extolling humankind as much more than a world, the speaker moves on 'to consider the immensitie of the creatures this [human] world produces; our *creatures* are our *thoughts*, *creatures* that are borne *Gyants*: that reach from *East* to *West*, from *earth* to *Heaven*, that doe not onely bestride all the *Sea*, and *Land*, but span the *Sunn* and *Firmament* at once' (*Devotions* 20). Again, humanity is elevated only to be destroyed utterly at the end of the same meditation: 'Call back therefore thy Meditations again, and bring it downe; [...] whats become of [man's] soaring thoughts, his compassing thoughts, when himselfe brings himselfe to the ignorance, to the thoughtlesnesse of the *Grave*?' (*Devotions* 20–1). Mortality puts an end to the possibility of communicating with the world through one's thoughts, let alone communicating these same thoughts to other human beings.

Expostulating to communicate

Despite the transience of human glory and communication, the speaker is never too sick to continue communicating with God himself – as he does predominantly in the expostulations. Nor does he accept that, bound to his sick bed, he shall no longer be able to converse with other human beings, not even to communicate, as preacher and priest, God to his congregation. He challenges God: 'Why callest thou me from my calling? *In the grave no man shall praise thee*; In the doore of the grave, this sicke bed, no Man shal heare mee praise thee' (*Devotions* 17). The speaker is not content to communicate but with God, for '[t]hou hast not opened my lips, that my mouth might shew *thee* thy praise, but that my mouth might shew *foorth* they praise' (*Devotions* 17). Earlier on, the speaker had already accused God of excluding him from inter-human communication by striking him with sickness: 'Thy first breath breathed a *Soule* into mee, and shall thy breath blow it out? Thy breath in the *Congregation*, thy *Word* in the *Church*, breathes *communion*, and *consolation* here, and *consummation* hereafter; shall thy breath in this Chamber breathe *dissolution*, and *destruction*, *divorce*, and *separation*?' (*Devotions* 13). God's breath communicates itself through his minister's mediation – but the '*communion*' which the preacher was able to create and share with the congregation is ruptured by the speaker's confinement to his sick-chamber.

Much as the speaker complains that his sickness separates him from God, the majority of Donne's *Devotions* constitute 'the *fruit* of a Christian's spiritual quest inspired by a struggle with a dangerous illness' (Raspa in *Devotions*, 1975: xxi, my emphasis). Body and soul are here no less closely interlinked than the material and immaterial dimensions of Donne's letters. Generally, the speaker conceives of his illness as God's attempt to communicate with him (cf. Goldberg, 1971: 508). In order to participate in this divine communication, the speaker has to make an effort. Whereas in the meditations the speaker focuses upon himself and the human condition, he now responds to God's initiative of making him sick by his endeavours to align his position typologically with that of various Biblical situations (cf. Raspa in *Devotions*, 1975: xxxvi). God engages in communication with human beings: 'My *God*, my *God*, Thou art a *direct God*, may I not say, a *literall God*, a *God* that wouldest bee understood *literally*, and according to the *plaine sense* of all that thou saiest? But thou art also (*Lord* I intend it to thy *glory*, and let no *prophane mis-interpreter* abuse it to thy *diminution*) thou art a *figurative*, a *metaphoricall God* too' (*Devotions* 99); and his actions, such as striking the speaker with illness, are also thus: 'The *stile* of thy *works*, the *phrase* of thine *Actions*, is *Metaphoricall*' (*Devotions* 100).

Even some minor details of his illness may be read typologically: 'in which manner I am bold to call the comfort which I receive now in this sicknesse, in the *indication* of the *concoction* and *maturity* thereof, in certaine *clouds*, and *residences*, which the *Physitians* observe, a discovering of *land* from *Sea*, after a long, and tempestuous *voyage*' (*Devotions* 100). There is some daring in associating one's clouded urine with the promise of rain indicated by the clouds the prophet Elijah made people see 'in a time of *desperate drought*' (*Devotions* 103, cf. Parr, 2007: 82). Such boldness is typical of the speaker's self-confident remarks as he communicates with God during the expostulations (cf. Janel Mueller, 1968: 15). The expostulations insist on their right to speak with God. The speaker protests: 'But I am more then *dust* & *ashes*; I am my best part, I am my *soule*. And being so, the *breath* of *God*, I may breath back these pious *expostulations* to my *God*' (*Devotions* 8). In relation to God, all people are alike in their inferiority, 'therefore how little soever I bee, as *God calls things that are not, as though they were*, I, who am as though I were not, may call upon *God*' (*Devotions* 12). Some self-confidence grows even from nothingness, and as the speaker elaborates in another expostulation, never should fear dissuade us from praying to God: 'I must then *speak* to thee, at all times, but when must I *feare* thee? At all times to' (*Devotions* 30). All communications with God should be accompanied by reverent fear, yet this humility does not always distinguish the expostulations: 'I have not the *righteousnesse* of *Job*, but I have the desire of *Job, I would speake to the Almighty, and I would reason with God*' (*Devotions* 21, cf. *Essays* 96). His insistence on reasoning with God tempts the speaker into self-aggrandisement, when he, however playfully and ironically, articulates a threat towards the Lord himself: 'My *God*, my *God*, my *God*, thou mightie *Father*, who hast beene my *Physitian*; Thou glorious *Sonne*, who hast beene my *physicke*; Thou blessed *Spirit*, who hast *prepared* and *applied* all to mee, shall *I alone* bee able to overthrow the worke of *all you*, and *relapse* into those *spirituall sicknesses*, from which your infinite *mercies* have withdrawne me?' (*Devotions* 122–3).

Praying (for) communion

Only in the concluding prayers 'assent becomes real, and the devotee addresses God in a spirit of love, humility, and acceptance, rather than in a spirit of rational inquiry' (Andreasen, 1964–65: 212). Whereas in the meditations the speaker communed but with his 'own heart' (cf. Psalms 4.4; 77.6), the prayers document the change of perspective he has undergone in the course of the particular devotion: 'O most gracious *God*, who [. . .] clothd me with thy selfe, by stripping me of my selfe, and by dulling my bodily senses, to the meats, and eases of this world, hast whet, and sharpned my spiritual senses, to the apprehension of thee' (*Devotions* 13–14). Thus does the prayer of the second devotion elevate God – while the meditation had mourned the 'Miserable distribution of *Mankind*' and then moved on to expostulate with God about why his anger had manifested itself with such sudden and overwhelming might.

The figure of Christ enables the speaker's participation in God's saving grace, allowing him a communion with the Highest rather than with his own human heart. Asking the Lord to prevent him from sinning again, the speaker begs God to do so 'for his sake, who knows our naturall infirmities, for he had them; and knows the weight of our sins, for he paid a deare price for them, thy *Sonne, our Saviour, Chr: Jesus, Amen*' (*Devotions* 10). Just as the intimate communion of God and Christ had not been severed by that great separator sin, so does the speaker hope that the favour in which Christ stands with God translates itself to him. In another prayer, God is asked to 'transferre my sinnes, with which thou art so displeased, upon him, with whome thou art so well pleased,

spiritual bread so as to make himself eternally one with Christ.
(A. J. Smith, 1991: 148)

Johnson even claims that, for Donne, the concern with the real presence had shifted from Christ's presence in bread and wine to the saviour's presence in the communicant himself: 'It is the crucified Christ that is reborn in those who receive the bread and wine' (Johnson 1999, 142; DiPasquale, 1999: 6, McNees, 1987: 99). This view reflects the early modern insight that you are what, or rather, who you eat: according to Galenic physiology, each person was 'to conceive all acts of ingestion and excretion as very literal acts of self-fashioning' (Schoenfeldt, 1997b: 243). In promising that '[h]e that eateth my flesh, and drinketh my blood, abideth in me and I in him', Thomas à Kempis aligns the Eucharist with an *imitatio Christi* (Kempis, 1934: 111), and the larger part of his treatise *Imitation of Christ* constitutes a manual on how the body of Christ should be received by communicants. 'For Donne, Real Presence results from man's recognition of reciprocity with Christ through suffering' (McNees, 1987: 94) – and such is the presence of Christ wherever Donne's speakers meditatively engage in imitations of Christ.

Young insists on Donne's preoccupation 'with the Catholic teaching regarding the real presence of Christ's body and blood' (Young, 2000: 95), yet such assignations appear problematic. Issues of Eucharistic presence and representation remained a bone of contention for virtually all Christians. Young himself precisely warns against an overemphasis of doctrinal difference (Young, 2000: 219) – a charge he raises, however, only against Protestant readings of Donne. Whenever a critic takes an unambiguous stance on the author's Roman Catholic affiliations, someone else will come up with good arguments for Donne's staunchly reformed convictions: Conti, for example, reads the *Devotions* as a warning against and confession of the dangers of idolatry (Conti, 2003; Salenius, 2001; Abrahamson, 1983). Simpson's explanation, according to which Donne denies transubstantiation, yet appreciates the real presence of Christ in the Eucharist (Simpson, 1948: 104–5), still appears most convincing. Such a view corresponds to the Thirty-Nine Articles, where the Lord's Supper is assumed to be merely 'the *sign* or sacrament of so great a thing [the body and blood of Christ]' only when received by the wicked

– for faithful Christians, by contrast, 'the bread which we break is a partaking of the body of Christ; and likewise the cup of blessing is a partaking of the blood of Christ' (Cressy/Ferrell, 1996: 67, my emphasis).

In the celebration of the Eucharist, signifier and signified are meant to coincide. In that their speaker is striving to find equivalents for his external situation in his inner state (cf. Webber, 1968: 34), the *Devotions* as a whole function as a sacrament. A lie, by contrast, which occurs wherever signifier and signified are deliberately dissociated from one another, constitutes the worst sin a person is capable of. It originates directly from the serpent's interference with humanity: 'For the first, the hiding of our sins from other men, hee hath induc'd that, which was his *off-spring* from the beginning, *A lye*' (*Devotions* 53). As long as one is busy concealing one's sins, one is still aware of one's trespasses and the gap between innocent appearance and rotten core, but there may be instances where this awareness is lost: 'The *bodie*, the *sinne*, is the *Serpents*, and the *garment* that covers it, *the lye*, is his too. [. . .] but the hiding of sinne from our selves, is *Hee himselfe*' (*Devotions* 53). Once our lies deceive even ourselves, the serpent's blood has entered our veins – where the Eucharist would allow only Christ's blood to flow. Having eaten the apple, man is suffering from the after-effects of an inverted communion: just as, after Holy Communion, celebrants do not only have Christ 'in their blood' but partly even have become the Son of God, so we, once we no longer recognise our own lies, 'are become *devils* to our selves, and we have not only a *Serpent* in our bosome, but we our selves, are to our selves that *Serpent*' (*Devotions* 53).

Such a state is beyond redemption, since the only remedy for our sins, to have God 'know them by my *Confession*' (*Devotions* 54), is blocked. By confession, we declare our sins, hence reinstating the balance of signifier, that is external utterance, and signified, our internal disposition – but this presupposes we be aware of any disequilibrium beforehand. Keeping what is internal in balance with what is external is one of the major premises of early modern humoral theory. The *Devotions* engage in making sense of the speaker's sickness by putting it into relation with his inner, spiritual state, through an identification with the body of Christ (Kuchar, 2001: 17). However, there are passages in the *Devotions* where the humoral model is threatened by a later, more mechanistic concept, which confronts the speaker with 'a radically alienated, solipsistic experience of self that is often represented through the fragmented or dismembered body' (Kuchar, 2001: 19). Once one fails to recognise one's own lies, one's identity is fragmented beyond redemption, whereas, as long as one is still aware of the (humoral) disequilibrium caused through lying, confession still offers to restore the balance. The *Devotions*' entanglement of the speaker's health with his spiritual state explains why he keeps 'envisioning confession as a cure for *physical* sickness' (Conti, 2003: 158).

No less crucial here is the metaphor of *'bodie'* and *'garment'*. Although we cannot choose or change our body, we make decisions with regard to the garments we wear: it is up to us if we want to lie and dress up in clothes more innocent than our bodies are in fact worthy of. Hence the powers of disguise, which, though to some extent permissible in the context of a carnivalistic feast or in the theatre, are intrinsically bound up with lying and intrigue in most other settings (Matt, 2008: 85). According to early modern sumptuary laws, status determined what clothes one was supposed to wear. Trusting in 'a congruence between the inner and the outer man' (Jagodzinski, 1999: 4), one would have been judged by external appearance – so that, with time, one was tempted to believe oneself that these clothes really fitted and forget about the lie which initiated the choice of a falsely impeccable or elegant outfit.

Nakedness precedes the creation of an appearance that belies what is inside: *'Adam was afrayde, because hee was naked.* They who have put off *thee,* are a prey to all' (*Devotions* 32). Before the Fall, Adam had nothing to hide and was unashamed of his nakedness. Eating the forbidden fruit, Adam and Eve become aware of their nudeness: 'And the eyes of them both were opened, and they knew that they were naked; and they sewed fig leaves together, and made themselves aprons' (Gen. 3.7). Clothes become necessary only once one finds that there is something to hide. As soon as Adam and Eve put off God, they need to conceal their nakedness, just as they hide themselves from God (Gen. 3.8). The Biblical account of the genesis of clothes suggests that no garment can ever be as good as nakedness. Clothes cannot but hide, belie and dissemble what is underneath. Humanity's Fall manifests itself in the recognition of its nakedness and the ensuing discomfort (cf.

Matt, 2008: 82). Confession amounts to making oneself naked again before God, of revealing one's sinful parts. Having thus put off one's sins, one is ready to put on Christ and be as naked as he had been on the Cross. Achieving such correspondence with Christ, in body and passion, a nakedness no longer ashamed of itself, is what each Christian must aspire to. Adam's and Christ's nakedness correspond to one another typologically – but Christ constitutes that which Adam – common man – is but meant to be, the signified with whom Adam, the signifier, ought to make it his life-long effort to coincide (cf. Clements, 1990: 13; Altizer, 1973: 100).

A letter of Donne's *'To Sir* H. R.' promotes tolerance of all religious denominations: 'You know I never fettered nor imprisoned the word Religion; nor straightning it Frierly, *ad Religiones factitias*, (as the *Romans* call well their orders of Religion) nor immuring it in a *Rome*, or a *Wittenberg*, or a *Geneva*; they are all virtuall beams of one Sun' (*Letters* 29). No matter of what denomination, '[r]eligion is Christianity, which being too spirituall to be seen by us, doth therefore take an apparent body of good life and works, so salvation requires an honest Christian. These are the two Elements, and he which elemented from these, hath the complexion of a good man, and a fit friend' (*Letters* 29). Wherever the Christian spirit is present in a person, it cannot but 'take an apparent body of good life and works' – nor, it is implied, can there be a 'body of good life and works' which does not originate from a Christian soul. Faith cannot but manifest itself in an individual's life and works, and these deeds then 'mean' his or her faith. The letter does not want 'to slack [the addressee] towards those friends which are religious in other clothes then we', but to warn him against those 'which are not onely naked, without any fashion of such garments, but have neither the body of Religion, which is morall honesty, and sociable faithfulness, nor the soul, Christianity' (*Letters* 30). What primarily distinguishes Christians is that their body correspond to their souls, that their works reflect their faith, that the ensemble of signifiers making up their lives in the world coincide with the thing signified, their Christian souls, that there be a communion, an at-oneness between abstract faith and concrete action, a communion as pregnant with signification as that between the body of Christ which constitutes the meaning of the consecrated host.

This insistence on action features also in the approach Donne's *Devotions* take to God himself. Devotion 20 meditates on the superiority of action over counsel: 'Though *counsel* seeme rather to consist of *spirituall parts*, than *action*, yet *action* is the *spirit* and the *soule* of *counsell*' (*Devotions* 104). Moreover, '*counsels* are not *counsels*, but *illusions*, where there is from the beginning no purpose to execute the determinations of those *counsels*' (*Devotions* 105). Language and action are sometimes very closely related to each other. Whereas the '*arts* and *sciences*' may be limited to the head only, 'yet the *art* of *proving*, *Logique*, and the *Art* of *perswading*, *Rhetorique*, are deduced to the *hand*, and *that* expressed by a *hand* contracted into a *fist*, and *this* by a *hand* enlarged, and expanded; and ever more the *power of man*, and the *power of God* himselfe is expressed so, *All things are in his hand*' (*Devotions* 105). When God speaks and advises, his language is performative, it does not merely say, it does something. As in rhetoric, it translates itself from head to hand, to divine (inter)action. God the Creator is the archetypical word-doer.

Whereas the meditation treats the relationship between God's counsel and action rather neutrally, the expostulation no longer remains contemplative and reminds God that, in the Bible, 'in the most eminent, and obvious, and conspicuous places, stands *doing*. Why then, O my *God*, my blessed *God*, in the waies of my *spirituall strength*, come I so slow to *action*?' (*Devotions* 107). God is challenged to live up to his word, that it may actually become manifest in his actions. Much more implicitly, the meditation already dropped a similar hint: 'Neither is *God* so often presented to us, by names that carry our consideration upon *counsel*, as upon *execution of counsel*; he is oftner called the *Lord of Hosts*, than by all other *names*, that may be referred to the other signification' (*Devotions* 105). God is expected to live up to his name, to live up to that which is said of him, to make the signified correspond with the signifier and enforce action. Just as one may expect it of each Christian, so also ought God to make himself known by 'a body of good life and works' (*Devotions* 29).

Communion as *imitatio Christi*

That the writer of Donne's *Devotions* should expect not only professed Christians to act according to their faith but also God himself to verify his word establishes a parallel between God and human beings, which makes it all the more plausible that Donne's speakers should so often assume for themselves the part of Christ. The Son of God provides the link between Godhead and humankind, and believers experience his presence as emblematic especially during the Eucharist, and meditations or devotional reading enforce similar processes of Holy Communion (cf. Young, 2000: 82; Jagodzinski, 1999: 28). The *Devotions'* '[s]uffering within the body and in imitation of Christ's suffering conforms [their speaker] to Christ' (Johnson, 1999: 59; Wilcox, 2007: 393).

The speaker of expostulation 14 intends to 'consider *seven daies, seven critical daies,* and *judge my selfe, that I be not judged by thee*' (*Devotions* 75). He accompanies the Son of God on the last days of his life on earth and the first day of his life after death. Although this procedure recalls the spiritual exercises of Ignatius of Loyola, this observation should not be mistaken as evidence of Donne's religious affiliation (cf. Narveson, 1998: 107). Devotional reading instead aimed at the self's turning away from itself and towards heaven: '*The Imitation of Christ*, a byproduct of the *Devotio Moderna*, is the premier example of this model of self-abnegation, and continued to be popular for devotional reading into the post-Reformation period by Catholics and Protestants alike' (Jagodzinski, 1999: 26; Young, 2000: 88). Even the Thirty-Nine Articles, which had to be subscribed to by all members of the clergy, allude to an *imitatio Christi* when promising to the elect that 'they be made sons of God by adoption: they be made like the image of his only-begotten Son Jesus Christ' (Cressy/Ferrell, 1996: 64).

The third stage of the *imitatio Christi* exhibited in Devotion 14 constitutes the speaker's 'day of preparing, & fitting my selfe for a more especial *receiving* of thy *Sonne*, in his institution of the *Sacrament*' (*Devotions* 75). The idea of meditating upon Christ's final days is intrinsically linked to the Eucharist, to the possibility of knowing 'that that *Bread* and *Wine*, is not more really assimilated to my *body*, & to my *blood*, then the *Body* and *blood* of thy *Sonne*, is communicated to me in that action, and participation of that *bread*, and that *wine*' (*Devotions* 75). On the one hand, the speaker passively receives Christ, who 'is communicated' to him in the Eucharist; on the other hand, this exercise relies on the speaker's own initiative and demands that he be actively 'preparing, & fitting [his] selfe' for Christ (cf. Oliver, 1997: 232). A similar active passiveness or passive action seems to be at work when the sick speaker of the *Devotions* styles himself or his sick body as an offering: 'As thou hast made this *bed*, thine *Altar*, make me thy *Sacrifice*; and as thou makest thy *Sonne* Christ Jesus the *Priest*, so make me his *Deacon*, to minister to him in a cheerful surrender of my body, & soule to thy pleasure, by his hands' (*Devotions* 18). On the one hand, the speaker is unauthorised to make himself a sacrifice and depends on God's help to do so. On the other, he hopes to minister even to Christ – if only 'in a cheerful surrender', and not himself, but 'by his [Christ's] hands'. Yet, whatever the speaker can do is minimal, for he has 'sacrificed a little, of that litle which thou lentst me, to them, for whom thou lentst it' (*Devotions* 22). He has done nothing, either more or less, than what God asked him to do.

Prayer 3 succinctly points out what contribution one can make to one's communion with God: 'I come unto thee, *O God, my God*, I come unto thee, (so as I can come, I come to thee, by imbracing thy comming to me)' (*Devotions* 18). There is some ingenuity in arguing that God or Christ themselves will come to fetch each human being. In expostulation 13, the speaker makes it clear that it is not he who links himself to Christ, but that '[e]ven my *spots* belong to thy *Sonnes* body, and are part of that, which he came down to this earth, to fetch, and challenge, and assume to himselfe' (*Devotions* 69–70). Christ takes what is his own anyway, so the speaker is perfectly justified in his reassurance that, '[w]hen therefore thou seest them [i.e. the spots] upon me, as *His*, [. . .] they shall not appear to me, as the *pinches of death*' (*Devotions* 70). Nevertheless, the question as to who has to approach whom in order to bring into effect such (comm)union seems to be a complex and subtle one. In hearing the bells toll, the speaker of *Devotions* believes to 'heare thy *Sonne* himselfe saying, *Let not your hearts be* troubled; Only I heare this *change*, that whereas thy *Sonne* saies there, *I goe to prepare a place for you*, this man in this *sound* saies, *I send to prepare you for a place, for a grave*' (*Devotions* 88). Christ's preparation of a grave is what comes first, but the speaker's own ensuing preparation for that place appears to be of similar significance.

The ambiguity and instability of Holy Communion

The speaker's attempts at imitations of Christ are often imagined as liminal experiences. The question as to whether Christ takes us to himself, or whether we are able to make him our own keeps recurring in Donne's *Devotions*. It is vital for the speaker to understand how communication may successfully conclude in communion with God. Too much presumptuousness in wanting to commune with God may be just as damaging as too weak an initiative of one's own. This issue of give-and-take is discussed most prominently in the expostulations. At the beginning of expostulation 11, the speaker is wondering whether or not he should give his heart to God: 'My *God*, my *God*, all that thou askest of mee, is my *Heart, My Sonne, give mee thy heart*; Am I thy *sonne*, as long as I have but *my heart*? Wilt thou give mee an *Inheritance*, a *Filiation*, any thing for *my heart*?' (*Devotions* 58). The speaker appears concerned about what he will gain from this exchange, but, as he hastily explains, he hesitates only because his heart may not be good enough: there are '*straight* hearts, no perversnesse without, and *cleane* hearts, no foulenesse within; [...] and if my *heart* were such a *heart*, I would give thee my *Heart*' (*Devotions* 59). But then there are '*stonie* hearts too, and I have made mine such', and the occasional '*Heart* into which the *Devill* himselfe is entred, *Judas heart*' (*Devotions* 59). Thus the speaker's dilemma: 'The first kind of heart, alas, my *God*, I have not; The last are not *Hearts* to bee given to thee; What shall I do? Without that present I cannot bee thy *Sonne*, and I have it not' (*Devotions* 59).

The speaker's desire to belong to God is linked to being '*thy Sonne*', the way towards communion is again associated with *imitatio Christi*. This time, the speaker's dilemma can be resolved: 'There is then a middle kinde of *Hearts*, not so perfit, as to bee given, but that the very giving, mends them: Not so desperate, as not to bee accepted, but that the very accepting dignifies them. This is a *melting* heart, and a *troubled* heart; and a *wounded* heart, and a *broken* heart, and a *contrite* heart; and by the powerfull working of thy piercing spirit, such a *Heart* I have' (*Devotions* 59). It will not do for the speaker simply to give his heart to God, nor for God merely to take it: 'the very giving', 'the very accepting', 'mends' and 'dignifies' – just as, in the Eucharist, Christ's body becomes manifest as gift only if it meets with the appropriate receptiveness in the communicant. The interfusion of the two parties' responsibilities is further elaborated in the remainder of the quotation: to commune with God, the speaker's heart has to be soft, responsive and, by implication, passive, but it is actively fashioned thus by the speaker who styles it as *'melting'*, *'troubled'*, *'wounded'*, *'broken'* and *'contrite'*. Immediately afterwards, these properties are attributed to 'the powerfull working of [God's] piercing spirit' (*Devotions* 59). Once the speaker's heart enters into communion with God, there is no more distinguishing as to who is consenting to, approaching, seizing upon whom, and the only way of translating this desired experience into language is through a constant oscillation between the two poles of speaker and God.

The same oscillation occurs wherever the *Devotions* make reference to the Eucharist as the primary instance of (holy) communion. The seventh prayer, which follows upon the speaker's definition of the Eucharist as the association not only of *'the signe* with the *thing signified'*, but also of the recipient with Christ, further develops this topic, by the Biblical story of heavenly manna, which has traditionally been interpreted as an Old Testament foreshadowing of Christ's instantiation of the Eucharist in the Last Supper: 'O *eternall*, and *most gracious God*, who gavest to thy servants in the wildernes, thy *Manna*, bread so conditiond, qualified so, as that, to every man, *Manna tasted like that, which that man liked best*, I humbly beseech thee, to make this correction, which I acknowledg to be part of my *daily bread*, to tast so to me, not as I would but as thou wouldest have it taste, and to conform my tast, and make it agreeable to thy will' (*Devotions* 39). By the example of heavenly bread whose taste adapts itself to the preferences of each of its consumers, the speaker insinuates that this is what God's daily and life-saving bread will hopefully also taste like. This assumption is immediately withdrawn by the speaker's plea to have that bread 'not as I would but as thou wouldest have it taste' – yet these potential differences in taste are then blurred again, as the speaker asks to have his taste conformed to that of God, so that the bread of correction will eventually taste as sweet as heavenly manna to him. Submitting his own taste to God's judgement is in the speaker's own interest and does not constitute any submission at all. By the end of this prayer, the positive effects of subordinating himself to God's taste become abundantly clear: 'whether thy *Mercy*, or thy *Correction*, were thy primary, and original intention in this sickness, I cannot conclude, though death conclude me; for as it must necessarily appeare to bee a *correction*, so I can have no greater argument of thy *mercy*, then to die in *thee*, and by that death, to bee united to him, who died for me'

(*Devotions* 40). As the speaker's own taste is no longer distinct from God's, he tastes with delight whatever it is that God offers him to eat – but because his taste is thus no longer his own, he cannot take all the credit for bearing God's corrections so well.

The presumption inherent in the speaker's demand that his own taste be conformed to that of God and the implication that thus he will, to some extent, become as him, is not considered problematic here, nor is it in Donne's letter *'To all my friends: Sir H. Goodere'*, where the writer argues: 'And certainly despair is infinitly worse, then presumption: both because this is an excesse of love, that of fear; and because this is up, that down the hill; easier, and more stumbling. Heaven is expressed by singing, hell by weeping' (*Letters* 46). The letter discusses people's place in society, in particular with regard to their superiors. A similar preference for presumption over despair is typical of Donne's *Devotions*, whose speaker claims for himself the right to approach God *'with holy importunitie, with a pious impudencie'* (*Devotions* 52).

Another letter of Donne's refers even more directly to the relationship between God and man, but with much less self-confidence:

> Yea words which are our subtillest and delicatest outward creatures, being composed of thoughts and breath, are so muddie, so thick, that our thoughts themselves are so, because (except at the first rising) they are ever leavened with passions and affections: And that advantage of nearer familiarity with God, which the act of incarnation gave us, is grounded upon Gods assuming us, not our going to him. And, our accesses to his presence are but his descents into us; and when we get any thing by prayer, he gave us before hand the thing and the petition. (*Letters* 110–11)

Whereas, elsewhere, the writer praises the value of words both in letters and prayers and stresses how they help to cultivate the bond between speaker and addressee, this passage questions the value of whatever words may be hoped to achieve. There is no point in presuming to speak with God as there is nothing one can do but attend his leisure to descend 'into us'. Not even our prayers are our own. Such wavering between passive prostration before God and active attempts for his presence are typical not only of Donne's letters and *Devotions* but of his writing in general (cf. Wilcox, 2007: 397).

Most of the time, God's and the speaker's interests are intermingled with one another, for example when the speaker prays that he may 'never fall into utter *darknesse, ignorance of thee*, or *inconsideration of my selfe*' (*Devotions* 77). These entanglements of human beings with God are brought about primarily through language, as in the following conclusion to a prayer: 'Doe this, *O Lord*, for his sake, who did, and suffered so much, that thou mightest, as well in thy Justice, as in thy Mercy, doe it for me, thy *Sonne*, our *Saviour*, *Christ Jesus*' (*Devotions* 19). Thanks to the fact that words are 'so muddie, so thick', 'thy *Sonne*' grammatically refers not only to '*Christ Jesus*' but also to the speaker himself. With linguistic subtlety, the speaker effects a communion of himself first with the Son of God, who is, of course, also 'our *Saviour*', who in turn cannot be anyone else but '*Christ Jesus*' (cf. Frost, 1990: 36).

Since the *Devotions* centre upon the occasion of the serious illness Donne was suffering from in 1623, God is repeatedly addressed as humankind's physician, as in expostulation 21, where the speaker re-enacts the story of Christ healing the lame man with what may indeed be considered '*holy importunitie*' or '*pious impudencie*' (*Devotions* 52). As regards his worldly physicians, 'I open my infirmities, I anatomise my *body* to them' (*Devotions* 48), and 'So I do my *soule* to thee, O my *God*, in an humble confession, That there is no *veine* in mee, that is not full of the bloud of thy *Son*, whom I have crucified, & Crucified againe, by multiplying many, and often repeating the same sinnes' (*Devotions* 48). The speaker's confession is not so very abject: although he takes upon himself the blame of crucifying Christ, he also assumes his identity when he claims the blood of Jesus is running in his veins. Likewise, the speaker's supposed modesty with regard to his worldly physicians – 'I offer not to counsel them' (*Devotions* 48) – becomes dubious when, after declaring his soul altogether infected by sickness before God, he continues: 'Yet, *O blessed and glorious Trinity, O holy, & whole Colledge*, and yet but one *Phisician*, if you take this confession into a *consultation*, my case is not desperate, my destruction is not *decreed*' (*Devotions* 48). The display of his soul does, after all, have an advisory dimension, although, a few lines earlier, the speaker denied that intention.

The hierarchical separation between patient and physician is similarly deconstructed in the sixth meditation, where the speaker assumes the physician's place for himself:

> I observe the *Phisician*, with the same diligence, as hee the *disease*; I see hee *feares*, and I feare with him: I overtake him, I overrun him in his feare, and I go the faster, because he makes his pace slow; I feare the more, because he disguises his fear, and I see it with the more sharpnesse, because hee would not have me see it. He knowes that his *feare* shall not disorder the practise, and exercise of his Art, but he knows that my *fear* may disorder the effect, and working of his practise. (*Devotions* 29)

Initially, the speaker empathises with the physician only by making the latter's fear his own. But soon he outdoes and even offsets him as the physician's attempts to hide his concern are thwarted by the patient whose fears may counteract the physician's best efforts. For the patient's recovery, the physician has to rely on adequate co-operation no less than on his own skill. The speaker hence features as patient and physician simultaneously, and if we recall that not only in the *Devotions* but also in the Bible God is often addressed as humankind's physician, this passage constitutes yet another instance of the speaker's ambiguous and ambitious (comm)union with the divine.[7]

Donne's speakers are eager to bring about divine communion, but most of the time, these communions are rather ambiguous, as it is never quite clear how the parties involved relate to each other, and how each depends on or dominates the other. In addition, their communions are often acknowledged to be only temporary. Whereas, after death, a human being's communion with Christ will be perfected, this is not true for his life where one always runs the risk of relapsing into one's old ways. Humankind's physical and spiritual frailty parallel each other: 'my *bodily strength* is subject to every *puffe of wind*, so is my *spirituall strength* to every *blast of vanitie*' (*Devotions* 115). Whatever strength the speaker gathers from his communions, there is no certainty as to how long it may last, which is why he prefers to remain in a state of conscious and constant dependency: 'Keepe me therefore still, O my gracious *God*, in a such a *proportion* of both *strengths*, as I may still have something to thanke thee for, which I *have received*, & still something to *pray for*, and aske at thy hand' (*Devotions* 115). The unwillingness to be free of one's superiors is also familiar from Donne's letters, where the writer explains that 'there is some degree of thankfulnesse in asking more (for that confesses all former obligations, and a desire to be still in the same dependency)' (*Letters* 95). Just as social contacts must be cultivated by repeated letters, so should one's faith become manifest in recurring attempts at communion. The speaker of prayer 22 asks God: 'let mee alwaies so apprehend *thee*, as *present* with me, and yet to *follow* after thee, as though I had not apprehended thee' (*Devotions* 120).

The desire to remain within a state of dependency and to repeat compulsively those efforts at communion which never seem to last for long is ambiguous as it strives to turn the speaker's insufficiencies into supposed advantages for his benefactor, whose lasting superiority is thus acknowledged. To some extent, Donne's speakers are aware of this dilemma: in the above prayer, the speaker recognises that God's generosity in having the patient recover from his sickness, and, by implication, from his sins this time should not encourage him to presume upon God's mercy on future occasions also. Yet a few pages later, the speaker comforts himself: 'and thou who hast commanded me *to pardon my brother seventy times seven*, hast limited thy self to no *Number*' (*Devotions* 125–6) – a statement immediately qualified as the speaker protests: 'But I speak not this, O my *God*, as preparing a way to my *Relapse* out of *presumption*, but to *preclude* all accesses of *desperation*, though out of *infirmity*, I should *Relapse*' (*Devotions* 126). It almost appears as if, given the choice, the speaker would have opted 'rather for death' and thus final salvation (Papazian, 1992: 616). He is, however, aware that his recovery must be accepted as God-given. As we read also in *Pseudo-Martyr*, 'hee which [. . .] entertaines not those overtures of escape, which God presents him, destroyes himselfe, especially if his life might be of use and advantage to others' (*Pseudo-Martyr* 155), as, for example, that of a preacher. Christ's death, by contrast, was even more useful than his life, which is why *Biathanatos* not only presents Christ as the arch-martyr but scandalously imagines him as suicidal: 'without doubt, no man did, nor was there any other then his owne Will, the cause of his dying at that tyme' (*Biathanatos* 129).[8]

The fear of relapsing into sickness, into a sin once forgiven before, dominates the last prayer of Donne's *Devotions*: 'I know that this comes to neare, to a making thy holy *Ordinances*, thy *Word*, thy *Sacraments*, thy *Seales*, thy *Grace*, instruments of my *Spirituall Fornications*' (*Devotions* 126). The most vivid instance of communion, the celebration of the Eucharist, must not be abused deliberately by returning to one's sinful ways. Yet this danger is imminent, and the speaker begs '[t]hat if my *infirmitie* overtake mee, thou *forsake* mee not' (*Devotions* 126). Relapse must be shunned, but it is lurking everywhere, even in the very last lines of the *Devotions*, which express the hope that 'thy *long-livd*, thy *everlasting Mercy*, will visit me, though *that*, which I most earnestly pray against, should fall upon mee, a *relapse* into those *sinnes*, which I have *truly repented*, and thou hast *fully pardoned*' (*Devotions* 127). For now, the occasion of the speaker's illness is past, but its potential return will send the reader to the beginning of Donne's *Devotions* and their repeated efforts at communion as 'the purpose of the text is to create a narrative of sickness and recovery that can, in every reading, be renewed' (Targoff, 2008: 153). This cyclical element is built into each individual devotion itself, as it proceeds from meditation and expostulation towards prayer: as a whole, the *Devotions* come across as 'both progressive and cyclical' (Seelig, 1989: 106) – thus their implicit encouragement to reread, and not just silently, for 'Donne seems to be imagining his audience reading his words aloud or speaking them along with him' (Conti, 2003: 151).

The *Devotions* as efforts at communion

There are parallels between the discourses of individual *Devotions* and the context within which the whole of the *Devotions* is couched. Whereas Ignatius of Loyola's *Spiritual Exercises* provide merely a guideline for personal application, Donne's text constitutes a set of actual *Devotions* for the reader to share in (Raspa in *Devotions*, 1975: xxxviii–xxxix). Both the *Devotions* and the Ignatian exercises acknowledge that one's contact with God must be cultivated on a regular basis. In that they are meant to be used whenever the danger of sinful and feaverish relapse arises, the *Devotions*, too, constitute exercises whose value can be appreciated only when they are practised repeatedly. Religious faith needs constant attention: no matter whether Roman Catholic or reformed, these religions 'are all virtuall beams of one Sun, and wheresoever they finde clay hearts, they harden them, and moulder them into dust; and they entender and mollifie waxen' (*Letters* 29). '[W]axen' suggests that, whenever hearts have been moulded into the right faithful shape, they are easily distorted again and should be exposed to religious 'sunlight' in order to be re-formed.

Presenting themselves as intended for repeated application, the *Devotions* acknowledge the instability of humanity's devotional communion with God. The same holds true for the ambiguity of their writer's communion with his reader – although this aspect is not quite as openly acknowledged. In his dedication 'To The Most Excellent Prince, Prince Charles', Donne gives his reasons for making the *Devotions* public and for dedicating them to the heir to the throne: '*It might bee enough, that* God *hath seene my* Devotions: *But* Examples *of* Good Kings *are* Commandements' (*Devotions* 3). After characterising the *Devotions* as primarily Donne's own, the second part of this sentence is simultaneously humble and presumptuous. On the one hand, it suggests the writer's subservience to the dedicatee by stressing the enormous influence of a King's example in contrast with the writer's efforts. On the other, the writer implies that any king may and ought to profit from the *Devotions* by subordinating himself to them and making them his example. In pointing out that the *Devotions* are primarily addressed to God, the writer suggests that the dedicatee ought to be flattered that those petitions are now accessible also to him. With all due humility, he self-confidently points out the educational value of his work for readers who are less than God. In dedicating his work to Prince Charles, Donne is giving something to him, but at the same time he has to rely on the dedicatee's acceptance (cf. Parry, 2002: 118) – much as God himself, offering us the body of Christ in the host, depends on the recipient's appropriate mindset for communion to take place at all. However, in a letter to the Queen of Bohemia which accompanies a copy of the *Devotions*, the writer turns even his dependency on the Prince's acceptance into a virtue and advantage over his present addressee: 'Now [. . .] I surprise your majestie, I take you at an advantage, I lay an obligation upon you, because that which your Brother's Highnesse hath received, your Majestie cannot refuse' (Simpson *Prose* 157).

A similar ambiguity is exploited in the eighth expostulation where the speaker pays tribute to the King's generosity in sending his own physician to attend upon him: 'To *give* is an approaching to the Condition of *Kings*, but to give *health*, an approaching to the *King*, of *Kings*, to *thee*' (*Devotions* 43). A few lines later, the speaker points out that it is God's capacity 'not only to send *Phisicians* for *temporall*, but to bee the *Phisician* for *spirituall* health' (*Devotions* 44). Temporal and physical health is subordinate to spiritual health – and the priest, not the King, comes closest to providing this kind of well-being for his brethren. The hierarchies between monarch and minister, King James and Dr John Donne, are discreetly blurred here. Such obscuration is reminiscent of the communions between the *Devotions'* speaker and his God: the process of reading the *Devotions* should result in a communion of speaker and reader, too, however unstable and ambiguous. By communing with the speaker and, to some extent, subordinating their identities to his, readers retrace the suffering patient's steps towards communion with God, towards physical recovery and spiritual regeneration. In demanding that the reader identify with the speaker, the *Devotions* differ from Donne's sermons: whereas the latter 'deliver the messages of God to your self', the reading of the former amounts to 'the hearing of me deliver my messages to God' (Simpson *Prose* 157, cf. Stein, 1984: 85). But although the *Devotions* allow for 'more concentrated doubts and fears than he could have permitted himself to voice in public', they were none the less also intended to serve their readers' edification (Webber, 1963: 201).[9]

The *Devotions* promote a concept of 'communal' reading which conforms and identifies the reader to and with the speaker (cf. Webber, 1968: 7, 13): 'All *mankinde* is of one *Author*, and is one *volume*' (*Devotions* 86), hence all that the speaker of the *Devotions* suffers in his sickness ought to be considered by readers as if it concerned them personally. In this sense, 'the *Devotions* is intimate rather than merely didactic, "experiential" rather than prescriptive' (Pender, 2003: 216). Their model is to be personalised and appropriated by each reader, so that a compromise between set prayer and extempore meditation is achieved (cf. Strier, 1996: 103). The *Devotions* herein resemble a letter writing manual; there, too, letter writers are encouraged to adapt general models to the individual context of a particular epistle. Devotions 16–18 read like a mise en abyme of what it means to read 'communally'. As a whole, the *Devotions* constitute a bell-ringing service or sermon of their own (cf. Conti, 2007: 368). Their bells are tolling, their meditations, expostulations and prayers are articulated upon the occasion of the speaker's own impending death. Just as 'The *Bell* doth toll for him that *thinkes* it doth' (*Devotions* 86), so are the *Devotions* written for him that thinks they are – they are 'both a record of one man's often fearful journey towards assurance and a guide for all those troubled by the "variable, and therefore miserable condition of man"' (Cox, 1973: 351; Pender, 2003: 226). This larger dimension is suggested once more when the speaker speculates whether it was God's intention 'To make *him* for whom this *bell* tolls, now in this dimnesse of his sight, to become a *superintendent*, an *overseer*, a *Bishop*, to as many as heare his *voice*, in this *bell*, and to give us a *confirmation* in this action' (*Devotions* 87–8). Shortly before his death in 1631, Donne himself was considered for a bishopric.

The role of Biblical example in the *Devotions* must not be underestimated (Raspa in *Devotions*, 1975: xl), especially since their speaker is emblematic of Hezekiah whose illness is reported in Isaiah 38. Typology is predominant also in expostulation 20, where the speaker assumes the role of the lame man who, in Matthew, is healed by Christ who orders him to take up his bed and walk. However, the indignant questions with which the speaker confronts God ('But when wilt thou doe *more*? when wilt thou doe *all*? when wilt thou speake in thy *loud voice*? when wilt thou bid mee *take up my bed and walke*?', *Devotions* 114) mark this as a problematic appropriation of Biblical example. Nor is the famous bell sequence sufficiently accounted for through Biblical typology.

The ways in which Devotions 16–18 interlink the speaker's fate with that of his deceased brother, and that of all readers with the speaker's, are best accounted for by the concept of communion. Notably, the Eucharist implies not only communion with God, but also communion among the brethren belonging to him. Immediately before extolling the merits of Holy Communion with Christ, the speaker of expostulation 7 thanks God that his help comes 'from the assotiation, & communion of thy *Catholique Church*, and those persons, whom thou hast always furnished that *Church* withal' (*Devotions* 39). Likewise, in the bell sequence, sharing in the assumed communion of the deceased with God is linked to each person's communion with the one for whom the bell tolls. The communicative situation of the *Devotions* is emblematic of the celebration of the Eucharist; they 'share in the power of God's "effectutall signes of grace" (Article 25) and prove spiritually efficacious for those who received them with faith' (DiPasquale, 1999: 15).

Like the sacrament, the *Devotions* constitute 'a celebration not only of the Christian's communion with his Redeemer, but also with his fellow Christians' (Young, 2000: 89; Duffy, 1992: 93). The Book of Common Prayer defines the Lord's Supper as a communion with one's fellow human beings, and *'those betwixt whom he* [the curate] *perceiveth malice and hatred to reign'* should not be allowed *'to be partakers of the Lord's table until he know them to be reconciled'* (Cressy/Ferrell, 1996: 45). The twenty-eighth of the Thirty-Nine Articles stresses that '[t]he supper of the Lord is *not only* a sign of the love that Christians ought to have among themselves one to another; but rather it is a sacrament of our redemption by Christ's death' (Cressy/Ferrell, 1996: 67, my emphasis). Reading Donne's *Devotions* 'comes as close as possible to the experience of having the illness ourselves' (Targoff, 2008: 137). Donne's sermons, by contrast, rarely invite listeners to identify as immediately with the preaching persona who tends to remain more aloof than the speaker of the *Devotions* – possibly not least because sermon audiences would have included people of much lower standing than would have been among the readers of Donne's *Devotions*. The immediate empathy encouraged by this work is typical also of the epistolary genre (cf. Altman, 1982: 124). Through communion, the individual's experience of embracing and being embraced by God coincides with each man's community with his fellow men – just as, for Donne, identification with Christ constitutes 'not so much a distortion as a stretching of the self, assimilating the individual into all of humanity through the *imitatio Christi*' (Frost, 1990: 162).

The *Devotions* take into account both individual and Christian community. That they should be 'both private and public is neither a contradiction nor an indication of bad taste: It is a necessary requirement of Christian spiritual autobiography' (Frost, 1990: 77). In the *Devotions*, 'Donne hovers between the medieval exemplum and early modern individuality' (Wilcox, 2000: 171), as he makes his highly individualised experience available for everyone (cf. Roston, 2007: 207–10).[10] Despite the difficulty of identifying with someone else's pain or sickness, Donne seems to have thought that the written communication of his personal experiences of communion would induce similar sensations in his readers. A notion of the self as humoral, and thus more sensitive and responsive both to its general environment and to its fellow humans, may account for his trust in his readers' abilities to empathise with the speaker of his *Devotions* in spiritually profitable ways. The speaker of Donne's *Devotions* keeps wavering between centring on himself and focusing on his fellow humans (cf. Wilcox, 2000: 171–6).

Donne's letters likewise were concerned with both self-fashioning and social networking, and these endeavours mutually conditioned one another. Community with society and the world was one of their greatest preoccupations: 'but to be no part of any body, is to be nothing. At most, the greatest persons, are but great wens, and excrescences; men of wit and delightfull conversation, but as moales for ornament, except they be so incorporated into the body of the world, that they contribute something to the sustentation of the whole' (*Letters* 51). Donne intended his *Devotions* to be printed so that they might indeed be 'incorporated' into society. *In* the *Devotions*, the speaker hopes to enjoy communion with God and be part of him – and *through* the *Devotions*, Donne meant to enable this communion for his readers, by way of creating a communion between them and himself. As the *Devotions'* dedication to Prince Charles and the dedicatory letter 'To the Queen of Bohemia' suggest, Donne's offering of his work was not altogether disinterested. To some extent at least, the *Devotions*, no less than Donne's letters, constituted a stake and a commodity in social discourses of patronage. Donne's letter writers aimed to align their own persons with those of their addressees, particularly at the end of a letter – equations that have their counterparts in the numerous imitations of Christ which conclude the prayers of many individual *Devotions*. Moreover, although Donne's letters were more private than his *Devotions*, they were occasionally read out loud. The addressee would have appropriated them to his own voice and made the writer's experience his own, an attitude desirable also in the reader of the *Devotions*: 'the original *you* becomes the *I*' not only 'of a new utterance', but also of the present letter at hand (Altman, 1982: 117). In both Donne's letters and *Devotions*, communication with the addressee, with God as an Other, gradually gives way to communion. And just as Donne's *Devotions* rely on him for whom the bell tolls or the speaker himself as a mediator, so do the writers of Donne's letters often depend on a third person to further their interests with a socially superior personage. Considering the prayers' attempts at imitations of Christ, in the *Devotions*, the Son of God appears to function as the arch-intercessor for the speaker's petitions towards God.

This is not to say that Donne's writers were aware of these parallels. In one letter, the writer refuses to enclose an epithalamion to the addressee instead of directly sending it to the patron who ordered it: 'If it be done, I see not how I can admit that circuit of sending them to you, to be sent hither; that seems a kinde of praying to Saints, to whom God must tell first, that such a man prays to them to pray to him' (*Letters* 181). Ironically, the same letter ends: 'J. Donne *Which name when there is any empty corner in your discourse with that nobel Lady at* Ashby, *I humbly beseech you to present to her as one more devoted to her service then perchance you will say*' (*Letters* 181). The letter in which the writer declines to transfer the practice of praying to saints to his suits for patronage concludes as precisely such an intercessional prayer. Furthermore, this writer's concern to be present(ed), and the letters' general eagerness 'to transmute into emotional presence the absence of writer and addressee and to strengthen the bonds of friendship' (Gibbson, 2000: 616), echo the *Devotions*' concern with the real presence of Christ both in the celebration of the Eucharist and in the suffering speaker: 'Donne wants to see as manifestly in his life as in the administration of the sacraments that the physical [dimension of his illness] conveys the metaphysical' (Janel Mueller, 1968: 6).

Poetry versus prose

Donne's prose letters and *Devotions* resemble each other in many respects. The *Devotions* also share many characteristics with the sermons, as both aim to perform a communion with God through Christ, which readers or listeners are invited to share. The two genres differ with regard to the strategies they employ towards that end. The *Devotions* place much more emphasis on (inter) personal bonds than is usual in the sermons where humanity's attitude towards God is considered yet far more superior to relationships between human beings and where these two dimensions are hardly as closely bound up with each other as in Donne's

Devotions. Also, whereas the sermons encourage identification primarily with Biblical example, the *Devotions* draw attention to how one ought to empathise with one's (real-life) neighbour. Likewise, as Chapter 3 has shown, Donne's erotic and divine poems are closely related to each other, but the question of how Donne distinguishes between prose and verse has not been touched upon so far. Whereas, both as a group but also as individual poems, Donne's *Songs and Sonets* are too idiosyncratic to lend themselves easily to a comparison with any of the writer's prose, a strong connection exists between his letters in verse and prose. Critics have pointed out the parallels between Donne's two kinds of letters (cf. Maurer, 1976: 235; Guillén, 1986: 80–2), but, except for Ramie Targoff's contrastive analysis of Donne's letters in prose and verse (Targoff, 2008: 45), the differences between them have gone largely uncommented.

Admittedly, the common features of these two epistolary modes are more striking: in a verse letter '*To the Countesse of Bedford*', the writer treats letters as commodities when he describes the need to respond to his addressee as a 'debt' (l. 5). His indebtedness to the addressee can never be sufficiently made up for – as in the prose letters, it further increases by thanking the addressee, because the writer believes to 'owe more / By having leave to write so, then before' (l. 9–10). As in many prose letters, the writer also alludes to a religion of epistolarity when he describes his writing as 'bare Sacrament' (l. 12). Moreover, the writer's identification with his own writing works even better in verse than prose, for only metrical language may convey not only the writer's 'name, words, hand' but also his 'feet' (l. 6). Similarly, when, in the '*Letter written by Sr. H. G. and J. D. alternis vicibus*', the writers ask their addressees to 'Admit our magique then by which wee doe / Make you appeere to us, and us to you' (l. 16–17), it is quite plausible that rhyme, since ancient times the medium of witchcraft and oracle, may better lend itself to such 'magique' than prose. Rhyme's 'magique' also makes it probable that Donne's verse letters were read out loud more frequently than his epistolary prose. Like their counterparts in prose, they had 'two audiences: the ostensible recipient of the epistle and a general audience' (Storhoff, 1977: 11; Cameron, 1976: 375).

At the same time, many letter manuals connect the letter's conveyance of the writer's person with a plain style of writing

(Müller, 1980: 150). Selves transmitted via verse may have appeared more artificial than those communicated by prose. This may be one of the reasons why Donne generally preferred to write his letters in prose. The scant commentary we have from him derives mostly from his prose letters, whose writing personae repeatedly articulate their reluctance to go back to writing verse:

> but for the expressing it [the praise] to her [presumably the Countess of Huntington], in that sort as you seem to counsaile, I have these two reasons to decline it. That that knowledge which she hath of me, was in the beginning of a graver course, then of a Poet, into which (that I may also keep my dignity) I would not seem to relapse. The Spanish proverb informes me, that he is a fool which cannot make one Sonnet, and he is mad which makes two. The other stronger reason, is my integrity to the other Countesse [. . .]: and for her delight (since she descends to them) I had reserved not only all the verses, which I should make, but, all the thoughts of womens worthinesse. (*Letters* 103–4)

The addressee apparently was aware of the writer's reluctance to verse: as the beginning of this quotation suggests, he avoided mentioning it directly. The argument which follows, however, is slightly contradictory: on the one hand, the writer wants to keep his 'dignity' by avoiding the foolish lightness of the verse medium, but, on the other, the writing of poetry for a patron is esteemed highly, which is why the writer feels it ought to be reserved for his former patroness, the Countess of Bedford. In another letter, apparently accompanying a piece of verse to be forwarded by the addressee (probably Goodyer) to the Countess of Bedford, the writer describes his patroness as the only one who 'hath power to cast the fetters of verse upon my free meditations: It should give you some delight, and some comfort, because you are the first which see it, and it is the last which you shall see of this kinde from me' (*Letters* 117). Since Donne's writers identify themselves with their written works, writing in verse imprisons the letter-producer, who considers the writing of epistolary verse a humiliation and a danger to his dignity. Only when he feels extremely obliged to the party in question does the writer of the letter '*To my worthy friend* G. K.' agree to verse rather than prose or a sermon: 'My poor study having lyen that way, it may prove possible, that my weak assistance may be of use in this matter, in a more serious fashion, then an Epithalamion. This made me therefore abstinent in that kinde; yet by my troth, I think I shall not scape. I deprehend in my self more then an alacrity, a vehemency to do service to that company; and so, I may finde reason to make rime' (*Letters* 180–1).

His reluctance to write verse does not have anything to do with an inability to do so. In a letter referring to the plan of publishing some poems, probably written at a time of particular pecuniary strain, the writer complains that it 'cost me more diligence, to seek them, then it did to make them' (*Letters* 197). Yet even in answer to a verse letter from a friend, the writer thinks up some rather lame excuse for his failure to respond in like manner: 'At least, to write presently, were to accuse my self of not having read yours so often as such a Letter deserves from you to me' (*Letters* 88). On the one hand, it surely would have been inappropriate for an ordained priest to correspond in verse, instead of articulating himself in 'a more serious fashion', that is, a sermon. In addition, around or slightly after his ordination, Donne seems to have considered the medium of verse beneath him. What is also implied, however, is that verse letters demonstrate a greater servility towards the addressee. Prose is more egalitarian in that it places writer and addressee on the same level. Whereas Donne wrote a number of verse letters to his patrons and patronesses, it is fairly unlikely that they would have responded in verse, too. However, even if, with a friend, this would have been more common, some differences remain between these two epistolary genres. For one thing, Donne's verse letters are more open in giving advice. Both the letter '112: To Sr. *Henry Wotton*' and '113: To Mr. *Rowland Woodward*' constitute frank admonishments against worldly entertainment and company and advise their addressees to concentrate on themselves instead: 'Be thou thine owne home, and in thy selfe dwell' (112, l. 47); 'Manure thy selfe then, to thy selfe be'approv'd, / And with vaine outward things be no more mov'd' (113, ll. 35–6). Such direct exhortations seem to be more easily amenable to the greater formality of verse.

In a letter 'To Mr. *Rowland Woodward*', the writer disparages 'love-song weeds, and Satyrique thornes' (l. 5) in favour of 'better Arts' (l. 6) which the addressee, according to the writer, tends to neglect: 'Though to use, and love Poëtrie, to mee, / Betroth'd to no'one Art, be no'adulterie' (ll. 7–8). The writer tries to wheedle some verse letters out of his addressee, and praises epistolary verse as an example of 'better Arts' (l. 6) – whereas the term 'art' would hardly ever be used for Donne's prose letters. A verse letter to 'Mr. T. W.' begins with the words 'All haile sweet Poët' (l. 1) and admires the addressee's poetic abilities which the writer claims to esteem far higher than his own, so much so that he asks him to ignore his own modest efforts at verse: ' "Twill be good prose, although the verse be evill, / If thou forget the rime as thou dost passe' (ll. 27–8). Despite the writer's polite compliment, some poetic competition is at stake here. Donne does not even hesitate to use the sonnet for his verse letters 116, 117 and 120, a form which, except for his 'Holy Sonnets', he carefully avoided. Addressing 'H. W. in Hiber. Belligeranti.', the writer explains what kind of letter he expects:

> I aske not labor'd letters which should weare
> Long papers out: nor letters which should feare
> Dishonest carriage: or a seers art:
> Nor such as from the brayne come, but the hart.
>
> (ll. 17–20)

Verse seems to encourage the writer to be quite straightforward in announcing his precise demands for a letter of response. Writing in verse, he will be satisfied only by a poetic letter, too. Such a letter may be fairly short, and, owing to its greater stylisation, need not fear censorship. Although using metrical language, such a letter may still come from the heart rather than the brain – this time, the greater polish of verse is not experienced as the imposition of 'fetters' on the writer's 'free meditations'.

The writing of verse letters seems to have been a site of sporty competition between Donne and his friends, enabling them to measure their poetic abilities. There are various instances where the writer addresses his verse letter directly: '115 To Mr. T. W.' begins with the words 'Hast thee harsh verse' (l. 1). '133 To Mrs. M. H.' exclaims: 'Mad paper stay' (l. 1). More than the prose letters, Donne's letters in verse seem to have an existence of their own, as they appear to have been treated less as a means towards an end than their prose counterparts. Whereas most prose letters rely on an already established relationship, the verse letters are still involved in the mutual positioning of their respective correspondents and the formation of their relationship; the genre enables the poet 'to create a relationship [...] where none existed before' (Faust, 1993: 79).

More than the prose letters, they seem to engage in building up and establishing a connection in the first place. This holds also for the verse letters dedicated to Donne's patrons and patronesses, especially in the ways in which they employ courtly idiom in order to demonstrate the poet's eligibility for introduction into those courtly circles he is begging his patroness to help him enter (Maurer, 1980: 212; Faust, 1993: 80). Many of Donne's verse letters work like 'a sign or seal that determines the sender's and receiver's shared identity even as it generates the community that unites them' (DiPasquale, 1999: 200). Since verse not only indicates greater formality but bestows more honour on its addressee, Donne would have used it to establish a relationship with a social superior. The poet's demonstration of his admiration through his verse letters was the basic element of Donne's relationship to the Countess of Bedford, a recognition which '136 *To the Countesse of* Bedford' makes no secret of. The Countess is refined through poetry, just as she, so the writer argues, has 'refin'd mee' (137, l. 2). The foundational moment of their relationship is poetic, as the patroness's fame is preserved and spread by the poet whose 'Verse embalmes vertue' (139, l. 13, cf. Maurer, 1980: 207–8). It is thanks to Donne's poetry that the Countess is still known today, and benefactresses like Lucy of Bedford were quite aware of these profits of patronage (cf. Parry, 2002: 133; Brennan, 1988: 9). More importantly, 'the true measure of a patron's position was not the actual powers he wielded, but the show of power evident in a swarm of followers' (Faust, 1993: 85). Yet the present letter's suggestion that the mutual creation of speaker and addressee depends on poetry is rather daring, as it insinuates not only that the writer's but also the addressee's social standing are inherently performative and not related to any given values (Aers/Kress, 1981a: 25–8).

Once the poet sings the praise of other women in his verse, his former correspondent may well feel neglected, as the poet seems to be striving for a similar relationship with someone else. This is what happened when Donne wrote the Anniversaries in favour of the young and recently deceased Elizabeth Drury, a poetic disloyalty which is the subject of '143 *To the Countesse of* Bedford. *Begun in France but never perfected'*. Parallels exist between relations of patronage and friendship: true friendship, which amounts to an identification of oneself with one's friend, cannot extend itself to more than one person (Montaigne, 1946: I, 205). Doubtless, the relationship of patroness and poet is one of mutual dependence: 'the patron's disgraces have consequences for his retinue' (Maurer, 1980: 217), and poetry may aid in repairing a patron's ruined reputation. The verse letter's generic position between poetry and letter is illustrative of its mediating function and reflects the patron's role as a go-between to the next-higher authority (cf. Faust, 1993: 81).

Donne's verse letters far more rarely mention financial matters than his letters in prose. Presumably, their being written in verse already marks them as unmistakable pleas for patronage. Epistolary poetry to a patron(ess) unambiguously places its writers in the position of a seeker of material support. Depending on the particular occasion, the context and the state of the relationship of writer and addressee, either verse or prose may be the adequate mode of address. When, in a prose letter to Goodyer, the writer declines to write in verse, although admitting to a past 'occasion of versifying' (*Letters* 104), the implication is that there may be occasions on which verse is appropriate. The fact that the writer has occasionally written verse letters should not lead to his being 'esteemed light' in general (*Letters* 104). As Donne moves from the position of dependent seeker to that of a comparatively well-established and dignified chaplain, he gradually shifts away from verse towards prose. By the time he took orders, Donne's relationships to his friends and (former) patronesses had long been established – not least through his verse letters. He then used the greater familiarity of the prose letter to maintain and further cultivate these already reliable friendships. Although we may consider both Donne's verse and prose letters as 'phatic utterances' (Marotti, 1986: 228), prose engages in maintaining a relationship, verse in striving to establish that connection in the first place.

A similar argument can be made for Donne's 'Holy Sonnets' in comparison with his *Devotions*. It would be too simple to say that, as an ordained priest, Donne was no longer able or willing to write verse. The 'Holy Sonnets' should not only be read as testimonies of their speakers' dependency on their ultimate addressee, God or Christ, but are instead illustrative of a need to establish a relationship to God. The speaker of the *Devotions*, by contrast, already considers himself closely related to God, because he interprets his illness, and all the symptoms attendant upon it, as divine messages: contact has already been established, and, owing to this greater familiarity, the speaker feels justified to use prose. But also as regards their worldly readers, the humility of the 'Holy Sonnets' by far exceeds that of the *Devotions*. Even if the dedication to the *Devotions* observes all the codes of honour and politeness, its author is fairly confident about the benefits his dedicatee Prince Charles may gain from reading his work. The sonnet 'To E. of D. with six holy Sonnets', by contrast, is far more submissive and suggests that the poems it accompanies must be improved by their reader: 'You are that Alchimist which alwaies had / Wit, whose one spark could make good things of bad' (ll. 13–14). Such humility is reminiscent of a number of Donne's verse letters, for some of which Donne likewise used the sonnet form, whose strictness he considered an adequate framework for approaching even the highest authority of all, God himself. In addition, the sonnet gives shape to the speakers' outpourings, whose otherwise chaotic formlessness would be inappropriate for a petition to the divine. It also fashions them in a way that easily makes them recognisable as the commodity of a sacrifice.

The speakers of the 'Holy Sonnets' prostrate themselves before God in a gesture of offering. In the *Devotions*, by contrast, the speaker trusts that his sacrifice has already been accepted, as he believes his illness to be initiated by God, who thus himself prostrated the speaker. Their emergent 'Occasion' not only means the situation which gave rise to this work but also describes it as one that connects a fall or death (*'occasus'*) with a rising (*'emergo'*), hence fashioning Donne's sickness as typological of Christ's passion (Shuger, 1985: 39–40). The speaker's illness, the spectacle of his own body, is already given, and the largest part of the *Devotions* is devoted to making sense of its details (cf. Sawday, 1997: 39). All this takes place in the awareness that his suffering already indicates God's acceptance; his sickness puts him in the right mood for approaching God (cf. Doerksen, 2004: 158): 'Donne encounters God in the "emergent" occasion that is the subject of the *Devotions*; God speaks to him through the various stages of his illness and recovery' (Doerksen, 2004: 158; Papazian, 1992: 604–8). Since the 'emergent' in the title may be interpreted as 'pressing' (Partridge, 1978: 199), God even appears to be addressing the speaker quite urgently. The 'Holy Sonnets', by contrast, constitute self-created and self-creating theatres and do not function as 'the speaker's particular response to affliction' (Papazian, 1992: 610). Instead, they still have to create that sickness, that affliction which is needed to face God adequately, in the first place, and out of themselves. Because sickness is cured either through recovery or through death and salvation, the 'spiritual malaise' of the 'Holy Sonnets' 'is considerably ameliorated, if not cured in his *Devotions*' (Rollin, 1994: 51). Whereas the *Devotions* are initiated by the 'emergent occasion' of Donne's illness, in the case of the 'Holy Sonnets' each poem itself functions as its own emergent occasion, or rather the occasion that it causes to emerge out of itself. Less a moment's monument, they strive to be that moment itself. While the *Devotions* compare and contrast their speaker's spiritual mood with his state of health, the 'Holy Sonnets' strive to make sense, with dubious success, of the tensions and ruptures their speakers experience within themselves – such as in 'Oh, to vex me, contraryes meete in one'. It is probably no coincidence either that, in the concluding couplet, the speaker aligns his wavering disposition with the 'fantastique Ague' (l. 13) of a fever, and that he should end on a note of yearning for just such an illness as consumes the speaker of the *Devotions*; for 'Those are my best dayes, when I shake with feare' (l. 14).

In the *Devotions*, the occasion of the speaker's illness brings him much closer to death and his God, whereas a poem such as 'Oh, to vex me' still has to produce and stage these feverish shakings. The 'Holy Sonnets' are still busy establishing their speakers' relation towards God, whereas, in the sickness of the speaker, that relatedness is already given in the *Devotions*. As we have seen in Donne's letters, a relationship is begun in verse, before it can move on to the lesser formality of prose. Once a relationship is established, it still needs to be cultivated and tended to – but that may be done in the more familiar mode of prose. The less one knows the other party, and the greater the gap between the two correspondents, the more attention must be paid to form, and the more advisable is it to ingratiate, locate and place oneself through (the value of) one's own poetry. By the time Donne wrote the *Devotions*, he had been a revered divine of the Church of England for eight years, and probably felt not only fairly certain of his election but also slightly closer to God than the ordinary layman who wrote the majority of the 'Holy Sonnets'. This, too, may have lent him the self-confidence to address God in the less formal mode of the *Devotions*, and it also explains the slightly lecturing tone they sometimes slip into. Donne's prose is much more bound to given occasions or relationships than his poems. And this is probably why Donne's verse has been and will remain so much more popular with us than his prose – just as Jack Donne, rather than the dignified Dr Donne, has long been the favourite of literary critics. Both of them, however, strove for and used communication as a means for communion.

Notes

1 I hence do not share Schwartz's claim that, in Donne, communion between this world and the next is taken to be possible (cf. Schwartz, 2008: 89).
2 This passage may have constituted a veiled warning concerning the implications of a potential Spanish match for Prince Charles (cf. Gray/Shami, 1989).
3 The speaker's identification with his neighbour has been seen critically by Ellrodt (2000: 29) and Oliver (1997: 229), whereas Sherwood (1984: 189), Stein (1984: 86), Friederich (1978: 63) and Andreasen (1964–65: 215) are more benevolent.
4 For a thorough account of the interpersonal dimensions of early modern subjectivity, cf. Selleck (2008).
5 Such attempts at communion with Christ are the origin also of Jesuit spiritual exercises, under which the speaker's individuality is subsumed (cf. Van Laan, 1963; Cox, 1973: 332). With varying emphasis, other critics have considered the speaker of Donne's *Devotions* as both individualised and generally representative (cf. Andreasen, 1964–65: 209; Janel Mueller, 1968: 3; Sullivan, 1988: 52–3; Wilcox, 2007: 389; Conti, 2007: 372).
6 For the *Devotions'* precarious oscillation between the praying speaker's self and his God, cf. H. C. White, 1966.
7 The metaphor of patient and physician features also in *Pseudo-Martyr* and *Essays in Divinity* where the speaker thanks God that 'by the inhabitation of thy Spirit, and application of thy merit, hast made me mine own Christ; and contenting thy self with being my Medicine, allowest me to be my Physician' (*Essays* 76).
8 For Donne's doubts as to whether he should imitate Christ through martyrdom or rather endure earthly life, cf. Migan, 2007: 380.

9 For further parallels between Donne's sermons and *Devotions*, cf. Webber, 1968: 37; Janel Mueller, 1968: 4, 8; Nelson, 2003: 259.
10 For more details as to whether the *Devotions* constitute a literarily self-absorbed or an adequately devotional and generally accessible piece of writing, cf. D. W. Harding, 1972; Johnson, 1999: 180; Narveson, 2004: 121.

Conclusion – Being Don(n)e

> Here where by All All Saints invoked are,
> 'Twere too much schisme to be singular,
> And 'gainst a practise generall to warre.
> [. . .]
> May therefore this be'enough to testifie
> My true devotion, free from flattery;
> He that beleeves himselfe, doth never lie.
> ('A Letter to the Lady Carey, and Mrs. Essex Riche, From
> Amyens', ll. 1–3, 61–3)

In the field of Donne studies, there is much to learn not only about this writer's amorous and religious desires but also about the desires latent in literary criticism. Many Donne scholars both want to be Donne and to be done (Saunders, 2006: 3–4). By approaching his writings as denominationally more or less neutral performances, I have refrained from assigning Donne to any particular religious confession. I have taken care to avoid projecting on to him any of my own convictions, and creating a Donne in the image of my own religious desires. Such evasion is, of course, not a virtue in itself, and one may criticise my reading precisely because it fails to take a stand with regard to Donne's religious allegiances – undoubtedly one of the most relevant, if most contested, interests. But the general thrust of my argument actually does make a statement on Donne's religious identity: a theory of performativity goes hand in hand with a particular conception of language and identity that also has consequences for religious discourse and personal faith. Religion, as, for example, my interpretation of Donne's 'Holy Sonnets' has suggested, is a matter of performance. By this I do not mean to imply that religious faith is pretentious or illusory;

my intention has been to emphasise that personal and religious identity develop through processes in which 'saying' and 'playing' 'make it so'.

The preceding chapters, different as they are in their generic and theoretical emphases, consider Donne's poetry and prose in a performative dimension. Donne's sermons adopt some of the dramatic force of traditional ritual since they function as homiletic theatres which invite their listeners to personally re-enact the roles and examples suggested by their texts. Donne's 'Pulpit performances' manage to make vivid and perform an idea of conversion to God that relies on each person's willing co-operation. In so far as the preacher's persona features both as 'director' and (en)actor in the play he is producing, he recreates the Christian dogma of God's taking on a human form in Jesus Christ. Although, most of the time, the sermons' speakers rely quite confidently on the powers of language and identification, there are instances where the notion of (play-)acting by example is questioned and put into perspective.

Donne's worldly poetry is much more varied and even contradictory as regards the different 'plots' of each poem's individual performance. Here, too, however, each poem's internal communicative situation is in important ways reflected by the external performance context of a (predominantly) male coterie. Against the background of Austin's speech act theory, I have tried to show how the illocutionary force of a poetic speaker's utterance, for example that of persuading a woman to partake in sexual intercourse, may have the perlocutionary effect of gaining the poet the love and respect of his audience. Donne's poetic speakers engage not only in Promethean performances, as they linguistically create world, truth and self, but also in protean role-play and shape-shifting. The poems themselves function as stakes for (verbal) competition in a coterie context.

Many of Donne's worldly poems are not only uttered in a highly passionate vein, they are also exemplary of a notion of love as passion as it has been articulated both by Niklas Luhmann and similarly by Roland Barthes. The speakers of Donne's divine poetry are likewise passionate, most clearly so wherever they align themselves with the suffering Christ. However, much as Donne's 'Holy Sonnets' have in common with his *Songs and Sonets*, their performances are far more unstable and problematic since the communicative situation differs strikingly from that of their worldly counterparts. In that their external and internal communicative systems coalesce, the 'Holy Sonnets' function as theatres of their own, in which their speakers feature as actor and audience simultaneously. The emotional turmoil of these poems can often be explained by the speakers' doubts about their utterances' performative efficacy – a doubt much more prevalent here than in Donne's sermons.

Early modern epistolography conceives of the letter as an image of the writer's soul, but, at the same time, letter writing remained importantly shaped by convention, so that, depending on context and addressee, the writing persona still needed to adopt a certain role. Donne's letter writing personae take epistolary theory at its word by literally equating themselves with their own utterances. Not infrequently, they also attempt to create greater interdependency and intimacy with their addressees, whether patron(esse)s or friends, by identifying with them. When they do so, they often introduce parallels between the letter genre and spiritual discourse. These similarities are illustrative of a veritable religion of letters, whose doctrine, however, does not at all times bear out.

As each of the *Devotions* moves from initial meditation towards concluding prayer, it rehearses a development from communication towards communion that is reminiscent of Donne's epistolary performances. More than in the letters, however, the idea of communion is here related to contemporary theories of the Eucharist and Holy Communion as *imitatio Christi*. Not only are the *Devotions* more articulate as concerns the ambiguities and instabilities surrounding the Eucharist than are Donne's sermons – they also place greater emphasis on the Lord's Supper in particular and Christian devotion in general as a communal event and process respectively, in both of which the speaker considers himself more thoroughly implicated than is the case with Donne's preaching personae.

Apart from employing similar communicative strategies, the prose letters and the *Devotions* also have something else in common. Donne's oeuvre provides a poetic counterpart for each of these prose genres: the verse letters and the 'Holy Sonnets' respectively. The writing of poetry places the speaker in a more humble position than his addressee whereas prose comes across as more democratic. Moreover, while verse is more commonly used to establish a relationship in the first place, prose assumes the relationship between speaker and addressee, writer and God, to be in existence already and uses language to maintain and cultivate it further. As this final comparison illustrates, the performative parallels between Donne's various genres can hardly be denied: with various emphasis and for different motives, all of his writing uses language not only to say but to do something, and engages in theatricality and role-play from an interest not only in seeming but in being.

Performance and performativity are phenomena typical not only of Donne's writing but also of literary criticism. If it is true that, as critics, we 'change and even *create* our desires', or, more generally, our focus and thesis of research, 'in their formal articulation' (Saunders, 2006: 10), this implies that the study of literature significantly depends on how to do things with words. There is much space for each member of the 'Communitie' of Donne critics to perform as one finds one's 'fancy bent' ('Communitie', l. 6). The fancies of biographers such as Dennis Flynn and John Stubbs, or of critics such as Louis Martz and Barbara Lewalski, are bent towards different, if not opposite directions – and much as one may side with Flynn or Martz rather than Stubbs or Lewalski, or vice versa, there is no denying that criticism lives and thrives on such contradictory impulses. The controversy over Donne's religious affiliation importantly contributed to the theoretical thrust of the present study. Reading Barbara Lewalski's and Louis Martz's interpretations of Donne's divine poetry, I was stunned at how it was possible to agree with either approach. That each of these two monographs should come across so convincingly is due to these critics' abilities both to do things with words and vividly to create a Donne in the image of their particular argument – and as I realised that this was what Donne's own writings also endeavoured, the larger idea of *John Donne's Performances* was conceived. My own book cannot claim to be exempted from the performative strategies of literary criticism either: having invoked, if not 'All Saints', then at least nearly all of the most canonised of Donne critics, "[t]were too much schisme to be singular, / And 'gainst a practise generall to warre'. In reading Donne performatively, I, too, have created a particular kind of Donne, one who suits both my professional and personal interests in theories of performativity. What I have said of Donne, that, in the major part of his writings, both 'saying' and 'playing' importantly contribute to making it so, is true as well of my own work – but also of studies as influential and profound as Martz's and Lewalski's, and of Greenblatt's *Shakespearean Negotiations*: there, too, the critic confesses that, 'if I wanted to hear the voice of the other, I had to hear my own voice' (Greenblatt, 1990: 20).

It is in the nature even of the best criticism to make something true by saying that it is so. The more, the longer and the better one has argued a point, the more it may become convincing not only to oneself but eventually also to others. As Donne himself wrote, since '[h]e that beleeves himselfe, doth never lie', convincing both oneself and others through words may well testify to one's 'true devotion, free from flattery'. In arguing in favour of reading Donne performatively, I have suggested an image of John Donne as a man who put considerable trust in the powers of saying and play(-act)ing. Such an idea of the writer has the advantage of accommodating all of his works, since it enables us to include the multiple and divergent characters of his many writing and speaking personae.

Just as the speakers of Donne's 'Holy Sonnets' still have to await God's and Christ's verdict as to the persuasiveness and efficaciousness of their performance, this study of *John Donne's Performances* attends judgement by the 'Communitie' of readers and critics. I hope that since I 'beleeve [my]selfe', I 'never lie' in this book – but, as we read in Donne's *Devotions*, there may be instances where one internalises one's own lies so thoroughly that one is no longer able to recognise them as such (*Devotions* 53). Nevertheless, although I do not presume that this study will be as 'good' as to be loved by all critics, I hope that, neither, it will be hated as all 'ill' things must be. Once it forms part of the enormous body of Donne studies, it belongs to its 'fruits': 'He that but tasts, he that devours, / And he that leaves all, doth as well' ('Communitie', ll. 19–21). If each critic approaches this book 'as he shall find his fancy bent', it will reflect the ways in which Donne's writings, too, have been received, and thus hopefully likewise engender lively discussion, whether of Donne's works or of the writings of other metaphysical poets – as performances.

Bibliography

Primary literature

Donne, John, 1952, *Essays in Divinity*, ed. Evelyn M. Simpson (Oxford: Clarendon Press).
Donne, John, 1953–64, *The Sermons of John Donne*, ed. George R. Porter and Evelyn M. Simpson, 10 vols (Berkeley and Los Angeles: University of California Press).
Donne, John, 1967, *The Complete Poetry of John Donne*, ed. John T. Shawcross (New York: Anchor Books).
Donne, John, 1967, *Selected Prose*, chosen by Evelyn Simpson, ed. Helen Gardner and Timothy Healy (Oxford: Clarendon Press).
Donne, John, 1969, *Ignatius His Conclave*, ed. T. S. Healy (Oxford: Clarendon Press).
Donne, John, [1651] 1974, *Letters to Severall Persons of Honour* (Hildesheim, New York: Georg Olms Verlag).
Donne, John, 1975, *Devotions Upon Emergent Occasions*, ed. Anthony Raspa (Montreal and London: McGill-Queen's University Press).
Donne, John, 1980, *Paradoxes and Problems*, ed. Helen Peters (Oxford: Clarendon Press).
Donne, John, 1984, *Biathanatos*, ed. Ernest W. Sullivan II (Newark: University of Delaware Press/London and Toronto: Associated University Presses).
Donne, John, 1993, *Pseudo-Martyr*, ed. Anthony Raspa (Montreal: McGill-Queen's University Press).

Secondary literature

Abrahamson, R. L., 1983, 'The vision of redemption in Donne's *Devotions Upon Emergent Occasions*', *Studia Mystica*, 6:1.
Adlington, Hugh, 2008, 'Donne and diplomacy', in Jeanne Shami (ed.), *Renaissance Tropologies: The Cultural Imagination of Early Modern England* (Pittsburgh: Duquesne University Press).

Aers, David and Gunther Kress, 1981a, ' "Darke Texts Need Notes": Versions of self in Donne's verse epistles', in David Aers, Bob Hodge and Gunther Kress (eds), *Literature, Language and Society in England 1580–1680* (Dublin: Gill and Macmillan).
Aers, David and Gunther Kress, 1981b, 'Vexatious contraries: A reading of Donne's poetry', in David Aers, Bob Hodge and Gunther Kress (eds), *Literature, Language and Society in England 1580–1680* (Dublin: Gill and Macmillan).
Aers, David, Bob Hodge and Gunther Kress, 1981, *Literature, Language and Society in England 1580–1680* (Dublin: Gill and Macmillan).
Albrecht, Christian and Martin Weber, 2002a, 'Einführung', in Christian Albrecht and Martin Weber (eds), *Klassiker der protestantischen Predigtlehre* (Tübingen: Mohr Siebeck).
Albrecht, Christian and Martin Weber (eds), 2002b, *Klassiker der protestantischen Predigtlehre* (Tübingen: Mohr Siebeck).
Althoff, Gerd, 2003, *Die Macht der Rituale: Symbolik und Herrschaft im Mittelalter* (Darmstadt: Wissenschaftliche Buchgesellschaft).
Altizer, Alma B., 1973, *Self and Symbolism in the Poetry of Michelangelo, John Donne, and Agrippa d'Aubigne* (The Hague: Martinus Nijhoff).
Altman, Janet Gurkin, 1982, *Epistolarity: Approaches to a Form* (Columbus: Ohio State University Press).
Alvarez, A., 1961, *The School of Donne* (London: Chatto and Windus).
Andreasen, N. J. C., 1963, 'Theme and structure in Donne's Satyres', *Studies in English Literature*, 3.
Andreasen, N. J. C., 1964–65, 'Donne's *Devotions* and the psychology of assent', *Modern Philology*, 62:3.
Aughterson, Kate (ed.), 1998, *The English Renaissance: An Anthology of Sources and Documents* (London, New York: Routledge).
Augustine, St, 1991, *Confessions*, trans. and introd. Henry Chadwick (Oxford: Oxford University Press).
Austin, J. L., [1962] 1975, *How to Do Things with Words: The William James Lectures Delivered at Harvard University in 1955*, 2nd ed., ed. J. O. Urmson and Marian Sbisà (Cambridge, MA: Harvard University Press).
Bach, Rebecca Ann, 2005, '(Re)Placing John Donne in the history of sexuality', *English Literary History*, 72:1.
Bacon, Francis, [1605] 1947, 'The nature of poetry', in Edmund D. Jones (ed.), *English Critical Essays (Sixteenth, Seventeenth and Eighteenth Centuries)* (London: Oxford University Press).
Bacon, Francis, [1587, 1625] 1972, *Essays*, introd. Michael J. Hawkins (London: J. M. Dent & Sons Ltd).
Baker, David J., 2004, ' "The religion I was born in": Forgetting Catholicism and remembering the King in Donne's *Devotions*', in Christopher Ivic and Grant Williams (eds), *Forgetting in Early Modern English Literature: Lethe's Legacies* (London: Routledge).

Baker, Sir Richard, 1641, *A Chronicle of the Kings of England* (no place, no publisher).
Baker, Sir Richard, [1662] 1972, *Theatrum redivivum, or The theatre vindicated*, introd. Peter Davison (New York, London: Johnson Reprint Corporation).
Bakhtin, M. M., 1981, *The Dialogic Imagination: Four Essays*, ed. Michael Holquist, trans. Caryl Emerson and Michael Holquist (Austin, London: University of Texas Press).
Bald, R. C., 1970, *John Donne: A Life* (Oxford: Clarendon Press).
Baldick, Chris, 1996, *Concise Oxford Dictionary of Literary Terms* (Oxford, New York: Oxford University Press).
Barber, C. L., 1988, *Creating Elizabethan Tragedy* (Chicago: The University of Chicago Press).
Barish, Jonas, 1981, *The Antitheatrical Prejudice* (Berkeley: University of California Press).
Bartenschlager, Klaus, 1970, *Die Situation des Sprechers im Gedicht: Wyatt, Sidney, Spenser: Ein historisch-typologischer Versuch* (Munich: Kurfürstendruck).
Barthes, Roland, [1977] 1979, *A Lover's Discourse: Fragments*, trans. Richard Howard (New York: Hill and Wang).
Bates, Catherine, 2007, *Masculinity, Gender and Identity in the English Renaissance Lyric* (Cambridge: Cambridge University Press).
Bauer, Robert J., 1977, 'Donne's letter to Herbert re-examined', in Gary A Stringer (ed.), *New Essays on Donne* (Salzburg: Universität Salzburg).
Baumbach, Sibylle, 2007, *Let me behold thy face: Physiognomik und Gesichtslektüren in Shakespeares Tragödien* (Heidelberg: Winter).
Baumlin, James S., 1991, *John Donne and the Rhetorics of Renaissance Discourse* (Columbia, London: University of Missouri Press).
Beer, Gillian, 1997, 'The making of a cliché: "No Man is an Iland"', *European Journal of English Studies*, 1.
Bell, Catherine, 1992, *Ritual Theory, Ritual Practice* (New York, Oxford: Oxford University Press).
Bell, Ilona, 1986, '"Under Ye Rage of a Hott Sonn & Yr Eyes": John Donne's love letters to Ann More', in Claude J. Summers and Ted-Larry Pebworth (eds), *The Eagle and the Dove: Reassessing John Donne* (Columbia: University of Missouri Press).
Bell, Ilona, 1996, '"if it be a shee": The riddle of Donne's "Curse"', in M. Thomas Hester (ed.), *John Donne's 'desire of more'. The Subject of Anne More Donne in His Poetry* (Newark, London: University of Delaware Press).
Bellette, Anthony F., 1975, '"Little Worlds Made Cunningly": Significant form in Donne's *Holy Sonnets* and "Goodfriday, 1613"', *Studies in Philology*, 72.

Belsey, Catherine, 1994, *Desire: Love Stories in Western Culture* (Oxford: Blackwell).
Benet, Diana Treviño, 2001, ' "This Booke, (thy Emblem)": Donne's *Holy Sonnets* and biography', in Mary Ellen Henley and W. Speed Hill (eds), *Wrestling with God: Literature & Theology in the English Renaissance* (no place, no publisher).
Bennett, Roger E., 1941, 'Donne's *Letters to Severall Persons of Honour*', *Papers of the Modern Language Association*, 56.
Berley, Mark (ed.), 2003, *Reading the Renaissance: Ideas and Idioms from Shakespeare to Milton* (Pittsburgh, PA: Duquesne University Press).
Bermingham, Ann and John Brewer (eds), 1995, *The Consumption of Culture 1600–1800: Image, Object, Text* (London, New York: Routledge).
Berry, Paul, 1975, *The Essential Self: An Introduction to Literature* (New York: McGraw-Hill Book Company).
Berry, Philippa, 1989, *Of Chastity and Power: Elizabethan Literature and the Unmarried Queen* (London, New York: Routledge).
Blackmur, R. P., 1954, *Language as Gesture: Essays in Poetry* (London: George Allen & Unwin Ltd).
Blissett, William, 2001, ' "The strangest pagant, fashion'd like a court": John Donne and Ben Jonson to 1600 – Parallel lives', in Mary Ellen Henley and W. Speed Hill (eds), *Wrestling with God: Literature & Theology in the English Renaissance* (no place, no publisher).
Booth, Stephen, 1998, 'On the aesthetics of acting', in Jay L. Halio and Hugh Richmond (eds), *Shakespearean Illuminations: Essays in Honor of Marvin Rosenberg* (Newark: University of Delaware Press).
Boutcher, Warren, 2002, 'Literature, thought or fact? Past and present directions in the study of the early modern letter', in Toon Van Houdt, Jan Papy, Gilbert Tournoy and Constant Matheeussen (eds), *Self-Presentation and Social Identification: The Rhetoric and Pragmatics of Letter Writing in Early Modern Times* (Leuven: Leuven University Press).
Branaman, Ann, 1997, 'Goffman's social theory', in Charles Lemert and Ann Branaman (eds), *The Goffman Reader* (Oxford: Blackwell).
Brennan, Michael, 1988, *Literary Patronage in the English Renaissance: The Pembroke Family* (London, New York: Routledge).
Brett, Julia, 1999, 'Distance, demystification, and Donne's divine Poetry', *John Donne Journal*, 18.
Bridge, G. Richmond, 2001, 'Trumpet vibrations: Theological reflections on Donne's Doomsday Sonnet', in Mary Ellen Henley and W. Speed Hill (eds), *Wrestling with God: Literature & Theology in the English Renaissance* (no place, no publisher).
Bristol, Michael D. and Arthur F. Marotti (eds), 2000a, *Print, Manuscript, Performance: The Changing Relations of the Media in Early Modern England* (Columbus: Ohio State University Press).

Bristol, Michael D. and Arthur F. Marotti, 2000b, 'Introduction', in Michael D. Bristol and Arthur F. Marotti (eds), *Print, Manuscript, Performance: The Changing Relations of the Media in Early Modern England* (Ohio: Ohio State University Press).

Brooks, Cleanth, [1947] 1968, *The Well Wrought Urn: Studies in the Structure of Poetry* (London: Methuen).

Brown, Cedric, 2008, 'Presence, obligation and memory in John Donne's texts for the Countess of Bedford', *Renaissance Studies*, 22:1.

Brown, Meg Lota, 1995, *Donne and the Politics of Conscience in Early Modern England* (Leiden, New York, Cologne: Brill).

Brown, Piers, 2009, 'Donne's hawkings', *Studies in English Literature*, 49:1.

Bryan, Robert A., 1962, 'John Donne's use of the anathema', *The Journal of English and German Philology*, 61.

Buc, Philippe, 2001, *The Dangers of Ritual: Between Early Medieval Texts and Social Scientific Theory* (Princeton, Oxford: Princeton University Press).

Burke, Peter, 1997, 'Representations of the self from Petrarch to Descartes', in Roy Porter (ed.), *Rewriting the Self: Histories from the Renaissance to the Present* (London: Routledge).

Burnham, Douglas and Enrico Giaccherini (eds), 2005, *The Poetics of Transubstantiation: From Theology to Metaphor* (Aldershot: Ashgate).

Burrow, Collin, 2006, 'Recribations': Review of *Donne: The Reformed Soul* by John Stubbs, *London Review of Books*, 28:19.

Bush, Douglas, 1962, *English Literature in the Earlier Seventeenth Century 1600–1660*, 2nd ed. (Oxford: Clarendon Press).

Butler, Judith, 1990, *Gender Trouble: Feminism and the Subversion of Identity* (London, New York: Routledge).

Butler, Judith, 1997, *Excitable Speech: A Politics of the Performative* (London, New York: Routledge).

Cameron, Allen Barry, 1976, 'Donne's deliberative verse epistles', *English Literary Renaissance*, 6.

Carey, John, [1981] 1990, *John Donne: Life, Mind and Art* (London: Faber).

Carlson, Marvin, 1996, *Performance: A Critical Introduction* (London, New York: Routledge).

Carrithers, Gale H., 1972, *Donne at Sermons: A Christian Existential World* (Albany: State University of New York Press).

Carrithers Jr, Gale H. and James D. Hardy, Jr, 1992, 'Love, power, dust royall, gavelkinde: Donne's politics', *John Donne Journal*, 11.

Castiglione, Baldassare, 1966, *The Book of the Courtier*, trans. Sir Thomas Hoby, introd. W. H. D. Rouse (London: Dent).

Chamberlin, John S., 1976, *Increase and Multiply: Arts-of-Discourse Procedure in the Preaching of Donne* (Chapel Hill: University of North Carolina Press).

Cheney, Patrick, Andrew Hadfield and Garrett A. Sullivan, Jr (eds), 2007, *Early Modern English Poetry: A Critical Companion* (Oxford: Oxford University Press).
Chuilleanáin, Eiléan Ní, 1984, 'Time, place and the congregation in Donne's sermons', in John Scattergood (ed.), *Literature and Learning in Medieval and Renaissance England: Essays Presented to Fitzroy Pyle* (Blackrock: Irish Academic Press).
Clark, Ira, 1982, *Christ Revealed: The History of the Neotypological Lyric in the English Renaissance* (Gainesville, FL: University Presses of Florida).
Clements, Arthur L., 1990, *Poetry of Contemplation: John Donne, George Herbert, Henry Vaughan, and the Modern Period* (Albany: State University of New York Press).
Colclough, David (ed.), 2003, *John Donne's Professional Lives* (Cambridge: Brewer).
Conti, Brooke, 2003, 'Donne, doubt, and the *Devotions Upon Emergent Occasions*', *John Donne Journal*, 22.
Conti, Brooke, 2007, 'The *Devotions*: Popular and critical reception', *John Donne Journal*, 26.
Cooper, Robert M., 1977, 'The political implications of Donne's *Devotions*', in Gary A. Stringer (ed.), *New Essays on Donne* (Salzburg: Universität Salzburg).
Cormican, John D., 1978, 'The letter as a genre in early modern English', *USF Language Quarterly*, 16:3–4.
Corns, Thomas N. (ed.), 1993, *The Cambridge Companion to English Poetry: Donne to Marvell* (Cambridge: Cambridge University Press).
Corthell, Ronald J., 1981, '"Friendships Sacraments": John Donne's familiar letters', *Studies in Philology*, 78.
Corthell, Ronald, 1997, *Ideology and Desire in Renaissance Poetry: The Subject of Donne*, (Detroit: Wayne State University Press).
Cox III, Gerard H., 1973, 'Donne's *Devotions*: A meditative sequence on repentance', *Harvard Theological Review*, 66.
Crane, David, 1975, 'English translations of the *Imitatio Christi* in the sixteenth and seventeenth centuries', *Renaissance History*, 13.
Cressy, David and Lori Anne Ferrell (eds), 1996, *Religion and Society in Early Modern England: A Sourcebook* (London, New York: Routledge).
Crockett, Bryan, 1995, *The Play of Paradox: Stage and Sermon in Renaissance England* (Philadelphia: University of Pennsylvania Press).
Crockett, Bryan, 2000, 'Thomas Playfere's poetics of preaching', in Lori Anne Ferrell and Peter McCullough (eds), *The English Sermon Revised: Religion, Literature and History 1600–1750* (Manchester, New York: Manchester University Press).
Culler, Jonathan, [1982] 1994, *On Deconstruction: Theory and Criticism after Structuralism* (London: Routledge).

Cummings, Brian, 2002, *The Literary Culture of the Reformation: Grammar and Grace* (Oxford: Oxford University Press).
Davies, Horton, 1986, *Like Angels from a Cloud: The English Metaphysical Preachers 1588–1645* (San Marino, CA: Huntington Library).
Davies, Horton, 1996, *Worship and Theology in England*, 3 vols (Cambridge: Eerdmans).
Davies, Stevie, 1994, *John Donne* (Plymouth: Northcote House Publishers).
Davis, Walter R., 1986, 'Meditation, typology, and the structure of John Donne's sermons', in Claude J. Summers and Ted-Larry Pebworth (eds), *The Eagle and the Dove: Reassessing John Donne* (Columbia: University of Missouri Press).
Davison, Peter (ed.), 1972, 'A short treatise against stage-plays, 1625' [anonymous], in *Critics and Apologists of the English Theatre: A Selection of Seventeenth-century Pamphlets in Facsimile* (New York, London: Johnson Reprint Company).
Dawson, Anthony B. and Paul Yachnin, 2001, *The Culture of Playgoing in Shakespeare's England: A Collaborative Debate* (Cambridge: Cambridge University Press).
Day, Angel, [1599] 1967, *The English Secretary Or Methods of Writing Epistles and Letters With A Declaration of such Tropes, Figures, and Schemes, as either usually or for ornament sake are therein required*, introd. Robert O. Evans (Gainesville, FL: Scholars' Facsimiles & Reprints).
Dean, Paul, 2007, 'Donne's "Dialogue of One"', *New Criterion*, 25:5.
Derrida, Jacques, [1972] 1986, 'Signature, event, context', in Alan Bass (trans.), *Margins of Philosophy* (Brighton: The Harvester Press).
Deubel, Volker, 1971, *Elisabethanische Bauformen in der Dichtung von John Donne: Untersuchungen zum Stilwandel in der englischen Lyrik* (Stuttgart: Kohlhammer).
Diehl, Huston, 1997, *Staging Reform, Reforming the Stage: Protestantism and Popular Theater in Early Modern England* (Ithaca: Cornell University Press).
DiPasquale, Theresa M., 1993, 'Donne's Catholic Petrarchans: The Babylonian captivity of desire', in Claude J. Summers and Ted-Larry Pebworth (eds), *Renaissance Discourses of Desire* (Columbia, London: University of Missouri Press).
DiPasquale, Theresa M., 1995, 'Receiving a sexual sacrament: "The Flea" as profane Eucharist', in Raymond J. Frontain and Frances M. Malpezzi (eds), *John Donne's Religious Imagination: Essays in Honor of John T. Shawcross* (Conway: University of Central Arkansas Press).
DiPasquale, Theresa M., 1999, *Literature and Sacrament: The Sacred and the Secular in John Donne* (Pittsburgh, PA: Duquesne University Press).
DiPasquale, Theresa M., 2008, *Refiguring the Sacred Feminine: The Poems of John Donne, Aemilia Lanyer, and John Milton* (Pittsburgh, PA: Duquesne University Press).

Docherty, Thomas, 1986, *John Donne, Undone* (London, New York: Methuen).
Doerksen, Daniel W., 1995, ' "Saint Pauls Puritan": John Donne's "Puritan" imagination in the sermons', in Raymond J. Frontain and Frances M. Malpezzi (eds), *John Donne's Religious Imagination: Essays in Honor of John T. Shawcross* (Conway: University of Central Arkansas Press).
Doerksen, Daniel W., 1997, *Conforming to the Word: Herbert, Donne, and the English Church before Laud* (Lewisburg: Bucknell University Press).
Doerksen, Daniel W., 2004, 'Discerning God's voice, God's hand: Scripturalist moderation in Donne's *Devotions*', in Daniel W. Doerksen and Christopher Hodgkins (eds), *Centered on the Word: Literature, Scripture, and the Tudor-Stuart Middle Way* (Newark: University of Delaware Press).
Doerksen, Daniel W. and Christopher Hodgkins, 2004a, 'Introduction', in Daniel W. Doerksen and Christopher Hodgkins (eds), *Centered on the Word: Literature, Scripture, and the Tudor-Stuart Middle Way* (Newark: University of Delaware Press).
Doerksen, Daniel W. and Christopher Hodgkins (eds), 2004b, *Centered on the Word: Literature, Scripture, and the Tudor-Stuart Middle Way* (Newark: University of Delaware Press).
Dolan, Kathleen H., 1979, '*Materia in Potentia*: The paradox of the quintessence in Donne's "A Nocturnall Upon S. Lucies Day"', *Renascence*, 32.
Döring, Tobias, 2005, 'Introduction', in Susanne Rupp and Tobias Döring (eds), *Performances of the Sacred in Late Medieval and Early Modern England* (Amsterdam, New York: Rodopi).
Döring, Tobias, 2006, *Performances of Mourning in Shakespearean Theatre and Early Modern Culture* (Basingstoke: Palgrave).
Dubrow, Heather, 1979, 'Donne's satires and satiric traditions', *Studies in English Literature*, 19.
Dubrow, Heather, 1982, *Genre* (London, New York: Methuen).
Dubrow, Heather, 1995, *Echoes of Desire: English Petrarchism and Its Counterdiscourses* (New York: Cornell University Press).
Duffy, Eamon, 1992, *The Stripping of the Altars: Traditional Religion in England c. 1400–c. 1580* (New Haven, London: Yale University Press).
Dyson, A. E. and Julian Lovelock, [1973] 1985, ' "Contracted thus": "The Sunne Rising"', in Julian Lovelock (ed.), *Donne: Songs and Sonets: A Selection of Critical Essays* (London: Macmillan).
Earle, Rebecca, 1999a, 'Introduction: letters, writers and the historian', in Rebecca Earle (ed.), *Epistolary Selves: Letters and Letter-writers 1600–1945* (Aldershot: Ashgate).
Earle, Rebecca (ed.), 1999b, *Epistolary Selves: Letters and Letter-writers 1600–1945* (Aldershot: Ashgate).

Easthope, Anthony, 1983, *Poetry as Discourse* (London, New York: Methuen).
Eliot, T. S., [1932] 1939, *Selected Essays* (London: Faber).
Ellrodt, Robert, 2000, *Seven Metaphysical Poets: A Structural Study of the Unchanging Self* (Oxford: Oxford University Press).
Engemann, Wilfried, 2002, *Einführung in die Homiletik* (Tübingen: Francke).
Erasmus, [1536] 1985, *On the Writing of Letters: De conscribendis epistolis*, trans. and ann. Charles Fantazzi, *Collected Works of Erasmus: Literary and Educational Writings 3: De Conscribendis Epistolis / Formula / De Civilitate*, ed. J. K. Sowards (Toronto: University of Toronto Press).
Erne, Lukas, 2001, 'Donne and Christ's spouse', *Essays in Criticism*, 51:2.
Esterhammer, Angela, 1994, *Creating States: Studies in the Performative Language of John Milton and William Blake* (Toronto, Buffalo, London: University of Toronto Press).
Estrin, Barbara L., 1988, 'The Lady's gestures and John Donne's gestes', *Forum for Modern Language Studies*, 24:3.
Faust, Joan, 1993, 'John Donne's verse letters to the Countess of Bedford: Mediators in a poet-patroness relationship', *John Donne Journal*, 12.
Faust, Joan, 2002, 'Donne on love: Sometimes the end just doesn't justify the means', in Claude J. Summers and Ted-Larry Pebworth (eds), *Fault Lines and Controversies in the Study of Seventeenth-Century English Literature* (Columbia: University of Missouri Press).
Ferrell, Lori Anne, 1992, 'Donne and his master's voice, 1615–1625', *John Donne Journal*, 11.
Ferrell, Lori Anne, [2002] 2004, 'Religious persuasions, c. 1580–c. 1620', in Arthur F. Kinney (ed.), *A Companion to Renaissance Drama* (Malden, Oxford, Victoria: Blackwell).
Ferrell, Lori Anne and Peter McCullough, 2000a, 'Revising the study of the English sermon', in Lori Anne Ferrell and Peter McCullough (eds), *The English Sermon Revised: Religion, Literature and History 1600–1750* (Manchester, New York: Manchester University Press).
Ferrell, Lori Anne and Peter McCullough (eds), 2000b, *The English Sermon Revised: Religion, Literature and History 1600–1750* (Manchester, New York: Manchester University Press).
Ferry, Anne, 1983, *The 'Inward' Language: Sonnets of Wyatt, Sidney, Shakespeare, Donne* (Chicago, London: The University of Chicago Press).
Fischer-Lichte, Erika, 2002, 'Grenzgänge und Tauschhandel: Auf dem Wege zu einer performativen Kultur', in Uwe Wirth (ed.), *Performanz: Zwischen Sprachphilosophie und Kulturwissenschaften* (Frankfurt am Main: Suhrkamp).
Fischer-Lichte, Erika, 2004, *Ästhetik des Performativen* (Frankfurt am Main: Suhrkamp).

Fish, Stanley E., 1972, *Self-Consuming Artifacts: The Experience of Seventeenth-Century Literature* (Berkeley, Los Angeles: University of California Press).

Fish, Stanley, [1990] 1999, 'Masculine persuasive force: Donne and verbal power', in Andrew Mousley (ed.), *John Donne: Contemporary Critical Essays* (Basingstoke: Macmillan).

Fisher, Sheila and Janet E. Halley (eds), 1989, *Seeking the Woman in Late Medieval and Renaissance Writings: Essays in Feminist Contextual Criticism* (Knoxville: The University of Tennessee Press).

Fitzmaurice, Susan M., 2002, *The Familiar Letter in Early Modern English: A Pragmatic Approach* (Amsterdam, Philadelphia: John Benjamins Publishing Company).

Flynn, Dennis, 1989, 'Donne and a female coterie', *Lit: Literature Interpretation Theory*, 1.

Flynn, Dennis, 1995, *John Donne and the Ancient Catholic Nobility* (Bloomington, Indianapolis: Indiana University Press).

Franssen, Paul J. C. M., 1996, 'Donne's jealous God and the concept of sacred parody', in Helen Wilcox, Richard Todd and Alasdair Macdonald (eds), *Sacred and Profane: Secular and Devotional Interplay in Early Modern British Literature* (Amsterdam: VU University Press).

Friederich, Reinhard H., 1978, 'Strategies of persuasion in Donne's *Devotions*', *Ariel*, 9.

Frontain, Raymond J., 1987, 'Redemption typology in John Donne's "Batter My Heart"', *Journal of the Rocky Mountain Medieval and Renaissance Association*, 8.

Frontain, Raymond J., 1992. ' "With Holy Importunitie, with a Pious Impudencie": John Donne's attempts to provoke election', *Journal of the Rocky Mountain Medieval and Renaissance Association*, 13.

Frontain, Raymond-Jean, 1994, 'Donne's emblematic imagination: vision and reformation of the self in "The Crosse"', *Publications of the Arkansas Philological Association*, 20:1.

Frontain, Raymond J., 1995, 'Introduction: "Make all this All": The religious operations of John Donne's imagination', in Raymond J. Frontain and Frances M. Malpezzi (eds), *John Donne's Religious Imagination: Essays in Honor of John T. Shawcross* (Conway: University of Central Arkansas Press).

Frontain, Raymond-Jean, 1996, 'Translating heavenwards: "Upon the Translation of the Psalmes" and John Donne's poetics of praise', *Explorations in Renaissance Culture*, 22.

Frontain, Raymond-Jean, 2004, ' "the man which have affliction seene": Donne, Jeremiah, and the fashioning of lamentation', in Daniel W. Doerksen and Christopher Hodgkins (eds), *Centered on the Word: Literature, Scripture, and the Tudor-Stuart Middle Way* (Newark: University of Delaware Press).

Frontain, Raymond J., 2006, 'Donne, Spenser, and the performative mode of Renaissance poetry', *Explorations in Renaissance Culture*, 32:1.

Frontain, Raymond J. and Frances M. Malpezzi (eds), 1995, *John Donne's Religious Imagination: Essays in Honor of John T. Shawcross* (Conway: University of Central Arkansas Press).

Frost, Kate Gartner, 1990, *Typology, Numerology, and Autobiography in Donne's Devotions Upon Emergent Occasions* (Princeton: Princeton University Press).

Gardner, Helen, 1957, 'Introduction', in Helen Gardner (ed.), *The Metaphysical Poets* (Harmondsworth: Penguin).

Gardner, Helen, [1959, 1973] 1985, 'The argument about "The Ecstasy"', in Julian Lovelock (ed.), *Donne: Songs and Sonets: A Selection of Critical Essays* (London: Macmillan).

Geyer, Paul and Roland Hagenbüchle (eds), 1992, *Das Paradox: Eine Herausforderung des abendländischen Denkens* (Tübingen: Stauffenburg).

Gibbson, Jonathan, 2000, 'Letters', in Michael Hattaway (ed.), *A Companion to English Renaissance Literature and Culture* (Oxford: Blackwell).

Goffman, Erving, [1959] 1976, *The Presentation of Self in Everyday Life* (Harmondsworth: Penguin).

Goffman, Erving, 2002, 'Moduln und Modulationen', in Uwe Wirth (ed.), *Performanz: Zwischen Sprachphilosophie und Kulturwissenschaften* (Frankfurt am Main: Suhrkamp).

Goldberg, Jonathan, 1971, 'The understanding of sickness in Donne's *Devotions*', *Renaissance Quarterly*, 24:4.

Goldberg, Jonathan, 1983, *James I and the Politics of Literature: Jonson, Shakespeare, Donne, and Their Contemporaries* (Baltimore, London: The Johns Hopkins University Press).

Goldberg, Jonathan, 1990, *Writing Matter: From the Hands of the English Renaissance* (Stanford: Stanford University Press).

Gosse, Edmund, 1899, *The Life and Letters of John Donne*, 2 vols (London: Heinemann).

Gray, Dave and Jeanne Shami, 1989, 'Political advice in Donne's *Devotions*: No man is an island', *Modern Language Quarterly*, 50:4.

Greenblatt, Stephen, 1980, *Renaissance Self-Fashioning* (Chicago: The University of Chicago Press).

Greenblatt, Stephen, 1990, *Shakespearean Negotiations: The Circulation of Social Energy in Renaissance England* (Oxford: Clarendon Press).

Greenblatt, Stephen, 1991, *Marvelous Possessions: The Wonder of the New World* (Oxford: Clarendon Press).

Greene, Thomas M., 1996, 'Ritual and text in the Renaissance', in Jonathan Hart (ed.), *Reading the Renaissance: Culture, Poetics, and Drama* (New York: Garland Publishing).

Grimes, Ronald L., 1990, *Ritual Criticism: Case Studies in Its Practice, Essays on Its Theory* (Columbia: University of South Carolina Press).

Guibbory, Achsah, [1990] 1999, ' "Oh, Let Mee Not Serve So": The politics of love in Donne's elegies', in Andrew Mousley (ed.), *John Donne: Contemporary Critical Essays* (Basingstoke: Macmillan).

Guibbory, Achsah, 1993a, 'Sexual politics/political sex: Seventeenth-century love poetry', in Claude J. Summers and Ted-Larry Pebworth (eds), *Renaissance Discourses of Desire* (Columbia: University of Missouri Press).

Guibbory, Achsah, 1993b, 'John Donne', in Thomas N. Corns (ed.), *The Cambridge Companion to English Poetry: Donne to Marvell* (Cambridge: Cambridge University Press).

Guibbory, Achsah (ed.), 2006, *The Cambridge Companion to John Donne* (Cambridge: Cambridge University Press).

Guibbory, Achsah, 2007, 'Donne's religious poetry and the trauma of grace', in Patrick Cheney, Andrew Hadfield and Garrett A. Sullivan, Jr (eds), *Early Modern English Poetry: A Critical Companion* (Oxford: Oxford University Press).

Guillén, Claudio, 1986, 'Notes toward the study of the Renaissance letter', in Barbara Kiefer Lewalski (ed.), *Renaissance Genres: Essays on Theory, History, and Interpretation* (Cambridge, MA, London: Harvard University Press).

Gundersheimer, Werner L., 1981, 'Patronage in the Renaissance: An exploratory approach', in Guy Fitch Lytle and Stephen Orgel (eds), *Patronage in the Renaissance* (Princeton: Princeton University Press).

Guss, Donald L., 1966, *John Donne, Petrarchist: Italianate Conceits and Love Theory in The Songs and Sonets* (Detroit: Wayne State University Press).

Hadfield, Andrew, 2007, 'Donne's *Songs and Sonets* and artistic identity', in Patrick Cheney, Andrew Hadfield and Garrett A. Sullivan, Jr (eds), *Early Modern English Poetry: A Critical Companion* (Oxford: Oxford University Press).

Hall, Michael L., 1983, 'Circles and circumvention in Donne's sermons', *Journal of English and Germanic Philology*, 82.

Halley, Janet E., 1989, 'Textual intercourse: Anne Donne, John Donne, and the sexual poetics of textual exchange', in Sheila Fisher and Janet E. Halley (eds), *Seeking the Woman in Late Medieval and Renaissance Writings: Essays in Feminist Contextual Criticism* (Knoxville: The University of Tennessee Press).

Halpern, Richard, [1993] 1999, 'The lyric in the field of information: Autopoiesis and history in Donne's *Songs and Sonets*', in Andrew Mousley (ed.), *John Donne: Contemporary Critical Essays* (Basingstoke: Macmillan).

Hamilton, Donna B. and Richard Strier (eds), 1996, *Religion, Literature, and Politics in Post-Reformation England, 1540–1688* (Cambridge: Cambridge University Press).

Harding, D. W., 1972, 'The *Devotions* now', in A. J. Smith (ed.), *John Donne: Essays in Celebration* (London: Methuen).

Harding, Robert, 1981, 'Corruption and the moral boundaries of patronage in the Renaissance', in Guy Fitch Lytle and Stephen Orgel (eds), *Patronage in the Renaissance* (Princeton: Princeton University Press).

Harland, Paul W., 1986, 'Dramatic technique and personae in Donne's sermons', *English Literary History*, 53.

Harland, Paul W., 1987, 'Imagination and affections in John Donne's preaching', *John Donne Journal*, 6:1.

Harland, Paul W., 1995, 'A true transubstantiation: Donne, self-love, and the Passion', in Raymond J. Frontain and Frances M. Malpezzi (eds), *John Donne's Religious Imagination: Essays in Honor of John T. Shawcross* (Conway: University of Central Arkansas Press).

Harris, Victor, 1962, 'John Donne and the theatre', *Philological Quarterly*, 41.

Hart, Jonathan (ed.), 1996, *Reading the Renaissance: Culture, Poetics, and Drama* (New York: Garland Publishing).

Hartwig, Joan, 1995, 'Donne's horse and rider as body and soul', in Raymond J. Frontain and Frances M. Malpezzi (eds), *John Donne's Religious Imagination: Essays in Honor of John T. Shawcross* (Conway: University of Central Arkansas Press).

Harvey, Elizabeth D. and Katharine Eisaman Maus (eds), 1990, *Soliciting Interpretation: Literary Theory and Seventeenth-Century English Poetry* (Chicago: The University of Chicago Press).

Haskin, Dayton, 1993, 'A history of Donne's "Canonization" from Izaak Walton to Cleanth Brooks', *Journal of English and Germanic Philology*, 92:1.

Hattaway, Michael (ed.), 2000, *A Companion to English Renaissance Literature and Culture* (Oxford: Blackwell).

Haugen, Kristine, 2002, 'Imaginary correspondence: Epistolary rhetoric and the hermeneutics of disbelief', in Toon Van Houdt, Jan Papy, Gilbert Tournoy and Constant Matheeussen (eds), *Self-Presentation and Social Identification: The Rhetoric and Pragmatics of Letter Writing in Early Modern Times* (Leuven: Leuven University Press).

Healy, Thomas, 2005, 'Performing the self: Reformation history and the English Renaissance lyric', in Susanne Rupp and Tobias Döring (eds), *Performances of the Sacred in Late Medieval and Early Modern England* (Amsterdam, New York: Rodopi).

Henderson, Judith Rice, 1993, 'On reading the rhetoric of the Renaissance letter', in Heinrich F. Plett (ed.), *Renaissance-Rhetorik: Renaissance Rhetoric* (Berlin, New York: De Gruyter).

Henderson, Judith Rice, 2002, 'Humanist letter writing: Private conversation or public forum?', in Toon Van Houdt, Jan Papy, Gilbert

Tournoy and Constant Matheeussen (eds), *Self-Presentation and Social Identification: The Rhetoric and Pragmatics of Letter Writing in Early Modern Times* (Leuven: Leuven University Press).

Henley, Mary Ellen and W. Speed Hill (eds), 2001, *Wrestling with God: Literature & Theology in the English Renaissance* (no place, no publisher).

Herz, Judith Scherer, 1986, ' "An Excellent Exercise of Wit that Speaks so Well of Ill": Donne and the poetics of concealment', in Claude J. Summers and Ted-Larry Pebworth (eds), *The Eagle and the Dove: Reassessing John Donne* (Columbia: University of Missouri Press).

Herz, Judith Scherer, 2000, 'Of circles, friendship, and the imperatives of literary history', in Claude J. Summers and Ted-Larry Pebworth (eds), *Literary Circles and Communities in Renaissance England* (Columbia and London: University of Missouri Press).

Herz, Judith Scherer, 2006, 'Reading and rereading Donne's poetry', in Achsah Guibbory (ed.), *The Cambridge Companion to John Donne* (Cambridge: Cambrige University Press).

Hester, M. Thomas, 1982, *Kinde Pitty and Brave Scorn: John Donne's Satyres* (Durham, NC: Duke University Press).

Hester, M. Thomas, 1987, 'Re-signing the text of the self: Donne's "As due by many titles"', in Claude J. Summers and Ted-Larry Pebworth (eds), *'Bright Shootes of Everlastingnesse': The Seventeenth-Century Religious Lyric* (Columbia: University of Missouri Press).

Hester, M. Thomas, 1996a, ' "Let me Love": Reading the sacred "Currant" of Donne's profane lyrics', in Helen Wilcox, Richard Todd and Alasdair Macdonald (eds), *Sacred and Profane: Secular and Devotional Interplay in Early Modern British Literature* (Amsterdam: VU University Press).

Hester, Thomas (ed.), 1996b, *John Donne's 'desire of more': The Subject of Anne More Donne in His Poetry* (Newark, London: University of Delaware Press).

Hester, M. Thomas, 2000, ' "Like a spyed Spie": Donne's baiting of Marlowe', in Claude J. Summers and Ted-Larry Pebworth (eds), *Literary Circles and Communities in Renaissance England* (Columbia and London: University of Missouri Press).

Hillman, David and Carla Mazzio (eds), 1997, *The Body in Parts: Fantasies of Corporeality in Early Modern Europe* (New York, London: Routledge).

Hobby, Elaine, 1993, 'The politics of gender', in Thomas N. Corns (ed.), *The Cambridge Companion to English Poetry: Donne to Marvell* (Cambridge: Cambridge University Press).

Hodgson, Elizabeth M. A., 1999, *Gender and the Sacred Self in John Donne* (Newark: University of Delaware Press).

Höfele, Andreas, 1985, 'Rollen-Ich und lyrisches Ich: Zur Poetik des dramatic monologue', *Literaturwissenschaftliches Jahrbuch im Auftrag der Görres-Gesellschaft*, 26.

Höfele, Andreas, 1991, '"... As farre as doth the mind of man": Das elisabethanische Theater – ein heiliger Ort, ein unheiliger?', *Shakespeare-Jahrbuch West*.

Holmes, Michael Morgan, 2001, *Early Modern Metaphysical Literature: Nature, Custom and Strange Desires* (Basingstoke: Palgrave).

Horace, [1926] 1966, *Satires, Epistles and Ars Poetica*, trans. H. Rushton Fairclough (London: Heinemann).

How, James, 2003, *Epistolary Spaces: English Letter Writing from the Foundation of the Post Office to Richardson's Clarissa* (Aldershot: Ashgate).

Hudson, Elizabeth K., 1988, 'English protestants and the *imitatio Christi*, 1580–1620', *Sixteenth-Century Journal*, 19:4.

Humphrey, Caroline and James Laidlaw, 1994, *The Archetypal Actions of Ritual: A Theory of Ritual Illustrated by the Jain Rite of Worship* (Oxford: Clarendon Press).

Hunt, Clay, 1954, *Donne's Poetry: Essays in Literary Analysis* (New Haven: Yale University Press).

Hurley, Ann Hollinshead, 2005, *John Donne's Poetry and Early Modern Visual Culture* (Selinsgrove: Susquehanna University Press).

Hyatte, Reginald, 1994, *The Arts of Friendship: The Idealization of Friendship in Medieval and Early Renaissance Literature* (Leiden, New York, Cologne: Brill).

Ignatius of Loyola, 2004, *Personal Writings*, trans. and introd. Joseph A. Munitiz and Philip Endean (London: Penguin).

Ivic, Christopher and Grant Williams (eds), 2004, *Forgetting in Early Modern English Literature: Lethe's Legacies* (London: Routledge).

Jagodzinski, Cecile M., 1999, *Privacy and Print: Reading and Writing in Seventeenth-Century England* (Charlottesville and London: University Press of Virginia).

Johnson, Jeffrey, 1995, 'Wrestling with God: John Donne at prayer', in Raymond J. Frontain and Frances M. Malpezzi (eds), *John Donne's Religious Imagination: Essays in Honor of John T. Shawcross* (Conway: University of Central Arkansas Press).

Johnson, Jeffrey, 1999, *The Theology of John Donne* (Cambridge: Brewer).

Jones, Edmund D. (ed.), 1947, *English Critical Essays (Sixteenth, Seventeenth and Eighteenth Centuries)* (London: Oxford University Press).

Juvenal and Persius, 2004, ed. and trans. Susanna Morton Braund (Cambridge, MA: Harvard University Press).

Kaufman, Peter Iver, 1996, *Prayer, Despair, and Drama: Elizabethan Introspection* (Urbana and Chicago: University of Illinois Press).

Kawasaki, Toshihiko, 1971, 'Donne's Microcosm', in Earl Miner (ed.), *Seventeenth-Century Imagery: Essays on Uses of Figurative Language from Donne to Farquhar* (Berkeley: University of California Press).

Kelly, David, 1995/96, 'The Canonization of John Donne', *Sydney Studies in English*, 21.

Kempis, Thomas à, [1441] 1934, *The Imitation of Christ*, ed. Brother Leo, F. S. C. (New York: The Macmillan Company).
Kerins, Frank, 1984, 'The "business" of satire: John Donne and the reformation of the satirist', *Texas Studies in Literature and Language*, 26.
Kernan, Alvin, 1959, *The Cankered Muse: Satire of the English Renaissance* (New Haven and London: Yale University Press).
Kerrigan, William, [1974] 1999, 'The fearful accommodations of John Donne', in Andrew Mousley (ed.), *John Donne: Contemporary Critical Essays* (Basingstoke: Macmillan).
Kinney, Arthur F. (ed.), [2002] 2004, *A Companion to Renaissance Drama*, 2nd ed. (Malden, Oxford, Victoria: Blackwell).
Klawitter, George, 1992, 'Verse letters to T. W. from John Donne: "By You My Love Is Sent"', in Claude J. Summers (ed.), *Homosexuality in Renaissance and Enlightenment England: Literary Representations in Historical Context* (Binghamton: Haworth).
Klawitter, George, 1994, *The Enigmatic Narrator: The Voicing of Same-Sex Love in the Poetry of John Donne* (New York: Peter Lang).
Klawitter, George, 1995, 'John Donne's attitude toward the Virgin Mary: The public versus the private voice', in Raymond J. Frontain and Frances M. Malpezzi (eds), *John Donne's Religious Imagination: Essays in Honor of John T. Shawcross* (Conway: University of Central Arkansas Press).
Knapp, Jeffrey, 2002, *Shakespeare's Tribe: Church, Nation, and Theater in Renaissance England* (Chicago, London: The University of Chicago Press).
Korhonen, Kuisma, 2006, *Textual Friendship: The Essay as Impossible Encounter: From Plato and Montaigne to Levinas and Derrida* (New York: Humanity Books).
Krämer, Sibylle, 2001, *Sprache, Sprechakt, Kommunikation: Sprachtheoretische Positionen des 20. Jahrhunderts* (Frankfurt am Main: Suhrkamp).
Krämer, Sibylle, 2002, 'Sprache-Stimme-Schrift: Sieben Gedanken über Performativität als Medialität', in Uwe Wirth (ed.), *Performanz: Zwischen Sprachphilosophie und Kulturwissenschaften* (Frankfurt am Main: Suhrkamp).
Kuchar, Gary, 2001, 'Embodiment and representation in John Donne's *Devotions Upon Emergent Occasions*', *Prose Studies*, 24:2.
Kuchar, Gary, 2008, 'Petrarchism and repentance in John Donne's *Holy Sonnets*', *Modern Philology*, 105:3.
Labriola, Albert C., 1995, 'Sacerdotalism and sainthood in the poetry and life of John Donne: "The Canonization" and Canonization', *John Donne Journal*, 14.
Labriola, Albert C., 2003, '"Vile harsh attire": Biblical typology in John Donne's "Spit in my face yee Jewes"', *John Donne Journal*, 22.

Lake, Peter and Michael Questier, 2002, *The Antichrist's Lewd Hat: Protestants, Papists and Players in Post-Reformation England* (New Haven: Yale University Press).

Lange, Marjory E., 1996, *Telling Tears in the English Renaissance* (Leiden, New York, Cologne: Brill).

Lauritsen, John R., 1976, 'Donne's *Satyres*: The drama of self-discovery', *Studies in English Literature*, 16.

Leech, Geoffrey N., 1969, *A Linguistic Guide to English Poetry* (London: Longman).

Leishman, J. B., [1951, 1973] 1985, 'Logical structure in the *Songs and Sonets*', in Julian Lovelock (ed.), *Donne: Songs and Sonets: A Selection of Critical Essays* (London: Macmillan).

Lemert, Charles and Ann Branaman (eds), 1997, *The Goffman Reader* (Oxford: Blackwell).

Levy-Navarro, Elena, 2003, 'Breaking down the walls that divide: Antipolemicism in the *Devotions Upon Emergent Occasions*', in Mary Arshagouni Papazian (ed.), *John Donne and the Protestant Reformation: New Perspectives* (Detroit: Wayne State University Press).

Lewalski, Barbara Kiefer, 1973, *Donne's Anniversaries and the Poetry of Praise: The Creation of a Symbolic Mode* (Princeton: Princeton University Press).

Lewalski, Barbara Kiefer, 1979, *Protestant Poetics and the Seventeenth-Century Religious Lyric* (Princeton: Princeton University Press).

Lewalski, Barbara Kiefer (ed.), 1986, *Renaissance Genres: Essays on Theory, History, and Interpretation* (Cambridge, MA, London: Harvard University Press).

Linsley, Joy L., 1995, 'A holy puzzle: Donne's "Holy Sonnet XVII"', in Raymond J. Frontain and Frances M. Malpezzi (eds), *John Donne's Religious Imagination: Essays in Honor of John T. Shawcross* (Conway: University of Central Arkansas Press).

Lobsien, Eckhard, 2004, 'Aspekte der Krise und poetische Krisenbewältigungsstrategien in der englischen Renaissance', *Poetica*, 36.

Lobsien, Verena Olejniczak, 1999, *Skeptische Phantasie: Eine andere Geschichte der frühneuzeitlichen Literatur* (Munich: Fink).

Loewenstein, David and Janel Mueller (eds), 2002, *The Cambridge History of Early Modern English Literature* (Cambridge: Cambridge University Press).

Lovelock, Julian (ed.), [1973] 1985, *Donne: Songs and Sonets: A Selection of Critical Essays* (London: Macmillan).

Low, Anthony, 1978, *Love's Architecture: Devotional Modes in Seventeenth-Century English Poetry* (New York: New York University Press).

Low, Anthony, 1993, *The Reinvention of Love: Poetry, Politics and Culture from Sidney to Milton* (Cambridge: Cambridge University Press).

Low, Anthony, 1997, 'Recent studies in the English Renaissance', *Studies in English Literature*, 37.
Lowe, Irving, 1961, 'John Donne: The middle way. The reason-faith equation in Donne's sermons', *Journal of the History of Ideas*, 22.
Luhmann, Niklas, 1994, *Liebe als Passion: Zur Codierung von Intimität* (Frankfurt am Main: Suhrkamp).
Lukken, Gerard, 2005, *Rituals in Abundance: Critical Reflections on the Place, Form, and Identity of Christian Ritual in Our Culture* (Leuven, Dudley, MA: Peeters).
Lytle, Guy Fitch and Stephen Orgel (eds), 1981, *Patronage in the Renaissance* (Princeton: Princeton University Press).
Maassen, Irmgard, 2001, 'Text und/als/in der Performanz in der frühen Neuzeit: Thesen und Überlegungen', *Paragrana*, 10:1.
Maassen, Irmgard, 2005, 'Canonized by love? Religious rhetoric and gender-fashioning in the sonnet', in Susanne Rupp and Tobias Döring (eds), *Performances of the Sacred in Late Medieval and Early Modern England* (Amsterdam, New York: Rodopi).
Magnusson, Lynne, 1999, *Shakespeare and Social Dialogue: Dramatic Language and Elizabethan Letters* (Cambridge: Cambridge University Press).
Mahler, Andreas, 1991, 'Profanisierung des Sakralen – Sakralisierung des Profanen: Beobachtungen zur Entsubstantialisierung des religiösen Diskurses in der Frühen Neuzeit', *Shakespeare-Jahrbuch West*.
Mahler, Andreas, 1992, *Moderne Satireforschung und elisabethanische Verssatire: Texttheorie, Epistemologie, Gattungspoetik* (Munich: Fink).
Malpezzi, Frances, 1995, 'Donne's transcendent imagination: The divine poems as hierophantic experience', in Raymond J. Frontain and Frances M. Malpezzi (eds), *John Donne's Religious Imagination: Essays in Honor of John T. Shawcross* (Conway: University of Central Arkansas Press).
Malzahn, Manfred, 2003, 'The flea, the sun, and the critic: A communicational approach to John Donne's poetry', *Symbolism*, 3.
Marotti, Arthur F., 1981, 'John Donne and the rewards of patronage', in Guy Fitch Lytle and Stephen Orgel (eds), *Patronage in the Renaissance* (Princeton: Princeton University Press).
Marotti, Arthur F., 1986, *John Donne, Coterie Poet* (Madison: University of Wisconsin Press).
Marotti, Arthur F., 1993, 'Manuscript, print, and the social history of the lyric', in Thomas N. Corns (ed.), *The Cambridge Companion to English Poetry: Donne to Marvell* (Cambridge: Cambridge University Press).
Marotti, Arthur F. (ed.), 1994, *Critical Essays on John Donne* (New York: Macmillan).
Marotti, Arthur F., 1995, *Manuscript, Print, and the English Renaissance Lyric* (Ithaca and London: Cornell University Press).

Marotti, Arthur F., 2002, 'John Donne's conflicted anti-Catholicism', *Journal of English and Germanic Philology*, 101:3.

Marotti, Arthur F., 2005, *Religious Ideology and Cultural Fantasy: Catholic and Anti-Catholic Discourses in Early Modern England* (Notre Dame, IN: University of Notre Dame Press).

Marotti, Arthur F., 2006, 'The social context and nature of Donne's writing: occasional verse and letters', in Achsah Guibbory (ed.), *The Cambridge Companion to John Donne* (Cambridge: Cambridge University Press).

Martin, Catherine Gimelli, 1995, 'Pygmalion's progress in the garden of love, or The wit's work is never Donne', in Claude J. Summers and Ted-Larry Pebworth (eds), *The Wit of Seventeenth-Century Poetry* (Columbia, London: University of Missouri Press).

Martin, Raymond and John Barresi, 2006, *The Rise and Fall of Soul and Self: An Intellectual History of Personal Identity* (New York: Columbia University Press).

Martz, Louis, [1954] 1962, *The Poetry of Meditation: A Study in English Religious Literature* (New Haven and London: Yale University Press).

Martz, Louis, 1969, *The Wit of Love* (Notre Dame: The University of Notre Dame Press).

Martz, Louis L., 1994, 'The poetry of meditation: Searching the memory', in John R. Roberts (ed.), *New Perspectives on the Seventeenth-Century English Religious Lyric* (Columbia and London: University of Missouri Press).

Masselink, Noralyn, 1992, 'A matter of interpretation: Example and Donne's role as preacher and as poet', *John Donne Journal*, 11.

Matt, Peter von, 2008, *Die Intrige: Theorie und Praxis der Hinterlist* (Munich: dtv).

Maule, Jeremy, 1996, 'Donne and the past', in Helen Wilcox, Richard Todd and Alasdair Macdonald (eds), *Sacred and Profane: Secular and Devotional Interplay in Early Modern British Literature* (Amsterdam: VU University Press).

Maurer, Margaret, 1976, 'John Donne's verse letters', *Modern Language Quarterly*, 37.

Maurer, Margaret, 1980, 'The real presence of Lucy Russell, Countess of Bedford, and the terms of John Donne's "Honour is so sublime perfection"', *English Literary History*, 47.

Maurer, Margaret, 1982, 'The poetical familiarity of John Donne's letters', *Genre*, 15.

Maus, Katharine Eisaman, 1995, *Inwardness and Theater in the English Renaissance* (Chicago: The University of Chicago Press).

McCullough, Peter, 1998, *Sermons at Court: Politics and Religion in Elizabethan and Jacobean Preaching* (Cambridge: Cambridge University Press).

McEachern, Claire and Debora Shuger (eds), 1997, *Religion and Culture in Renaissance England* (Cambridge: Cambridge University Press).
McNees, Eleanor, 1987, 'John Donne and the Anglican doctrine of the Eucharist', *Texas Studies in Literature*, 29.
McNees, Eleanor J., 1992, *Eucharistic Poetry: The Search for Presence in the Writings of John Donne, Gerard Manley Hopkins, Dylan Thomas, and Geoffrey Hill* (Lewisburg: Bucknell University Press).
McRae, Andrew, 2007, 'Satire and the politics of the town', in Patrick Cheney, Andrew Hadfield and Garrett A. Sullivan, Jr (eds), *Early Modern English Poetry: A Critical Companion* (Oxford: Oxford University Press).
Migan, Neal E., 2007, '*Apologia Pro Vita Sua*: Martyrdom in Donne's prose', *Prose Studies*, 29:3.
Milgate, Wesley, 1967, 'General Introduction', in Wesley Milgate (ed.), *John Donne: The Satires, Epigrams and Verse Letters* (Oxford: Clarendon Press).
Miner, Earl (ed.), 1971, *Seventeenth-Century Imagery: Essays on Uses of Figurative Language from Donne to Farquhar* (Berkeley: University of California Press).
Mitchell, W. Fraser, 1962, *English Pulpit Oratory from Andrewes to Tillotson: A Study of Its Literary Aspects* (New York: Russell & Russell).
Moloney, Michael F., [1950, 1973] 1985, 'Donne's metrical practice', in Julian Lovelock (ed.), *Donne: Songs and Sonets: A Selection of Critical Essays* (London: Macmillan).
Montaigne, Michel Lord of, 1946, *Essays*, 3 vols. introd. A. R. Waller, trans. John Florio (London: Dent & Sons Ltd).
Montrose, Louis, 1980, 'The purpose of playing: Reflections on a Shakespearean anthropology', *Helios*, 7.
Mousley, Andrew (ed.), 1999, *John Donne: Contemporary Critical Essays* (Basingstoke: Macmillan).
Mousley, Andy, 2005, 'Transubstantiating love: John Donne and cultural criticism', in Douglas Burnham and Enrico Giaccherini (eds), *The Poetics of Transubstantiation: From Theology to Metaphor* (Aldershot: Ashgate).
Mueller, Janel M., 1968, 'The exegesis of experience: Dean Donne's *Devotions Upon Emergent Occasions*', *Journal of English and Germanic Philology*, 67.
Mueller, Janel, [1989] 1994, 'Women among the Metaphysicals: A case, mostly, of being Donne for', in Arthur F. Marotti (ed.), *Critical Essays on John Donne* (New York: Macmillan).
Mueller, William R., 1962, *John Donne: Preacher* (Princeton, NJ: Princeton University Press).
Muir, Edward, 1997, *Ritual in Early Modern Europe* (Cambridge: Cambridge University Press).

Müller, Wolfgang G., 1976, 'Die Definition in John Donnes Liebesdichtung', *Anglia*, 94:1/2.

Müller, Wolfgang G., 1980, 'Der Brief als Spiegel der Seele: Zur Geschichte eines Topos der Epistolartheorie von der Antike bis zu Samuel Richardson', *Antike und Abendland: Beiträge zum Verständnis der Griechen und Römer und ihres Nachlebens*, 26.

Müller, Wolfgang G., 1983, ' "My selfe, the hardest object of the sight": The problem of personal identity in John Donne's poetry', in Roland Hagenbüchle and Laura Skandera (eds), *Poetry and Epistemology: Turning Points in the History of Poetic Knowledge*, Eichstätter Beiträge: Sprache und Literatur, 20 (Regensburg: Pustet).

Müller, Wolfgang G., 1986, 'Liturgie und Lyrik: John Donne's "The Litanie" ', *Literaturwissenschaftliches Jahrbuch*, 27.

Müller, Wolfgang G., 1992, 'Das Paradoxon in der englischen Barocklyrik: John Donne, George Herbert, Richard Crashaw', in Paul Geyer and Roland Hagenbüchle (eds), *Das Paradox: Eine Herausforderung des abendländischen Denkens* (Tübingen: Stauffenburg).

Müller-Zettelmann, Eva and Margarete Rubik, 2005a, 'Introduction', in Eva Müller-Zettelmann and Margarete Rubik (eds), *Theory into Poetry: New Approaches to the Lyric* (Amsterdam, New York: Rodopi).

Müller-Zettelmann, Eva and Margarete Rubik (eds), 2005b, *Theory into Poetry: New Approaches to the Lyric* (Amsterdam, New York: Rodopi).

Nardo, Anna K., 1986, 'John Donne at play in between', in Claude J. Summers and Ted-Larry Pebworth (eds), *The Eagle and the Dove: Reassessing John Donne* (Columbia: University of Missouri Press).

Narveson, Kate, 1998, 'Piety and the genre of Donne's *Devotions*', *John Donne Journal*, 17.

Narveson, Kate, 2004, 'Publishing the sole-talk of the soule: Genre in early Stuart piety', in Daniel W. Doerksen and Christopher Hodgkins (eds), *Centered on the Word: Literature, Scripture, and the Tudor-Stuart Middle Way* (Newark: University of Delaware Press).

Nelson, Brent, 2003, '*Pathopoeia* and the Protestant form of Donne's *Devotions Upon Emergent Occasions*', in Mary Arshagouni Papazian (ed.), *John Donne and the Protestant Reformation: New Perspectives* (Detroit: Wayne State University Press).

Nelson, Brent, 2005, *Holy Ambition: Rhetoric, Courtship, and Devotion in the Sermons of John Donne* (Arizona: no publisher).

Norbrook, David, 1990, 'The monarchy of wit and the republic of letters: Donne's politics', in Elizabeth D. Harvey and Katharine Eisaman Maus (eds), *Soliciting Interpretation: Literary Theory and Seventeenth-Century English Poetry* (Chicago: The University of Chicago Press).

Nutt, Joe, 1999, *John Donne: The Poems* (Basingstoke: Macmillan).

O'Connell, Michael, 1985, 'The idolatrous eye: iconoclasm, antitheatricality, and the image of the Elizabethan theater', *English Literary History*, 52.
O'Connell, Patrick F., 1986, ' "La Corona": Donne's Ars Poetica Sacra', in Claude J. Summers and Ted-Larry Pebworth (eds), *The Eagle and the Dove: Reassessing John Donne* (Columbia: University of Missouri Press).
Oliver, P. M., 1997, *Donne's Religious Writing: A Discourse of Feigned Devotion* (London, New York: Longman).
Oxford English Dictionary Online, 2008, www.dictionary.oed.com (Oxford: Oxford University Press).
Papazian, Mary Arshagouni, 1992, 'Donne, Election, and the *Devotions Upon Emergent Occasions*', *Huntington Library Quarterly*, 55.
Papazian, Mary Arshagouni (ed.), 2003, *John Donne and the Protestant Reformation: New Perspectives* (Detroit: Wayne State University Press).
Parker, T. H. L., 1992, *Calvin's Preaching* (Westminster: John Knox Press).
Parr, Anthony, 2007, 'John Donne, travel writer', *The Huntington Library Quarterly*, 70:1.
Parry, Graham, 2002, 'Literary patronage', in David Loewenstein and Janel Mueller (eds), *The Cambridge History of Early Modern English Literature* (Cambridge: Cambridge University Press).
Partridge, A. C., 1978, *John Donne: Language and Style* (London: André Deutsch).
Paster, Gail Kern, 1993, *The Body Embarrassed: Drama and the Discipline of Shame in Early Modern England* (Ithaca, NY: Cornell University Press).
Paster, Gail Kern, 2004, *Humoring the Body: Emotions and the Shakespearean Stage* (Chicago: The University of Chicago Press).
Patrides, C. A., 1981, 'The epistolary art of the Renaissance: The Biblical premises', *Philological Quarterly*, 60:3.
Patterson, Annabel, 1990, 'All Donne', in Elizabeth D. Harvey and Katharine Eisaman Maus (eds), *Soliciting Interpretation: Literary Theory and Seventeenth-Century English Poetry* (Chicago: The University of Chicago Press).
Patterson, Annabel, [1993] 1994, 'Quod oportet *versus* quod convenit: *John Donne, Kingsman?*', in Arthur F. Marotti (ed.), *Critical Essays on John Donne* (New York: Macmillan).
Pebworth, Ted-Larry, 1989, 'John Donne, coterie poetry, and the text as performance', *Studies in English Literature*, 29.
Peck, Linda Levy, 1981, 'Court patronage and government policy: The Jacobean dilemma', in Guy Fitch Lytle and Stephen Orgel (eds), *Patronage in the Renaissance* (Princeton: Princeton University Press).
Pender, Stephen, 2003, 'Essaying the body: Donne, affliction, and medicine', in David Colclough (ed.), *John Donne's Professional Lives* (Cambridge: Brewer).

Petrey, Sandy, 1990, *Speech Acts and Literary Theory* (New York, London: Routledge).

Pfister, Manfred, [1988] 2000, *Das Drama: Theorie und Analyse*, 10th ed. (Munich: Fink).

Pfister, Manfred, 2001, 'Skalierung von Performativität', *Paragrana*, 10:1.

Pfister, Manfred, 2005, '"As an unperfect actor on the stage": Notes towards a definition of performance and performativity in Shakespeare's *Sonnets*', in Eva Müller-Zettelmann and Margarete Rubik (eds), *Theory into Poetry: New Approaches to the Lyric* (Amsterdam, New York: Rodopi).

Pfister, Manfred and Kurt Tetzeli von Rosador, 1991, 'Desakralisierung und Resakralisierung', *Shakespeare-Jahrbuch West*.

Piesse, A. J. (ed.), 2000, *Sixteenth-Century Identities* (Manchester: Manchester University Press).

Pinka, Patricia Garland, 1982, *This Dialogue of One: The Songs and Sonets of John Donne* (Alabama: The University of Alabama Press).

Plett, Heinrich F. (ed.), 1993, *Renaissance-Rhetorik: Renaissance Rhetoric* (Berlin, New York: De Gruyter).

Plett, Heinrich F., 2004, *Rhetoric and Renaissance Culture* (Berlin, New York: De Gruyter).

Porter, Roy (ed.), 1997, *Rewriting the Self: Histories from the Renaissance to the Present* (London: Routledge).

Post, Jonathan F. S., 1999, *English Lyric Poetry: The Early Seventeenth Century* (London, New York: Routledge).

Pritchard, R. E., 1994, 'Donne's image and dream', *John Donne Journal*, 13:1–2.

Puttenham, George, [1589, 1904] 1959, 'The Arte of English Poesie', in Gregory Smith (ed.), *Elizabethan Critical Essays*, 2 vols (Oxford: Oxford University Press).

Questier, Michael C., 1996, *Conversion, Politics and Religion in England, 1580–1625* (Cambridge: Cambridge University Press).

Quinn, Dennis B., 1962, 'John Donne's principles of Biblical exegesis', *Journal of English and Germanic Philology*, 61.

Radzinowicz, Mary Ann, 1987, '"Anima Mea" psalms and John Donne's religious poetry', in Claude J. Summers and Ted-Larry Pebworth (eds), *'Bright Shootes of Everlastingnesse': The Seventeenth-Century Religious Lyric* (Columbia: University of Missouri Press).

Rajan, Tilottama, [1982] 1999, '"Nothing sooner broke": Donne's *Songs and Sonets* as self-consuming artifact', in Andrew Mousley (ed.), *John Donne: Contemporary Critical Essays* (Basingstoke: Macmillan).

Rawson, Claude (ed.), 1984, *English Satire and the Satiric Tradition* (Oxford: Basil Blackwell).

Reiss, Timothy J., 2003, *Mirages of the Selfe: Patterns of Personhood in Ancient and Early Modern Europe* (Stanford, CA: Stanford University Press).
Richmond, H. M., 1973, 'Donne's master: The young Shakespeare', *Criticism*, 15.
Ricks, Christopher, 1988, 'Donne after love', in Elaine Scarry (ed.), *Literature and the Body: Essays on Populations and Persons* (Baltimore, London: The Johns Hopkins University Press).
Roberts, John R. (ed.), 1994, *New Perspectives on the Seventeenth-Century English Religious Lyric* (Columbia: University of Missouri Press).
Rollin, Roger B., 1986, '"Fantastique Ague": The Holy Sonnets and religious melancholy', in Claude J. Summers and Ted-Larry Pebworth (eds), *The Eagle and the Dove: Reassessing John Donne* (Columbia: University of Missouri Press).
Rollin, Roger B., 1994, 'John Donne's *Holy Sonnets* – The sequel: *Devotions Upon Emergent Occasions*', *John Donne Journal*, 13.
Rössler, Dietrich, 1994, *Grundriß der Praktischen Theologie*, 2nd ed. (Berlin: De Gruyter).
Rössler, Dietrich, 2002, 'Beispiel und Erfahrung: Zu Luthers Homiletik', in Christian Albrecht and Martin Weber (eds), *Klassiker der protestantischen Predigtlehre* (Tübingen: Mohr Siebeck).
Roston, Murray, 1974, *The Soul of Wit: A Study of John Donne* (Oxford: Clarendon Press).
Roston, Murray, 2007, *Tradition and Subversion in Renaissance Literature: Studies in Shakespeare, Spenser, Jonson, and Donne* (Pittsburgh, PA: Duquesne University Press).
Ruf, Frederick J., 1997, *Entangled Voices: Genre and the Religious Construction of the Self* (Oxford: Oxford University Press).
Rupp, Susanne, 2001, *'From Grace to Glory': Himmelsvorstellungen in der englischen Theologie und Literatur des 17. Jahrhunderts* (Heidelberg: Winter).
Rupp, Susanne, 2005, 'Performing heaven: The state of grace in seventeenth-century Protestant theology', in Susanne Rupp and Tobias Döring (eds), *Performances of the Sacred in Late Medieval and Early Modern England* (Amsterdam, New York: Rodopi).
Rupp, Susanne and Tobias Döring (eds), 2005, *Performances of the Sacred in Late Medieval and Early Modern England* (Amsterdam, New York: Rodopi).
Salenius, Maria, 2001, 'The circle and the line: Two metaphors of God and His works in John Donne's *Devotions Upon Emergent Occasions*', *Neuphilologische Mitteilungen*, 102:2.
Sanders, Wilbur, 1971, *John Donne's Poetry* (Cambridge: Cambridge University Press).

Saunders, Ben, 2006, *Desiring Donne: Poetry, Sexuality, Interpretation* (Cambridge, MA, London: Harvard University Press).
Sawday, Jonathan, 1997, 'Self and selfhood in the seventeenth century', in Roy Porter (ed.), *Rewriting the Self: Histories from the Renaissance to the Present* (London: Routledge).
Scarry, Elaine, 1988a, 'Donne: "But yet the body is his booke"', in Elaine Scarry (ed.), *Literature and the Body: Essays on Populations and Persons* (Baltimore, London: The Johns Hopkins University Press).
Scarry, Elaine (ed.), 1988b, *Literature and the Body: Essays on Populations and Persons* (Baltimore, London: The Johns Hopkins University Press).
Scattergood, John (ed.), 1984, *Literature and Learning in Medieval and Renaissance England: Essays Presented to Fitzroy Pyle* (Blackrock: Irish Academic Press).
Schalkwyk, David, 2002, *Speech and Performance in Shakespeare's Sonnets and Plays* (Cambridge: Cambridge University Press).
Schechner, Richard, 1988, *Performance Theory: Revised and Expanded Edition* (New York, London: Routledge).
Schleiner, Winfried, 1970, *The Imagery of Donne's Sermons* (Providence: Brown University Press).
Schneider, Gary, 2005, *The Culture of Epistolarity: Vernacular Letters and Letter Writing in Early Modern England, 1500–1700* (Newark: University of Delaware Press).
Schoenfeldt, Michael, 1997a, 'The gender of religious devotion: Amelia Lanyer and John Donne', in Claire McEachern and Debora Shuger (eds), *Religion and Culture in Renaissance England* (Cambridge: Cambridge University Press).
Schoenfeldt, Michael, 1997b, 'Fables of the belly in early modern England', in David Hillman and Carla Mazzio (eds), *The Body in Parts: Fantasies of Corporeality in Early Modern Europe* (New York, London: Routledge).
Schoenfeldt, Michael C., 1999, *Bodies and Selves in Early Modern England: Physiology and Inwardness in Spenser, Shakespeare, Herbert, and Milton* (Cambridge: Cambridge University Press).
Schoenfeldt, Michael, 2001, '"That spectacle of too much weight": The poetics of sacrifice in Donne, Herbert, and Milton', *Journal of Medieval and Early Modern Studies*, 31:3.
Schwartz, Regina Mara, 2008, *Sacramental Poetics at the Dawn of Secularism: When God Left the World* (Stanford, CA: Stanford University Press).
Scodel, Joshua, 1991, *The English Poetic Epitaph: Commemoration and Conflict from Jonson to Wordsworth* (Ithaca and London: Cornell University Press).
Scodel, Joshua, 1995, 'John Donne and the religious politics of the mean', in Raymond J. Frontain and Frances M. Malpezzi (eds), *John Donne's Religious Imagination: Essays in Honor of John T. Shawcross* (Conway: University of Central Arkansas Press).

Scodel, Joshua, 2005, ' "None's Slave": Some versions of liberty in Donne's *Satires 1* and *4*', *English Literary History*, 72:2.
Searle, John, 1969, *Speech Acts: An Essay in the Philosophy of Language* (Cambridge: Cambridge University Press).
Searle, John, 1979, *Expression and Meaning: Studies in the Theory of Speech Acts* (Cambridge: Cambridge University Press).
Seelig, Sharon Cadman, 1989, 'In sickness and in health: Donne's *Devotions Upon Emergent Occasions*', *John Donne Journal*, 8.
Seigel, Jerrold, 2005, *The Idea of the Self: Thought and Experience in Western Europe since the Seventeenth Century* (Cambridge: Cambridge University Press).
Selleck, Nancy, 2001, 'Donne's body', *Studies in English Literature*, 41:1.
Selleck, Nancy, 2008, *The Interpersonal Idiom in Shakespeare, Donne, and Early Modern Culture* (Basingstoke: Palgrave).
Sellin, Paul R., 1996, 'The mimetic poetry of Jack and John Donne: A field theory for the amorous and the divine', in Helen Wilcox, Richard Todd and Alasdair Macdonald (eds), *Sacred and Profane: Secular and Devotional Interplay in Early Modern British Literature* (Amsterdam: VU University Press).
Sessions, William A., 1987, 'Abandonment and the English religious lyric in the seventeenth century', in Claude J. Summers and Ted-Larry Pebworth (eds), *'Bright Shootes of Everlastingnesse': The Seventeenth-Century Religious Lyric* (Columbia: University of Missouri Press).
Shami, Jeanne, 1984, 'Anatomy and progress: The drama of conversion in Donne's men of a "Middle Nature"', *University of Toronto Quarterly*, 53:3.
Shami, Jeanne, 1992, 'Introduction: Reading Donne's sermons', *John Donne Journal*, 11.
Shami, Jeanne, 2000, 'Anti-Catholicism in the sermons of John Donne', in Lori Anne Ferrell and Peter McCullough (eds), *The English Sermon Revised: Religion, Literature and History 1600–1750* (Manchester, New York: Manchester University Press).
Shami, Jeanne, 2003, 'Labels, controversy, and the language of inclusion in Donne's sermons', in David Colclough (ed.), *John Donne's Professional Lives* (Cambridge: Brewer).
Shami, Jeanne, 2008a, 'Introduction: Renaissance Tropologies', in Jeanne Shami (ed.), *Renaissance Tropologies: The Cultural Imagination of Early Modern England* (Pittsburgh, PA: Duquesne University Press).
Shami, Jeanne (ed.), 2008b, *Renaissance Tropologies: The Cultural Imagination of Early Modern England* (Pittsburgh, PA: Duquesne University Press).
Shell, Alison, 1999, *Catholicism, Controversy and the English Literary Imagination, 1558–1660* (Cambridge: Cambridge University Press).

Shell, Alison and Arnold Hunt, 2006, 'Donne's religious world', in Achsah Guibbory (ed.), *The Cambridge Companion to John Donne* (Cambridge: Cambridge University Press).

Sherwood, Terry G., 1972, 'Reason in Donne's sermons', *English Literary History*, 39.

Sherwood, Terry G., 1984, *Fulfilling the Circle: A Study of John Donne's Thought* (Toronto: University of Toronto Press).

Shuger, Debora, 1985, 'The title of Donne's *Devotions*', *English Language Notes*, 22:4.

Shuger, Debora K., 1989, *Sacred Rhetoric: The Christian Grand Style in the English Renaissance* (Princeton, NY: Princeton University Press).

Shuger, Debora, 2000, 'Absolutist theology: the sermons of John Donne', in Lori Anne Ferrell and Peter McCullough (eds), *The English Sermon Revised: Religion, Literature and History 1600–1750* (Manchester, New York: Manchester University Press).

Shullenberger, William, 1993, 'Love as a spectator sport in John Donne's poetry', in Claude J. Summers and Ted-Larry Pebworth (eds), *Renaissance Discourses of Desire* (Columbia, London: University of Missouri Press).

Sidney, Sir Philip, [1595] 1947, 'An Apology for Poetry', in Edmund D. Jones (ed.), *English Critical Essays (Sixteenth, Seventeenth, and Eighteenth Centuries)* (London: Oxford University Press).

Simpson, Evelyn, 1948, *A Study of the Prose Works of John Donne*, 2nd ed. (Oxford: Clarendon Press).

Slater, Michael, 2006, ' "Invoking" Donne: A grammatical reconstruction of "The Canonization" ', *Notes and Queries*, 53:2.

Sloane, Thomas O., 1985, *Donne, Milton, and the End of Humanist Rhetoric* (Berkeley, Los Angeles, London: University of California Press).

Sloane, Thomas O., 2006, 'Dr. Donne and the image of Christ', *Rhetorica*, 24:2.

Smith, A. J., 1991, *Metaphysical Wit* (Cambridge: Cambridge University Press).

Smith, A. J. (ed.), 1972, *John Donne: Essays in Celebration* (London: Methuen).

Smith, Dan Noel, 1973, 'The artistry of John Donne's *Devotions*', *University of Dayton Review*, 10:1.

Smith, Gregory (ed.), [1904] 1959, *Elizabethan Critical Essays*, 2 vols (Oxford: Oxford University Press).

Smith, Jonathan Z., 1987, *To Take Place: Toward Theory in Ritual* (Chicago, London: The University of Chicago Press).

Sowards, J. K., 1985, 'Introduction', in J. K. Sowards (ed.), *Collected Works of Erasmus: Literary and Educational Writings 3: De Conscribendis Epistolis/Formula/De Civilitate* (Toronto: University of Toronto Press).

Stachniewski, John, 1991, *The Persecutory Imagination: English Puritanism and the Literature of Religious Despair* (Oxford: Clarendon Press).
Stampfer, Judah, 1970, *John Donne and the Metaphysical Gesture* (New York: Funk & Wagnalls).
Stanwood, P. G. and Heather Ross Asals, 1986, *John Donne and the Theology of Language* (Columbia: University of Missouri Press).
Stanwood, P. G., 1995, 'Donne's earliest sermons and the penitential tradition', in Raymond J. Frontain and Frances M. Malpezzi (eds), *John Donne's Religious Imagination: Essays in Honor of John T. Shawcross* (Conway: University of Central Arkansas Press).
Stanwood, P. G., 2002, 'Critical directions in the study of early modern sermons', in Claude J. Summers and Ted-Larry Pebworth (eds), *Fault Lines and Controversies in the Study of Seventeenth-Century English Literature* (Columbia: University of Missouri Press).
Stanwood, Paul G., Diana Treviño Benet, Judith Scherer Herz and Debora Shuger, 1993, 'Excerpts from a panel discussion', in Claude J. Summers and Ted-Larry Pebworth (eds), *Renaissance Discourses of Desire* (Columbia, London: University of Missouri Press).
Steen, Sara Jayne, 2001, 'Reading beyond the words: Material letters and the process of interpretation', *QUIDDITAS*, 22.
Stein, Arnold, 1962, *John Donne's Lyrics: The Eloquence of Action* (Minneapolis: University of Minnesota Press).
Stein, Arnold, 1984, 'Voices of the satirist: John Donne', in Claude Rawson (ed.), *English Satire and the Satiric Tradition* (Oxford: Basil Blackwell).
Stewart, Alan and Heather Wolfe, 2004, *Letterwriting in Renaissance England* (Washington, DC: Folger Shakespeare Library).
Stewart, Stanley, 2003, 'Reading Donne: Old and new his- and her-storicisms', in Mark Berley (ed.), *Reading the Renaissance: Ideas and Idioms from Shakespeare to Milton* (Pittsburgh, PA: Duquesne University Press).
Storhoff, Gary P., 1977, 'Social mode and poetic strategies: Donne's verse letters to his friends', *Essays in Literature*, 4.
Strier, Richard, 1989, 'John Donne awry and squint: The "Holy Sonnets" 1608–1610', *Modern Philology*, 86.
Strier, Richard, 1995, *Resistant Structures: Particularity, Radicalism and Renaissance Texts* (Berkeley: University of California Press).
Strier, Richard, 1996, 'Donne and the politics of devotion', in Donna B. Hamilton and Richard Strier (eds), *Religion, Literature, and Politics in Post-Reformation England, 1540–1688* (Cambridge: Cambridge University Press).
Stringer, Gary A. (ed.), 1977, *New Essays on Donne* (Salzburg: Universität Salzburg).
Stubbs, John, [2006] 2007, *Donne: The Reformed Soul* (London: Penguin).

Sugg, Richard, 2006, *John Donne* (Basingstoke: Palgrave).
Sullivan, David L., 1988, 'The structure of self-revelation in Donne's *Devotions*', *Prose Studies*, 11.
Summers, Claude J. (ed.), 1992, *Homosexuality in Renaissance and Enlightenment England: Literary Representations in Historical Context* (Binghamton: Haworth).
Summers, Claude J., 2001, 'W[illiam] S[hakespeare]'s *A Funeral Elegy* and the Donnean moment', in Mary Ellen Henley and W. Speed Hill (eds), *Wrestling with God: Literature & Theology in the English Renaissance* (no place, no publisher).
Summers, Claude J. and Ted-Larry Pebworth (eds), 1986a, *The Eagle and the Dove: Reassessing John Donne* (Columbia: University of Missouri Press).
Summers, Claude J. and Ted-Larry Pebworth, 1986b, 'Introduction', in Claude J. Summers and Ted-Larry Pebworth (eds), *The Eagle and the Dove: Reassessing John Donne* (Columbia: University of Missouri Press).
Summers, Claude J. and Ted-Larry Pebworth (eds), 1987, *'Bright Shootes of Everlastingnesse': The Seventeenth-Century Religious Lyric* (Columbia: University of Missouri Press).
Summers, Claude and Ted-Larry Pebworth, 1991, 'Donne's correspondence with Wotton', *John Donne Journal*, 10.
Summers, Claude J. and Ted-Larry Pebworth (eds), 1993, *Renaissance Discourses of Desire* (Columbia, London: University of Missouri Press).
Summers, Claude J. and Ted-Larry Pebworth (eds), 1995, *The Wit of Seventeenth-Century Poetry* (Columbia, London: University of Missouri Press).
Summers, Claude J. and Ted-Larry Pebworth (eds), 2000, *Literary Circles and Communities in Renaissance England* (Columbia and London: University of Missouri Press).
Summers, Claude J. and Ted-Larry Pebworth (eds), 2002, *Fault Lines and Controversies in the Study of Seventeenth-Century English Literature* (Columbia: University of Missouri Press).
Targoff, Ramie, 1997, 'The performance of prayer: Sincerity and theatricality in early modern England', *Representations*, 60.
Targoff, Ramie, 2001, *Common Prayer: The Language of Public Devotion in Early Modern England* (Chicago: The University of Chicago Press).
Targoff, Ramie, 2008, *John Donne: Body and Soul* (Chicago: The University of Chicago Press).
Thomson, Patricia, 1972, 'Donne and the poetry of patronage: The *Verse Letters*', in A. J. Smith (ed.), *John Donne: Essays in Celebration* (London: Methuen).
Turner, Viktor, 1989, *Vom Ritual zum Theater: Der Ernst des menschlichen Spiels*, trans. Sylvia M. Schomburg-Scherff (Frankfurt am Main, New York: Campus).

Ueding, Gerd (ed.), 1992–2005, *Historisches Wörterbuch der Rhetorik* (Tübingen: Niemeyer).
Van Houdt, Toon and Jan Papy, 2002, 'Introduction', in Toon Van Houdt, Jan Papy, Gilbert Tournoy and Constant Matheeussen (eds), *Self-Presentation and Social Identification: The Rhetoric and Pragmatics of Letter Writing in Early Modern Times* (Leuven: Leuven University Press).
Van Houdt, Toon, Jan Papy, Gilbert Tournoy and Constant Matheeussen (eds), 2002, *Self-Presentation and Social Identification: The Rhetoric and Pragmatics of Letter Writing in Early Modern Times* (Leuven: Leuven University Press).
Van Laan, Thomas F., 1963, 'John Donne's *Devotions* and the Jesuit Spiritual Exercises', *Studies in Philology*, 60.
Vickers, Brian, 1988, *In Defence of Rhetoric* (Oxford: Clarendon Press).
Walton, Izaak, [1675] 1928, *Lives of Donne & Herbert*, ed. S. C. Roberts (Cambridge: Cambridge University Press).
Wayne, Don E., 1995, 'The "exchange of letters": Early modern contradictions and postmodern conundrums', in Ann Bermingham and John Brewer (eds), *The Consumption of Culture 1600–1800: Image, Object, Text* (London, New York: Routledge).
Webber, Joan, 1963, *Contrary Music: The Prose Style of John Donne* (Madison: The University of Wisconsin Press).
Webber, Joan, 1968, *The Eloquent 'I': Style and Self in Seventeenth-Century Prose* (Madison, Milwaukee, London: The University of Wisconsin Press).
Whalen, Robert, 2002, *The Poetry of Immanence: Sacrament in Donne and Herbert* (Toronto, Buffalo, London: University of Toronto Press).
White, Helen C., 1966, *English Devotional Literature [Prose] 1600–1640* (New York: Haskell House).
White, Paul Whitfield, 1993, *Theatre and Reformation: Protestantism, Patronage, and Playing in Tudor England* (Cambridge: Cambridge University Press).
Wiggins, Peter DeSa, 2000, *Donne, Castiglione, and the Poetry of Courtliness* (Bloomington: Indiana University Press).
Wilcox, Helen, 1995, ' "No More Wit than a Christian?": The case of devotional poetry', in Claude J. Summers and Ted-Larry Pebworth (eds), *The Wit of Seventeenth-Century Poetry* (Columbia: University of Missouri Press).
Wilcox, Helen, 2000, ' "The birth day of my selfe": John Donne, Martha Moulsworth and the emergence of individual identity', in A. J. Piesse (ed.), *Sixteenth-Century Identities* (Manchester: Manchester University Press).
Wilcox, Helen, 2007, ' "Was I not made to *thinke*?": Teaching the *Devotions* and Donne's literary practice', *John Donne Journal*, 26.

Wilcox, Helen, Richard Todd and Alasdair Macdonald (eds), 1996, *Sacred and Profane: Secular and Devotional Interplay in Early Modern British Literature* (Amsterdam: VU University Press).

Wirth, Uwe, 2002a, 'Der Performanzbegriff im Spannungsfeld von Illokution, Iteration und Indexikalität', in Uwe Wirth (ed.), *Performanz: Zwischen Sprachphilosophie und Kulturwissenschaften* (Frankfurt am Main: Suhrkamp).

Wirth, Uwe (ed.), 2002b, *Performanz: Zwischen Sprachphilosophie und Kulturwissenschaften* (Frankfurt am Main: Suhrkamp).

Wollman, Richard B., 1993, 'The "Press" and the "Fire": Print and manuscript culture in Donne's circle', *Studies in English Literature*, 33.

Wright, Thomas, [1601] 1973, *The Passions of the Minde* (Hildesheim, New York: Georg Olms Verlag).

Yen, Julie W., 1995, ' "What doth Physicke profit thee?": The pharmakon of praise in Donne's *Ignatius His Conclave* and the *Holy Sonnets*', in Raymond J. Frontain and Frances M. Malpezzi (eds), *John Donne's Religious Imagination: Essays in Honor of John T. Shawcross* (Conway: University of Central Arkansas Press).

Young, R. V., 2000, *Doctrine and Devotion in Seventeenth-Century Poetry: Studies in Donne, Herbert, Crashaw, and Vaughan* (Cambridge: Brewer).

Young, R. V., 2007, 'Theology, doctrine, and genre in *Devotions Upon Emergent Occasions*', *John Donne Journal*, 26.

Zunder, William, 1982, *The Poetry of John Donne: Literature and Culture in the Elizabethan and Jacobean Period* (Brighton: John Spiers).

Index

Please note: Works not assigned to an author are by Donne

act/acting/actor(s) 10–12, 26–7, 30, 36, 41, 43–4, 49–52, 54–6, 58, 60, 75, 79, 105, 108–9, 116–17, 126, 130, 131, 133, 140–1, 143, 154, 158–60, 168, 170, 172, 174–6, 178–80, 182, 272–3, 275
  see also audience; drama; enact; perform; spectacle; spectator(s); stage; theatre; theatrical
addressee(s) 3, 5, 14, 22, 28, 81, 84–5, 87, 89, 91, 94–7, 99–103, 108–13, 115, 118, 123–6, 128, 130–3, 135n.12, 141, 144–6, 151, 154, 159, 167–72, 174, 178, 180–2, 186, 188–90, 192–3, 195, 197, 199–203, 205, 207–23, 226–7, 234, 239, 244, 250, 255, 259–66, 273–4
  see also audience; coterie; listener(s); reader(s); spectator(s)
'Aire and Angels' 93–4
Andrewes, Lancelot 9
Anniversaries 142, 265
  see also 'The Second Anniversary'
'The Apparition' 84, 87, 131
audience 5, 12–15, 18, 21, 27, 29–30, 32, 36, 38–40, 44, 47–52, 54, 57–9, 68–9, 73–5n.6, 76n.9, 77, 80–1, 99–100, 107–10, 124–8, 130–34, 146, 151, 158, 167–70, 172–83, 222, 232, 254, 258, 261–3
  see also addressee(s); coterie; listener(s); reader(s); spectator(s)
Augustine, St 34, 53, 160, 168, 181–2, 240
Austin, J. L. 2–3, 5–7, 21, 40–1, 77, 79, 80–2, 109, 125, 134n.1, 142, 151, 272
  see also Searle, John; speech act

Bacon, Sir Francis 82–9, 92, 99, 104–5, 128, 136n.27, 174, 206
'The Baite' 176
Baker, Sir Richard 15, 27, 49
Bakhtin, Mikhail 76n.10, 123
Bald, R. C. 27, 109, 167–8, 224n.1
Barthes, Roland 21, 138–40, 142–5, 149–50, 153–4, 163, 170, 172–4, 272
Bell, Ilona 121, 176
Biathanatos 20, 45, 155, 168, 174, 253
Bible 3, 7–9, 17, 21, 25–7, 31–2, 37, 41–2, 44, 48, 51–3, 59, 62, 65–6, 69–71, 75n.3, n.4, 76n.12, 92, 118, 132–3, 139, 160, 175, 182–3, 214, 227, 230, 237, 240, 243, 245, 249, 252, 257, 261
body/bodies 4–6, 10, 12, 16, 34, 37, 40–3, 48–9, 52, 56, 60, 67, 72, 76n.13, 88, 93–5, 104, 106, 113, 117, 126, 131, 135n.12, 149, 156–7, 194, 205, 216, 224n.4, 230–1, 236, 239–48, 251, 255, 259, 267, 275

308 Index

'Breake of day' 131
'The broken heart' 151–2, 162–3
Brooks, Cleanth 78, 123
Butler, Judith 4, 41, 118, 121

Calvin/Calvinism/Calvinists 6, 33, 36, 167, 203, 218
'The Canonization' 7–8, 14–15, 21, 64, 77–9, 81, 91, 110, 117–19, 122–3, 125, 127, 134n.2, 136n.19, n.20, n.22, 142–4
Carey, John 17, 23n.2, 77, 102, 127, 134n.5, 135n.15, 154, 184n.6
Castiglione, Baldassare 162
Catholicism/Catholic 5–8, 12, 15–19, 28, 36, 40, 44–5, 55–6, 63–5, 82, 103–4, 107, 112, 123, 135n.13, 136n.19, 171, 173, 184n.6, 190, 210, 227, 240–1, 246, 254
'Change' 91
character 14, 46, 55, 59, 108, 131, 133–4, 154–5, 166, 182–3, 230, 275
Christ 5–7, 9, 16, 18–19, 21–2, 25, 30–1, 33, 35–9, 44, 48–9, 51–2, 57, 60–4, 66–75n.3, n.5, 76n.12, n.13, 87, 93, 111, 135, 138, 154–60, 162, 166–8, 171, 173–7, 179, 183, 226, 229, 231–2, 235, 238–42, 244, 246–7, 249, 251–3, 255, 257–60, 266, 269n.5, n.7, n.8, 272
church 2, 8–10, 12, 15–17, 19, 26, 28, 32, 44–5, 49–50, 67, 71, 73, 93, 112, 118, 123, 171, 183, 228, 236, 240, 257, 268
code 21, 139, 142–9, 151, 153, 165–6, 170, 178–9
commendatory poetry 21, 80, 109–10, 133, 177
commodity 22, 110–11, 199–200, 204, 259, 261, 267
communicate/communication 2, 12–13, 21–2, 26, 28, 32, 49, 56, 61, 72, 80–1, 109, 127, 139, 146–7, 150, 155, 167, 175, 181, 184, 189, 191, 194–6, 198–9, 206–7, 211, 214–16, 218, 220–1, 225–6, 229–30, 232–7, 246, 248, 258–9, 262, 269, 273
communicative situation 5, 21, 46, 51, 69, 81, 99, 124–5, 167, 172–3, 175, 182, 257, 272–3
communicative system 5, 13–14, 26, 69, 81, 109–11, 124–5, 130–33, 136n.22, 139, 167, 178, 273
communion 13, 22, 56, 77, 189, 190–1, 198, 216, 218, 221, 223–7, 229–30, 232–4, 236, 238–40, 242, 244–5, 247–9, 251–60, 269, 269n.1, n.5, 273
  Holy Communion 22, 29, 30, 56, 67, 136n.26, 226, 234, 239–41, 245–7, 249, 257, 273
  see also Eucharist
'Communitie' 1, 90, 274–5
confession 17–19, 57–8, 72, 75n.7, 104, 194, 241–4, 251, 271
  see also denomination
'Confined Love' 91
conform/conformist/conformity 9, 17, 40, 246, 249–50, 256
convention 5, 7, 10, 21–2, 75n.4, 80–1, 88, 104, 118, 142, 147, 151, 166, 185–6, 189, 197, 204–5, 225, 273
conversion/convert 10, 15, 18, 20–1, 23n.5, 25, 27, 30–1, 33–42, 46, 51, 55–8, 61–3, 65–71, 74–75n.5, n.7, 105–7, 131–5, 155, 160, 183, 226, 259, 272
  see also transubstantiation
co-operate/co-operation 32, 35, 37–8, 82, 103, 207–9, 216, 252, 272
coterie 13, 21, 79, 81, 110, 123–8, 132, 136n.25, n.27, 153–4, 160, 167, 170, 176–7, 272
  see also addressee(s); audience; listener(s); reader(s); spectator(s)

Index

create/creation/creator 2–4, 7–8, 10, 12, 18, 21, 31, 34, 37, 42–3, 48, 54, 58–9, 61, 64, 80, 82–7, 90, 93–9, 109–10, 123, 125–7, 130, 132–3, 134n.6, 137n.28, 140–1, 146–7, 149, 166, 168, 173–6, 181, 192, 208, 212, 214, 217–18, 222, 235–6, 243, 245, 250, 254, 259, 265, 268, 271–4
criticism/critics 1, 4, 14–15, 17–19, 23n.2, 37, 45, 77–8, 134n.7, 136n.22, 138, 185, 241, 246, 261, 269, 271, 274–5
'The Crosse' 157–8
crucifixion 64, 66, 76n.13, 157, 239
Culler, Jonathan 3, 79, 123, 198
'The Curse' 21, 81, 110, 117–23, 126

Davies, Horton 4, 18, 45, 51
Day, Angel 22, 86–7, 216
death 37, 43–4, 57, 62–4, 67–8, 77, 84, 88, 96–101, 111, 114–17, 120, 124, 135n.10, n.17, 138, 144, 154–5, 158–9, 175, 178, 198, 218, 221, 225, 228–33, 235, 240, 246–7, 249, 252–3, 256–9, 267–8
'Death' 178
deconstruction 88, 198, 205
denomination 12, 16–19, 171–2, 184n.2, 244, 271
Derrida, Jacques 3, 79, 142, 212
desire 17–18, 40, 83, 85, 88, 115, 125, 127, 130–1, 138, 143–4, 147–50, 154, 159, 162, 166–7, 174, 176, 178, 202, 206, 208, 210, 215, 217, 220, 223, 225, 228–9, 237, 240, 248–9, 252–3, 271, 274
despair/desperate 32, 68, 104, 139, 146, 152, 168, 174–5, 179, 199, 203, 219, 237–8, 250–1, 253
devotion/devotional 9–10, 12, 22, 50, 63–4, 77, 110–11, 138, 150, 153, 158–9, 162, 164, 166, 170–2, 174–6, 179, 183, 197, 202, 215, 218, 224–6, 228–9, 231–5, 238–9, 246, 254–5, 270n.10, 271, 273, 275

Devotions Upon Emergent Occasions 2, 4, 8, 10, 13–14, 17, 19–20, 22, 41, 56, 137n.28, 184, 187, 191, 193, 199, 202–3, 216, 223–4, 224n.6, 225–70 *passim*, 273, 275
dialogue/dialogisation 15, 26, 31, 48–9, 57, 70, 102, 130, 185, 198
DiPasquale, Theresa 2, 33, 82, 148, 165–6, 182, 184n.6, 189, 241, 258, 265
director 51, 58, 60, 63, 76n.11, 272
disease 68, 140, 213, 227, 252
  see also illness; sickness
dissemble/dissimulation 10, 41, 101, 104–5, 160–2, 179, 243
Docherty, Thomas 23n.2, 134n.7, 136n.20, 154, 174
Donne, Anne More 121, 136n.25, 171, 204
Döring, Tobias 13, 27–8, 179
drama/dramatic 13–15, 26–8, 37–8, 41, 44–6, 48–9, 51, 54, 57–60, 66, 70–1, 75–6, 80, 98–9, 110, 127, 130–4, 139, 154, 161, 167, 181–2, 184n.7, 272
  see also act; audience; perform; theatre; theatrical; spectacle; spectator(s); stage
'The Dreame' 84–8, 94, 125, 134n.4
Dubrow, Heather 105, 135n.13, 184n.1
Duffy, Eamon 8, 10, 12, 258

effect/efficaciousness 2–10, 14, 18, 21, 29–30, 33, 37–40, 42, 44, 47–8, 53, 57, 59–60, 62, 65, 67–8, 74–5, 78, 81–2, 86, 95, 97–8, 102, 109, 112–14, 118, 120–3, 125, 127, 129–30, 132, 146, 152–3, 156, 158, 160–1, 165, 173, 175–7, 180, 183, 190, 194, 199, 202–3, 207, 213–14, 218, 226, 229, 232, 234–5, 240, 242, 247, 249, 251–2, 257–8, 272–3, 275
  see also enact/enactment

Egerton, Sir Thomas 22, 221–3
elegies 127, 132
    see also individual titles
Eliot, T. S. 1, 98
Elizabeth I 16, 49, 82, 135n.13, 166
embodiment 5, 29, 126, 216, 240
empathise/empathy 14, 56, 166, 252, 258–9, 261
    see also identification
enact/enactment 7–9, 15–16, 21, 26–7, 41, 54–5, 57, 60, 62–4, 70, 75, 109–10, 116, 131, 133, 139, 141, 147, 153–8, 160, 162, 175, 177, 189, 240, 251, 272
    see also effect/efficaciousness; perform; re-enact
encomiastic poetry 80–1, 177
    see also commendatory poetry
epistolography 13, 22, 208, 273
'Epitaph on Himselfe' 96–8
'Epithalamion made at Lincolnes Inne' 95
Erasmus 22, 161, 185–8, 204, 208, 216
Essays in Divinity 20, 30, 135n.8, 232, 238, 269n.7
essence/essentialism/essentialist 4, 10, 27, 31, 35, 39, 41, 55, 74, 89, 92, 96–100, 106, 128, 157, 172, 175, 178, 203–4, 219
    see also perform
eternal life 36, 69, 136n.18, 159
Eucharist 5–8, 12, 16, 22, 25, 28–30, 32, 36, 52, 56, 67, 76n.13, 136n.26, 137n.27, 219, 233, 239–42, 246, 248–9, 253, 257, 260, 273
    see also Holy Communion
example 9, 26–7, 38–40, 44, 51, 53, 61, 65–75 *passim*, 114, 145, 158–60, 175, 222, 228, 231, 255, 257, 261, 272
excess 21, 61, 110, 130, 140–4, 146, 148–9, 151–3, 170, 194, 209, 250, 267

expostulation 22, 226–7, 231–4, 236–8, 245–8, 251, 254–7
'The Expostulation' 81, 124, 140–1, 147
'The Extasie' 93–4
external/externality/exterior/exteriority 3–5, 9–11, 13–14, 41, 69, 81, 88, 104, 109, 111, 124–5, 132–3, 136n.22, 149, 157, 160–2, 167, 169, 178–9, 181, 183, 242–3, 272–3

faith 9, 16–19, 23n.5, 31–2, 35–7, 39–41, 48, 52, 55, 69, 75, 91–3, 117, 124, 155, 162, 164, 180–1, 186, 209, 215, 225, 242, 244–5, 253–4, 258, 271
Fall, the 32, 101, 239–43
fashion 9, 18, 89, 95, 98, 112, 124, 132, 152–3, 155–6, 165, 189, 205, 215, 217, 232, 249, 267
    see also self-fashioning
fictional/fictionalise/fictionality 12, 81, 88, 127, 133, 161
Fischer-Lichte, Erika 4–5, 12, 160
Fish, Stanley 1, 64, 120, 146, 154, 163–4, 179, 184n.4
'The Flea' 148
friendship 33, 124, 128, 136n.27, 137n.27, 153, 188–90, 193–9, 201, 204, 209, 217–21, 224n.5, 225, 227, 260, 266
    see also patronage
Frontain, Raymond 44, 75n.2, 77, 82, 154, 165, 175, 184n.3

Gardner, Helen 82, 169
gender 2, 21, 41, 46, 163–7
Genesis 3, 157, 243
generic/genre 10, 20, 22, 26, 29, 77, 81–2, 84, 88, 93, 96, 117, 119–20, 127, 134, 182–3, 185–6, 189, 193, 198, 204, 218, 223, 226, 233, 258, 260, 263–4, 266, 272–4
Goffman, Erving 79, 184n.7

'Going to Bed' 95, 133, 138, 165
Goldberg, Jonathan 45, 134n.2, 194, 204, 220, 237, 239
'The good-morrow' 19, 83–4, 87, 91, 126, 143
Gosse, Edmond 23n.4, n.5, 36, 224n.1
grace 4–6, 33–4, 36, 93, 126, 145–6, 155, 166, 175, 183, 203, 216, 220, 238, 253, 257
Greenblatt, Stephen 4, 9, 11–12, 18–19, 78, 179, 275
Grierson, Herbert 1
Guibbory, Achsah 127, 150, 175

Harland, Paul W. 34, 37–8, 45–6, 56, 61–2, 76n.12, 157, 184n.4
Hester, Thomas 103, 107, 153, 176
'Holy Sonnets' 8, 10, 13, 17–18, 20–2, 28, 65, 95, 138–84 *passim*, 191, 226, 235, 264, 266–9, 271–3, 275
'Holy Sonnet: "At the round earths"' 181
'Holy Sonnet: "Batter my heart"' 138, 150, 159, 165–6
'Holy Sonnet: "Death be not proud"' 99
'Holy Sonnet: "Father, part of his double interest"' 167
'Holy Sonnet: "I am a little world"' 175
'Holy Sonnet: "If faithfull soules"' 162, 181
'Holy Sonnet: "If poysonous mineralls"' 163
'Holy Sonnet: "O Might those sighes"' 151–3, 175
'Holy Sonnet: "O my blacke Soule!"' 161, 167
'Holy Sonnet: "Oh, to vex me"' 149, 164–5, 170, 178, 182, 268
'Holy Sonnet: "Show me deare Christ"' 19, 93, 167
'Holy Sonnet: "Since she whome I lovd"' 166, 171
'Holy Sonnet: "Spit in my face"' 65, 138, 156–7
'Holy Sonnet: "This is my playes last scene"' 167–8
'Holy Sonnet: "Thou hast made me"' 8, 175, 269n.7
'Holy Sonnet: "What if this present"' 162, 166
'Holy Sonnet: "Why are wee"' 174
'Holy Sonnet: "Wilt thou love God"' 157
homiletic/s 7, 20, 22, 25, 28–9, 44, 46, 49–50, 59, 133, 139, 179, 183, 272
humankind 20, 25, 33, 35, 38, 40, 42, 51, 56, 60, 62, 69, 82, 136n.26, 157, 166, 227, 229, 235, 246, 251–2
humor/humoral 10–11, 18, 34–5, 41, 72, 100–2, 108, 113, 135n.11, 149, 164, 189, 242–3, 259
'A Hymne to Christ, at the Authors last going into Germany' 170–1
'A Hymne to God the Father' 155
'Hymne to God my God, in my sicknesse' 154, 159, 165, 168
'An hymne to the Saints, and to Marquesse Hamylton' 87

identification/identify 9, 14, 18–19, 22, 36, 38–40, 43–5, 54, 58, 64–71, 76n.12, n.13, 80, 108–9, 111–14, 116, 127, 135n.8, 136n.18, n.26, 138–9, 147, 149, 153–6, 168, 171, 176–7, 185, 189–90, 205, 207, 212–13, 217, 224n.3, 226, 228–9, 231, 240, 242, 256, 258, 261–2, 266, 269n.3, 272–3
  see also empathise
identity 3–4, 9–11, 18, 41, 55, 59, 83, 94–8, 100, 102, 107, 112–13, 117, 121–2, 127, 135n.8, 136n.26, 139, 158, 166–7, 177–8, 181, 192–3, 208, 223, 224n.3, 243, 251, 256, 265, 271–2

Ignatius His Conclave 20, 45
Ignatius of Loyola 17, 54, 171–4, 176, 181, 184n.3, 246, 254
illness 34, 119, 148–9, 205, 225–7, 251, 254, 257–8, 260, 267–8
  see also disease; sickness
illocution 5, 21, 29, 40, 80–1, 109, 127, 272
'Image of her whom I love' 84–8
imitate/imitation 8, 49, 60, 79, 160, 195, 222–3, 233
Imitatio Christi/Imitation (of Christ) 18, 62–4, 154–7, 159, 184n.2, n.3, 239–41, 245–8, 258–60, 269, 273
'The Indifferent' 19, 89, 91–2, 126
individual/individuality 1, 5, 8, 10–11, 16, 20, 22, 27, 30–44, 48, 51–6, 59, 64, 66, 76n.13, 78, 91, 93, 113, 128, 134, 142, 145–6, 160, 165, 169, 178, 183, 185–6, 195, 197–8, 203, 225–6, 230, 232–4, 244, 254, 256, 258–9, 261, 269n.5, 272
inside *see* interior
intercede/intercession/ intercessor 123, 210–11, 217, 221–2, 260
interior/interiority/internal/ internality 4–5, 10–11, 13–14, 32, 41, 43, 69, 81, 96, 109–10, 124–5, 127, 131–3, 136n.22, 148–9, 160–2, 167, 174, 176, 178–9, 181, 234, 242–3, 272–3, 275

James I 28, 49, 166, 190, 211, 256
Jonson, Ben 142

Kempis, Thomas à 18, 154–5, 157, 241
Kuchar, Gary 10, 179, 242–3

Labriola, Albert 136n.19, 156–7
'La Corona' 111, 135n.16, 168
'The Lamentations of Jeremy' 175

language 2–4, 7–8, 14, 21, 23n.1, 28, 42, 48, 76n.10, 78–83, 94–5, 97–8, 120, 122–4, 126, 129, 131, 134n.1, n.2, 142, 144, 146–7, 153, 161, 163, 173, 183, 187, 191, 197–9, 245, 249, 251, 261, 264, 271, 274
'Lecture upon the Shadow' 181
'The Legacie' 144, 162–3
letters 2, 4, 13–15, 19–20, 22, 27, 45, 71, 142, 145, 169, 184, 185–224 *passim*, 225–7, 231–2, 236, 239, 244, 250, 252–4, 256, 259–68, 273
Letters to Severall Persons of Honour 22, 189–90, 200, 218
Lewalski, Barbara 2, 17, 44, 82, 112, 135n.17, 159, 168, 174, 183, 184n.2, n.6, 274–5
lie/lying 110, 242–3, 271, 275
listener(s) 5, 9, 15, 20–1, 25–7, 30–1, 33, 35, 37–41, 44, 46–9, 51–8, 62–74, 100, 108, 119, 125, 128, 130–3, 159, 168–9, 175, 182–3, 258, 260, 272
  see also addressee; audience; coterie; reader(s); spectator(s)
'A Litanie' 92, 139, 151
literary/literature 1, 3–5, 8, 13, 17, 20, 48–51, 57, 79, 83, 117, 123, 127, 145, 148, 153, 167, 185, 189, 233, 269, 270n.10, 271, 273–4
liturgical/liturgy 8, 12, 17, 19, 29–30, 76n.13
  see also Holy Communion; Eucharist
love 1–2, 8, 12, 14, 19, 21, 24, 65, 73, 77–184 *passim*, 188, 190–3, 200–1, 203, 206–7, 210, 215–17, 223, 227–8, 235, 238, 250, 258, 263, 272, 275
'Loves Alchymie' 144, 158
'Loves Deitie' 143, 151
'Loves diet' 10, 141, 144
'Loves growth' 143
'Loves infiniteness' 143
'Loves Progress' 94–5

'Loves Warre' 166
Low, Anthony 136n.22, 165, 173, 184n.4
Luhmann, Niklas 21, 138–9, 143–9, 151, 272
Luther, Martin 6, 37, 44, 161

manuscript 125–6, 136n.24, 145, 167
Marlowe, Christopher 27
Marotti, Arthur 16, 75n.7, 76n.10, 85, 107, 117, 125–8, 133, 136n.18, n.22–4, 137n.27, 153, 167, 178, 182, 188, 191, 194, 213, 224n.2, 266
martyr/martyrdom 15, 67, 143, 151, 165, 174, 253, 269n.8
Martz, Louis 2, 17, 54, 153–4, 168, 171, 173, 181–2, 274–5
material/materiality 10, 13, 22, 32, 34, 47, 79, 96, 177–8, 190–1, 193–7, 199–201, 204, 224n.4, 225, 233, 236, 239, 266
Maurer, Margaret 187, 204, 211–12, 261, 265–6
meditation/meditative 13, 21–2, 41, 44–5, 64, 112, 156, 167–74, 176–84n.3, 193, 206, 214, 226–8, 230–8, 241, 245–6, 251, 254, 256, 262, 264, 273
metaphor 12, 33, 42–3, 51, 68, 75n.4, 80, 82, 85, 99, 128, 138, 147–9, 184n.7, 195, 198, 214, 237, 240, 243, 269n.7
metaphysical conceit 3, 46, 79–80, 82, 84, 114, 147–8
metre 99, 142
misogyny 81, 94, 109, 121, 126, 132, 144, 180
Montaigne, Michel de 100, 135n.10, 160, 172, 175, 189–90, 266
More, Sir George 22, 217, 221–3
Muir, Edward 5–6, 8–9, 11, 99
mutual/mutuality 11, 20, 25, 36, 40, 68, 76n.9, 87, 109, 118, 127, 130, 140, 146, 162, 183, 188–9, 197, 201, 203, 208, 213–16, 231–3, 259, 264–6

Müller, Wolfgang G. 82, 135n.15, 136n.20, 156, 170, 185, 187, 203, 208, 262

'Negative love' 129
Neoplatonism 118, 127, 171
'A nocturnall upon S. Lucies day, Being the shortest day' 95–8

object/objectivity 32, 35, 52, 92, 95–6, 113, 119–21, 125, 130–1, 133, 140, 147–8, 150, 164–5, 170, 172, 178
'Obsequies to the Lord Harrington' 80, 109–17, 135n.17
Oliver, P. M. 23n.2, 70, 75n.1, 76n.10, 155, 175, 246, 269n.3
'On the untimely Death of the incomparable Prince, Henry' 117
outside see external
Ovid 127

papism/papist/papistry 157, 228
paradox 20–1, 35, 67, 73–4, 78, 93, 142–3, 147–9, 151, 157, 163, 185, 195, 205
passion 10, 21, 27, 32, 34, 46–7, 59, 61, 77, 104, 107–8, 138–84 *passim*, 250, 272
  of Christ/Christ's 27, 62–5, 71, 76n.13, 138, 156–9, 173, 176–7, 240, 244, 267
passive/passiveness/passivity 8, 35, 52, 141, 148–50, 159, 165, 246, 248, 250
  see also active; object
Paster, Gail Kern 10, 12, 122, 135n.15, 149
patriarchal/patriarchy 127
patronage/patron(ess) 20–2, 76n.9, 80, 109–10, 112, 136n.25, 160, 177, 185–224 *passim*, 259–6, 273
  see also friendship
Paul, St 15, 21, 26–8, 40, 44, 50, 57, 61, 63, 65–71, 183

Index

perform/performance/performative/performativity 1–23, 271–5 *and passim*
  see also act; audience; drama; essence; spectacle; spectator(s); stage; theatre; theatrical
perlocution 5–6, 21, 39–40, 81, 109, 127, 272
persona(e) 3, 8, 14, 19–20, 22, 27, 38, 58–61, 68, 71, 76n.12, 109, 125, 127, 134n.6, 178, 187, 190, 205, 210–11, 252, 258, 272–3, 275
Petrarch/Petrarchan/Petrarchism/Petrarchist 118, 127, 136n.20, 143, 148, 150–1, 179, 181–2, 184n.1
Pfister, Manfred 3, 10–11, 15, 30–2, 46, 109, 124–5, 132, 162, 182, 233
play/player/playing 4–5, 9–16, 18, 22, 26, 28, 36, 45–51, 55–60, 62, 64, 74–5, 77, 80–1, 83, 89, 98–100, 103–13, 124–34, 137n.28, 138–43, 145, 150, 156–8, 160–1, 164, 167–8, 172, 178, 184n.7, 186–7, 194, 208, 212, 216–19, 223, 238, 240, 272–5
  see also act
Playfere, Thomas 45, 64
plot 21, 55, 57, 76n.8, 134, 154, 272
poetological 77, 118
  see also poetic/poetry
poetic/poetry 1–4, 7–8, 13–14, 17, 19–23n.2, 27–8, 46–50, 59, 64, 75n.6, 77–184 *passim*, 187–93, 204, 224n.2, n.3, 226, 233, 260–9 *passim*, 272–5
  see also poetological
politics 76n.14, 132, 166, 188
post-structuralism 138–9
pray/prayer 4, 22, 25–6, 28, 42, 49, 52, 59, 61, 72–4, 111, 117, 139, 164, 167, 169–70, 176, 182–3, 202, 204, 210–11, 213, 217, 220–2, 225–6, 230–40, 247–60, 269n.6, 273

preach/preacher/preaching 6, 12, 15, 20–1, 23n.5, 25–76 *passim*, 88, 104–7, 133, 159, 166, 168, 183, 219, 223, 228, 236, 253, 258, 272–3
predestination 33, 36, 203
presence 6–8, 10, 16, 29, 60, 64, 86, 104, 137n.28, 145, 155, 198, 204, 207, 211, 215, 240–1, 246, 250, 260
pretend/pretence 11, 99, 103, 107, 158, 162, 169, 179, 209, 271
print 125–6, 136n.24, 189, 259
'The Prohibition' 144
prose 2, 8, 13, 20, 22–3, 127, 184, 187, 193, 226, 260–9, 272–4
Protestant/Protestantism 6, 8–9, 16–18, 27–8, 44–6, 49, 55–6, 63, 82, 171, 184n.6, 241, 246
Psalm(s) 27–8, 32, 47–8, 118, 183, 228, 238
Pseudo-Martyr 20, 93, 156, 253, 269n.7
public/publication/publish 12, 17, 34, 84, 115, 123, 129, 136n.23, 146–7, 170, 178, 182–5, 188–91, 213, 223–5, 233, 255–6, 258, 263
Puttenham, George 7–8, 11, 81–2, 88, 95, 124, 178–9

reader(s) 5, 8, 14–15, 20–2, 41, 74, 77–8, 82, 97–8, 100, 111, 112–13, 117–19, 125–6, 130, 134n.7, 136n.25, 149, 161, 168, 170, 176–8, 189, 207, 215, 218, 226, 254–60, 267, 275
  see also addressee(s); audience; coterie; listener(s); spectator(s)
redemption 60, 157–61, 230–1, 242–3, 258
  see also salvation
re-enact/re-enactment 8–9, 15–16, 21, 26, 41, 57, 60, 62, 64, 70, 75n.3, 155–8, 160, 189, 240, 251, 272
  see also enact

Reformation 6–8, 10–12, 15–18, 23n.5,
  27–30, 32, 36–7, 44–6, 49–50, 67,
  72, 76n.12, 82–4, 107, 138, 161,
  219, 225, 227, 240–1, 246, 254
religion/religious 2, 4, 7, 10, 12–13,
  16–19, 22, 36, 40, 45, 48, 50,
  55–9, 76n.10, 82, 84, 92–3, 103,
  133–4, 134n.5, 138–9, 143, 150–1,
  153, 159–60, 162, 164–7, 169–72,
  174–6, 180, 183–4n.6, 190–1, 195,
  209–10, 212, 218–21, 223, 225–6,
  228, 244, 246, 254–5, 261, 271–4
  see also theological
representation 6–7, 9–10, 16, 28,
  55–6, 66, 71, 75, 99, 119, 123,
  143, 148, 172, 185, 191, 199, 206,
  241, 243, 269n.5
ressurection 26, 37–8, 57, 62, 68,
  75n.3, 76n.12, 77, 113, 157–9,
  176, 183, 221, 239–40
'Ressurection, imperfect' 158
rhetoric 6, 20–1, 26, 34, 40, 46–8, 52,
  58–60, 62, 66, 72, 97, 123, 130,
  133–4, 150, 172, 183, 185, 188,
  204, 245
rhythm 163
  see also metre
rite(s) 6, 9, 12, 31, 40, 123, 231
  see also ritual
ritual 5–9, 11–12, 16, 20, 25, 28–32
  passim, 35–6, 39–41, 43, 46–7,
  54–6, 62–3, 76n.8, n.11, 118, 123,
  134n.1, 171, 176–9, 184n.7, 239,
  272
  see also rite(s)
role/role-play 10–11, 13, 16, 18, 21,
  36, 41, 43, 46, 52–64, 70–1, 74–5,
  80–1, 98, 100, 102, 108–10, 113,
  116–17, 124, 128, 131–4, 138–40,
  143, 150, 153–4, 158–61, 164–5,
  168, 170, 172, 174, 176–80, 183,
  206–8, 212, 217, 240, 257, 266,
  272–4

sacrament 7–8, 28–9, 32, 36, 43, 52,
  61, 67, 192, 219, 240–2, 246, 253,
  258, 260–1

sacrifice 9, 26, 68, 76n.13, 116, 157,
  219, 225, 247, 267
salvation 25, 30–1, 34–9, 41, 44,
  61–4, 72, 77, 138, 155, 158, 167,
  183, 239, 244, 253, 268
  see also redemption
'Sapho to Philaenis' 131
satire 100–8, 135n.14, 136n.19, n.21,
  191
'Satyre I' 80, 100–3, 107–8, 135n.12
'Satyre III' 92–3
'Satyre IV' 80, 100, 103–8, 135n.13,
  n.14, 141
Saunders, Ben 17–18, 89, 124, 129,
  131, 142, 156, 166, 184n.5, 271,
  274
say/saying 3–5, 7, 9, 11, 18, 26,
  30–1, 33, 39, 45, 51, 57–8, 60–7,
  70–1, 75–82, 94, 98, 107, 109,
  115–18, 120, 129, 142, 146, 152,
  160, 162, 169, 173, 187, 200–1,
  208–11, 214–15, 223, 237, 240,
  245, 247, 260, 266, 272–5
  see also language
Schalkwyk, David 109
Schechner, Richard 176–8
Schoenfeldt, Michael 10, 34–5, 39,
  41, 72, 163, 165, 184n.5, 241
Scodel, Joshua 96, 102, 106, 117
Searle, John 21, 80–1, 99
  see also speech act; Austin, J. L.
'The Second Anniversarie' 99, 111
self 3–4, 7, 10, 13–16, 18, 23n.1, n.2,
  25–6, 32–46 *passim*, 52, 58, 60,
  62, 68–9, 71–2, 74, 78–80, 85,
  93–8 *passim*, 100, 102, 107–9,
  113–17, 127–8, 135n.10, n.15,
  139–40, 150, 154–60, 163–4,
  168–70, 172–81, 183, 185, 187,
  193, 196–7, 203–6, 209, 211, 213,
  216, 218, 221, 223, 225, 228,
  231–4, 242, 253, 256, 258–9, 263,
  269n.6, n.7, 272
  see also identification; identity;
  individual; subject; perform
self-confidence 113, 183, 209, 237,
  250, 269

self-consciousness 9, 18, 106, 179, 208
self-contradiction 46, 91, 148, 206
self-fashioning 11, 83, 100, 103, 164, 189, 204, 239, 241
  see also Greenblatt, Stephen
self-interest 21, 154–60 *passim*, 188
self-presentation 97, 136n.23, 204
self-reflexiveness 72, 129, 148, 179–80, 193–4, 220
'Selfe Love' 131
Selleck, Nancy 10, 34–5, 41, 160, 164–5, 269n.4
sermons 2, 4, 6–7, 9–10, 12–14, 17, 19–21, 25–76 *passim*, 81, 83–4, 88, 92–3, 132–4, 136n.26, 137n.28, 139, 158–9, 168–9, 175–6, 182–3, 188, 203, 218–19, 222–3, 228–9, 256, 258, 260–3, 270n.9, 272–3
  Death's Duel 37, 63–4
sex/sexuality 10, 94–5, 119, 124, 126, 130–2, 134n.5, 138, 147–8, 165–7, 180, 224n.4, 272
Shakespeare, William 11, 13, 27, 75n.2, 134n.3, 151, 182, 275
  Hamlet 13
  Henry V 99
Shami, Jeanne 23n.3, 45, 76n.10, 269n.2
Shuger, Debora 20, 33–4, 46–8, 267
Shullenberger, William 95, 109, 135n.2
sickness 4, 43, 58, 68, 97, 105, 149, 154, 159, 161, 164–5, 168–9, 213–14, 222–224n.6, 225, 227, 230, 234–39, 242–3, 247, 249, 251, 253–4, 256, 258, 267–8
  see also disease; illness
Sidney, Sir Philip 7, 75n.6, 92, 120
sin 9, 28, 35, 37, 39–40, 42–3, 48, 52–4, 57–9, 63–4, 68, 72, 103, 121, 153, 155–6, 161, 168, 171, 231, 238, 242, 244, 253

sincere/sincerity 4, 13, 23n.4, 162, 174, 179, 204
social context/dimension/function 5, 21, 79–80, 123, 125, 128, 135n.13, 136n.23, 169, 171, 224n.2
'Song: Goe, and catch a falling starre' 88, 91
Songs and Sonets 2–3, 20–2, 77–137 *passim*, 167–8, 178–80, 182, 261, 272
sonnet 65, 78, 86–7, 111, 134n.3, 151–2, 156, 164–5, 167, 173, 181–2, 184n.4, 262, 264, 267
soul 4, 13, 17, 22, 30, 32, 34, 39, 42–3, 63, 68, 72–3, 80, 85, 88, 94, 96, 99, 101, 109, 111–16, 135n.12, 147, 159, 161–3, 167–71, 181–8, 192–4, 196, 198, 204, 207, 212–13, 216, 218, 220–1, 230–2, 236–7, 244–7, 251, 273
spectacle 12, 45–6, 56, 70, 104, 125, 131, 267
  see also act; audience; drama; perform; spectator(s); stage; theatre; theatrical
spectator(s) 49, 55, 106, 108, 141, 150, 176, 179
  see also addressee(s); audience; coterie; listener(s); reader(s); act; audience; drama; perform; spectacle; stage; theatre; theatrical
speech act 3, 5–6, 21, 39–40, 57, 77, 80, 99, 108–9, 127, 132, 134n.1, 151, 196, 272
  see also Austin, J. L.; Searle, John
stage 11–14, 26–7, 42–57, 63, 69, 79, 99–100, 103–5, 108, 110, 128–31, 133–4, 141, 147–8, 156, 168, 172, 178–82, 215, 246, 267–8
  see also act; audience; drama; perform; spectacle; spectator(s); theatre; theatrical
Stanwood, P. G. 49, 61, 138
'The Storme' 224n.3

Index

St Paul's (Cathedral) 15, 27, 65
style 28, 47–8, 141, 165, 169, 185–7, 198, 225, 247, 249, 261
subject/subjectivity 1–2, 10, 17, 19, 29, 33–5, 41–2, 45, 52, 55, 59, 61, 66, 84, 87–8, 90, 95, 98, 109–12, 114–22, 125, 139, 142–3, 149–50, 154, 156, 167, 170, 173, 186, 196, 202, 234, 252, 265, 267, 269n.4
 see also identification; identity; individual; self
suicide 123, 168, 210, 253
'The Sunne Rising' 14, 84, 99, 130, 134n.2
system theory 139

Targoff, Ramie 4, 9, 12–13, 19, 28, 32, 64, 173, 175, 182–4n.4, 189, 194, 206, 216, 219, 225, 231, 235, 254, 258, 261
theatre 4–5, 11–13, 20, 22–23n.3, 26–7, 46–7, 49–51, 54–5, 70, 75n.2, 81, 99, 103, 105–6, 108, 126, 128, 130–1, 137n.28, 168, 171–2, 176–9, 243, 268, 272–3
 see also drama; perform; spectacle; spectator(s); stage; theatrical
theatrical/theatricalisation/theatricality 5, 12–16, 21, 23n.3, n.4, 26–7, 41–2, 45–56, 62–3, 74–5, 80, 98–100, 103–10, 127–30, 132–5n.9, 138–9, 141, 155, 157, 160–1, 171, 174, 176, 179, 182–3, 187, 204, 208, 274
 see also drama; perform; spectacle; spectator(s); stage; theatre
theological/theology 8, 22, 28, 36, 43, 55, 82, 88, 171, 219, 226
 see also religion
Thirty-Nine Articles 203, 241, 246, 257–8
'To E. of D. with six holy Sonnets' 267
'To the Lady Magdalen Herbert, of St. Mary Magdalen' 111, 135n.16

'To Mr. Tilman' 166
transform/transformation 9, 12, 32, 35, 78, 99, 132, 134, 177–8, 187
transubstantiation 5–6, 12, 30, 52, 67–8, 241
 see also conversion
Trinity, the 31, 46, 76n.12, 92–3, 119, 251
'The triple Foole' 129
truth 2–3, 21, 31, 45, 80, 83–95, 98, 110, 134n.6, 140, 162, 181, 214, 272
Turner, Viktor 176
'Twicknam garden' 89

'Upon Mr. Thomas Coryats Crudities' 191–2
'The undertaking' 128

'A Valediction forbidding mourning' 147
'Valediction of the booke' 145, 153
'A Valediction of my name, in the window' 123, 191–3, 197
'A Valediction of weeping' 83–4
'Variety' 91
verse 22–3, 25, 53–4, 64, 70, 87, 107, 109–11, 129, 136, 150, 167, 191–2, 224, 226, 260–70 *passim*, 273–4
 see also prose
verse letter(s) 107, 109–10, 192, 224n.3, 260–70 *passim*, 273
via media 6, 56
vigour 4, 47, 79
vitality 14, 58

Walton, Izaak 20, 23n.5, 37, 59
Webber, Joan 23n.1, 29, 51, 74, 187, 229, 235, 242, 256, 270n.9
Wilcox, Helen 139, 179, 193, 239, 246, 250, 258–9, 269n.5
'The Will' 144
wit 126, 139, 144, 259, 267
'Womans constancy' 89
Wright, Thomas 59, 104, 107–8, 149, 154–5, 157, 160–1

EU authorised representative for GPSR:
Easy Access System Europe, Mustamäe tee 50,
10621 Tallinn, Estonia
gpsr.requests@easproject.com

www.ingramcontent.com/pod-product-compliance
Lightning Source LLC
Chambersburg PA
CBHW030117240426
43673CB00041B/1306